THE
BLACK BOOK
OF POLISH
CENSORSHIP

THE
BLACK BOOK
OF POLISH
CENSORSHIP

Translated and Edited by
Jane Leftwich Curry

Vintage Books
A Division of Random House / New York

To My Parents

FIRST VINTAGE BOOKS EDITION, April 1984

Copyright © 1984 by The Rand Corporation

The documents translated in this book were gathered by Tomasz Strzyżewski and first published in Polish by ANEKS, Copyright © 1977, 1978 by ANEKS— Polish Political Quarterly, Uppsala-London.

Library of Congress Cataloging in Publication Data

Main entry under title:
The Black book of Polish censorship.

Translation of Czarna księga cenzury PRL.
Includes bibliographical references.
1. Mass media—Poland—Censorship. I. Curry, Jane Leftwich, 1948–
P96.C42P7313 1984   302.2′34′09438   83-47813
ISBN 0-394-71734-1

Manufactured in the United States of America

9 8 7 6 5 4 3 2

FOREWORD

The Polish censorship documents translated in this book provide a unique inside view of censorship in Communist systems. They are the first such documents available in the West since publication of Soviet documents from the 1930s captured in Smolensk during World War II.* The Polish documents (as Dr. Curry explains in Chapter 1) were collected by Tomasz Strzyżewski, an official of the censors' office in Kraków, who then smuggled them out of the country. The documents were published in Polish in London by *Aneks,* the journal of the younger Polish emigration. They were later smuggled back into Poland, where they received wide underground circulation. This book makes available to the English-speaking reader, by arrangement with *Aneks,* a translation and analysis of the Polish censorship documents. Preparation of this book was sponsored by The Rand Corporation as part of its program of research on Eastern Europe and Communist media.

Jane Leftwich Curry was uniquely qualified to prepare this volume. Dr. Curry wrote her doctoral dissertation on Polish journalism and interviewed many Polish journalists in Poland. She subsequently participated in a project on intra-élite communication in Communist countries and interviewed a number of former Polish censorship officials. She has thus been able to draw on the experiences of both censors and censored in analyzing and interpreting the Polish censorship documents.

*Merle Fainsod, *Smolensk Under Soviet Rule* (Cambridge, Mass.: Harvard University Press, 1958). A Rand Corporation Research Study.

Censorship in Poland, as Dr. Curry explains in Chapter I, is not limited to the official censor who edits copy according to his book of rules. The official censor is only one part of a whole system of media control intended to make the media responsive to the wishes of the Communist Party leadership. That system is supervised by the Politburo and by the party Central Committee Press Department. It requires politically reliable chief editors. It engenders self-censorship by journalists, who learn to follow the "rules of the game." Yet, as these documents testify, in Poland official censors have needed a strong hand to control presumably reliable editors and journalists ostensibly loyal to the regime.

This book contains two different kinds of censorship documents. It draws from the *Book of Rules and Recommendations*, informally called "The Black Book" because of the black loose-leaf folder in which the regulations were kept, and supplemental guidelines (Informative Notes). The detailed directives translated in this book are only a part of the censor's rulebook. Tomasz Strzyżewski smuggled out only a fraction of the censorship regulations he was required to observe, and in any case the printed regulations were supplemented with regular oral briefings. These detailed regulations were kept secret even from trusted editors. One prominent former Polish editor, now in the West, who had dealt with censors for years, said after reading the documents: "I knew all this, but I didn't know that the regulations were so precise and so detailed. . . . I didn't know that all my movements were inside the censorship book. I didn't know that everything I could imagine [publishing] had been anticipated by the censors. . . ."

This book also contains documents that are reviews of censorship compiled by the censorship office itself in *Report on Materials Censored*. These reviews were conducted periodically to inform the censors' superiors in the party leadership and to instruct individual censors how they had been too lenient (or harsh). These documents offer fascinating testimony as to how censorship works in practice. They reveal the absurd lengths to which the Gierek leadership went to foster so-called "propaganda of success." Censored texts included a discussion of inadequate facilities for container ships in the seaport of Gdańsk; a review of problems with shoes manufactured from synthetics; statistics on national coffee consumption; and a satire on the national housing shortage. They demonstrate that there was widespread resistance to the party leadership's conception of a monolithic media system from within the ruling Communist establishment itself. And they contain numerous censored warnings of the political earthquake that was to hit Poland in August 1980 and give birth to Solidarity—warnings the party leadership suppressed and ignored. Thus one prophetic article was censored because, as the censors' bulletin reported, ". . . the author pointed to the supposed existence of a 'kindling point' resulting from the 'unrealized democratic ambitions of the workers, who are anxious to have their voice be heard in fact, not just in theory.' "

September 1983   A. ROSS JOHNSON
                                    Associate Director
                International Security Policy Research
                            The Rand Corporation

ACKNOWLEDGMENTS

This book could never have been conceived without the moral outrage and courage of Tomasz Strzyżewski, who realized the absurdity of his work as a censor. He took the risk of squirreling away over a period of three years the materials on which this book is based. Then he boarded the ferry to Sweden, not knowing if he would see his family again, bearing these official documents with him—a legal offense that could have meant a long prison term had he been caught.

The book is also very much a reflection of the determination and independence of many so-called regime journalists. They tried to write about failures and inconsistencies of the system and about other public concerns even though, in most cases, they knew they ran the risk of not being published. If they had not dared to challenge the system, there would have been no need for a censors' office; nor would we have this record of the "truth" not considered safe for Poles to read. I owe many of these men and women, whom I came to know in Poland and abroad, an overwhelming debt of gratitude. They tried to translate their world to me—a task that was not only time-consuming but, I am sure, taxing. And they often took me on as a friend. This has been a very special experience.

In a negative sense, this volume exists only because of the failures of the Gierek leadership. Instead of solving problems, the leadership created a bureaucracy to write and enforce regulations denying that those problems existed. In the end, this ensured that the message of the Polish media departed so dramatically from reality that, far from being believed, it served to incense the Poles.

Finally, this book exists thanks to the efforts of *Aneks,* which issued a Polish-language version of the censorship documents in 1977–78, and thanks to The Rand Corporation, which undertook to sponsor preparation of an English-language interpretive translation. My own research in Poland in 1975–76 and again in 1983, which provided me with a base for my understanding of Poland, was funded by the International Research and Exchanges Board.

On a personal level, I owe a debt of gratitude to those who read all or part of this manuscript and tried to straighten out my misimpressions and misstatements: Ross Johnson, Abraham Brumberg, Joseph Fiszman, Andrzej Korboński, Kazimierz Brandys, Małgorzata Dymek-Karpińska and a number of Poles whose names must go unmentioned but whose help is more than appreciated. I am also grateful to Joan Dassin, who gave me a broader perspective. As always, none of these kind people is responsible for my interpretations or any mistakes.

I am grateful to my editor, Klara Glowczewski, for her patience and guidance, to Robert Scott for his help in translating the documents, and to Theresa Czajkowska, for her care for details.

This book was completed only because my family and friends kept me in touch with the real world. I am especially grateful to my husband, who has shared many of my fondest Polish experiences with me, my sons, Andrew and Matthew, who grew up along with this volume and kept me truthful with their questions. To those who gave my sons special time while I worked on this book, my special thanks: my parents, Bill Balderston, Betsy Closs, Nina Bernstein and Donna Crotty.

CONTENTS

I / THE WORLD OF THE CENSORS

1 / **INTRODUCTION**

IN FEBRUARY 1977 Tomasz Strzyżewski, censor no. C-36 of the Kraków Main Office for Control of Press, Publications and Public Performances, boarded the ferry to Sweden at Świnoujście, Poland, for what his passport described as a two-week vacation. His real purpose, though, was quite different. Strapped in plastic bags to his back and legs, mixed in with pages from newspapers and stuffed in his pockets, were some 700 pages of classified censors' documents. These he had collected, copied and slipped out of his office between the summer of 1975 and February 1977. His goal was to let the world and the Poles themselves, for whom the very word "censorship" had been ruled unprintable, know how the Communist Party bureaucracy under Edward Gierek was distorting the truth about their world by denying the reality of such events as the massacre of 8,000 Polish army officers by the Soviets in the Katyń forest during World War II, excising simple reports on day-to-day problems in Poland and orchestrating propaganda campaigns. In fact, it was the regulation requiring him to prevent any publication of the names of soldiers massacred at Katyń, among them his own grandfather's, and to ensure that the Polish media treated the incident just as the *Great Soviet Encyclopedia* did—dismissing it "in a few lines and attributing the crime to the Nazis"—that convinced him "that was the limit of what I could take . . . and the result is here before you."*

*Leopold Unger, "Censorship: Polish Defector Describes How It Works," *Herald Tribune*, June 5, 1978, p. 8.

What he carried with him out of Poland in 1977 was far more than a collection of classified documents. It was a record of the very fears of the Polish political leadership about its own failings and weaknesses, a record of the rot that pervaded Polish politics, economic life and social welfare long before the appearance of Solidarity unmasked the total failure of Gierek's politics and thrust the reality of censorship into the open. The regulations and censored articles tell the story of bureaucratic communism and the struggle of those caught in the system to survive, by exposing its failings or manipulating the truth. These documents are evidence of the concerns of the rulers and their attempts to create their own world in the media. They are also evidence of the specific failure of the Polish regime to convince, coopt or coerce the very journalists who, according to Lenin, were supposed to serve as its link with the population.* For Poland is the only country in the Communist world that has had to make such an exhaustive list of taboo subjects and maintain a mammoth bureaucracy of censors and supervisors outside the media to monitor and control what journalists do. Ultimately, then, these documents and the insights they provide into the history of Poland in the mid-seventies are the answer to the questions "Why Solidarity?" and "Why in Poland?"

For over thirty years Poles had lived with media that could not answer or address their questions or concerns because they either lied or told only part of the truth. People read newspapers and listened to radio and television, but they could not believe what they read and heard. With time, no information or promise coming from the Communist leadership rang true, and the very leaders who manipulated the media to maintain their public image lost almost all credibility. In an official 1980 poll, only 36 percent of the population said it trusted the Communist Party.† The writing was on the wall.

Significantly, when the workers in the Gdańsk shipyards organized and presented their demands to the government in August 1980, gaining access to accurate and complete information was almost as important a demand to them as the right to strike and the right to have independent unions.

Censorship, as it grew in direct proportion to the failures of govern-

---

*V. I. Lenin, "What Is to Be Done?" in *Collected Works* (Moscow: Progress Publishers, 1967), 1:233.
†1981 Survey by the School of Journalism and the Center for Public Opinion Research of Polish Radio and Television. Mimeographed copy.

ment policies, deprived not only the population of information, but the leadership as well. Journalists knew what they could not publish and avoided those subjects and problems. This left the party leadership dependent on its bureaucrats and policy makers to report their own failures—hardly something they did willingly or accurately. Yet losing control of the mass media was for the Polish leadership one of the most frightening of the concessions Solidarity demanded, and the one they fought hardest against making.

When the regime's declaration of "a state of war" on December 13, 1981, brought an end to the new workers' Poland and to the considerable freedom the media achieved after August 1980, it was not only Solidarity leaders who were frontally attacked in the immediate aftermath and in the various acts of repression. Journalists and editors, many of whom had worked in the system for years, were detained, fired and attacked as traitors and enemies. Many refused to further submit themselves and their work to the distortions of censorship and so left the field of journalism. The censors, after eighteen months of restraint while Solidarity was allowed to flower, had their full power restored to them. They now work basically as they did before, and the hopes of Poles that the media would someday independently reflect reality have been dashed.

This book is a social history of Gierek's Poland; its material evidence comes not from the "truth" that was allowed to appear in the media, but from that which could not appear. For by the mid-seventies, the truth was so troubling to the Gierek leadership, and the world they wanted Poles to believe existed was so far from reality, that the censors' own biweekly publication, *Report on Materials Censored*, comes closer to being an accurate image of the world of Communist rule than what was left to appear in the media.

The documents on which this book is based are far more than a picture of the Poland that frightened its leaders and alienated its population in the seventies: the Polish leadership is not alone in trying to deny its failures and blind its population with images that outshine reality. The other Communist states have also, in less systematized ways, redesigned the reality that appears in their media. Furthermore, though the Gierek leadership had probably one of the most complex and developed bureaucracies of media control in the world, its goals and sensitivities were not that different from those of authoritarian leaders, both Communist and non-Communist, who seek to rule not simply by terror but also by trying to convince their populations to see them as respectable. In all such societies the media, however unwilling, are the most viable tools of propaganda. And in all these systems the harder the leaders have pushed to control and mold the media, the more they have lost contact and control of their populations. So, while the examples here come from nearly three years of censors' records from Poland, the fears and frailties of rule that they illustrate have existed in differing degrees under conditions as diverse as the American occupation of Japan, the early years of military rule in Brazil and party rule in the rest of the Communist world.*

For the most part, the documents are those that Tomasz Strzyżewski found most representative and most offensive and, therefore, saved and smuggled out. There are no documents here pertaining to regulations protecting military or state secrets, for example. That responsibility of censorship Strzyżewski accepted when he took his job and continued to respect as legitimate. He brought with him, first of all, over seventy pages of rules that were regularly inserted in black loose-leaf notebooks of *Rules and Recommendations from the Main Office for Control of Press, Publications and Public Performances* (the so-called *Black Book*) from which each censor got his instructions on specific subjects and pieces of information that had to be removed. He also carried out the instructions given to novice censors and some sheets of special instructions (Informative Notes) that dealt with important issues in detail so that the censors would better understand what they needed to do to appropriately handle these issues or see to it that the media followed the "party line." And he brought out records of what the censors had to handle and how they did it. For the Main Office for Control of Press, Publications and Public Performances (GUKPPiW), Poland's official censorship apparatus, kept records of all its work. This it published in carefully numbered copies for the censors, the Central Committee officials in charge of the media and, presumably, party leaders who were interested in the semimonthly "red bulletins" reprinting the material that was censored or questioned by the censors in the two preceding weeks. Strzyżewski also smuggled out one example of a quarterly "brown bulletin" published by the GUKPPiW, summarizing the themes that had had to be censored in the preceding quarter and giving a full statistical analysis of what subjects and media organs were censored. Finally, the

---

*Jane Curry and Joan Dassin, eds., *Press Control Around the World* (New York: Praeger Publishers, 1982).

censors received, and Strzyżewski brought out, copies of long directives circulated by the Central Committee Press Department on the appropriate orchestration of media coverage for such events as the American Bicentennial and the Polish United Workers' Party (PZPR) Congress, held after much fanfare in December 1975.

All of this material was made exact because of the fact that, from all accounts, the censors were not especially dedicated or ideologically sophisticated people. They were—as their identity papers said, to shroud their work for the Main Office for Control—"bureaucrats," who most often took the job because they could get no other. (Strzyżewski, in fact, had no special training for his position; his brother, well placed in the municipal administration of Kraków, got him the job.)* The position of censor carried perquisites, but hardly enough to make up for its negative image in the society. Furthermore, whatever commitment any of them might have had to communism when they began work was eroded rapidly because they, after all, saw more than almost anyone else what was really going on in Poland and what had to be left unsaid. As a result, the Central Committee officials personally charged with media supervision and the directors of the Main Office for Control, whom the Politburo itself appointed, formulated regulations and in all ways carefully monitored the work of the censors. These documents, then, are a reflection not of the minds of the censors—many of whom often told journalists that they did not agree but followed the rules to keep their jobs—but of the top party leadership.

Under the leadership's direction, little escaped the censors' eyes. There were divisions in the Main Office for Control in Warsaw and in its various regional branch offices that approved business cards, rubber stamps, sheet music, concert, theater and exhibit programs, posters and even the private reproduction done in the British-licensed photocopying concession in Warsaw. Other employees of the Main Office worked with the post office to see that no unacceptable or untoward publications came to Poles from abroad. Above them in status were divisions that monitored films, theater performances, books, radio, television, newspapers and periodicals, no matter who their publisher and what their circulation. (In the material Strzyżewski brought out there are reports of major national or regional publications being questioned and "cleansed" as well as of articles and

*Interview, 1979.

statements being removed from tiny factory publications, amateur productions, student publications and academic writing.) In all, the censors intervened over 10,000 times each year in what appeared or was printed in Poland. Of course, only a fraction of the interventions are recorded here. Not only did the censorship officials who compiled surveys of their bureaucrats' work have to limit themselves to reporting that which would instruct their workers or interest their superiors, but Strzyżewski himself selected only those instances of censorship he thought were most important and objectionable. Furthermore, the very nature of the censorship process for television, performances and books—an ongoing consultation process among censors, producers and party officials that could not be recorded as clearly as examples of articles written and questioned—kept these kinds of impositions on Polish culture out of the reports that we now have in the West.

While censorship deeply affected everything that appeared in Poland's official media, from obituaries to intellectual discussions, and though the falseness of the mass media was no secret to anyone, the censorship documents themselves were shrouded in secrecy. Any revelation of or allusion to the existence of censorship in Poland had to be censored, and even the instructions given the censors were secret. Instructions were telegraphed in code from the Main Office for Control in Warsaw to regional police and then brought to the regional censors' offices to be decoded; limited numbered copies were made by the censor on duty and placed under lock and key until they were distributed to the censors. Many of the most significant regulations included the additional proviso that

> This is only for the use of the censors. Its existence may not be revealed or referred to as a reason for censorship to anyone.

It was only the sloppiness of a bureaucracy of uncommitted bureaucrats that enabled Strzyżewski to stay after work and copy regulations or documents by hand, or simply pick up outdated reports and guidelines inadvertently left around the office instead of being locked in the safe, as they were supposed to be.

As a result of the secrecy that was supposed to surround the censors' decisions, many leading editors claimed that even they had no idea of the extent of the regulations under which they worked in the Gierek era. The full truth about censorship came to be known only when the British émigré publishing house ANEKS published them in

Polish and sent them back to Poland to be reprinted by NOWA, the independent publishing house that in 1978 took it upon itself to send copies of the documents to all the major government and media officials. The revelations for those who had access to the NOWA reprints partially set the stage for later (1980) journalists' and writers' discussions of the tragedy of censorship during the Solidarity period. Then workers' demands that, along with free unions and the right to strike, the society be guaranteed freedom of the media, with censorship strictly regulated under law, opened the door for discussion of censorship.

Censorship in Poland was a far more insidious phenomenon than the regulations and the summaries of interventions would indicate. It became a part of the subconscious of every journalist. Not only did Polish journalists work under the media production constraints that affect all journalists everywhere—getting work out on time, wrestling with information blocks, pleasing editors and publishers who can hire and fire—but the majority of those in the journalistic profession had worked for thirty years under censorship. They had learned what could not be reported and they ceased to look at those areas, censoring themselves before they even began. Journalists in conversation in the mid-seventies would often say that there was no specific topic they could not write about, then admit that they did not even consider trying to write about the Soviet Union, the top Polish leadership or the most glaring problems in the society. They knew that any writing about these subjects would end up in their own desk drawers. And since they were paid for what they published, most could not afford the luxury of writing for themselves and their friends. In reaction to the long years of censorship, journalists had also developed a whole unspoken code to communicate to their audiences ideas that they had no hope of expressing directly. As a result, so that they could appear, ideas were elaborately veiled and often ultimately obfuscated.

Editors also exercised a kind of preemptive self-censorship. Only those strong enough to fight the censors and those unaware of the barriers they faced failed to exert more caution than even the censors themselves with respect to what they tried to publish. The bulk of the censorship recorded in these documents therefore applies to either the most prominent intellectual journals with powerful and established editors (either in the party or in the Catholic intellectual community) or to factory and student papers and small professional journals. Little if anything came from the dailies or the mass weeklies and monthlies whose editors had neither the time nor the prestige necessary to do battle with the censors. The censors had to do little more than speak and most editors obeyed. In 1976 top editors who were also members of the Communist Party Central Committee were given the formal right to make their own decisions on whether to follow the censors' orders or not, but according to *Report on Materials Censored* and the editors themselves, there was never an equal balance of forces even for them. Whether or not they had the ostensible right to make their own decisions, it soon turned out that in practice they still had to follow the censors' orders unless they were able to muster enough support in the party leadership to override the censors' negative decisions. For other editors, whether the censors "challenged" and "questioned" what they wanted to publish or whether they explicitly "censored" or "blocked" an article or passage or "ordered it removed," the effect was the same. Editors followed the censors' directions whether they were presented as suggestions or as orders.

In this book, the censors' rules and directives and the deliberate and inadvertent failures of the journalists' self-censorship paint a picture of Poland on the crest—after three years of government promises of success and just before the rapid collapse of the economy and political authority that took place in the late seventies. To show the Poland that existed but that could not be admitted to in the media, the various documents have been divided by topic. The picture that appears is very different from that reflected in the media, but it is far from complete: the more than 700 pages of documents and copies of documents that Tomasz Strzyżewski brought with him out of Poland represent but a fraction of the masses of regulations, instructions, reports and other information that circulated in the Main Office for Control and all its branches. This volume reflects a further selection of documents, but on the whole those dealing with all the basic issues confronting the censors are included here. Documents that were repetitious were cut.

The regulations that Strzyżewski took from the *Rules and Recommendations from the Main Office for Control of Press, Publications and Public Performances* are presented as evidence of the concerns of the leadership and those who protected its interests. These appear in the text as they did in the looseleaf notebooks from which Strzyżewski took them. They are not, however, identified individually as coming from the *Rules and Recommendations*. Some are dated and also show the date of cancellation when a restriction was lifted. (The ending of

a prohibition did not necessarily mean that publication was possible
—substitute regulations that may not have been smuggled out or the
general caution of the censors often continued to impose similar restrictions.) Others are undated because they were in effect for a long
period of time or because the date was simply not included with the
documents. In some cases, issues were complicated enough that the
wishes of the censorship bosses had to be spelled out more clearly; this
was done in detailed memos called Censors' Information (with supple-
mentary information that provided background on an issue) and
shorter Informative Notes. The smuggled documents also include
instructional materials in which poor judgment on the part of censors
is presented and discussed, as well as plans for handling some of the
major events for Polish propaganda in the mid-seventies: the Helsinki
Conference, the American Bicentennial and the Seventh Party Congress.

The volume also contains documents that show the concerns and
efforts of those on the other side of the censorship system—the writers
and journalists: the excerpts from the forty- to seventy-page *Report
on Materials Censored* and the forty-five-page *Bulletin of Themes of
Materials Censored in the Second Quarter of 1974* are the censors'
records of what journalists had to be blocked from saying. In line with
the style of the actual reports, when only part of a passage was
censored, the entire passage is included and the censored section is
underscored. Such examples show not only what was unacceptable,
but also how strategic cuts enabled censors to restructure what the
journalists wrote. When an entire passage is questioned and ordered
removed, the passage is presented without underscoring. In addition
to the challenged sections, the censors' own explanations as to why
a passage was objectionable or what it revealed are included as windows on the minds of those who direct censorship.

Censorship is as much a part of the history of Poland as are failed
promises and unwelcome rulers. It did not come merely with the
imposition of Communist rule on Poland after World War II. Since
Poland's partitioning among Prussia, Russia and Austria in the eigh-
teenth century, censorship has been an important element of rule.
During the partitions, it was imposed by each of the empires to
prevent intellectual journals from spreading revolutionary sentiments
among the tiny literate urban population. In the Prussian section, it

was also designed to destroy Polish nationalism by forbidding the very language and culture of the Poles. In the years just before World War I, the most restrictive practices of censorship had ended as a result of the liberalization of Russian and Prussian policies. But journals still had to be licensed by the administrators of the empires, and journalists and editors of the all too financially marginal journals knew a single article that was too critical might be cause for the confiscation of an entire issue, leaving them with nothing to sell to pay their publication's bills. Nevertheless, despite the restrictions under which they worked, those who dedicated themselves to journalism during the partitions were national leaders. After all, the press was the only forum for debate, however tiny, allowed to Poles.

The Versailles peace treaty at the end of World War I brought Poles what they had longed for: their own sovereign nation. Bringing a nation ruled by three separate empires for over a century, a nation that had been a battleground during World War I, together into the kind of democratic government Polish exiles had campaigned for proved difficult. For the press, the shift to a Polish government was not totally liberating. They were dependent on government advertisements for the funding they needed to survive, and these were offered only to journals that supported the government. The press laws of the partitions remained in force, allowing displeased politicians and administrators to confiscate journals that angered them. And journalists themselves were trapped by their own commitment to the survival of Poland: pleas for restraint in discussions in order to protect the interests of the fragile new state worked to make most journalists exercise self-censorship.

The Nazi German attack on Poland in 1939 brought with it the ultimate censor. Aside from the Polish-language papers put out by the Germans, Polish papers went underground. Journalists and editors from the prewar period and from the organization of underground resistance fighters strove to support the battles of the underground against the Germans to prevent them from destroying Poland and its population. To do this, in part, they used a press that could provide both inspiration and leadership to "Fighting Poland"—as the underground, which involved most of the Polish population, came to call itself. The German censorship that they knew was a simple and brutal one. To be caught carrying or printing these underground papers was tantamount to sabotaging German operations. The punishment was death or shipment to a concentration camp.

At the end of the war, most of the Polish underground turned from fighting the Germans to trying to prevent a Communist takeover in Poland either by the pro-Communist underground, which had been increasingly active during the war, or by the Soviet-controlled and -sponsored troops advancing from the Soviet Union. In this the underground was unsuccessful. The Soviet troops came through Poland as they pushed the defeated German troops westward. Rather than aid the Polish underground in its last battles with the Germans, the Soviets let the underground be defeated and brought with them a government of loyal Communists who had spent the war years in the Soviet Union, and installed them at first in Lublin to rule the newly liberated Poland.

What they had to rule was a devastated battleground. Little had survived unscathed and the population had been decimated. For this battle-scarred country, a Communist takeover was palatable only to the extent that it promised to get the nation on its feet again and protect it from another German attack. But Poles were not willing to concede to the Polish Communists the kind of political control they wanted. As a result, from the end of the war until 1948, when the Polish United Workers' Party formalized its total control, there was a vitriolic civil war in Poland as the nation sought to reestablish itself on its own terms.

Control of the media was an important part of the Communists' plan to take control of the country. In the early days of chaos, the Communists made no declarations. After all, the Communist government had access through its sponsor, the Soviet army, to the paper, portable presses and ink that were virtually unavailable in the rubble of Poland. No one knew and no one could control how those things were distributed. The Communist government had popular support for forbidding the reappearance of prewar rightist newpapers, but its definition of "rightist" fit its own needs more often than it did popular perceptions. As they installed their own people in each region in the wake of the Soviet army, the Communists opened new regional papers with editors they could trust. As the civil war progressed, the Communist forces targeted anti-Communist papers for mysterious attacks on their paper supplies, newly printed editions, journalists and distributors. These tactics left the pro-Communist press far stronger than the non-Communist journals that managed to survive, just as similar tactics against non-Communist parties and politicians in postwar Poland decimated those parties and their leadership.

Almost incidentally, the Main Office for Control of Press, Publications and Public Performances was established by ministerial decree in 1946. This regulation gave the Main Office the right and responsibility to protect the Polish state from any revelation of state secrets or "material which would be potentially damaging to the Polish state and its international posture."* To monitor the media of Poland, the new leadership relied on loyal Communists who had come with them from the Soviet Union or fought in the Communist underground during the war. Most of these were people without skills, many of them women, who were needed nowhere else in People's Poland. Censorship was a safe sinecure for them.

In the early years of Communist rule, these censors had little guarding to do. This was the period of Stalinism, and the society was ruled by a combination of fear and fervor. Young peasants and workers were drawn by the promises and possibilities of Poland's reconstruction and industrial growth. For many, the opportunities seemed breathtaking. At the same time, fear became a basic element of Polish life. Wartime fighters in the anti-Communist underground were hounded from their jobs. Professionals and academics who were ready to resume their work and help rebuild Poland were blocked from jobs and attacked because they were not loyal Communists. Those who criticized the system or somehow crossed those with political connections found themselves publicly purged and jailed.

All of this, however, did not give the Polish Communists real control over Poland. Communism itself had little real or widespread support in the society. Before and during the war, communism had been simply a Russian import. Nor was the Polish United Workers' Party, as the Polish Communists began calling themselves after 1948, strong. It was torn apart by ideological and personal conflicts. Those who came in with Soviet troops ousted and jailed many who had fought with the pro-Communist underground. The party's legacy was a leadership destroyed by Stalin because of its independence before the war began. As a result, the Polish Communists engaged in much less brutal repression than did the other East European leaderships. There were no purge trials where the defendants were put to death. Unable to thoroughly communize the population, the Com-

---

*"Dekret z Dnia 5 Lipca 1946 o Utworzeniu Głównego Urzędu Kontroli Prasy, Publikacji i Widowisk" (Decree of July 5, 1946, on the Establishment of the Main Office for Control of Press, Publications and Public Performances), *Dziennik Ustaw* (Gazette of current legislation), No. 34, p. 210.

munists satisfied themselves with getting support by offering jobs.

Journalists working in this atmosphere of fear and propaganda fervor were constantly caught in the conflicting demands made by the Stalinist system. Most of what their journals published came from press releases of the official press agency, from various government and party offices, and from reports by peasant and worker correspondents, so there was little space for them to publish in their own journals. Furthermore, though they were supposed to uncover problems, they were unwelcome in most enterprises, where NO JOURNALISTS WELCOME signs frequently appeared. Consequently, even when journalists could get their articles printed, they seldom were able to get any critical information to put in them—information that also might have been subject to censorship. And no matter how much the party propagandists told them they were the friends of readers, the readers treated them as regime spies. Also, like other professionals, journalists were expected to be political activists and spend their time working not in their profession but on political meetings. All of this left them with little time to write things that needed to be censored and with an acute sense of dissatisfaction about their situations.

During this time censorship became as much an act of monitoring as of terrorizing and controlling. Neither the censors nor the journalists had yet acquired skill in their crafts. For journalists to go beyond the narrow confines of what was sought was, they clearly understood, almost impossible, and when it wasn't, it was too frightening. The Central Committee Press Department and the censors who worked under it therefore had little need to give detailed instructions. Instead, they monitored the work of journalists and editors so that they could find those who would be trustworthy and competent leaders in producing propaganda.

The death of Joseph Stalin in 1952 and that of Poland's own party leader, Bolesław Bierut, at the Soviet Party Congress following Stalin's death brought a gradual end to the fear that had gripped Poland. As the Polish party leaders jockeyed with each other for more powerful positions, news of the paralyzing battles for power began to leak out. This, in turn, encouraged journalists and writers, university professors and artists to test their limits. By 1954 words that had been unspeakable even at private gatherings were being uttered at public conferences of journalists and writers. By 1956 these spoken words had become printed criticisms of the Polish system, its corruption, failures and repression, which in turn signaled to workers that they too could act. In June 1956 the city of Poznań was rocked by massive worker demonstrations and riots behind banners calling for "bread, truth and freedom for Poland." The battles between the police and the rioters put an end to the demonstrations in Poznań, but not to the unrest in Poland, which continued in public meetings and press discussions on subjects that had been taboo since the Communist takeover less than ten years before.

Soon the Polish United Workers' Party leadership was itself locked in a struggle for power. Ultimately, the majority agreed that the party's only hope was for Władysław Gomułka to return to the leadership and head the party. A leader in the Communist underground during World War II and, most importantly, jailed for his nationalism during the Stalinist period, Gomułka was the closest to a national hero the party could offer.

As the party leaders had hoped, Gomułka's return to power was heralded as a new beginning. The Poland he was to rule when he took over in October 1956 seemed irrepressible. Even the censors had been so caught up by the spirit of reform, and paralyzed by the cross-pressures of party leaders battling out their own desires for power by using the press, that they had voted themselves out of existence. In a stormy all-night meeting they sought a way out of what one of them was later to call a "brothel." Party officials, journalists and editors all joined in the discussion, and by morning a majority of the censors had voted to go on strike against censorship and to declare the Main Office disbanded. Thus censorship ended in Poland in September 1956 just as the Soviets were warning Hungary that its uncontrolled liberalization and press freedom had to be stopped. Polish journalists feared that their freedoms would be lost if there was no control over what was said in the media, so they took it upon themselves to form their own Board of Press Review. This group of senior journalists and government officials made a few fruitless attempts to have radical student journals calm their anti-Communist and anti-Soviet rhetoric, and tried to guide Poland's press away from excessive radicalization.

All of this apparent freedom of the press and society ultimately lasted only a matter of months, for Gomułka was more a traditional Communist than he was a nationalist. He watched over the dissolution of Soviet-style collectivized farming and the return of Polish peasants to their own plots; he conceded to the Catholic Church a protected position in Poland; the Polish Cardinal, Stefan Wyszyński, was released from house arrest and appeared as a public figure; religious education began again; and Catholic journals opened up after having been shut down in the Stalinist move to control the society. At the same time, however, Gomułka made it clear that these were concessions to stubborn Polish traditions, not signs of a new freedom. As he made these concessions, he also put a stop to the intellectual freedom that had convulsed Poland in the fall and winter of 1956. The most critical journals were closed down and new, controllable journals opened in their place as forums for whatever public debate was allowed. Censorship began again in 1957 and by the end of the decade was in full force at its old offices on *ulica Mysia* (Mouse Street, a tiny, alley-like passage across from party headquarters in Warsaw) and in regional centers all over Poland. Those who refused to make any concessions to Communist control were blacklisted; other critics were tolerated.

Politics under Gomułka came to be not a game of winning or losing, but a game of coexistence. Gomułka led a party of opponents and supporters. He saw press criticism, like internal party criticism and discussion, as a tolerable if unfortunate fact of life in any modern society. And so he largely left the press to its own devices just as he left the economy and his party to follow their own paths.

Insofar as censorship was concerned, party leaders under Gomułka wanted peace, not change; because they were not trying to mobilize the population, they felt no need to try and force the media to speak in one voice. The Main Office for Control made its own rules. If a ministry or party official called and wanted something blocked or included, the censors picked their way through the thicket of conflicting demands as best they could. Otherwise, censors had to decide individually what was acceptable and what was not. At the same time, journalists and editors knew that if they could find an ally in the party leadership, they could get a censor's decision overruled. What all this meant, for journalists and editors, was that what went on in the Main Office was unpredictable and mysterious, not definitive.

This communism of disinterest nearly ended in the mid-sixties when one of the party factions sought to oust Gomułka and his supporters. Formed around Mieczysław Moczar, the Minister of the Interior, the "Partisans," as this faction was called, saw control of the mass media as the road to control of the party and the government. Their attacks on journalists and officials made use of the Poles' traditional hatred of Russians and the strains of anti-Semitism that had grown in peasant Poland and been fanned before

World War II by the close ties Poles saw between the Polish Communist Party, the Soviet Union and Poland's Jewish community. All of this was compounded and made a ready point of attack by the fact that many Poles of Jewish origin had escaped to the Soviet Union when the Germans invaded Poland, spent the war years there, and returned with the Soviet forces as trusted Communists to run the new government. Many held high-level jobs in the media and the Main Office for Control, preventing young, better-trained Poles from moving into positions of power.

Members of the Moczar faction tapped this frustration and these traditional hatreds. They used their control over the Ministry of the Interior and its secret police to push older Communists of Jewish origin out of the Main Office and install their own supporters. Because censors until then had been left largely to their own devices, there was no existing organized system of decision making and the Moczarists could easily step in, give orders and use their own people. By doing this and by engaging in a similar assault on the staffs of various journals, this faction used the press as its assault weapon and orchestrated what became a full-scale condemnation and expulsion of Poles of Jewish origin. Moczar's bid for control of the party failed, however, and Gomułka, whose wife and some of whose lieutenants were ethnically Jewish, continued as its leader.

The Moczar attack was not the last for the Gomułka regime. An ill-timed pre-Christmas attempt to reduce subsidies on food brought workers to the streets all over Poland in December 1970. Even as troops shot striking shipyard workers in the Baltic towns of Gdańsk and Szczecin, it was clear that Gomułka could no longer maintain himself as the head of his party or the nation—especially since there was a savior waiting anxiously in the wings. Edward Gierek, head of the party in the prosperous Silesian coal basin, had long promoted himself as Poland's independent miracle worker. And since few went to Silesia to see what was actually happening there, it was easy for him to maintain the myth that, in Silesia, prosperity and economic and intellectual freedom went hand in hand—just as they seemed to in Western Europe, where Gierek had spent much of his childhood.

When he became the head of the Polish United Workers' Party, Gierek promised the Poles prosperity. Nearly every group in Poland got instant wage increases and promises of the kinds of changes in working conditions and benefits that they had called for all during the Gomułka period. The nation as a whole was promised that it would be listened to by the new leaders. Gierek's plan was to rapidly develop Poland's industrial base by importing technology, equipment and materials from the West, paid for with the low-interest loans that were being proffered by Western nations moving to cement the political détente that had been established and to invest their petrodollars. To get workers to increase their productivity, Gierek promised massive reforms in living standards and also imported sought-after Western goods as a short-term reward. To pay back Poland's loans and to provide the improvements in the living standard that he had promised, he counted on being able to use what the factories that were being built would produce.

An unspoken correlate of these economic reforms was the centralization and control of Polish politics. In the minds of the social and economic "engineers" who dominated the Gierek leadership, questions and discussions about alternatives were counterproductive. To get the population to work harder, the media had to be engineered to convince the workers that this was the best and only alternative for Poland and would definitely bring them the gains they were promised. The party, too, could no longer be an organization of supporters and opponents, as it had been under Gomułka, but had to be a cohesive body working for their leaders' goals. Gierek knew from experience how regional politicians could use their positions to get control, so he made sure that no regional leader would be able to displace him as he had displaced Gomułka. The party was therefore centralized and its leadership cleansed of all but Gierek's men. And since journalists and writers could not be convinced to speak only in superlatives about Gierek's plans, most of which they had advocated originally, the Party Press Department and the Main Office for Control had to be strengthened and given direct orders.

In the early seventies, the political and economic changes that Gierek was making appeared to be bringing prosperity to Poland. But by the mid-seventies, when the documents in this book were issued, the "economic miracle" was failing, and the Gierek regime came more and more to talk of the "economic maneuver" (manipulating the economy without making deep structural changes) as a way to survive until the economy caught up with itself. With this came the "propaganda of success," the decision that no matter what disasters befell Poland and its economy, the government would claim success and, by so doing, convince the population that it was indeed successful.

To this end, the powers of the Central Committee Press Department and its "instructors" (officials in charge of specific papers or broadcast media) were increased. The instructors had the right to decide what could appear in the media, the responsibility of designing media campaigns and the job of regularly reviewing each individual paper, magazine and broadcast program. Television news was given the special position of being an outright organ of the party leadership. The censors in the Main Office for Control were tied more closely than ever to the Press Department and subordinated to it. Only Press Department officials could approve the regulations according to which censors made their decisions. The Main Office itself was enlarged and centralized so that censors acted under orders and with constant supervision rather than being left to make their own judgments, as they had in the Gomułka era. For journalists and editors, all this meant that they could no longer use their political connections to push through articles they wanted published. They were trapped by the bureaucracy that had come to control their publication.

This strictly controlled propaganda bureaucracy only served increasingly to isolate and close off the official media. As the failures of Gierek's economic plan became more and more apparent, a whole series of unofficial, open publications began to appear from the intellectual opposition that developed and grew in strength in the wake of the workers' strikes of 1976. The worse the situation became, the less the official media were allowed to reflect reality and the less negative information Gierek and his men wanted to either share or hear. And instead of trying to deal with the difficult economic situation that was developing in Poland, they busied themselves with fulfilling their own personal needs and ambitions. While Poles were facing increasingly painful shortages of food and consumer goods, these men provided themselves with the goods and services they wanted, setting a standard of ostentatious corruption.

By the mid-seventies, Poland had become a land of two separate worlds: a leadership that lived well and held tightly to its bureaucratic reigns of power, and a population that spent its time coping with the realities of constant shortages and media that could not be believed. So, even though the Gierek leadership had ousted its opponents in the party leadership and consolidated all of the power in the central bureaucracy run by Gierek's own men, the population was coming to ignore that leadership and to rely on its own world of gossip and underground journals, personal connections and under-the-counter purchases, all the while nurturing a silent fury over the bureaucracy they saw living well and ruling badly.

What would have been the link between the governed and the governors—the mass media—was destroyed by Gierek's "propaganda of success" and the restraints that it put on any public expression of the true state of affairs. As journalists were all too well aware, no one believed the "propaganda of success" or those associated with it as either its executors or its orchestrators of discussion. What was even more important, a social or economic problem that could not be addressed in the mass media did not disappear; often it grew worse since there was no outside control, and, furthermore, the population's own ignorance about the causes and extent of the problem merely made them more bitter than they would have been had they been told the facts. The results were clear: in 1976, in industrial areas all over Poland, a sudden increase in prices triggered riots that could only be stopped by a return to the old prices; in 1980, when the government tried again to raise prices, the workers struck again. But in 1980 they were unwilling to settle for only temporary economic gains. They wanted their hunger for information to be filled as well.

The fury that existed over the falseness of the mass media was something journalists had warned about in 1974 and 1975, only to have their criticisms of Gierek's "propaganda of success" removed by the censors. One writer's observations in 1974, on the growing distance between media images and reality, was red-penciled out by the censors:

> . . . radio programs and some press publications are increasingly "favoring what we should be on our guard against—cheerfully smiling stupidity. . . . The reality coming out of the speaker is too joyful and noisy to be bearable," the same writer added. In another item it was noted that "there is resistance to recognizing the right of reporters and journalists to represent public opinion. . . . Reporting is avoiding research in favor of more or less safe prepackaged materials . . . where wishful thinking is confused with reality." Such a situation exists at the present time, according to the author, and is a threat to all the mass media. (*Bulletin of Themes of Materials Censored*, February 1974)

The censors made it clear that articles like the one submitted to them by *Odgłosy* (a weekly from the city of Łódź, one of Poland's oldest and poorest industrial centers), in which "the author was critical of the role of radio, television and much of the press structuring our way of thinking about basic problems," would not appear and tarnish the image of the media that Gierek sought. The censors removed the following sections from "Games and Politics," as well as its title:

"Only a small, negligible portion of our press appears to view reality as one great, joyous game. But this, after all, is precisely what we get over the radio waves. It would be interesting to know whether the people who constantly listen to our radio programs are more familiar with the name of the candidate of the United Left in the French presidential campaign or the director of the Paris Olympia [a music hall theater], with a famous political activist or a leading figure in the entertainment industry. . . . I have the impression that while the press provides a lot of information and commentary on general world problems, the radio has tried to keep such things to a minimum and, even if it does give a few minutes of its precious time to these matters, it follows them immediately with music for entertainment, as if to suggest to its listeners: 'Gentlemen, it's all a joke, the conflicts, the problems, the conferences, and so on. The world is one great show.' . . . Some are sorry and others relieved that the press has not yet created such an image for itself, that there are still some objective parts, that a newspaper, until now at least, cannot sing. . . . However, has it not been possible of late to observe signs that the press is beginning to lean toward mass taste? Now the specialized periodical, hitherto known for its courage and uncompromising nature, is beginning to publish rewritten material here and there." (*Report on Materials Censored,* May 1–15, 1974)

The most direct attack on this practice of presenting reality only as gleaming perfection came from Stefan Kisielewski, Poland's leading lay Catholic critic and one of the censors' most frequent adversaries. Kisielewski used the contrast between the positive images presented in Polish films and the negative pictures presented in American films like *The Effect of Gamma Rays on Man-in-the-Moon Marigolds* to attack the falseness of the "propaganda of success." The final paragraphs in his article consisted of criticism so explicit that Kisielewski must have known (as both he and censors claim he has in many other cases) that it would be censored and appear only in the report made by the censors for their superiors to read and consider:

In Issue No. 50 of *Tygodnik Powszechny* [the major Catholic intellectual weekly], an article by Kisiel [Kisielewski's pen name] entitled "An Exhibition of Mournfulness or Rejoicing?" criticizing our system of propaganda, was challenged. Extensive paragraphs from this article are quoted below:

". . . In Warsaw I saw an interesting American film with the paraphrased Polish title *Defenseless Marigolds*. The film was preceded by a Polish short from the series celebrating the 30th anniversary of the Polish People's Republic, this one devoted to Łódź. The short, a beautifully photographed, wide-screen color production, was bursting with joy, energy and images of prosperity. Of course, it started off by showing a little bit of the ghetto ruins and a couple of scenes adapted from the martyrology of the occupation, but everything that followed was sweetness and light: construction, expansion, bright, spacious factory halls, smiling faces, good-looking, nicely dressed girls, colorful streets, new theaters and hotels. After this, the American film turned out to be a dreadfully sad experience . . . a stark contrast to the unrestrained joyfulness of Łódź. . . .

"And in this same regard, I was struck by something else about this otherwise coincidental contrast. Here you have the world's most affluent great power showing us a film about its way of life that is embittered and self-doubting, and here we are whistling tunes about 'the merry lads of Kraków,' marching off into a world without doubt and sadness. Someone will say that this is not the great power the United States, but rather film director Paul Newman, private citizen, describing his own observations and doubts. True, but he wanted to and was able to do this. Nobody was worried about creating a bad impression or negative propaganda. I have also witnessed this sort of thing in an 'official' context. Warsaw recently played host to an American gala: a screening of the film *The Sting*, which was honored by Hollywood with a number of 'Oscars' (and in which Paul Newman played a leading role). The performance was attended by all of Warsaw's 'fashionable society,' led by several official personages. Illustrated albums commemorating Edward Gierek's visit to Washington were handed out to the guests as they entered the theater. The evening began with a very cordial welcome from the U.S. ambassador himself. And what about the film? It was an amusing but perfidious tale of gangsters, murderers, blackmailers, cardsharps and racetrack swindlers. . . . Well, this was all fine, even healthy. No one was shocked. No one was worried that the audience would generalize this view of life in America, that the film would discredit the United States, denigrate it or present it in a bad light. Just imagine what a portrait of sublime happiness, optimism and self-confidence we would present on this kind of occasion! And yet which approach would be more convincing?

"The view that art which portrays the realities of everyday life (not the kind of abstract, 'sublime' art that Mr. Andrzej Sulikowski has been rattling on about in *Tygodnik*) is the display window of a system, a government, a nation or a fatherland, and that such a display window should be decorated only with things that are proper and uplifting, this view remains unproven, but its consistent application over the years has already done us an incalculable amount of harm. But, most importantly, it has deprived us of a literary and cinematic record and testament of our age, the loss of which has been described more precisely by Kornhauser and Zagajewski in their extraordinary book. [*Unknown World,* a study of Polish literature, was considered objectionable by the censors and, though technically published, was never actually made available for sale in Poland; Kornhauser and Zagajewski are themselves Polish writers and experts in Polish literature.] This is a painful loss, and serves no purpose whatsoever, since the consistent optimism has still not persuaded anyone, and may have even achieved quite the opposite effect. It is inconceivable that we would exhibit bad machine tools at the Essen Exposition. We can only exhibit good ones. The same goes for novels, but a good novel cannot portray only the bright side of life. It has to have elements of black and white, light and dark. This is why *Ashes and Diamonds,* a book which in my view is historically inaccurate, continues to be such a popular novel when so many others have faded into oblivion: because its author divided the light and distributed equal portions to both sides." (*Report on Materials Censored,* December 1–15, 1974)

2 / THE POLISH MEDIA AND THE MECHANICS OF CENSORSHIP

THE WORLD of the Polish censors was not a simple one. In journalists and editors they faced strong adversaries who, after more than thirty years of working under censorship, had by the mid-seventies developed not only a sixth sense of what could be written, but also an arsenal of maneuvers for getting their material published despite the censors. The directors of the Main Office for Control of Press, Publications and Public Performances (GUKPPiW) and their superiors in the PZPR Press Department sent the censors a plethora of rules, instructions and examples of good and bad censorship. These the censors had to adjust to fit the whole panoply of newspapers, magazines, scholarly journals, radio, television, theatricals and books. For even as the Gierek propaganda bosses depleted the Poles' supply of information and silenced criticism in the media, they maintained a media system that was the most diverse in the Soviet bloc: for a population of over 30 million people, Poland had 56 different daily newspapers and 595 magazines, 4 radio stations and 2 television channels, as well as 220 different factory newsletters and a lively world of theaters and cabarets. The circulation of Poland's print media ranged from two million copies for the weekly women's magazine *Przyjaciółka* and one and a half million copies for the weekend edition of the Party's own daily, *Trybuna Ludu* (with a weekday circulation of 900,000 copies), to less than 100,000 copies daily for some local papers that appeared only five times a week and 50,000 copies weekly of the much sought-after independent Catholic weekly *Tygodnik Powszechny*. Scholarly and professional journals as well as factory newspapers appeared in tiny editions that barely covered the needs of their membership. Polish television, by far the most used of the media in Poland, was seen everywhere. Among urban dwellers, there were 95 television sets for every 100 homes.

Just as the elaborate system of censorship was evidence of the failure of the Communist authorities to face problems squarely and lead the country, the stacks of different newspapers and magazines in corner newsstands were evidence of the leadership's own recognition of the divisions in the population and the need to recognize these differences to get some popular support. So, while Marxist ideology promised a society without class or conflict, these Marxist leaders, like their counterparts in the Soviet Union and the other East European countries, invested in diverse media with something targeted for almost every interest group and some kinds of information deliberately given to some but not others. Such extensive media exist in every Communist society and are a reflection of the principle that to divide is to conquer, by never allowing the population to think of itself as a huge mass with common interests and the numerical strength to realize them. But in Poland the diversification went further and brought with it a measure of openness. The post-Stalin period saw the appearance of Catholic periodicals independent of both the Church and Communist ideology, as well as formal Church publications. A group of intellectual weeklies, dealing critically with cultural, political and economic issues, also appeared, and it was these weeklies (*Polityka, Kultura, Życie Literackie, Literatura, Życie Gospodarcze* and *Prawo i Życie*) that set the tone for the Polish media as a whole.

These intellectual weeklies printed most of the critical discussion appearing in the media. Their contributors and staff comprised Poland's most respected and best-known journalists and intellectuals. Their editors were men of political prominence who, in most cases, used their journals as platforms for the policies they supported. As a result, articles in these weeklies were avidly read, and far more copies could have been sold than the 300,000 or fewer that each was authorized to print by government publishers.

For the censors, working with the weeklies was difficult at best. Rules that held for all the media were sometimes bent for these journals in recognition of their intellectual audience's tastes and their editors' own power. But this did not mean that they were above censorship. Even though the three that served as centers around which discussions revolved (*Polityka, Kultura* and *Życie Gos-*

podarcze) had been formed as "loyal equivalents" to the journals that lit the fires of the dramatic liberalization in 1956 *(Po Prostu, Nowa Kultura, Przegląd Kulturalny)*, they hardly spoke in the subservient voice that Gierek wanted in the mid-seventies. Because they were so prominent politically and personally, the editors of these journals took risks and submitted articles to which the censors could not help but object. They were also willing, on many issues, to appeal the censors' decisions to high-level censorship officials or to their friends in the political leadership. Even so, it was these journals that were the targets, along with the Catholic publications, of most of the objections raised by the censors.

The weeklies reflected Poland's prewar tradition of the press as a forum of intellectual debate and discussion, as well as the realities of its current politics. They were not intended to be vehicles for information or reviews of weekly events; like the intellectual journals that set the tone for the West European press before the advent of mass tabloids, they were primarily for exchanges of opinion and impressions and for advocacy. Each journal had its own special topics and ideological issues. And each cultivated its own special audience. The two most specialized were *Życie Gospodarcze* and *Prawo i Życie*. *Życie Gospodarcze* was primarily an economic affairs journal. But since economics was the stuff of politics and social welfare in a state where any private enterprise was limited and influenced by the state, this journal often dealt with politics and social affairs. *Prawo i Życie* was the organ of the Polish Lawyers' Association. When its editor was strong, however, it covered far more than legal issues and took stands that were often very different from those of the association.

Kultura, Literatura and *Życie Literackie* all had the task of handling Poland's cultural life. But they were far more than simply literary journals. Like Polish culture itself—which served writers and artists as a vehicle for political statements and which was dependent for its funding on the government and subject to censorship—these were journals with a political purpose. *Życie Literackie* is the oldest of Poland's cultural weeklies. Established in the old center of Poland's traditional intellectual life, Kraków, in the late forties, it represents an attempt to give intellectuals who refused to support the new regime something that would ease their acceptance of Communist rule. Its editor, Władysław Machejek, has fought—unsuccessfully—for the Kraków establishment to accept his journal and the Communist way. *Życie Literackie* has survived and become his personal fiefdom—

involved in factional battles within the party (during the late sixties, for example), when such involvement offered Machejek a chance to increase his political power, or limited to purely literary concerns when that suited his needs. His victories in the seventies lay in his ability to be left alone to publish who and what he wished—adherents of the dissident movement as well as prominent politicians whom Gierek had pushed out to protect his exclusive hold on the political establishment.

Kultura, the national equivalent of *Życie Literackie,* was a tool of the retrenchment process that occurred after Gomułka had taken power. Until the mid-seventies, this journal was considered the regime's attempt to control Polish culture: it had been formed when the two leading journals pushing for radical change in Poland, *Nowa Kultura* and *Przegląd Kulturalny,* were closed down. Its editors in the sixties were not interested in liberalization of cultural policies, as were most of Poland's leading intellectuals; they advocated a rethinking of Polish wartime history. By the mid-seventies, though on the surface it appeared to be the same journal of poetry, prose, literary reviews (by regular columnists and guest authors), historical articles and literary debates, with only one of its four four-page sections devoted to social and political affairs, *Kultura* began to change dramatically in its staff and public image. The editor who took over in 1974, Dominik Horodyński, had an entirely different mind-set from that of the former editors. His experiences as Poland's ambassador to Rome and as a member of Poland's prewar aristocracy were reflected in the new views that began to appear in the weekly: the need for socioeconomic reforms in Poland, demands for greater cultural freedoms and increased discussion of the experiences of other nations. Although the change in the journal's profile was hampered somewhat by the realities of a complicated editorial process that remained much as it had been in the sixties—numerous contributors and relatively autonomous section editors—*Kultura* did emerge in the mid-seventies as a respected intellectual journal and one that frequently alarmed the censors.

Kultura's competition, *Literatura,* was Gierek's major olive branch to the cultural intelligentsia. It was intended to be a journal for the writers and intellectual critics who had been blacklisted in the sixties, but it never "took off." Just after it was established in 1972, *Kultura* began to liberalize and draw the very audience that *Literatura* was to attract. Just as *Literatura* got established, however, the rapid expansion of media control denied its staff and contributors the ability to express the very things for which they had been blacklisted in the late sixties.

The most prominent of the intellectual weeklies is *Polityka,* which in the sixties gave Gierek his national platform and, through its party connections, pushed him forward as a contender for power with Gomułka. By the mid-seventies the *Polityka* staff and its editor, Mieczysław Rakowski, saw that the Gierek leadership had failed as competent modernizers and did not support, as it had at first seemed they would, a liberal media policy and professional involvement. Because Rakowski combined his editorial position with membership in the party's Central Committee, and because most of the staff had weathered their journal's good and bad times for twenty years, *Polityka* could afford to become—and soon became—the most continuously critical of the weeklies. In its departments and columns dealing with economic, sociopolitical, cultural, historical, foreign and national affairs, journalists took on issues as they saw them. Generally, they advocated Poland's modernization, the use of technology, liberal social and cultural policies, and an active role in international affairs—things Gierek said he supported even as he moved Poland backwards in each area. Rakowski himself often published tough critiques, supported his managing editors in their battles with the censors and, at the same time, kept the journal within the regime's limits of the tolerable by quelling certain criticism or directing journalists to write positive articles as well as critical ones. For these journalists, censorship was not to be feared. They had worked together for nearly twenty years, so they knew the rules of the game and how best to circumvent the censor's red pen. They helped each other. Also, *Polityka* had the generous policy of paying anyone whose article was accepted for publication whether or not the censors finally approved it, rather than following the customary pattern of paying only for what was published. And, ultimately, journalists counted on Rakowski's political power and connections to protect them and their articles.

In 1976 Rakowski's power and prestige, as well as his close relationship with the Gierek leadership, brought *Polityka* the promise that it could join the Central Committee's own journals (the daily *Trybuna Ludu* and *Nowe Drogi,* the party theoretical monthly, whose editors were trusted employees of the committee) and move above the rule of the censors. The Central Committee announced that Rakowski and his staff would be allowed to make their own decisions on what would appear in their journal. This proved to be a sham: in the first two weeks of its new independence, *Polityka* published articles considered so offensive by the censors that they quickly moved from making recommendations to giving orders again. And though the censors were told that freedom would be extended to other weeklies with prominent politicians as editors, in reality the weeklies continued to be ordered about by the censors and, increasingly, had little recourse for appeal. (In the ten weeks for which we have the censors' own statistical records of interventions, forty-nine articles from these journals were questioned and only five were published over the censors' objections.)

In 1976 the censors were given an Informative Note that attacked two articles published in *Życie Gospodarcze* on the editors' authority, for going beyond the limits of the tolerable. In these cases, the editors clearly had a very different picture of what should be allowed than did the Press Department and the GUKPPiW. The articles were in line with the European tradition of critical intellectual weeklies rather than with Gierek's goal of the media speaking in one voice. The Informative Note reprinted here lays out the limited flexibility that was given to three of the intellectual weeklies because of their special roles and their politically prominent editors. That editors could decide whether an article should appear only if it would have been acceptable to the censors anyway was also made clear:*

Main Office for Control of Press,
   Publications and Public Performances
Instruction, Evaluation and Control Group
No. ZI-Pf-134a/2/76

                    Warsaw, 6 July 1976
                    C O N F I D E N T I A L
                    Copy No. 48

Informative Note No. 2

The control formula for *Trybuna Ludu* and *Polityka* was recently extended to *Życie Gospodarcze*.

In keeping with the principles in effect with regard to this formula, the employees of the GUKPPiW are required, in the course of control-

*See also pages pp.265–66.

ling these publications, to confiscate without discussion all publications that violate existing regulations and instructions concerning protection of state secrets. On the other hand, in assessing controversial articles, they are required to communicate their reservations to the editorial leadership. In practice, the editorial leadership usually shares our views and, in the light of our suggestions, publications in dispute are corrected or deleted.

In the event the editorial leadership does not agree with the censors' reservations and does not wish to adopt our suggestions, and the difference of opinion concerns less important questions, such a publication is permitted to be printed, provided that the editor in chief assumes personal responsibility for printing unchanged the formulations or excerpts questioned by us.

Nonetheless, this solution may not be employed if the difference of opinion between the office and the editors concerns an item that is very important in our domestic or foreign policy. In such instances, both sides must appeal to the PZPR Central Committee's Press Department leadership or to *województwo** leaders [who hold the ultimate responsibility for what appears in the media].

The controversial items discussed here from *Życie Gospodarcze* concerned very important, difficult socioeconomic problems and should, therefore, have been assessed with proper care by both the editorial leadership and our office employees. It should be understood that the censor was mistaken in [only] stating a number of his reservations and calling for appropriate deletions and reediting but [then], to some extent, giving in to the editors' arguments. It is true that two minor corrections were made in the text and that it was stated that the leadership of *Życie Gospodarcze* had decided to publish the questioned items and take full personal responsibility for this decision, but, in this case, such a solution of the matter was wrong for general social reasons. In keeping with the regulations in effect, permission should not have been given to print the articles and the censor should have made his reservations known to his supervisors so that the editors would have had to make the necessary deletions and do the essential reediting.

Distributed according to the list

No such special treatment was even suggested for Catholic publications. Their very existence was considered a concession by the government, granted because of the Poles' commitment to the Church. The Catholic media were subject to special censorship regulations, and

*Voivodship. Regional governmental district, one level below the national government.

according to both former censors and Catholic journalists, specially trained censors scrutinized with great care everything that was to be published. Catholics only had permission to publish printed material. No Communist leadership was willing to permit the Church to have access to radio or television for fear that it would make the Church too strong and available. The press that existed in the seventies was divided into the publications of the Church hierarchy, for use in individual parish ministries, and the publications of lay Catholic intellectual groups. These groups were basically divided into those who supported the Communist regime in Poland and those who saw their role as one of preserving Polish values in the face of and against the communism that had been imposed on them.

The pro-Communist Catholic press was published by the PAX organization, established by the government right after the war to counter the Catholicism of the population by coopting it. Its daily, *Słowo Powszechne,* and its other periodicals were part of what became a major publishing enterprise in Poland, concentrating on foreign books and apolitical Catholic books. The independent Catholic group, Znak, was allowed far fewer resources and publishing rights. Its weekly, *Tygodnik Powszechny,* and the various periodicals that came out of its discussion groups (the Clubs of Catholic Intelligentsia) such as *Więź* and *WTK (Wrocławski Tygodnik Kulturalny)* were havens of criticism and independent thinking. They were also the most highly censored journals in Poland.

The rest of Poland's media establishment found itself somewhere between the bold example set by the intellectual weeklies and Znak journals and the more traditional roles of the media in a Communist system. Each journal *addressed* a different audience. Most were to serve the interests of a specific organization. There were journals formally published by various party organizations; journals published by unions and professional and social organizations; and the journals of Poland's two minority parties, the United Peasant Party and the Democratic Party, aimed at reaching the peasantry and the private tradesmen. There was also a category called "readership journals," which did not originate with a specific social group but were designed to appeal to a broad audience of readers with their fairly general and unideological presentations. Some of these were élite dailies like Warsaw's daily *Życie Warszawy,* others were afternoon tabloids put out in Poland's larger cities. Finally, there was a special-interest press that ranged from periodicals put out by large and small scholarly organizations to amateur factory newspapers. Whether they served students, workers, peasants or scholars and specialists, all these journals were ultimately controlled and directed by the party's Press Department and dependent on the government for approval, printing and distribution.

Party and government control was no lighter for radio and television programs, books, theater or film productions. Gierek made promises of increased funding for each of these areas, but at the same time party and government control and interest in these media increased dramatically. The nightly television news became not just a television program but the organ of the party leadership itself, and censors participated actively in the production process in all these areas.

Because the party leaders themselves ran the Main Office for Control of Press, Publications and Public Performances, their media were accorded special treatment. Party journals—from the monthly *Nowe Drogi* to the daily *Trybuna Ludu* and regional party dailies—appear in the censorship documents only as standards of coverage for the rest of the mass media. They were left to censor themselves under the direct supervision of a top party official assigned to them. Little active direction actually went on (except of television news, considered the most important medium by the Gierek leadership) simply because the editors were well-placed members of the political élite who knew what was to be said and what was to be left unsaid since they were privy to all the political discussions that went on in the upper echelons of the party. They and their journals were careful and circumspect about their work because they knew it was read as the party's own word both in Poland and abroad.

In fact, most of the journals and programs in Poland needed little outside censorship (though the censors still read them all closely). Their editors chose not to take risks and so avoided anything they thought might be censored. Normally, only journals with prominent editors and staff, books and productions with prominent backers; and tiny specialized journals or amateur papers and productions required cuts by the censors. For journals like the daily *Życie Warszawy* and the satirical weekly *Szpilki,* censorship was a risk that had to be taken cautiously, as it was for the minor Democratic Party weekly *Tygodnik Demokratyczny* (aimed at the private tradesmen and non-Communist urban populations) and for *Słowo Powszechne,* the pro-Communist Catholic PAX daily. The editors of these publications were established enough that censorship did not mean the loss of their positions, and their audiences required they not simply be carbon copies of the party line. Student papers were also among the most censored. The editors and journalists of as such weeklies as *ITD, Politechnik* and *Medyk* were not yet inculcated with all the limits that those who were more experienced placed on themselves. In this respect, their weeklies were like the tiny factory newspapers, professional association publications and occasional academic publications whose names appeared on the censors' reports. Beyond this, the student papers and factory newspapers were products of their audiences' expectations: had they not been critical, they would not have been read.

Because of the variations that are built into the mass media, censorship in Poland is, by design, inconsistent. As is clear from *Rules and Recommendations,* some things may be published in one journal and not in another, so journals that specialize are able to publish more than others in their area of specialization. The rule of thumb for censors—the smaller the audience, the larger the margin for criticism—allows sociopolitical weeklies more leeway than dailies and tiny-circulation scholarly journals even more room. Some topics are blocked from discussion for a specific period of time and then allowed, with no explanation for the change. Writing about some issues is simply not feasible at all; other matters may appear when the references are to low-level problems; and some issues may be discussed with no censorship whatsoever. In addition, articles may be blocked from one issue of a journal and then allowed in another. In these cases, the censor may simply feel that there is too much criticism in one issue of a journal or that the article, in the context of other articles in that issue, takes on too problematic a tone.

For the 10,000-plus journalists who worked in the Polish media in the seventies, as well as the writers, editors and producers responsible for Poland's output of books, films and theater, censorship began long before they had something finished and ready to be approved. No matter what role they wanted to play in society, each knew that he was expected to function as Lenin had said he would: "not only as a collective propagandist and collective agitator but also as a collective organizer,"* and as the eyes and ears of the party. In the words of

---

*V. I. Lenin, "What Is to Be Done?" in *Collected Works* (Moscow: Progress Publishers, 1967), 1:233.

Gierek, this meant that the main responsibility of the media and culture in the seventies was to

> win over public support for the policies of the party; deepen the bond between the party and the nation; with party members and nonmembers, participate in developing the party line, liberate social initiative and strengthen society's knowledge and discussions. . . . Its basic task is to increase the effectiveness of its political and ideological influence in the direction of developing a socialist world-view, national morality and a basic sense of responsibility for the development of the country and the joint management of the national riches.*

This role left little room for individual initiative and independence; it made journalism and artistic work political no matter what their topics. And it meant that however much they wanted to monitor and question policy decisions and administration, journalists knew they were limited by the government's demands on them.

Journalists were caught between the professional goals they set for themselves and the demands made on them by party and state leaders. They were also trapped between the professional world they controlled in their offices and the world of party and state media moguls who controlled what was to be published with formal and informal instructions: on the one hand, editors encouraged journalists to write creatively; on the other, those same editors had to send those articles out to be censored. The Main Office for Control of Press, Publications and Public Performances sat at the intersection of these two worlds. Above it sat the party's Press Department, the top party official charged with propaganda and, purely formally, the Prime Minister's office. Working with the Main Office were the various publishing houses, theaters, the Polish Radio and Television administration and the Ministry of Culture divisions responsible for approving publishers' book lists and production plans for theaters and the other artistic institutions that it supported. And seeking approval from the Main Office were various newspapers, journals, radio and television programs, book publishers and artistic institutions.

Ironically, even as Gierek expanded and strengthened this media-control hierarchy during his tenure in office, the whole media-control process was pushed further into the shadows. Under Gierek, the Main

*"O dalszym socjalistycznym rozwoju PRL, wytyczne KC PZPR na VI Zjazd partii," *Nowe Drogi*, October 1971, pp. 73–74.

Office for Control functioned independently of any ministry. The Press Department became one of the larger departments of the Central Committee. The Main Office and the Press Department were both listed in the Warsaw telephone book as regular government and party offices. Changes in their directors were routinely announced in the press. Yet their work was not public: only under extraordinary circumstances could censorship even be mentioned, and in theory (but not in practice) journalists and artists were not supposed to be told that their works were rejected or changed because they were censored.

At the same time, party leaders' interest in the mass media and their positions on most major issues were far from being secrets. Polish intellectuals read the pronouncements and public speeches of party leaders as barometers of what was publishable and what the political realities were. Journalists knew that each top party leader regularly received *Trybuna Ludu, Życie Warszawy, Polityka, Nowe Drogi* and *Życie Gospodarcze,* along with summaries of articles that appeared in the other Polish media, translations of foreign news and commentary, and reprints of censored materials like those that appear in this volume. Writers knew that the first 300 copies of their books went to research libraries and to the top party leadership (though there were few indications that they read any except the political books whose publication had been a matter of concern). The selection of an official from the party's top governing body, the Politburo, to supervise the media, as well as the naming of Press Department officials, chief editors of the party's own publications, the directors of the Main Office for Control and the Polish Press Agency (PAP), and the heads of the major publishing houses, were real concerns for the entire Politburo leadership.

On a day-to-day basis, the media were the realm of the Press Department bureaucracy. Under Gierek, this department ran the media as an industry: setting goals for what it should cover and how, monitoring its production and appointing its personnel. In years past, all of this had been managed by ten officials, called "instructors" in the party lexicon. But under Gierek the role of the Press Department and its powers not only to guide but to control all the media were so expanded that there were fifty instructors. These officials convened meetings of top journalists and editors with various party officials and the secretary for propaganda to tell them of the issues that should be raised and provide them with guidance as to how they should be handled. To reinforce these meetings, they put out explicit directives, some of which are reprinted in this book, on how various national and international events and issues should be handled. Each of the instructors was also responsible for personally supervising and instructing a group of journals or broadcast programs. Their authority was reinforced by the fact that editors and correspondents got their positions only after being approved by the Press Department (through the so-called *nomenklatura,* "personnel control system").

The Press Department's relationship to the Main Office for Control was particularly close in the seventies. Only the Press Department, a party organ, could order the Main Office to have material removed by the censors. (Before this, under Gomułka, ministries, various party departments and powerful figures all could take it upon themselves to push the censors directly for the removal of any piece of information they saw as damaging.) The directors and department heads of the censors' office were included in all meetings held by the Press Department for editors or journalists. They also received all printed instructions and guidelines sent to the editors, as well as more specific documents for their own use. In addition, they had direct telephone lines to top Press Department officials. The heads of the Main Office for Control met regularly with the party Central Committee secretary in charge of the Press Department and of their own office. In their meetings with him, they asked for and received specific and detailed information on what should and should not be published, and their most recent decisions were reviewed as guidance for future decisions.

Editors or artists who wanted to fight the censorship of their work had first to appeal to the Press Department. Then, if they needed to further argue their case, they could go to the Politburo member assigned to act as final arbiter. In practice, the battles that were waged were far less formal than the structure of the censorship would imply, since the entire media establishment was interconnected with the party authorities. Editors in chief often came from positions in the Press Department or left their editorships for party positions or government sinecures. The most prominent editors outside the Catholic media were high-ranking party politicians in their own right, such as *Polityka*'s Mieczysław Rakowski. The directors of the Main Office had all been instructors or Press Department officials earlier in their careers. This allowed all of them to build up a network of contacts and connections. So, as one former censor put it:

The really important transfer of information goes on daily in the party headquarters cafeteria and over coffee when our directors and their party pals talk together.*

For all but a few prominent and well-placed journalists and artists, it was their editor or producer who was the link to the officials who imposed the invisible and visible boundaries on their professional activities. It was the editors who were called most frequently to Press Department meetings. They were the ones who were contacted by party and state officials objecting to a journalist's coverage, or seeking more coverage. Censors talked to them when they wished to raise objections. Theoretically, these conversations were supposed to be confidential, with the editors or producers later presenting the objections or the suggestions for coverage as their own. Instead, since the editors also needed the support of their journalists, they tended to use their inside information about what had been censored and what comprised the issues of the day as currency to get information from journalists about what they had gleaned from their contacts. This inside information the editors often used to strengthen their position on the board of their publishing organization, or with their contacts in the party and state leadership. For both editors and producers knew that the stronger their personal position with both the political élite and the population, the harder it would be to prevent them from presenting what they wanted.

Editors and producers of radio and television broadcasts, as well as the directors of publishing houses, theaters and film studios, dealt with the technical details of funds, equipment and timing that often determine the audience for what is written or said. For the print media, the publishing houses are crucial. They make decisions about the distribution of paper to individual journals and about each journal's assignment to printing equipment. They also control the distribution of publications as well as their budgets for staffing and for special coverage (e.g., for foreign correspondents and travel). In these ways, they can determine whether a journal will be profitable for journalists to work on, how readable it will be and what its circulation will be. All of this is important to journals since all but the party journals are expected to be self-supporting. Technical decisions such as the printing equipment assigned, the time allotted for printing an edition and the kind of paper given a journal all affect its newsstand

*Interview with a former censor, 1979.

appeal and the time allowed for putting out the most up-to-date edition and lobbying for the publication of censored articles. Cutbacks in paper allocations force journals to cut down either their size (and therefore the amount of space journalists have to get articles published) or their circulation. This only reduces their readership and their earnings from sales—the journals' main source of independent income. Finally, without making any declaration, publishing houses can distribute journals so poorly that they never reach their readers and go unsold. For radio and television programs, the heads of Polish Radio and Television have the same powers as publishers do for the print media. They set the program and allocate time to each program. They also distribute film and equipment, with the best being given to the programs that serve their political needs. The worst time and equipment is given to programs of only marginal interest or those that are considered too independent. For books, theater and film, the Ministry of Culture is the bureaucracy on which they depend. This ministry has the right to approve production lists and plans, as well as to make decisions about funding. All these apparently technical concerns were and are still ultimately political decisions that affect the viability of the mass media and Polish culture. They were, in effect, the technical censors of the media and culture because they determined their links with their audiences.

Life in the news rooms, broadcast studios, book publishing houses, and theaters and film studios was an entirely different world from the bureaucratic world described above. Journalists and writers, individual book editors and directors knew what went on in the media-control circles only after the fact or through the reports—not always complete—of their editors or bosses. They did their work, as they had for over thirty years, in the way they had found to be the most productive and profitable. This was also the way that minimized their sense of outside control and maximized their ability to work around that control. When the Press Department commissioned a study in the early seventies on the possibility of reducing autonomy in the editorial process, the report came back: "Journalists are quite willing to talk about their work but are unwilling to deal with the possibilities of organizational change."*

---

*Bolesław Garlicki, *Organizacja pracy redakcji* (The organization of publishing work) (Kraków: Ośrodek Badań Prasoznawczych, February 19, 1972), p. 80.

The journalists who peopled the news rooms and studios of the Polish media were a varied lot. Most of them had come into the profession in the late forties and early fifties, so they had lived through Stalinism, the hopes of liberalization in 1956, and the stagnation and stabilization of the Gomułka years. Although journalists in prominent positions, as well as editors, were encouraged to join the party, this was not required. Instead, in most cases a high priority was placed on skill. Even *Trybuna Ludu* hired prominent writers who were not in the party:

> In RSW Prasa, the party publishing house, party membership is about 51 percent. In the Polish Press Agency [which handles all foreign news and the domestic wire reporting] party membership is about 56 percent; in the Polish Committee on Radio and Television, membership is about 44 percent. . . . Membership in political organizations is, of course, much higher among editorial boards. In RSW Prasa, the editorial boards are 80 percent party members. In radio and television, 70 percent are party members.
>
> The increase in journalism cadres from 1970 to 1977 did not show a notable increase in party membership. Of the current 3,994 employees [in RSW Prasa], 50.7 percent are in party organizations. In 1970, of the 2,865 journalists employed, 1,610 (56.2 percent) were in a party organization.*

Life for journalists, whether they were in the party or not, was not simple. Their salaries were raised significantly when Gierek first took over, but at least half their earnings was still based on how much they had actually published rather than on position or seniority. This made censorship not only an insult to their sense of professional competence and honesty, but also an economic penalty. Only *Polityka* and *Tygodnik Powszechny* paid for what they accepted, not what was finally accepted by the censors. Journalists were also caught in a bind because as they got established they had to specialize and build up contacts and expertise in a single area. To this end, they needed the respect of those about whom they wrote, which required having their articles published. It also required writing not simply propaganda tracts but thoughtful and critical analyses; these in turn were often tampered with by the censors, leaving the journalists look-

*Zbigniew Krzystek, "Kim Jesteśmy?" (Who are we?), *Prasa Polska*, August 1977, p. 30

ing ike lackluster reporters or regime apologists: their published articles would often not reflect what they had originally tried to say.

For the editors, no matter what their party connections, producing a newspaper or journal was no easy task. They had to have something that was interesting and new enough to attract readers since they needed the earnings from sales to be at least partially self-supporting. At the same time, most did not want to risk censorship since it was costly and time-consuming to reset pages or substitute stories to fill the spaces left blank by censored passages or articles.

These pressures, and the Polish tradition of analytical journalism, make for a far different process of journalism in Poland than exists in most newspapers in the United States. Even the staffs of dailies draft yearly plans for the themes they will cover. These plans, general guidelines for what the papers would concentrate on in each quarter, are drawn up by the editors and their staffs on each newspaper and journal. They allow and encourage journalists to think ahead about what they will write and to make long-term commitments rather than simply report daily events—the lowest-status journalistic work in Poland. All of these plans have to be submitted to the Press Department instructor responsible for the journal and to the governing board of the organization that sponsors the journal. Most often the plans are so general, based as they are on the editors' and journalists' knowledge of what the acceptable themes are, that little is said about them by either the Press Department instructors or the governing board of the sponsoring organization.

Using these plans and their own observations of life around them, journalists take on various writing projects. While they work, they discuss their topics with others in their cramped office space. In the course of their discussions, they get advice and guidance from their department editors and colleagues about the issues they raise and the tone of their articles. On most dailies and weeklies, they also attend staff meetings where recent issues are discussed, objections raised by the censors and other individuals are presented, and future issues are planned. In the course of these discussions, the editors frequently give at least general reports on their own contacts and impressions of the political situation. All of this provides journalists with a framework in which to think about what they are writing.

Once they have finished writing, journalists turn their articles in to department editors who specialize in various fields—economics, sports, politics, social welfare, culture—and who go over the articles before submitting them to the managing editor for review. If in their opinion an article might have problems getting past the managing editor or the censors, the department editors will usually discuss the alternatives with the journalist before sending it any further. The article is then reviewed by the managing editor. If he is concerned about it or if the editor in chief is particularly active, the latter will also review the article.

The edition is then set in type and the first copy off the press sent to the censors. Journalists and editors act on the supposition that the censors will be reluctant to make many interventions on an already printed page. After all, there is far less time to have changes made if the presses are waiting to run the full edition, and changes at this stage are costly at best. The censors have gone along with this tactic because it allows them to judge the edition as a whole—to look at the tenor of the entire publication and to determine how the various juxtapositions of articles and pictures might affect the reader. In the case of dailies, the censored copy comes back many hours later; for weeklies, it usually comes back in two days, unless the censors feel something needs to be reviewed by their bosses; for monthlies, the censors generally hold the copy for a month to approve it. Editors then have to decide whether to follow the censors' directives or appeal their decisions. Usually, they simply go along with the changes demanded by the censors. The reset copy goes back to the censors, who reread it to make sure that all the changes they requested have been made. Then the censors put their stamp on the first copy and it is okayed for printing, with the responsible censor's number on the masthead.

Polish radio and television journalists face many of the same problems as do print media journalists. Like their colleagues everywhere in the world, they have to submit their ideas and tapes for approval and review. In Poland journalists and editors plan long-term themes so they can schedule their work and get it approved by the directors of radio and television. These plans and the journalists' ongoing search for topics, as well as the demands for coverage made by party and government institutions, determine the content of the various programs. Before journalists go into the field to do their programs or begin to tape them, they draw up an outline of the issue and its planned coverage. This is approved, revised or rejected by their editors. Then the journalist is left to shoot the program and prepare the tapes, which are then reviewed by the editor responsible and, if he does not order it shelved as too sensitive, given to the censors. Only when a program is broadcast is the journalist paid.

For other programs, including numerous scheduled talk show features with well-known journalists, broadcasting live was an option until the mid-seventies, when the directors of Polish television tried to force even the most prominent journalists to submit scripts beforehand so the censors could exercise measures of control other than simply cutting off live programs. As a result, many media personalities, including Mieczysław Rakowski, then a Central Committee member, and Karol Małcużyński, a member of Parliament, left television rather than have their shows pretaped and edited.

Book publishing houses are involved in long-term financial enterprises, with books often funded years in advance of their publication dates. All have special fields of interest: some are geared to a large general audience; some are devoted to the publications of the PZPR and the minor parties; and some are tiny academic and special-interest houses that publish only a few books a year. There are also two Catholic publishing houses and a military publishing house that aims not only at the armed forces but at a general audience as well.

In the seventies each publishing house drew up five-year publishing plans and turned them in to the Ministry of Culture book department for approval. The ministry's responsibility was to see to it that the publishing plans did not overlap and that they took into account the interests of the regime and the needs of Polish culture. Often its decisions, couched in terms of the overall picture of Polish culture, were really political decisions for or against a given publisher or writer. The five-year plans were also used in the yearly decisions of the Ministry of Culture in regard to the allocation of funds to the various publishing houses and their ration of paper. These decisions, too, were often related not to the plans and needs of a given publisher, but to a publisher's position with the ministry and the political élite. Those who published material that displeased ministry or party officials found themselves with far less paper and funding than they needed. This meant that they could produce and sell fewer books, and so their own incomes, on which they also had to depend, were reduced.

Individual books and book ideas were often proposed and accepted even before the manuscripts were written. Editors and publishers based their decisions on their knowledge of the author and his presentation of his topic. As authors worked on their volumes, most were in contact with their editors for ongoing guidance. Individual editors went over each manuscript carefully not only for its quality, but also for its publishability. In most cases, books were also sent out for review by specialists in the field or by potential critics. This review was supposed to cover not only the book's quality but also whether it would be accepted by the censors. Only after all these checks would a manuscript be sent to the censors, and the long discussions with them about content would begin.

The book publication process offered more alternatives to the censors than did the editing process of newspapers and magazines. Sometimes, publishers simply dropped a book from their list with no explanation. In other cases, decisions were made to produce only a very small number or even to sell the few that were printed in "closed sales" where notices were put up or sent out advertising the impending publication of a book or series. Those who wished to could then pay in advance for the book or series and receive it directly when it was printed. For these books and for some others that were sold in bookstores, the audience was reduced by making the price unusually high. Ultimately, too, everyone involved knew that there was always the possibility that after a book had been printed and even distributed, it could be recalled because of some powerful leader's objections. All these possibilities increased the options for publication of something a publisher was committed to and yet made publishers very cautious about investing money in books that could never be sold.

Theatrical and film producers, like the editors and publishers of books, drew up plans for their seasons and then applied to the Ministry of Culture for financing. In their case, too, ministry decisions were based as much on past performance as on what the producers promised for the future. Each individual production was created with the demands and blind spots of the censors in mind, for the first audience that viewed a theatrical production, the screening of a film or a cabaret performance included the production's censors. And, for theaters and cabarets, there was always the possibility that the censors would return just to be sure that the staging had not been changed or new words written in after they had initially been passed.

It was during this production process that much of the real filtering of information and criticism went on. What the censors received had already been censored by writers, producers and editors in the course of their conception and preparation of an article, book or production.

The normal constraints of time, money and information were narrowed by the hold of the government and party over funding and the time demands of censorship itself. Most of the individuals involved knew they would be paid only if they produced something that could appear. That was, after all, their job.

Unconsciously, journalists were their own censors. The majority of Poland's journalists and writers, and almost all of the most prominent and established ones, had been writing and dealing with the censors since the Stalinist period. They simply ceased to think in terms of writing critically of the Soviet Union, proposing alternatives to the Polish way of socialism or revealing details of leaders' lives and internal party debates. Even if they had information that they could use in these areas, it seldom occurred to them even to try to use it. Censorship was so deeply ingrained that journalists no longer even recognized that they were censoring themselves.

What they tried to write was further controlled by officials and experts who often flatly refused to give journalists information. After all, it did not serve the interests of those responsible for problems in the economy and the bureaucracy to provide evidence of their failings to top party officials and to the public. Since most established journalists were specialists, they could sometimes counter this information censorship by going to personal friends in a certain area or using their own fund of knowledge as the basis for their reports. Nevertheless, this meant that many of their articles never had the kind of detail they would have liked. In fact, given the sensitivity of most journalists' internal censors, it was this access to information that they found to be their greatest problem in the mid-seventies.

However little information and criticism appeared in the media, the journalists' own world was full of information, gossip and criticism of their work and the policies of the government and party. This was the meat of a journalist's work and his lifeline. The dining room at the headquarters of the Association of Polish Journalists and the staff offices of programs and journals all over the country were always alive with talk. For, as one leading journalist explained in a conversation in 1976,

> What happens to any one of us is an indicator to all of us of what we can do and how far we can go. That's the way we keep track of changes in the rules of the game. We are much better off because we know what is happening between the lines—who did what to whom.

When something new appeared, journalists immediately checked to see if it was a possible precedent for allowing them to report and engage in criticism in that area.

Because top journalists and editors knew Poland's leading politicians, intellectuals and dissidents, or were involved in party work or consulting on various issues themselves, little happened that they did not know about. The information that did come the journalists' way might not be detailed or publishable, but for them it was certainly something to share with their friends and colleagues. What they found out gave them ideas about what the issues were that should and could be raised in the media and where the support lay for having information published. These bits of information were used by journalists to protect and position themselves.

Journalists' own self-guidance and censorship did not simply make them resign themselves to handling tiny shreds of uncensorable material. Their options were more complex than that. On the one hand, most journalists saw their work as far more than getting articles published or programs aired. Many who were concerned with political, economic or social issues felt that a part of their role was to influence policy by advocating issues behind the scenes when they met with policy makers and administrators. On the other hand, the rules of censorship were not consistent for all journals. Some, like the Znak Catholic press and a number of the socioeconomic weeklies, succeeded in publishing far more critical articles than did the mass dailies or weeklies. So journalists often wrote articles not for their own journals but for those where the chance of publication was higher. This encouraged variety in the Polish press and also gave journalists a chance to be heard and be paid for work that, under normal circumstances, would have ended up in their desk drawers.

The final stage for everything printed or shown in Poland (except the party's own publications) under Gierek was at the Main Office for Control in Warsaw or in its branch offices in every major city in Poland. Here the censors give final approval for everything from rubber stamps to encyclopedias. Censors in Warsaw and in the various regional offices were subordinated to a director and two assistant directors of the Main Office—men who were either on the party Central Committee or closely connected with it in the sixties and seventies. The directors supervise and guide individual censors through various department heads responsible for each media area. In addition, in the Warsaw office, there is a division for training censors, a personnel department and an administrative division. The office in Warsaw also had an Instruction, Evaluation and Control Group that sent out instructions, checked what had been censored, and pointed out and "explained" where errors in judgment were made by the censors. It was this group that issued most of the regulations and reports in this book. Finally, there is a military division in which a few officers delegated by the Defense Ministry to work for the Main Office check for military information and advise civilian censors about military regulations.

The men and women who work in the censorship offices are the gray figures of the media bureaucracy. Few admit to working there. Even their passports list them as simple "bureaucrats" rather than as censors. Under Gierek, the hope was that the censors' office would not only control the press but also school a whole new generation of journalists who would know clearly what they should and should not write because they had worked as censors. There were no special requirements for the job. Even party membership was not required. Below is part of an interview in which censors' qualifications are discussed.

INTERVIEWER: Can anyone be a censor?

CENSOR: Anyone with a college education and the desire to work in this business could get hired. Graduates with diplomas in the humanities are in the majority. . . . The profession is pretty well feminized, because it is a quiet and calm job. On the other hand, there is a big turnover; I don't think that more than one-fourth work in censorship for longer than a couple of years. . . . I would not like to create the impression that there is a definite censor personality. There is no such thing. . . . Some are guided by a peculiar interpretation of ideology; they think that censorship is the best way to protect socialism and the leading role of the party. Others think it is a super game. Like chess players. They enjoy getting the best of a journalist.

INTERVIEWER: Where would you place yourself?

CENSOR: Among the most numerous ones, those who take the job with the idea of leaving it in a few years. One keeps looking for one's place in life. It is easier if one has some talent, though. I have no feeling of mission or calling.*

---

*"I, The Censor," *Tygodnik Solidarność*, May 8, 1981. This interview took place in November 1980. Its inclusion in the Solidarity weekly, *Tygodnik Solidarność*, was ground for a major battle between the censors, and the issue was delayed by one day while the decision whether to allow the interview was thrashed out under the threat of a printers' strike if it was removed.

There are rewards for work in the censors' office. Although their salaries were low before the documents reprinted here were privately circulated in Poland (they received raises to make up for the embarrassment), censors did have valuable special privileges. Unlike most young Poles, who had to wait ten to fifteen years for an apartment of their own, censors were put first on the housing lists. High-ranking censors could use specially stocked party stores and vacation spots. And all censors were exempt from appearing in court on civil and criminal charges.

Those who got these special privileges were constantly supervised. According to Strzyżewski, in the Gierek era, formal training in censorship was required. Novice censors took a six-week course in groups of about thirty, attending classes from 8:00 A.M. to 3:00 P.M. daily and studying information on the actual economic policy and party positions in Poland, basic legal regulations for the Main Office for Control of Press, Publications and Public Performances, as well as current history. In addition, there was training in the area of military secrets. One-third of the course involved exercises in censoring based on specially designed texts where censors had to identify the passage that was to be censored. In the mid-seventies, according to Strzyżewski, the course was sometimes shortened to three weeks because such large numbers of new censors were being recruited. Both the full and concentrated programs were run by full-time instructors from the censors' office and by Press Department officials as well.

The initial courses were then followed by yearly month-long refresher courses in Warsaw for all censors; periodic meetings of the heads of censorship with groups of censors to give them verbal guidance and explanations on current issues and problems; and special courses for individuals specializing in difficult subjects such as economics or religion. The lectures and courses were constantly updated by materials from the Instruction, Evaluation and Control Group and the book of *Rules and Recommendations.*

Censors also had to work their way up through the hierarchy from minor popular journals for children and other noncontroversial items like stamps and printed personal or bureaucratic documents, to political and economic journals. In the vernacular of the censors themselves:

> There is a specialized group in the press unit that reads religious publications, and its actions are the outcome of relations between the

Office for Religious Denominations and the Episcopate. We call them the Saints. Another group, called the Funnies, would attend movie showings, theaters and cabarets. Work in the theater was easier, because one could hardly correct Musset or Fredro [playwrights]. One had to watch the staging. Censors of posters had an easy job; censors of books, terribly dull. The most noteworthy group, known as the aristocracy of censors, are the press people. The avant-garde. They are the foundation of the business. It is the largest and the brightest unit. The first in the line of fire.*

Once their training was over, the censors were on their own to decide what should appear and what should be cut. Their supervisors got involved only if the individual censors felt that the issue was too sensitive for them to handle or if they had been instructed in the regulations to refer any mention of a specific topic to the heads of the Main Office. Or, the censors' decisions were checked before publication if an editor or producer tried to appeal his cuts to a higher official.

Even with the plethora of detailed instructions and regulations, as well as all the other documents in circulation, individual censors were required to use their political intuition. According to Strzyżewski's own impressions, only about 30 or 40 percent of the more than 10,000 interventions made each year in the seventies were based on specific regulations. In effect, these regulations were not for the handling of major political issues (national and international issues that were important to Poland in the mid-seventies do not even appear in them) but for the details that the censors might not even recognize:

> If the text is not marked by the low-level censor, it goes to the printer unread. Because there can always be a lot of trouble if this happens, the rank-and-file censor simply keeps crossing out.†

This has always been done on the basis of the same internal censorship criteria that lead journalists to avoid various topics and the same kinds of signs of the political winds: the party publications, the gossip of what had and had not been cut and who had complained, and the issues that had been presented in the mass media.

In cases of military or security questions, the censors refer the entire piece to the military censor, who sits in a special office in the Warsaw headquarters. It is the military expert's responsibility to see that

---

*"I, the Censor," *loc. cit.*
†Ibid.

nothing related to Poland's military interests is reported in either the civilian or military press without approval. On these issues and on interventions made on the basis of regulations, there is little possibility of appeal by any editor or writer.

Concerning issues of interest to the Soviet Union in the mid-seventies, the censors knew that they were not working alone. According to Strzyżewski and others from the censors' office, under Ambassador Pilotowicz the Soviet embassy press department read everything that was published in Poland down to the tiniest local news sheet. This department circulated special lists of names of Soviet figures that should be censored, and when something displeased them, they called the censors and editors directly responsible and made their objections known. In one instance as reported by Strzyżewski, the Soviets said there should be no mention of Rudolf Nureyev or Vladimir Bukovsky (both Soviet artists who emigrated) in the Polish media. Another time, the Soviet embassy distributed a list of some twenty Soviet dissidents whose names were not to appear in the Polish press.

How censors did their work depended in large part on what they were assigned to review. Whatever the material, they did their work in ways that were intended to allow them very little contact with the people they censored. Only censors dealing with the daily press, radio or television, or wire agency reports worked outside the censors' office where they could see and be seen by journalists and editors. Censors who worked on specialized problems that required so much training and experience that they could not be rotated in and out got to know the people behind the words they read and cut. Even in these cases, though, their contacts were distant. Between the editors of *Tygodnik Powszechny* in Kraków and the censors' office in Warsaw there were long phone discussions during which editors and censors came to know each other's personal problems even as their jobs made them adversaries. *Tygodnik Powszechny*'s leading columnist would at times insert in the middle of his articles highly unorthodox and witty pleas for the censor to allow something he knew would be removed, but he never met with his censor. On the socioeconomic weeklies, phone conversations were also a regular part of an editor's work, but seldom did the average editors or journalists sit with a censor face to face. For other kinds of publications the censors were rotated frequently so they did not become personally identified with or too tolerant of what they censored.

Those who censor the daily press, radio and television, or the press agencies are the only censors who do not spend much time at the Main

Office. Carting material there and back would be too time-consuming. Instead the censors work alone or in pairs in locked offices at the printing houses or in rooms with only a window and slit through which material is pushed at the broadcast studios. As wire copy is prepared, program tapes are completed or pages printed up, they are given to the censor to review and return for corrections—sometimes with a few curt comments. Most censors of daily morning newspapers work at night, so they have little contact with anyone other than their partners. They simply read the proof sheets or, in the case of radio and late-breaking television news, the scripts for items that were not prerecorded. If a question arises, things are held until morning, when the department director at headquarters can review them. But since news is fresh for only a short time, there is seldom any interest in reviewing the decisions. As a result, the censors seldom have to deal with questions about what they have removed. No one has time to do anything but accept their cuts.

The censors of weeklies, monthlies and books work in the censors' building and go to their department heads constantly for advice. This they do not only because they have the time and because the material is often so much more complex, but also because the editors involved have far more time to appeal their decisions to their élite allies. So, rather than have their decisions reversed, censors try to get support from their superiors first.

As a final check on their work, the Instruction, Evaluation and Control Group and individual censors review one another's work in post-publication reviews. Any censor who finds a slip in material that has been censored receives a salary bonus. In addition, though articles of the Polish Press Agency are censored and cannot be rewritten by any editor, Strzyżewski reported that censors are instructed to check the PAP material for an error or oversight before it can be printed. A special award is given to any censor who can find an error in press agency material. Such instances are often used as instructional materials for the entire staff of the censors' office.

The Press Department and high-ranking administrators and politicians often respond to published articles and even phrases that have not been correctly censored. This is the ultimate threat. If a serious oversight is made, both the journal's editor and the censor responsible for that issue are fired. Writers or editors of articles with a questionable political tone may be temporarily blacklisted from publishing altogether, from publishing on a given topic, or from publishing in their own name. Censors, too, can lose their jobs or be demoted to simple and boring "guard duty." And to lose one's job as censor is to lose the possibility of any future employment in the so-called *nomenklatura* positions—party and state jobs that require party clearance for hiring.

In their review of what was censored, the Instruction, Evaluation and Control Group also engages in a tabulation of what is censored. Despite the detailed regulations sent to the censors and the directions to make greater allowances for criticism in journals with more specialized and smaller audiences, these data on the targets of the censors' attacks show little variation from report to report between 1974 and 1976. Whatever their legal role as guardians of state secrets and national security data, the censors do comparatively little in this area. Only 20 percent of the censors' interventions involved "state secrets." Often these interventions merely concerned details like requiring the removal of a bridge in the background of a picture or of a detail about some military installation which, for the Polish military, would have given too much information about troop deployments.* Instead, the articles and statements that deal with sociopolitical and economic issues require the most censorship. According to reports of the Instruction, Evaluation and Control Group, these so-called sociopolitical articles deal with social issues that are political because they concern the Gierek leadership rather than what would be political issues in the West.

REASONS FOR CENSORSHIP

KINDS OF MATERIAL CENSORED	PERCENTAGE OF CENSORED ARTICLES†
Sociopolitical issues	38
Economic issues	19
Cultural-historical discussions	14
Religious topics	9
State secrets	20

Editor's calculations based on statistics from *Report on Materials Censored* for the period from 1974 to 1976.

---

*For an example of the kinds of detailed "security" cuts the censors made, see "Informacja Nr 63 o ingerencjach z zakresu ochrony tajemnicy państwowej" (Censor's Information No. 63 on interventions in protecting national security), July 23, 1976, *Czarna księga cenzury PRL* (The black book of censorship of the Polish People's Republic) (London: ANEKS, 1978), 2:441–42.

†Articles showing intervention of any sort on the part of the censors.

The concentration of concerns that appear in these reports reflects the failings of the Polish system. The Communist party leaders had promised social welfare, political participation and economic success. Journalists, authors, dramatists and readers called them to account for their promises and were silenced, for the regime could not admit its shortcomings. Instead, the censors circulated among themselves and to the party élite the *Report on Materials Censored* that gave the true "Signals" (as the reports were called) of life in Poland. It is these documents that serve us now in mirroring the mind of Poland's Communist rulers and in laying out a social history of Poland in the mid-seventies, when the Gierek regime had begun its mad retreat from reality.

II / THE DOCUMENTS

3 / **POLISH POLITICS**

The Making of a Nonevent

HE YEARS between 1974 and 1976 were a time of great change in
Polish political life. Traditional institutions from before World
War II were suddenly transformed by law or fiat. The Party Congress
of December 1975 and the parliamentary elections three months later
brought Edward Gierek closer than any of his predecessors to total
control of the party and government élite. At the same time, clouds
began to appear over Gierek's glory. Intellectuals became increasingly
aware of the failures of his economic program and their own exclusion
from any real policy discussions. In the summer of 1976 workers rioted
in response to government attempts to raise food prices, an undeniable
demonstration of the failure of the politics of the seventies. From these
demonstrations and the repression that followed came the first real
organized attempt by intellectuals to aid workers in what was in
essence their common political struggle. KOR, the Workers' Defense
Committee, gradually grew into a group whose aim was nothing less
than the transformation of Polish political realities through grass-
roots change. Four years later KOR was to play a role in the dramatic
events of August 1980.

During these politically turbulent years, however, politics came to
be virtually nonexistent in the Polish media. To strengthen their hold
over the party and government, Gierek and his men had taken a very
tight grip on the media. Statements that detracted from the glory of
the Gierek image as a leader and of his political power were not
allowed to appear. Major policies were carried out with no public
discussion whatsoever. Individuals who criticized the actions of the

leadership became nonpersons in the press and on radio and television. When the leadership did wish to use a political event to rally support or to make a point, the Central Committee Press Department and the Main Office for Control of Press, Publications and Public Performances worked together to orchestrate it carefully in the media and the public mind. All other political information was generally unavailable, for the control that the Gierek leadership had on the party and its apparatus also meant that few individuals "in the know" were willing to be involved in public debates or to leak information to journalists. All of this tended to make journalists unwilling and/or unable to write what we consider prime political news. As a result, there was in fact very little "politics" to censor. So little was written on pure domestic politics, for example, that the censors did not even consider it a separate category. Instead, what the censors viewed as sociopolitical issues were matters that would at best be of marginal political sensitivity in the West. Yet the information that they were instructed to remove or that they rejected on the basis of their own "nose for news" is no less telling than if the subjects had been of major political import.

The Rulers and the Ruled

Censorship was intended at least in part to help the leadership mobilize the population to work for the glory of Gierek's Poland. That it achieved no such thing was clear long before the victory of the Solidarity movement in 1980. Journalists and political commentators not only pointed out that the media propaganda was not believed, but also attempted to show that propaganda blitzes succeeded only in dulling popular interest in, and knowledge of, the political process and leaders. In one such case, the censors forced *Polityka*'s editor to remove an entire article despite the fact that he had been granted the right to handle his own decisions about what to publish. The article reported on research conducted at the government's major public opinion research institute, information that was, obviously, made available by the institute itself:

> "It might seem that the recent reform of the people's councils was accompanied by a propaganda effort sufficiently comprehensive for everyone to be familiar with what it was all about. Information in a

variety of forms, ranging from schola¬ly explanations to a schematic plan drawn on the cover of *Perspektyw*ᵥ (Dec. 7, 1973), streamed forth in increasing intensity, particularly during the period just before the elections.

"However, research conducted at the end of last year by the Center for Public Opinion Research and Program Studies of Polish Radio and Television showed clearly that only one citizen out of three in this country has a very clear idea about the elections held on December 9, 1973, or about the sort of council to which he was electing representatives. Moreover, those questioned had their job made easier for them: the answers were already there. It was only necessary to choose the right one. Half of those questioned either showed some ability to fish —i.e., underlined *some* correct answers—or allowed themselves to be caught, claiming that on December 9 we elected *gmina* [lowest-level administration units] directors, heads of voivodships, presidents of towns, or . . . delegates to the National Unity Front.

"One out of every five adult citizens did not have any idea who he was electing or to what.

"Worse still were answers to more detailed questions, such as: who in the local leadership discharges legislative functions and who the executive? does a councilman work as a volunteer or receive pay? and so on.

"Barely one-third of the people examined made a distinction between the representative and administrative bodies of the local councils. Two-thirds correctly answered a question about the nature of a councilman's work.

"Altogether, 15 percent of those questioned answered the whole section of detailed questions correctly.

"An attempt was made to determine the causes of this state of affairs. We asked whether the subjects had received information about the elections and where they had gotten the information. Eleven percent indicated a lack of interest. The overwhelming majority, though, said the source of their information was the press, radio and television. The authors [of the study], understandably, are doubtful about this information. . . . 'the indications that information had been received should be treated rather skeptically. At the very least, the method of its reception should be considered to have been passive.'

"Questions were also asked about the quality of the preelection propaganda. Twenty-three percent of those questioned assessed it favorably ('the commentary and information were entirely convincing'). Exactly half said that they were 'pretty' or 'moderately' convincing. More than 20 percent replied 'hard to say.' People with higher education proved to be the most critical.

"Summing up, the authors of the research say that it shows that knowledge about the elections was limited, and that the elections were viewed 'more as a demonstration of the citizens' attitude than as the deliberate election of representatives to . . . representative bodies.' "

(*Report on Materials Censored*, May 1–15, 1974)

For Gierek, who had promised to institute a regime based on close ties between the rulers and the ruled, these criticisms were far more threatening than they would have been for other East European regimes where mutual tolerance was the goal. With the Gierek regime putting out propaganda aimed at mobilizing the population, the censors could not allow the reflections in Z. Kowalski's article "Shooting at Cuckoos," in *Kierunki*, about

. . . the allegedly compulsory nature of certain "instructions and guidelines" in the nation's sociopolitical life. The following observation was deleted: "All I have to do is this or that, and then I am a law-abiding and 'committed' individual. All I have to do is think thus and so, and I am thinking properly. All I have to do is to say this and not something else, and I am . . ." (*Report on Materials Censored*, May 16–31, 1974)

Nor could they allow articles that honored criticism and discontent, like "Concerning the Effects of the Different Velocities of the Hunted and the Hunters" by A. A. Mroczek in *Kierunki*, which argued

. . . that in every society "progress originates in criticism and discontent," for "the critic is the one who discovers the existence of needs, and by being critical he is the one who demands some kind of change." (*Report on Materials Censored*, May 16–31, 1974)

To illustrate the distance between the rulers and the ruled without being accused of attacking the Gierek leadership directly, Jacek Maziarski, a writer for *Polityka*, used letters from readers to "criticize the model of industrial democracy 'that has been in existence for over 15 years' " under Gomułka and Gierek. His argument was so objectionable to the censors that his editors had to withdraw the entire article. There was simply no one who would protect an article contending that the existing model of industrial democracy in Poland

. . . does not make it possible for the working class to fulfill its "structural role" as "co-manager and co-proprietor of industrial enterprises."

In the author's view, this state of affairs can be attributed, among other things, to the growing "trend toward an autocratic style of enterprise management," and a distortion of the chain of command between superiors and subordinates. Stressing that at the present time it is possible to observe a strong "sense of the need for democracy in the minds of the workers themselves" (compared with the end of the 1950s and the first half of the 1960s), the author wrote about the need to eliminate the "trouble spots" that are created "at the point of intersection between the discontent [of the workers] and the growing need for participation" in the decision-making process for enterprises. (*Report on Materials Censored,* May 16–31, 1974)

On one level, this article attacked the managerial mentality—the very philosophy—with which *Polityka* and its editor had traditionally been identified. In advocating the development of real and effective workers' councils, Jacek Maziarski was suggesting worker control and power over the decisions of *Polityka*'s traditional constituency and challenging the premise that workers counted in Gierek's Poland. The discontent over which Maziarski raised an alarm was realized, however, only two years later with the workers' strikes of 1976 and then took the form of active worker participation and organization with the appearance of Solidarity in 1980. But the article was aimed at mounting a far broader attack on society—a criticism shared by the very managers whom the article itself appeared to criticize. It was readers' letters pointing up individual managerial failings that veiled this broader attack. Beneath the veil was an attempt to promote the standard *Polityka* line that participation should be increased so that the population would have a reason to be responsible.

Similar concerns were raised by and removed from an article in *Tygodnik Kulturalny,* a less widely read journal published by the small ancillary Peasant Party targeted to appeal to those peasants who could not be reached by the Communist Party. Here again, statements of readers were utilized to remove the onus of criticism from journalists and to give greater immediacy to the discussion. In this case, the censors would not even allow criticism of Gomułka's political style because of its parallels with Gierek's style and because in fact nothing had changed in Polish political life despite Gierek's promises:

> Issue No. 21 of *Tygodnik Kulturalny* ran an article by Z. Grzelak entitled "A Sense of Hope and a Sense of Urgency." The author, using statements made by readers in a contest to describe daily life in the

course of a single month, organized by *Tygodnik Kulturalny* in 1962 and 1973, sought to comparatively examine the course of Poland's thirty-year development.

The following passages were censored:

—with regard to 1962:

". . . Material living conditions were not the only factor that left its stamp on the collective intellect in 1962. . . . Accounts of countless meetings, conferences, conventions and congresses all offer the same picture. Inflated oratory, long, drawn-out speeches, a failure to act on continually expressed demands, boastful talk, empty rhetoric, drowsiness, boredom and a lack of new faces among the discussants. The decline of the influence of public opinion is symptomatic of a breakdown of the spiritual bonds between citizens gathered together in a community. . . . The director of a general secondary school for workers in Poznań wrote in 1962: 'I do not know whether I am right or wrong, but I cannot think about so-called political issues without a profound sense of dread and sadness. I realize that the forces that are at work here are not the kinds of forces that are guided by rational motives or by some desire to ensure the happiness of the people. Politics is a broad forum in which a desperate struggle is being waged for power, influence and wealth. . . .' Analyzing the structures of public life, Stanisław Ossowski wrote in 1962 that in certain social circles these institutions give rise to a set of attitudes burdened with a 'Lilliputian' complex. This refers to a sense of helplessness beyond the sphere of personal affairs, to the conviction that high above the heads of us Lilliputians are Gullivers who are so so much more powerful than we are that we cannot exert any influence on the course of events on a larger scale."

(*Report on Materials Censored,* May 16–31, 1974)

In the same article, the censors also blocked characterizations of the Gierek period that went beyond a mere statement of the discouragement of low-level officials about the possibility that they could implement the grandiose Gierek plans. Explicit statements about the demoralization of the population and the failure of the government to live up to its promises had to be cut before the article could be published:

—with regard to 1973:

". . . The principal of a school located in the suburbs of Warsaw gave the most perceptive description of her doubts. She wrote: 'When one looks at the many initiatives undertaken by the party and government, one is led to expect that something wise and sensible is going to be done, that a splendid future is opening up before our eyes. But when we look at these things from below, from the position of those little organizational and administrative units that have the greatest impact on the actual implementation of assigned tasks, then we are overcome with a sense of profound melancholy.'

" 'I do not know whether the authorit es are aware of just how great the extent of the demoralization is in certain places. Over a period of several years people have grown accustomed to an atmosphere of impunity and indifference. Somehow things will get done. And it is hard for people to change. . . .

" 'The wise actions undertaken by the new government are long overdue. Are they perhaps too late? . . . A Warsaw office worker in the regional administration considers the struggle against deceptive practices to be the most important and most difficult part of the whole battle: 'If one has practiced deceit for this long, then he is already wearing a different skin, one that sticks to his body as well as his own.' "
(*Report on Materials Censored,* May 15–31, 1974)

In the 1970s, as politics came to mean falsehood and alienation from the political system, the demoralization of young people in Poland reached what journalists and intellectuals saw as crisis proportions. No mention of this readily evident phenomenon was allowed if it placed the blame not on young people themselves but on the system, or if it implied that these problems were not just among young people.

The editors of *Polityka,* in accordance with our suggestions, changed the following sections of J. Olek's article "Before the 30th Anniversary Strikes":

". . . For young people, everything is coming to be a matter of indifference. They are losing their enthusiasm and creative criticism. It makes no difference whether one is brilliant or just average: in terms of earnings and recognition, it comes out the same. Still worse, working at a level below one's knowledge, skills and capabilities is not risky. It is more profitable.

"This honoring of the average and mediocre, which has been going on for many years, has finally led to the creation of an antibody against ambition in the public mind, as a result of which the natural demand for recognition and advancement is increasingly disappearing.

". . . It is difficult to alter human attitudes that have been accustomed to mediocrity for years. In order to wipe out a deeply rooted attitude, resistance and the good will of young people are needed, but there is also a need to get rid of inertia, feudal patterns of behavior, senseless regulations, bureaucratic restrictions, cynicism, and egoistic, calculating pusillanimity." (*Report on Materials Censored,* March 16–31, 1974)

Party organizations and party members were themselves protected from attack by the Main Office for Control. When interviews with individual party members pointed to broad social and economic problems, the censors blocked publication lest individual party members sound less than fully satisfied with working conditions, food supplies, prices and consumer goods. The mass media were allowed to address only those problems caused by human error and could not speak along with much of the population in demanding, for instance, Saturdays off. Further, the media were barred from revealing that many party members were less than fully and permanently committed to and active in the party. Nor did the censors allow party members to appear as opportunists advancing their careers through party membership:

In an article entitled "The Organization" (*Kultura,* No. 49), A. Kantowicz described the activities of the Primary Party Organization of Department Nine of the Voivodship State Motor Transport Enterprise in Grójec [a small industrial town near Warsaw] on the basis of party meetings and private interviews conducted with members of the basic party organization. Interventions were made, *inter alia,* in the following passages dealing with:
—meetings of the Primary Party Organization:
". . . Organizational Matters, Point Four . . .
"Warehouse worker, age 24, skilled bricklayer by trade, working intelligentsia family background, member of the Union of Socialist Youth, knowledge of Russian language. I am applying to the Executive Committee of the Primary Party Organization of Department Nine of the Voivodship State Motor Transport Enterprise in Grójec for admission into the ranks of the PZPR. My sociopolitical growth has reached the point where there is nothing left for me to do but to join the PZPR. I have an excellent knowledge of the party statutes, and, in addition, my record of public service work in the Union of Socialist Youth ought to qualify me for the bonus of being admitted into the PZPR. . . .
"Discipline: a certain comrade has quit his job at the State Motor Transport Enterprise. He refused to be transferred, and he has not paid his dues. The Executive Committee recommends that he be expelled from the party. Perhaps he is ill? We checked, and found out that he is in good health. He was expelled by a unanimous vote. It was the same story with another comrade. I met him. He has some kind of health

problem. But that doesn't matter—he could have come. With one abstention, the committee voted to expel him too.

—private interviews with Primary Party Organization members:

". . . Interviewee A: the meals served here are not always nutritious, and they are not always hot. Wages are low, and nobody pays much attention to the workers. (After a while, the meals got better, but wages continued to be low.) . . .

"Interviewee B: a bad food supply situation in town, shortages of meat and meat products, obsolete sewer system. . . .

"Free Saturdays: The transportation industry is given more work to do then, since others are taking advantage of the achievements of our society. And we just keep slaving away. Theoretically, we are entitled to a day off in comp-time, but in practice half of us never get it. We just get paid. In any event, a day off in comp-time on Tuesday or Wednesday is never the same thing as having Saturday off. Saturday has its own inimitable flavor. One out of three drivers absolutely insists on having Saturday off. . . .

"Socialism never promised to make anybody happy. That depends on the individual. He has to make his own choices. If only there was something to choose from. But to be able to get something too easily isn't right either. . . .

"But the system *ought* to eliminate obstacles. Why, then, aren't there any spare parts?

"Does comrade editor have any idea why a certain brand of crackers is so expensive? After all, it's only 20 decagrams of flour, eggs and a few added ingredients, and yet altogether it costs 20 złotys!" (*Report on Materials Censored*, December 1–15, 1975)

Even when the criticism of political conditions in Poland was limited to a passing mention in the Christmas and New Year's greeting in a musicians' journal, and even though it concerned relations between the population and only strictly low-level government bureaucrats, the censors were unwilling to allow any negative view of such relations to appear. Although the government officials themselves had launched a campaign for greater civility on the part of government bureaucrats and shopworkers in order to reduce popular tensions, the censors eliminated the holiday wish:

"So, we hope that you will be able to forget as soon as possible about moments of disrespect and humiliation. About times when belittling the worth of one's neighbor was the universally accepted means of enhancing one's own sense of well-being. We hope that your basic human ambition will recover as soon as possible from the wounds inflicted on it from time to time in the streets, in stores, at work or in government offices. We hope that other people will simply be other people and cease to be opponents, rivals or threats. For health, success and money are no consolation and serve no purpose when we lack the respect of other people, that immeasurable and intangible bond which ties together all the elements of happiness." (*Report on Materials Censored,* December 1–15, 1975)

Suggestions, even vague ones, about the possibility that the Gierek policies might ultimately prove unsuccessful were unmentionable. Even a report in a factory newspaper on a conference held in 1975 at the factory itself could not repeat public criticism that had been made there. For example, this comment, made during the conference by a member of the Polish Academy of Sciences, was eliminated:

"At the present, our imaginative faculties are not strong enough to envision what society will be like twenty or even ten years from now. This lack of imagination is apparent both among scholars and among politicians, who are occupied with the task of laying the material and economic foundations of the future." (*Report on Materials Censored,* December 1–15, 1975)

Ironically, the failure of the Gierek regime to live up to any of its promises or to admit its problems, which led to its downfall in 1980, did not escape notice in the mid-seventies; but the censors would not allow warnings about this to appear even addressed to small groups of readers. In late 1975, for example, the opinion of an activist in the state-run Society for the Promotion of Secular Culture was cut from that organization's journal, *Argumenty:*

". . . In my opinion, the greatest danger to our society is the still persisting contradiction between words and deeds, the inconsistency between the preaching of *theories* and views and the way that they are put into practice in everyday life, and the failure to live up to and fulfill those many assurances and promises that are made by conferences, resolutions, and formal proposals. This alienates and discourages people, and they will grow distrustful or—in the case of the cleverer ones —hypocritical and, even worse, cynical." (*Report on Materials Censored,* September 16–30, 1975)

Images of the Leader

The Gierek leadership's interest in the propaganda of success involved much more than filtering out all but a positive image of Polish society. While some policy measures were kept out of the media, others were designated to receive extensive exposure and for still others clear and detailed plans for coverage were drawn up. Individuals in the leadership were protected from negative treatment by journalists' own sense of the feasible. Beyond this, the top leaders were still anxious to manipulate coverage in order to provide themselves with the best possible image. For example, censors were informed that:

> 1. Prior to publication, all pictures of the First Secretary of the Central Committee and other members of the party leadership must have the approval of the Department of Press, Radio and Television of the Central Committee of the PZPR. (Canceled December 17, 1976)

As if this were not enough, another special entry among the censors' directives was added at the time of the Seventh Party Congress, requiring that

> in the period preceding and during the Party Congress all pictures of the First Secretary, Comrade Gierek, proposed for magazine covers should be referred to the GUKPPiW administration before permission to publish is given.

For most journals, this regulation had little potential impact: the photographs they used were provided almost exclusively by the Polish Press Agency and the Central Photographic Agency.

For the Polish leadership, the key to the propaganda battle was television, especially the seven o'clock news. This was far too important, though, to be left to mere censors. There were censors who viewed the news program before it aired, but their job represented only token control. The real control came from Gierek's top lieutenants' constant attention to the program, its staff and its presentation of their work. Top party officials responsible for the national mass media, like the Central Committee's Secretary for Propaganda (Jerzy Lukaszewicz), Secretary for Party Administration (Edward Babiuch) and Secretary for Ideology (Jan Szydlak), all took it upon themselves to drop by frequently to view films and chat with the journalists and editors about what they were doing and how the news should look. Other top officials, including the heads of the police and the military, courted television news in their own interests by providing special aid (such as military planes if journalists needed to get reports flown into Warsaw quickly) and cultivating personal contacts with the journalists. And journalists made an effort to censor themselves even more carefully than their colleagues elsewhere did, since they knew that their program was being watched by the "200 top families of Poland," the families of the political élite, many of whom were given videotapes of the program so that they could watch it at their convenience.

The public appearances of Gierek and other Politburo members were not spontaneous events, and even though the orchestration of media events and television news coverage designed to show off party and government leaders did not go unnoticed by journalists, their criticisms of the orchestration went unpublished. One national student newspaper, for instance, tried to publish an editorial discussion on the "role of photography in the press, the concept of the profession of photoreporter and the causes of the crisis in the field of photojournalism." These passages were censored so that not only was the article no longer critical but its very meaning was changed:

> ". . . J. Rurański: In photographs in the press, why is Poland so well arranged, so <u>painted up</u>? Why are the pictures identical in every newspaper? <u>The same podiums, the same cutting of the ceremonial ribbons, the same smiles?</u> . . .
>
> "J. Borkiewicz: A voivodship paper fails to publish a fantastic, completely authentic photograph that is most effective as propaganda, <u>simply because one of the heroes, a local dignitary, is not smiling the way he is supposed to.</u> But we would like to photograph real, live people who react, <u>even if they are members of the Politburo.</u> . . .
>
> "K. Barański: <u>Documentation is one thing, but how do you define the everyday, joyous creativity of the editors, who determine the ultimate shape of what appears in the paper? For me, in many cases, this is anti-propaganda.</u>" (*Report on Materials Censored*, March 16–31, 1974)

Another journalist reported on his conversations with people from a small mountain community two days after Gierek had been there: since their impressions of the official visit were at best negative, the article was never published. A passage in a provincial journal criticizing the time and expense involved in setting up the "spontaneous" appearances of government and party officials was also censored:

> In a letter to the editors of *Pobrzeże* (Issue No. 12) a university student from Warsaw who worked "during the harvest in one of the large storage facilities of the State Grain Elevators enterprise in Koszalin Voivodship" as a "seasonal or contract employee" wrote, in part, as follows:
>
> ". . . During this hectic time of year, when, literally speaking, every available hand counted, a lot of work was also being done just 'for show.' For example, just before a government representative was expected to pay us a visit, a food bar was set up in the plant lounge, in spite of the fact that there was already one just on the other side of the fence. After the departure of our distinguished guest, the bar was closed down, since one sales area was naturally sufficient. On the occasion of this visit, a normal line of suppliers was also not permitted to form in front of the elevator. What did they want to prove by that?
>
> "The work done in the warehouse by the employees of various city institutions was simply comical. It was loudly proclaimed to be 'public service work'; as a matter of fact, it was done during working hours and, for that matter, for money." (*Report on Materials Censored,* December 1–15, 1974)

That these ceremonies fooled no one was clear to all involved. But the censors still knew that ceremonies and the rules of protocol that had been developed were beyond attack—to say nothing of the impermissibility of any lack of awe and respect for the work of the state prosecutor:

> In Issue No. 20 of *Życie Literackie,* the following passage from the column "Café Notes" [containing gossip related by Jerzy Urban] was challenged:
>
> ". . . The news has reached the café that the official ceremonial rulebook in use throughout Poland regulating rituals involving the decoration, welcoming and send-off of guests, which the press likes to make fun of, is an internal document of the Public Prosecutor's Office. This gives rise to rumors [which sound reasonable given the current situation] that this office is more interested in handing out decorations than in delivering verdicts, in praising people than in prosecuting them, and in shaking hands than in issuing indictments. The economic conditions have also arisen which can make it profitable to transform prisons

into vacation resorts. . . ." (*Report on Materials Censored,* May 16–31, 1974)

The arrangement of continual public ceremonies and media events for party and government leaders seems to have ended by 1975, just as the Gierek leadership began to institute drastic changes in the Polish political system—a regional reorganization, a major constitutional reform and a party congress glorifying the regime. The regulations that went into effect in 1975 and 1976, as well as the apparent absence of censored attacks on the growing personality cult, signaled a retreat of the leadership from being media personalities. The possibility that journalists would make them appear less than glorious increased as reality became harder and harder to square with their claims of glory and as opposition to Gierek and his policies became stronger, more open and more pervasive. Public ceremonies ran more of a chance of being reported as fiascoes simply because, for all but the most stark reports of the Polish Press Agency, there was no other way to describe them. Thus, from 1975 on, the regulations sought not so much to orchestrate press coverage of Gierek and his fellows as to block it, thereby keeping the public from getting the idea that it was the leaders who had made the policies and who were responsible for their failures. And finally, given the fact that politics in Poland was becoming more and more a matter of insignificant bureaucratic shuffling, Press Agency communiqués were most appropriate. Journalists who wished to discuss the leadership and the events of the day found themselves confronted more and more frequently with an impenetrable wall of censorship, and the verdict "Only Through PAP."

Party Action Days, during which party members were expected to do some symbolic manual labor, were resurrected in the early seventies and continued throughout the middle years of the decade. The very purpose of this activity—to show party members and leaders as workers at heart—was negated by a censorship rule from the mid-seventies:

No photographs are permitted of the party and state leadership performing social volunteer tasks.

The regulation went on to specify that "two Central Photographic Agency (CAF) photographs are to be used in *Trybuna Ludu, Życie Warszawy* and the regional *województwo* party newspapers." The reason for the rule? Perhaps the fact that these events, however they were viewed by those isolated at the top, were held in contempt by party rank and file and nonparty members alike and thus were better left unheralded or unreported than treated as they were in the censored passages of the following:

In an article entitled "Autumn in the Park and Public Service Work" (*Więź*, No. 11), I. Krzemiński criticized instances of ill-advised and pointless volunteer public service projects and pointed out how socially harmful this kind of activity is. The article read in part as follows:

". . . A couple of weeks ago I was awakened by the rustling of leaves, the shuffling of many feet and the din of many voices. The source of the commotion turned out to be schoolchildren (about two or three classrooms' worth) who were devoting their morning to cleaning up a large part of the park, diligently raking up leaves and dumping them in piles along the park's central pathways. . . . A week went by. . . .

"Then a new 'brigade' showed up, this time consisting of respectable gentlemen with neckties and ladies wearing patent leather shoes. The solemnity and seriousness with which they repeated the job done a week before by the schoolchildren left no doubt that this, too, was a 'public service project.'

"The social costs of these hapless projects are especially high, since, in addition to the loss of time and energy, they inflict more serious damage by undermining the very idea of public service work and by distorting the purpose and meaning of 'public service.' And once again it is possible to find support for this conclusion in the results of sociological studies which show that the individuals being studied, while aware of the need for someone to do public service, are not very enthusiastic about these so-called public service 'projects' or 'actions,' and, generally speaking, do not hold them in very high esteem. And yet the theoretical and sociological bases for efficient and, for the participants, effective public service work is well known. . . .

"The performance of genuinely effective public service work is feasible, but primarily when based on informal social bonds. Only this kind of social group, bound together by a desire to perform unselfish labor for its own community, is truly capable of carrying out projects that are of more than passing significance to larger social groups or even to society as a whole." . . . (*Report on Materials Censored,* December 1–15, 1975)

In the same vein, when Edward Gierek sent out New Year's greetings in 1976 to selected factories and institutions—greetings that were normally the high point of the New Year's propaganda—no information concerning them was permitted in the mass media. Ironically, the explanation given to the censors for this rule—however self-justifying —was an admission on the part of those who control the media and propaganda not only that there was a retreat from the personality cult, but also that there had been overkill in the propaganda battle:

> In the interests of maintaining a proper standing for good wishes (and thanks for good wishes) expressed in the mass media by the leadership of the party, the Sejm [Parliament], the Council of State and the government, on New Year's and other holidays and anniversaries, attempts to initiate this form of contact with society by representatives of various social organizations and lower-ranking administrative and party leaders should be eliminated from the press, radio and television.
>
> The various periodicals and radio and television may extend greetings on behalf of the editors to their public in the paid advertisements section, or as part of music requests.
>
> Plant newspapers may publish various forms of good wishes and thanks directed to the entire work force or to certain employees. (New version, October 3, 1976)

Other traditional "media opportunities" for party and state leaders to appear as leaders, figures who had been given top billing in the early seventies, were also ordered to be ignored. No one was permitted to write about the distribution of party cards—essentially a symbolic renewal of one's commitment to the party—to members of the party leadership (members and alternate members of the Politburo, members of the Central Committee Secretariat). All such information— heretofore, prime propaganda material for blitzing the media with pictures and statements from national and local leaders—could now come only from the central Polish Press Agency. In 1975, too, even the opportunity to portray Gierek as a national hero in eulogies to him on his sixty-second birthday was passed up.

Similarly, even regular party and state events about which the press received formal notification could not simply be written up in the media. Even when the topics of Politburo meetings were given to the press, they could only be published as directed by the Polish Press Agency. By the end of 1974, this national news agency had also become the only permissible source of information, at least while an event was still news, on the supposedly public news conferences given by Gierek that were ostensibly a major step toward open communication between the leaders and the led. These news conferences were also to bring journalists into closer contact with the party leadership and party life, provide them with authoritative and usable news, and allow them to play a more direct role in political discussion. Instead:

> No material referring to the meeting between the First Secretary of the Central Committee of the PZPR [Edward Gierek] and journalists on November 20, 1974, should be allowed to appear. The PAP information dated November 21, 1974, exhausted the subject. In the event of any doubt, please contact the censor's office. (November 22, 1974–January 13, 1975)

> No in-house discussions, commentaries or the like concerning the meeting the First Secretary of the Central Committee of the PZPR and journalists on January 28 should be permitted. In-house information must fit into the framework of the report issued by PAP. In the event that PAP issues any coverage of this meeting, any of the editor's own materials must fit within the framework of the PAP report.

Television cameras, already strictly controlled at these press conferences and closely watched by party officials, were placed under even greater control so no slips would be visible to the public:

> Film reporting for television is permissible only with approval from the Department of Propaganda, Press and Publications of the PZPR Central Committee.

The logic of the rules for a lower profile of the Gierek leadership after 1974 was never explained to the censors—at least not in the documents available to us. We do know, however, that these regulations appeared at a time of major political change in Poland and of a major propaganda campaign about Poland's successes—"successes" that, in fact, were increasingly failures. This suggests that Gierek and his leadership might have decided to make changes in the system they controlled without centering attention on, and therefore taking responsibility, themselves. Similarly, as economic problems became increasingly visible to the public, the leadership seems to have moved in general to an emphasis on "the system" rather than on the responsibility of individuals within that system's leadership. It was also as though the party leadership wanted to exclude any stories that could be twisted into jokes or lead to questions about national stability.

Hence the prohibitions against the kind of coverage that could permit suggestions of the mortality and competence of the leaders: their age, their ability to answer the questions of audiences, their ability and/or willingness to do physical or demanding labor. (When Gierek disappeared from view, there were rumors in Warsaw that he had serious back problems and had gone abroad for treatment, but no writer dared suggest in the mass media that human frailties could be attributed to Poland's leader.)

The censorship documents themselves only offer hints about the reasons for the end of the leader-as-hero theme, yet they indicate clearly that journalists seldom, if ever, tried to report on their own about "media events" staged for the top leadership, or about leaders' public appearances. Such high-level reports were almost always left to the Polish Press Agency, even without explicit directions. The individuals and institutions about which journalists were willing—and able—to write were at a far lower level. Indirect criticism of high-level officials and institutions had to be ferreted out by the discerning reader. No reports on Gierek's press conferences, for example, appear in the censorship documents available to us. Journalists seem to have simply assumed that these events were "off the record" and not to have attempted to quote press conferences directly as a source of information.

Orchestrating Political Events

The key political events of 1974–76 were handled by special guidance and censorship. Some were designated to receive maximum coverage; others were to be passed over in silence. Those that could be were planned far in advance, like the celebration of the thirtieth anniversary of the postwar Communist regime or the Seventh Party Congress in December 1975. Media coverage was carefully orchestrated, with every detail spelled out. The Press Department of the Central Committee had worked out plans for what was to be covered, how, when, where and to what extent. (The impact of these plans was limited, however, by their secrecy: the regulations for handling the thirtieth anniversary of the party were exclusively for the use of the censors, and even the instructions for covering the Party Congress were issued in numbered copies. Those who wrote stories could therefore only shadowbox, and politically powerful editors, who were often given only vague directions, were sometimes left to chart their own paths in what they submitted if not what was actually allowed to be used in the media.

For the celebration of the thirtieth anniversary of the Polish United Workers' Party, every detail was preplanned—down to the regulation specifying that the "printing or reproduction of emblems, posters, pennants and the like, or information on tourist events and competitions [were to be permitted only if] they were included in the Plan of Major Undertakings and Ceremonies Related to the 30th Anniversary ratified by the respective party committee." In addition, this plan specified that:

> No material (books, folders, albums, posters and so on) prepared in honor of the jubilees of various organizations, associations, unions, enterprises and so on should be permitted for publication, unless such anniversaries are included in the national or voivodship "Plan of Undertakings and Ceremonies" or have been approved by the PZPR voivodship committee.
>
> No information about these anniversaries should be permitted in the mass media. On the other hand, material may be permitted concerning the contributions and prospects for development of individual organizations, enterprises and institutions, but without reference to anniversary celebrations organized as purely internal affairs. An exception should be made for plant newspapers, which may include information about anniversary celebrations taking place within the enterprise.

Clearly, no local event was to overshadow the national celebrations or to seem to be a separate event. Nor could this glorification of the past and past leaders outshine the images and events of the present: if "commemorative programs, the creation of committees to celebrate the thirtieth anniversary of the Polish People's Republic, or other undertakings related to the jubilee" were not mentioned in the "Plan," the censors were instructed not to allow them to become a part of the media's picture of reality. Nor was approval to be "given for printing or reproduction of any greetings, thanks or letters of commendation either in the mass media or in the form of separate printings." In this way, the censors controlled not only what was reported but much of what was done. The issue itself was sensitive enough that censors were instructed to consult with the GUKPPiW leadership if they had any questions.

As a result of these instructions, the censors' Reports for 1974 indicate that a large number of materials on the thirtieth anniversary were ordered removed. In May, for instance, the censors excised 202 items on the much acclaimed national celebration. Even long-planned events honoring the party were kept out of the media in conformity with the regulations. For example:

> Reports on the erection of five new monuments and plans for the erection of two others were challenged. (*Report on Materials Censored*, May 16–31, 1974)

In line with the regulations, the censors removed even the most positive of reports from the tiniest of local journals. In a biweekly factory paper, all references to the thirtieth anniversary were deleted from an article on the initiatives of the factory party committee taken under the directions given them to commemorate appropriately the party's anniversary, since the regulations forbade the reporting of individual initiatives not included in the "Plan of Undertakings and Ceremonies":

> In the biweekly plant newspaper *Nasze Sprawy,* published by the Soda-Salt Combine in Inowrocław, W. Lewandowski wrote an article entitled "Current Problems of Internal Party Work in the Inowrocław Soda-Salt Combine," which reads in part as follows:
> ". . . the Plant Committee respectfully acknowledges the pledge according to which the youth organization, in commemoration of the 30th anniversary of People's Poland, committed itself to the preparation of thirty of its most outstanding members for entry into the ranks of the PZPR. . . ." (*Report on Materials Censored,* May 16–31, 1974)

The censors were also instructed to keep out any possible "leaks" of information about major events planned for the thirtieth anniversary celebrations. The foremost concern here was that "information about preparations for the military parade to take place in Warsaw on the occasion of the 30th anniversary of the Polish People's Republic" not outshine a planned interview with General E. Molczyk, the Vice-Minister of National Defense, by appearing in the media before he could announce it in his interview scheduled for mid-June. The censors were therefore instructed that, until the interview appeared,

> . . . all information should be cleared with the military censorship officer (telephone number is Ministry of Defense switchboard, 210-06,

extension 25-75), or with the independent military department of GUKPPiW (28-25-81 and GUKPPiW central number, extensions 20, 30, 31 and home phone numbers 28-64-19 and 58-97-30).

The fact that even home telephone numbers were supplied in a country where such numbers are almost never given out or used for conducting business indicates how seriously this matter was taken by the military.

The great rituals of public participation were likewise not matters about which information could appear without being carefully scripted. Coverage of parliamentary elections, regardless of how closely they were controlled, was not intended to be either spontaneous or timely:

> Until the publication of the official communiqué giving a full list of candidates to the Sejm, no names of candidates for deputy or for member of the People's Councils should be made public (even if they have already been agreed upon). Until the results of the elections are announced, no figures on the number of persons entitled to vote should be published.

Once these elections took place, the minuscule number of citizens who expressed their disapproval of the single list of party-approved candidates, either by not voting at all or by crossing out names on the list, could be given only in percentages. This number, at a casual glance, seemed far smaller than the absolute number of thousands of voters willing to take the risk involved in publicly demonstrating their disaffection.

National party events like the Seventh Party Congress and the various meetings of the Central Committee were, during the Gierek period, far more than occasions for formal ratifications of leadership policies or élite discussions of problems and policies. Highly confidential documents, circulated in numbered copies within the GUKPPiW offices and to a limited number of editors and party activists, provided clear directions for exploiting such party events as carefully orchestrated propaganda campaigns. These plans were drawn up by the Department of Press, Radio and Television of the Central Committee to guide the editors' choice of overall themes to be emphasized and of specific topics to be covered. Even more explicit instructions on coverage were provided verbally by Press Department officials at press conferences for editors and journalists specializing in key areas such as economics, culture and social welfare. Chief censors and censors specializing in related fields also attended these conferences so that they could better guide journalists and editors in following the instructions as closely as possible.

The process of control did not end with the issuance of coverage plans or the holding of press conferences. Specific instructions going far beyond a general outline of the issues and the desired tone of reporting were also distributed. Furthermore, Central Committee instructors assigned to each journal reviewed its compliance with the coverage guidelines, and editors and censors with questions were urged to consult with them.

Despite all the planning, however, coverage of these events often did not turn out to be what had been hoped for. Generally, the truly "mass" media like the daily, regional and national papers tended to stay closer to the projected themes than the sociopolitical weeklies and other "intellectual" journals. But even in the least independent publications, the journalists' own sense of what was an interesting and appropriate slant for their coverage, as well as the pressures of daily news reporting, made the media far less consistent and orchestrated than the carefully set-out plans had envisioned. The two plans cited below, dealing with the Third Party Plenum and the Seventh Party Congress, can therefore only be taken as evidence of the leadership's perception of what coverage was important and appropriate, not as indicators of what actually appeared.

The Third Plenum of the Central Committee

The Third Plenum of the Central Committee of the PZPR, which met on April 20, 1976, was concerned with improving the ideological and organizational work of the party. Sections of the Press Department's plan for coverage of this plenum were excerpted by the GUKPPiW's Instruction, Evaluation and Control Group on April 15 and printed for the censors in an edition of sixty-three copies. The general topics and conclusions of the plenum were specified before it ever happened. The tasks and schedule of events for educational and cultural institutions and the mass media in publicizing and promoting the decisions the plenum was slated to make were also preordained. Relevant portions of that document appear below.

Main Office for Control of Press,
. Publications and Public Performances
Instruction, Evaluation and Control Group
ZI-I-132/15/76

Warsaw, April 14, 1976
C O N F I D E N T I A L
Copy No. 24

Informative Note No. 15

We are attaching, for the information of censorship groups, excerpts
of the "Plan for the Popularization and Implementation of the Work
of the Third Central Committee Plenum."

Deputy Group Director
Janusz Buchalski

Copies made: 63
Distributed according to the list

. . . Taking into account the continuing importance of the resolutions
of the Third Party Plenum for programming and improving the
method and content of work to strengthen the nation's socialist consciousness throughout the period of the construction of an advanced
socialist society, the following plan includes both immediate and long-
term actions.

III. Work of the Mass Media
1. The popularization of the work and achievements of the Third
Party Plenum should be the object of systematic, long-range efforts
on the part of all of the mass media, through a theoretical elaboration
of the problems reflected in the deliberations of the plenum and, more
importantly, through wide-ranging ideological education. The media
should seek to awaken the nation's sense of social and national responsibility, and to encourage its active participation in the life of the
country. The basic tasks of the press, radio and television should be
to bolster the patriotic unity of the nation, to strengthen the Polish
state, to increase levels of efficiency and quality in all areas, and to
focus the attention of the whole society on the program and political
line of the party.

2 The Department of Press, Radio and Television is drafting guidelines
for the popularization of the subject matter of the Third Party Plenum
by the press, radio and television.

3. An evaluation of editors' plans for the treatment of the subject matter
of the Third Party Plenum is absolutely essential, and there should be

a discussion of current and projected coverage on this subject at the March meetings of editorial boards of local party dailies.

4. Editorial boards should hold meetings devoted to a thorough discussion of the tasks of journalists in covering the subject matter of the Third Party Plenum, and a several-day seminar to discuss the plenum should be organized this March for journalists specializing in ideological and political problems.

5. It is essential to conduct running evaluations of press, radio and television coverage of the subject matter of the Third Party Plenum.

6. The Association of Polish Journalists is organizing a series of meetings, discussions and seminars devoted to the Third Party Plenum.

7. The Main Office for Control of Press, Publications and Public Performances has stepped up its efforts to increase editors' political responsibility for texts presented for printing, increasing control over other periodicals and certain publishing houses according to the *Trybuna Ludu* formula [of editorial responsibility].

8. It is essential to adhere consistently to the principle that throughout the Polish press and nonperiodical publications, regardless of orientation or organizational affiliation, there is only one proper approach to interpreting the past.

9. Along with efforts to upgrade the qualifications and attitudes of administrative employees, it is essential that the mass media provide society with an image of the government official as a representative of authority, an employee subject to appropriate discipline, who has respect for legality and whose duty it is to serve society and individual citizens.

IV. Tasks of the Publishing Industry

1. All publishing plans and undertakings should be reviewed in light of the work of the Third Party Plenum, and appropriate additions should be made where needed. Publishing houses will influence authors to take up subjects concerned with progressive historical traditions, the creation and strengthening of the Polish state, and the building of socialism.

2. A mass deluxe edition of the Constitution of the Polish People's Republic and a special edition for state ceremonies should be published.

3. The Ideological Education Department and the Ministry of Culture and Art have drawn up a list of works basic to national culture and of the greatest educational value. These works should constantly be available for purchase. In the selection of titles for reprinting, particular

consideration should be given to items that emphasize the idea of a strong Polish state.

4. Ksiażka i Wiedza, Krajowa Agencja Wydawnicza, Wydawnictwo Ministerstwa Obrony Narodowej, Czytelnik, Nasza Księgarnia, Iskry and other publishing houses will set up a new series of works devoted to civic and patriotic education.

5. It is essential to produce albums devoted to the progressive traditions of the nation and the traditions of the workers' movement, as well as works portraying the achievements of socialist Poland. A documentary album dealing with World War II should also be prepared.

7. The Ministry of Education and Upbringing, in cooperation with the Committee on Radio and Television and the Chief Publishing Administration, will draw up publication and program plans to ensure the civic, patriotic and internationalist education of children and young people and the formation of a proper educational environment in the home.

8. Publishing houses will evaluate their activity in light of the Seventh, Thirteenth, Sixteenth and Third Party Plena, as well as in light of the resolution of the Politburo on the tasks and role of the publishing industry.

The Seventh Party Congress

The Seventh Congress, held in December 1975, was a triumph of media orchestration and of propaganda about the glories of Gierek's leadership. Its goal was clearly not the launching of new programs that would help the country: it was designed as a forum for the glorification of past accomplishments and for the strengthening of the political control of the Gierek leadership. Following the congress, the First Secretary consolidated his gains with new elections to the Sejm and amendments that brought the Polish constitution into line with others in the Soviet bloc. Simultaneously, the Press Department of the Central Committee moved to capitalize on the aura of success the Congress had sought to create by launching a campaign of post-congress propaganda.

No more than three weeks after the congress, the censors received a special set of elaborate instructions entitled "The Tasks of Press, Radio and Television Following the Seventh Congress of the PZPR." These were drafted by the Press Department and distributed in the censors' office January 6, 1976, to serve as a guide in assessing material in the media. This was, in many ways, a victory document: the congress had been preceded by the greatest campaign of glorification of the leadership and its policies ever undertaken in postwar Poland. (Undoubtedly, part of the reason for the heavy propaganda blitz was the realization by those in the leadership with access to accurate economic data that this was probably the last time the party's claims of an "economic miracle" would have any credibility. Difficult times lay ahead.)

Main Office for Control of Press,
   Publications and Public Performances
Instruction, Evaluation and Control Group
ZI-Pf-132/1/76

> Warsaw, January 6, 1976,
> C O N F I D E N T I A L
> Copy No. 29

Informative Note No. 1

I am attaching, for the information of censorship groups, material entitled "The Tasks of Press, Radio and Television Following the Seventh Congress of the PZPR," drafted by the PZPR Central Committee's Department of Press, Radio and Television.

> Deputy Director of the Group
> Janusz Buchalski

THE TASKS OF PRESS, RADIO AND TELEVISION
FOLLOWING THE SEVENTH CONGRESS OF THE PZPR

Our whole society has given its support to the rich achievements of 1971–75 in the socialist construction of our country under the leadership of the party, an achievement which confirms that the development strategy adopted by the Sixth Congress of the PZPR was a correct one. The Seventh Congress set new, ambitious, courageous goals for national socioeconomic development during the next five-year period, goals that represent a continuation of the strategy of dynamic development followed during the first half of the 1970s. They are aimed at the further rapid development of the socialist economy, the expansion and modernization of production potential, an increase in the social productivity of labor, scientific, technical and organizational progress, upgraded management effectiveness, an expansion of Poland's contribution to the socialist community, and a strengthening of her position in Europe and the world. 1976 will be the first period in the realization of the resolutions of the Seventh Party Congress. A very great deal depends on getting off to a good start in the implementation of the program of the party and the nation and on achieving good results this year. Hence, there is also a need to strengthen the belief of working people and society as a whole in the correctness of the path we have taken and in the unexhausted possibilities for well-organized and disciplined activity and the expansion of action and initiative. The growing consciousness of working people, their patriotic commitment and their increasing belief in their own strength and potential are a guarantee of further success in the building of an advanced socialist society in our country.

The mass media have an extremely important role to play in this connection. The tasks facing the mass media in the period following the Seventh Congress may be summed up as follows:

I. General Tasks

1. After the Seventh Party Congress, the basic task of the mass media is to disseminate throughout society the program described in the resolution "On the Further Dynamic Development of Socialist Construction—On a Higher Quality of Work and Living Conditions for the Nation" and in the resolution "On the Further Development of the Forces of Socialism, the Maintenance of Peace and the Further Strengthening of the International Position of the Polish People's Republic."

The aim of this activity should be to make every citizen aware of the political, ideological and socioeconomic foundations for the development of the country over the next five years, and thereby to mobilize the population to the full realization of these goals. It is a question of maintaining a high ideological temperature, productive work and a sense of commitment from the first few days after the Party Congress.

2. In the substantive activity of the mass media, special attention should be given to the following:

—Continued popularization of the record of achievement in national socioeconomic development during the current five-year plan in general and in 1975 in particular. This should touch upon overall macro-economic gains and on achievements in specific areas, with emphasis on the correctness of the developmental strategy laid down by the Sixth Party Congress, the high level of participation on the part of the working people and the leadership role of the party.

—An indication of the goals and tasks for 1976–1980, especially those for 1976, which follow from the strategy for development adopted by the Seventh Party Congress. In particular, society should be convinced of the need to maintain a high rate of national development, increased labor productivity, modernity and high production quality as preconditions for and guarantees of the building of an advanced socialist society, a rise in the people's material and cultural standard of living, and an increase in the power and prestige of Poland in the world.

II. Key Steps in the Promotion of National Economic Tasks

In light of the overall economic tasks, the press, radio and television should concentrate on the following:

1) Ensuring the proper dissemination throughout society of the basic tasks involved in the socioeconomic development plan for 1976. Here the major emphasis should be on convincing [the population] that this plan *will ensure* the implementation of the party's program, *a good beginning for the whole five-year period,* the further improvement of living conditions, dynamic growth of production and services, economic cooperation with other countries, and the continued expansion and modernization of the material base of the economy. Against this backdrop, it should be emphasized that it is important to begin immediately, without wasting a single day or hour, if the provisions of the plan are to be realized. It should also be *emphasized that the goals of the plan are ambitious and courageous,* and that all of its projected segments are subordinated to the goal of raising the standard of living of both society and its individual members. Special emphasis should be placed on the factors of intensive economic growth, particularly on labor productivity, modernization of productive assets and the need for further intensification of and exploitation of untapped reserves for housing construction.

2) Plans for the further modernization of the Polish economy. Here, the development of modern fields of production, including automation, electronics, chemicals, the automotive industry and others, should be portrayed, along with a discussion of the dynamics and effects of the modernization of the structure of production. There should also be an emphasis on the complexities involved in the development of various production sectors, including the fuel and raw materials complex, agriculture and food processing, and manufacturing.

3) Plans for the intensification of agricultural production. In particular, there should be a discussion of the ways of finding solutions to key problems like the expansion of grain and fodder production, the development of livestock breeding, and better land utilization. More coverage should be given to various initiatives of rural communities *(gminy)* and the successes they have enjoyed. Attention should also be given to highly productive agricultural methods and collective forms of agricultural production. There should be a portrayal of the correct, ever increasing role and tasks of the rural community *(gmina),* as well as its role in bringing the citizen into closer contact with the government

offices that have emerged from the reform of local administration. Informational and propaganda work should aid in the activizational work of the rural communities, but at the same time it should point to shortcomings that need to be overcome.

4) Plans for the production of consumer goods—both foodstuffs and manufactured items. In these days, marked by shortages of certain food items, the creation of new patterns of consumption and the use of substitutes have taken on new importance.

5) The popularization of plans for a continued policy of active investment to increase long-range prospects for the growth of the production potential of the national economy and a better satisfaction of the needs of the economy, the market and export. Modernization investments, one of the major aspects of the present five-year plan, should be given special emphasis.

6) The development of economic cooperation with other countries as an essential factor in successful and dynamic development. In this area, more effort should be made to popularize the export-oriented strategy of economic development and the need for exports to grow faster than imports. A key place should be given to indicating the significance of cooperation with the USSR and other Comecon countries for economic development and the significance of the even stronger forms of integration and cooperation with those [other Soviet bloc] countries (joint production as well as specialization to ensure greater export effectiveness and continued growth; joint investment ventures, an effective and genuine way to satisfy growing raw-materials needs). Greater attention should be given to the dynamic growth of imports of industrial goods from CMEA countries in 1976–80.

7) The need for rational management of labor resources as outlined in the plan for 1976. The rationalization of employment is an important course to be pursued by our economic policy, given the increasing exhaustion of labor resources. This problem should be taken up as a whole and in terms of its parts, with a presentation of actions taken in various sectors of the economy and the results achieved. The problem of the rationalization of employment policy should be related to technical and technological progress within the economy and to the need for the further upgrading of vocational qualifications through continuing education, the improvement of vocational standards and the improvement of vocational training, to an increase in labor productivity and to effective organization and management. The scientific organization of work, which represents the most important need at this moment in this area, should be given a key place [in coverage].

III. Main Tasks in the Area of Social Affairs

The overall approach to problems in this area should start from the need to ensure effective management, increased labor productivity and quality, and the development of the consciousness appropriate to the building of an advanced socialist society.

In the press, radio and television there is a need to deal with problems such as the following:

1. Effective Management

At the present stage of our nation's development, this is one of the most important factors in ensuring the successful implementation of production goals. It is a matter of better utilization of capital goods, improvement of investment procedures, the introduction of scientific and technological advances, the organization of work in all sectors of the economy, the better utilization of fuel, raw materials and other production materials, and the efficient use of imported goods. The mass media should mobilize the population to carry out these tasks, promoting good models and exposing inferior ones. An important element [to be stressed] is the need to ensure the high productivity of fixed assets and to increase the extent to which they are used. Of prime importance here is the effective use of shift labor, particularly in enterprises with new technology or new machinery. This also involves the problem of lowering material costs, the rational management of raw materials, etc. Of importance here is an awareness of the virtues of high production quality and, hence, the durability of the goods produced, which leads to savings in the social costs of production.

2. The Human Factor

In the effort to inspire society to realize the resolutions of the Seventh Congress and the goals for 1976, a central place should be devoted to the role of the individual, groups of people and society as a whole. Therefore, alongside numbers and indices, an effort should be made to emphasize the decisive role of people, of the working class, as implementers of our plans and as the crucial element in guaranteeing success in achieving our quantitative and qualitative goals. In this regard, the concept of the "open plan" needs to be fully explained. The idea is that the open plan provides working people and factory crews with the opportunity to shape and improve their own production goals. The plan is open to initiative, commitment, professional and personal ambition, higher quality and new creative possibilities and perspectives. It is closed to poor work, extravagance, passivity and egoistic attitudes, all of which should be condemned. A climate favorable to creative initiative on the part of working people—a climate favorable to innovation and dynamic action—should be created and permanently established. We must create a model of a man without complexes, courageous in his actions, who supports innovation, who seeks to do what is right and is satisfied with good work. The pressure of social needs should be confronted with the need for greater efforts toward their satisfaction.

3. Work Quality and Productivity

As in the pre–Party Congress period, there should be a continuing and developing effort to promote a sense of responsibility for the tasks that individuals have to perform, as well as an effort to demonstrate the direct link between the quality and quantity of work on the one hand and the quality of life on the other. Good, reliable and productive work is essential to the realization of the goals outlined above and is the basic means of an improvement in the standard of living. In promoting work quality, the meaning of the concept should be widely propagated, giving attention to its component elements: including product quality (modernity, utility, beauty, precision, solid workmanship, durability), labor productivity, an innovative and organized approach to work, a view of one's own tasks in terms of national needs, conscious discipline, the upgrading of qualifications, the bolstering of vocational ethics and the integration of employees into the plant.

The problems of work quality should be skillfully correlated with the quality of life, including material living conditions, social services, the socialist model of consumption and man's internal needs (the acquiring of knowledge, broader participation in cultural life), the inculcation of principles of socialist morality and behavior, the search for the deeper meaning of life within the framework of socialist ideals, a strengthening of family life as the basic unit of socialist society, the proper structuring of human relations and the promotion of secular ceremonies.

The mass media should create a climate for good work, the sharing of experience and new solutions, the publicizing of the best new undertakings and experiments of individual enterprises, effective organization and good administration. The effective use of work time should be particularly emphasized: official work time should coincide with actual work time at each work station. We should promote the idea that the time when work begins is the time when production should begin, and that the end of the working day is the moment when production equipment is left. Journalists' attention should also be directed to the role played in the production process by foremen, supervisors and the heads of production sections, as the people directly responsible for the organization and results of work. They should use their sense of responsibility, their moral attitudes and their authority to mobilize [those under them] to do better work. In a broader sense, this applies to the responsibility of the managerial staffs of enterprises and institutions for the organization and realization of the tasks assigned to the workers under them.

At the same time, criticism should be aimed at those factors and forces that interfere with the improvement of work quality: lack of discipline, laziness, the desire to avoid inconvenience, overcautiousness, kibitzing, wastefulness, disorganization, inertia, carelessness and so forth. Efforts should be made to stimulate worker motivation and a sense of satisfaction from work well done. We should foster the conviction that "in working for the country, you are working for yourself," that my wealth and my family are directly affected by the overall wealth and welfare of the country.

4. The Formation of Socialist Consciousness

The efforts of the mass media to popularize and explain the meaning, purpose and concept of the building of an advanced socialist society in this country. There is a real need to make people aware that an advanced socialist society is not only a society of producers and consumers of an abundance of material goods, but is also a society of broadly educated people with developed intellectual aspirations, a society based on modern technology, modern principles of management, a high level of sociopolitical consciousness and a profoundly rooted ideology. More attention should be concentrated on the strengthening of recognized social values and the formation of new attitudes, outlooks and habits. In particular, it is a matter of intensifying patriotism, in the sense of conscientious, creative work for the nation. It is also a matter of the economic education of society. It is a question of imparting greater importance to innovative attitudes, of reinforcing such moral values as good will, human dignity, solidarity and friendship, and of giving greater attention to the educational function of the family as the fundamental unit of any society.

Respect and politeness in dealing with other citizens is an essential element of all activities at all times.

In the context of ideological confrontation, the mass media must take a more aggressive stance in propagating and promoting socialist ideals and must more effectively combat bourgeois and petit-bourgeois attitudes and ideology, basing its defense on a profound scientific analysis.

Particular emphasis should be placed on an explanation of the crucial importance of fraternal cooperation with the USSR and other socialist countries for the economic development of the country and for the realization of the common goals of peace and social progress throughout the world.

IV. Tasks of Journalistic Activists

If the tasks outlined here are to be carried out, journalists will have to have a good grasp of the problems discussed by the congress as well as of the documents and resolutions issued by it. An important role in their study of the congress documents should be played by party organizations and the Association of Polish Journalists.

In carrying out information and propaganda work, which should be consistent yet varied, it will be extremely important to find an answer to the following questions: How can we reach our audience—readers, viewers and listeners—with an explanation of the tasks outlined by the Congress? How can we engage them in a dialogue and effectively inspire and mobilize them? How can we make these aims the goal and ideal of every Pole? The specific characteristics of individual enterprises and institutions as well as individual voivodships should be taken into account in the presentation of these materials.

It will be possible to accomplish these tasks if every journalist personally identifies with the goals of the party program and strives each day to make that program a reality. This means that journalists, as activists on the ideological front, must be in daily contact with the working class, the creator of all national successes and achievements.

Before the Seventh Party Congress took place, painstaking efforts were made to cleanse the media of anything that would detract from the carefully orchestrated campaign to reap the maximum propaganda on predetermined issues from the gathering. Reports on anything spontaneously proposed for the congress during the preceding months of discussion were therefore removed. In addition, basic rules were distributed for coverage of the congress and of pre-congress events whose purpose was to ensure that all the glory would accrue to the Warsaw leadership, not to others. For example, no discussion of the upcoming congress was allowed until Gierek's meeting with his party unit in Silesia could lead the way. Furthermore, the instructions stated:

> 19. In connection with the announced meeting of the Seventh Party Congress in the fourth quarter of 1975, the following principles should be adhered to in censorship practice:
>
> 1) Information concerning initiatives and undertakings of a character that does not correspond to the high level of an event like the Congress should not be included under the heading "Seventh Congress."
>
> 2) Information on production obligations, social volunteer projects and other socially beneficial undertakings carried out in honor of the Seventh Party Congress may appear in the press and on radio and television only if they are in keeping with the principles established by the secretary for propaganda of the voivodship committee.

This prohibition does not apply to obligations undertaken by plant workers in response to letters from Comrades E. Gierek and [Prime Minister] P[iotr] Jaroszewicz.

3) Slogans and symbols related to the Seventh Party Congress on various kinds of incidental publications, brief cases, book covers and book jackets, pennants, etc., are also not desirable. (February 7, 1975; canceled January 12, 1976)

The censors went so far in enforcing these instructions that even when *Tygodnik Powszechny,* normally the most critical journal in Poland, presented a generally positive view of the first five years of the Gierek regime, its references to specific shortcomings were considered unacceptable. Even more unacceptable was the article's sullying of the image of the Congress by suggesting that by the mid-seventies the quality of life was low and was impeding the regime's moves for labor productivity. The following shows the passages that were cut to transform the article into a statement positive enough to be publishable:

In the lead article of Issue No. 49 of *Tygodnik Powszechny,* which appeared on the eve of the Seventh Congress of the PZPR, it was stated, *inter alia,* that "this congress is placing a special emphasis on summing up the accomplishments of the period 1971–1975." The article went on to say:

". . . This was an economically unprecedented five-year plan, one that cannot be compared with any previous five-year plan. An enormous investment drive, which resulted in the achievement of a record-breaking (for Poland) rate of growth, was accompanied by an honest effort to provide for the material needs of both society and the individual. For the first time in the history of the Polish People's Republic, these needs were given top-priority attention and were the subject of long-range government programs. They turned out to be a motivating force which stimulated our economy and opened it up to the rest of the world. This was the right policy to pursue, even though no miracles were wrought; we were unable to satisfy many needs all at once, and indeed demand grew at a faster rate than did our economic capabilities. We did not accomplish as much as we should have in such an important area as housing construction. On the other hand, a great deal of progress was made in the area of social policy, i.e., in what might be termed a more equitable distribution of the national income. . . . Let us also remember that it was not so long ago that the so-called baby-boom generation, then approaching productive age, was openly regarded as a national disaster that was going to destabilize the economy and reduce living standards. Well, the eventual recognition of these young people as invaluable members of society, their assimilation into the nation's economic mainstream, and the realization that without their help it would be impossible for us to speed up our rate of growth all amounted to a revolution in the thinking of official circles. Now, we are deeply troubled by the fact that the age cohorts that have followed are smaller, as well as by the prospect that we may be faced with a population deficit before we succeed in raising labor productivity to a satisfactory level and find the means to automate industrial jobs. . . . It is fitting that the concept of work quality and the quality of life was such a frequently recurring theme in speeches before the congress. For if there is any one thing we should do for ourselves, it would probably be to promote the universal conviction that it is worthwhile to do one's job well, and that it is indeed possible to derive personal satisfaction from one's work. It has always been the case that the person doing a bad job is one who is in effect fed up with life. For work cannot be isolated from the rest of life. Work is in fact a function of the quality of life, not only in a material sense, but also in a cultural and—for some people—religious sense. Man functions as a synergistic system—i.e., it is not possible to speed up things in one area while there is stagnation and regression in another. The Marxists themselves have always claimed that the underdevelopment of the superstructure can retard the development of productive forces. It is only right that we should agree with this and work together to clear the way for all of the opportunities that now stand before us. . . ." (*Report on Materials Censored,* December 1–15, 1975)

Keeping Policy Quiet

Silence and noninformation were sometimes deliberately employed in preparing for the implementation of a new policy so that questions would not be raised. It was imperative for the Gierek administration to present its decisions not only as its own but also as the only valid and conceivable choices. This was the case in the "preparation" of the reform of regional administration that fragmented the old power bases into tiny, powerless units. Over eight months before Poland's seventeen traditional administrative regions were split into forty-nine smaller, weaker ones, the censors were instructed that before May 1975, when the reform was to be announced and lauded,

No material should be permitted concerning projects for changes in the administrative division of the country or the structure of state administration.

In addition, all works (books, handbooks) discussing the current structure and function of the state administration should be held up and referred to the leadership of the Main Office for Control of Press, Publications and Public Performances. (First version, October 10, 1974; second version, April 2, 1975; third version, April 8, 1975)

In accordance with these instructions, the following "leaks" were caught:

In one article it [the regional administrative division] was described as "artificial" and "obscuring the actual situation," and a new division was called for. Someone wrote concerning Warsaw Voivodship, for example: "in its present form . . . it cannot be maintained. Life itself will not permit it. Several separate regional units must be put in its place." (*Bulletin of Themes of Materials Censored,* Second Quarter, 1974)

This moratorium on discussion permitted the Gierek leadership to carry out a reform destroying traditional regional power bases and transferring all real authority to the central party and state bureaucracy—without allowing local party leaders to protect themselves until everything was in place. In fact, until the official announcement was made, almost no one in Poland knew the extent or the potential impact of all the changes planned. And because the issue had virtually not been discussed at all, even months after the redivision had been enacted the power this fragmentation would give to the central authorities was not fully comprehended; each group was only able to see the changes in light of their impact on its own particular interests.

Once the reforms had been announced, the media were to explain and promote them throughout the society, and not to question them in any way. Popularization was not left simply to the good sense and good will of journalists. It was carefully organized, and the guidelines laid down for coverage provide one of the best available examples of the basic principles of propaganda during the Gierek years. They reflect the regime's all-pervasive fear of uncontrolled and potentially critical public discussion of, and reaction to, political measures. The more things could be kept under wraps, the leadership reasoned, the better. Not only was no criticism of the new regional units to be permitted, but all attempts to explain and justify the reforms were to use only the arguments already set forth by the regime. Furthermore, even though the reform was officially touted as opening up possibilities for citizens to participate actively in local government, local communities were to be given no opportunities to reflect on precisely how they could benefit from the changes. Perhaps because of the importance of these issues to the leadership, the censors were also given more detailed reasons than usual for the regulations they were to enforce:

> In connection with the reform made in the structure of local government and the territorial division of the country, I should like to emphasize that, consistent with the text of Comrade Edward Gierek's address made at the 17th PZPR Central Committee Plenum [where these reforms were announced], it is the task of the press, radio and television to present the reforms throughout the society.
>
> Hence the mass media should not take up those problems that could evoke undesirable repercussions from the public.
>
> This applies in particular to the following problems:
>
> a. Goals and tasks of the reform
> In explaining the goals of the reform, the press, radio and television should be guided by the arguments contained in the speeches of Edward Gierek, Piotr Jaroszewicz and Edward Babiuch, given at the 17th PZPR Central Committee Plenum. Hence no "speculation" should be permitted concerning the reforms and seeking any sort of reasons for them other than those contained in the materials of the plenum;
>
> b. Evaluation of the old system
> In this matter, too, the assessments contained in the plenum materials must be followed. The key guideline in this matter is Comrade Gierek's statement that the *powiaty* [county seats] as a body of the state administration and the past *powiat* personnel played their role in the old organizational structure.
> It would therefore not be useful now to try to hold the old *województwa* [regional governments] accountable for past problems (bureaucracy, abuse of power and so on). On the other hand, it is all right to permit publications that, on the basis of the materials of the 17th Party Plenum, show that the old units are no longer needed now that the new ones have been created (shifting certain rights and authority downward) and two-level administration has been introduced;
>
> c. It is also with great care and in close consultation with the local government officials that an assessment should be made of the useful-

ness of publications concerning the savings to be accomplished from the reform that was introduced. This applies both to personnel matters and to vacated buildings or facilities.

For example, premature discussions, postulates and proposals concerning the use of these facilities are not desirable.

Information on the subject of using vacated facilities may be published only in the local press with the approval of the first secretary of the local PZPR committee;

d. All postulates, advice and so on concerning improvements in the new projected administrative division of the country are also undesirable. Hence any discussion concerning the possibility of a different way of ordering the individual units and so on from that proposed in the draft is useless.

e. The same applies to the names of the new *województwa* and their headquarters. Press discussion on possible changes in this matter is to no purpose.

Directors in the Main Office are requested to speak personally with the editors in chief in situations where press material presented for the censors' control conflicts with the above principles and, in the case of conflict, to refer the material to the GUKKPiW leadership. (May 14, 1975, version ends here.)

f. Maps of new *województwa* presented for publication must be approved by the first secretary of the PZPR *województwo* committee or the *województwo* head.

g. Before the Sejm or government accepts appropriate normative documents, no material containing detailed information on the work and decisions of the *województwo* staffs should be permitted.

Premature "laurels" and praise for their efficiency are also undesirable, to avoid creating the impression that "everything is already finished and decided."

h. Given the possibility of increased ambitions and possible resentment among people, to the extent possible, we should tone down publications that accentuate the benefits the previous *powiat* towns will obtain from the very fact of their promotion to headquarters of new *województwo* officials, and the euphoria and joy of the residents and activists of these towns should be subdued.

It is a question of avoiding having various instances of "awkwardness" create a sense of degradation and inferiority in other urban centers (not just *powiat* towns, after all).

They, too, have their objective and personnel values, which in the new administrative structure will permit them not only to maintain their previous character as centers with a positive effect on the given region, but also to even improve their standing in economic and social life.

i. These same considerations should also be taken into account in assessing the standing of the *gminy*. In the new administrative structure this term will change its historically based meaning. It is no longer merely a territorial cluster of rural hamlets, but the center of the economic and social life of a relatively large area, in which various types of changes have occurred.

Nonetheless, we should count on the fact that in certain groups (including journalists) the *gmina* is conceived of in the old way. For example, opinions that now instead of the so-called "*powiat* Poland" we are going to have a "*gmina* Poland" may crop up. If such comparisons serve to lead to final conclusions that are positive (for example, power closer to the population, more decisions and concern for the needs of the parish population, and so on) or that polemicize the old way of thinking, they may be permitted. On the other hand, if this type of digression leads to negative conclusions ("lowest common denominator," "becoming like peasants" and so on), then it should absolutely be eliminated and the editors should be advised of the need for a new look at the traditional word (*gmina*) and the need to find the new content hidden in it. (Canceled July 13, 1975)

The handling of the administrative reform precluded from publication even oblique references to the all too rapid enactment of some unspecified "Polish laws" in an article on legal awareness written for the regional managers' association bulletin:

". . . It is the duty of the state to instill in the subjects of the law (citizens) this essential minimum [of knowledge of legal principles], making use of the mass media, social and political organizations, propaganda campaigns, etc. The more quickly legal norms are rotated, i.e., the shorter the period of time during which they remain in effect and the more quickly they are replaced by new norms, the more difficult this task becomes. Our legislative policy is not beyond reproach in this regard. The hastiness with which laws are passed and an excessive faith in the effectiveness of problem solving by the issuance of administrative decrees and prohibitions has contributed to the present surfeit of regulations. At the present time, a great effort is being made to limit the number of laws on the books and to standardize them. . . ." (*Report on Materials Censored,* September 16–30, 1975)

In the months that followed the administrative reform, nothing was allowed in the media that might tarnish the image of the reforms as instantly bringing improved services and better administration. When a popular weekly tried to run an article on how the administrative reforms were affecting individual citizens, the censors excised quotations from peasants who complained not about administrative intransigence but about the corruption of local agricultural cooperative workers—quotations that clearly implied that transforming the administration neither increased its control nor provided the goods and services that were needed. The remarks could also be read as suggesting that the administrative reform was a sham reform, with many services still not decentralized. They were deleted even though the summation of the remarks was that the reform was a good thing and should simply be strengthened:

In Issue No. 40 of *Dookoła Świata,* in an article entitled "The Government Went to the Citizen," A. Tumialis presented the results of a journalist's poll on the subject of changes in the administrative style of governmental authorities and ways in which government offices take care of official business in the wake of the national administrative reform. The following statements made by farmers in Gołymin Gmina of Ciechanów Voivodship were challenged:

" '. . . I can take care of renewing my personal identity document once every 20 years right here in the *gmina,* but to get some lumber I have to travel to the *powiat,* just like always.

" 'And there's no saying that I'll get it even then. I need three pieces of lumber to build a feeding trough. I ran all over the *powiat* for nothing. And if there was any lumber to be had anywhere, they told me that I'd have to pay 100 złotys to the health care fund before they'd give it to me. That's more than the price of three pieces of lumber! . . .

" 'They say that the *gmina* manager is in charge of things. It depends on who you're talking about. I went over to the agricultural circle cooperative to ask about having my fields plowed. They said, "We'll be there in two weeks." Two weeks went by, and I had to start my planting right away. I couldn't afford to wait for them to do the plowing. They're clever. They leased some land from the State Land Fund to make a little income, and they do their own land before any one else's. If there's any time left over, then they'll come and help us out. So why am I paying 4,000 złotys to the agricultural circle?

" 'Not so long ago, acting as if they were lords of the manor, they kicked 50 peasants out of the agricultural circle cooperative, all because these peasants demanded that the machines be used to plow their land. " 'That's how it is. And when the tractor operator from the circle finally does get around to showing up, he puts in three hours of work and says: "The tractor broke down on me," and just takes off. Either the tractor really is a piece of junk, or he has work to do somewhere else that's—to be blunt—more profitable. And what's more, he'll say, "Hire yourself a privately owned tractor," or "Go complain to the village priest."

" 'The agricultural circle cooperative has only one threshing machine that is in working order. For the whole *gmina*!

" 'So, while we're still on the subject of the *gmina* office and the powers of the *gmina* manager, it would be a good thing if he could exercise those powers not only over the peasants, but over the cooperative chairman, too!

" 'Because the peasant will do his share anyway, since that's the way he's always done things, but the chairman of the cooperative does what he wants. So, let the manager tell him what he ought to be doing, because the chairman isn't afraid of us, even though we elect him.

" 'It's a very good thing that political authority and the whole administrative apparatus is now located in the *gmina*. But the *gmina* also needs to be kept supplied with goods and services. This is even more important to us than political authority.' " (*Report on Materials Censored*, September 16–30, 1975)

Guarding "the Polish Road to Socialism"

Although there are no available regulations concerning it, coverage of Poland's political system was kept relatively circumspect. Communist party rule was never a subject for discussion. But journalists did try to suggest, however subtly, that "the Polish Road to Socialism," with its private agriculture, tolerance of the Catholic Church and acceptance of popular resistance to communism, was littered with still unfulfilled promises. A journal on local government problems pointed out that at least on a local level one of the two minor parties, the Democratic Party (created after the war to coopt small tradesmen and white-collar workers who would not support the Polish United Workers' Party), was hardly a viable entity. The remarks were eliminated. Although the article made no mention of the position of the Democratic Party and its lack of real access to jobs and administrative positions on a national level commensurate with its membership or with the delegation it was allowed in parliament by the PZPR, the censors made sure that there were no statements about the fact that the Democratic Party also played no real role in political life and in government administration on a local level. Students of local government and local government officials were thus left with only what they knew from their own experiences. And Democratic Party officials could not push for more representation or make their point to party members because they had no access to the media.

Nor was it acceptable to suggest that the Catholic Church was an important force in Polish society and politics. This is reflected in the following attempt by the Catholic intellectual weekly to respond to an anti-Church roundtable printed in the Atheist Union weekly. The censor's deletions turned the article from one that made it clear the Church was a strong force in young peasants' lives to one that implied their ties to the Church had broken down and that criticized only the fact that there was nothing to replace it with.

> "Not 'What' but 'Who' Is Important" (*Tygodnik Powszechny*, No. 19) is the title of an item reporting on a roundtable, "In Pursuit of Ideals and Attitudes," set up by the editors of *Argumenty*. We deleted an excerpt that argues with a statement made by one of the parties to the discussion, K. Długosz, secretary of the Main Board of the Union of Rural Socialist Youth:
> ". . . He is not satisfied with the fact that the village is the last place 'where moral social pressure still functions perfectly well,' because this pressure has its roots in the activity of the Church. In other words, Długosz is not interested in the fact that people steal less because of the influence of the Church's teachings, but he is pleased by the 'recently noted weakening of parish ties.' Meanwhile, 'the gap which has been created by the disappearance of old bonds has not been filled.' He says in the discussion that we do not know much about what happens to a person who has broken off his religious affiliation. So what is there to be happy about here?" (*Report on Materials Censored*, May 1–15, 1974)

National documents, rules and laws were sacrosanct for the Polish media. When in 1974 a scholar questioned the authority and usefulness of the Polish constitution, the censors blocked all his statements that the constitution had become an outdated document which did not meet the needs of Poland's new legal system. (Ironically, this prohibition was made at a time when Poland was the last of the Soviet bloc states not to have amended its constitution to take into account the gains that the Communist leaderships all claimed to have made. And a year later, the article's criticisms were presented as those of the Polish leadership itself and the constitution was amended, in spite of the opposition of the Church and the intellectuals.) The censors also removed a passage from an article suggesting there should be a mechanism to review the laws that were passed to be sure they were in keeping with the constitution:

> After an interval of several months, the problem of the state's political and administrative structure has returned to the pages of certain publications. During the past quarter, there was intervention in several publications dealing with this subject, and, among other things, calls for changes in the constitutional system and a clearer delimitation of the competence of the highest organs of state were deleted.
>
> In Z. Jarosz's *Introduction to the Study of Government Law* we questioned, among other things, the author's reflection that "one of the characteristic features of our constitution is extreme abstractness, brevity and sometimes even vagueness of its provisions. This is one of the reasons why even profound changes in our system, including changes in the principles by which organs of state carry on their work, can be made to a great extent in an extra-constitutional fashion."
>
> This same issue was taken up by J. Zakrzewska, in a challenged article entitled "On the Constitutionality of Laws in a Socialist State." Referring to the fact that many bourgeois and socialist states have institutions to review the constitutionality of laws passed by the legislative branch, she proposed the creation of a similar body in Poland. In her view, in light of legislative practice, "it would be useful to introduce into the Polish legal system an opinion-rendering body that could clarify the consistency or inconsistency of ordinary legislation with the provisions of the constitution." (*Bulletin of Themes of Materials Censored,* Second Quarter, 1974)

The fact that the Polish Sejm, or Parliament, was for all practical purposes a powerless institution during this period, and that laws were in fact made by the executive branch, was also not a permissible subject for discussion. Nor was any reference to the de facto lawmaking power of the PZPR Politburo permitted. Officially, after all, the party was charged with providing overall direction, not with specific policy decisions and administration:

We also challenged the view that there is no formal or practical delineation of the respective prerogatives of the Sejm and the government. One author wrote the following on this question: "A rationalization of relations between the Sejm and the government would be aided by a clear delineation of the line between the areas under the jurisdiction of each of the supreme bodies." He justified his proposal with the statement that "A decision of the Sejm, expressed in law, is sometimes altered by a ministerial decision in a lower-ranking document." Elsewhere, he suggested that "another complicated issue in the socialist system" was in need of a solution, namely, "which of these two supreme organs of state should be linked with the center of political decision making—the Politburo or the Central Committee?" (S. Ehrlich: "Six Hypotheses About Political Decision-Making Experts and the Center of Political Decision Making" in *Prakseologia*) (*Bulletin of Themes of Materials Censored*, Second Quarter, 1974)

Unpleasant Surprises

Not all news was as the party had planned. The carefully orchestrated propaganda of the 1975 Polish United Workers' Party Congress and of the parliamentary elections that followed—intended to glorify Gierek and his achievements and the successes of Poland in the 1970s—was marred by two major acts of opposition signaling Eastern Europe's first open, worker-intellectual opposition movement and indicating for the first time that the Gierek regime could exclude alternative points of view from the media but could not stop opposition and discussion. In the spring of 1976, constitutional amendments legalizing Poland's ties to the Soviet Union, the obligations of citizens to the state and the leading role of the Polish United Workers' Party were announced and quickly passed. They provoked a spate of critical letters and petitions from the intellectuals and the Church and, ultimately, became a matter of Church-state negotiation. And, in June of that same year, the regime's attempt to raise food prices brought industrial workers in two factory towns near Warsaw out into the streets. The subsequent arrests and firing of the workers stimulated a group of intellectuals, many of whom had been involved in protests over the constitution, to form the Committee in Support of the Workers (KOR), which then became a major underground organization and publishing organ. KOR also forced the regime to retreat from its plans to increase food prices and maintain them at highly subsidized levels.

These events, the real seeds of what in August 1980 was to become Solidarity, were a major source of concern for the regime. Its reaction was to try to minimize their impact by giving them no coverage. They were so important to the political leadership that mere written regulations were used only as supplements to meetings held during and after the protests and strikes between censors from all over the country and the heads of the Main Office for Control. Censors, whose job it was to have a sixth sense about what was sensitive and what was not, treated all reports about these events with utmost seriousness. They knew without being told that the safest course was to reject the material and, if there were any questions, to let their bosses take responsibility. Editors, too, saw little hope of entering into the debate on these issues. They censored themselves and relied on Press Agency reports for their coverage—or simply resorted to silence. And those involved—the Ministry of Justice and the Ministry of the Interior— had little to gain and everything to lose by feeding the fire with information. As a result, journalists could find out little unless they went to the striking towns or had contacts among the officials involved. All of this meant that the censors saw little that was in fact censorable and took few chances. The regulations that they were issued dealt with the details and the players in the events that they needed to know about to keep them out of the media.

The Constitutional Amendments

Once the Gierek leadership decided to amend the old Stalinist constitution of 1952, it evidently resolved to orchestrate the amendment process in almost total silence. Rather than risk the appearance of opposition or discussion, the amendments were announced only as they were passed by the Sejm. Censors were simply told in meetings with their superiors that there was to be a blackout on all coverage of these amendments—their preparation, any discussion that did go on about them, and special reports of their passage. Trouble was rightly anticipated, and the decision was made beforehand not to admit its existence.

The need for revisions in the constitution had been mentioned in passing at the Sixth Party Congress in 1971, but no move had been made then toward drafting amendments. First, the media bosses wanted to make sure that the old constitution would not be enshrined before it had to be changed: the censors were instructed to keep studies of the Polish system and its constitutional base out of sight. Scholarly works dealing with such questions were published in limited quantities for an audience of experts. The censors were told to delete any mention in the media of these very works that had earlier been approved by their office. This was the case for much of 1975, when the censors were instructed, for example:

> 61. No information, mentions, reviews, etc., should be permitted concerning Jerzy Stembrowicz's *Structure, Organization and Operation of the Government of the Polish People's Republic,* published by the Chief Methodological Center for Studies in Political Science.
> This prohibition is intended solely for the information of the censors. (February 28, 1975; canceled October 23, 1975)

After the Seventh Party Congress in December 1975, as work to draft the amendments began, the silence surrounding the constitutional question became almost deafening. Verbal instructions were given, but no one was allowed to know the nature of the amendments Gierek planned to put into effect. Drafts of the amendments were not made public. Journalists had only word-of-mouth evidence to guide them in their responses and opposition to provisions that sanctioned the special position of the Soviet Union and the Polish United Workers' Party, made citizens' rights conditional on their fulfillment of unspecified obligations to the state, and eliminated any mention of the Church in the constitution. Articles hinting at these changes or dealing with these issues were simply removed by the censors in the months between the Party Congress and the amendments' ratification by the Parliament. When the amendments were announced on January 24, 1976, journalists were left with the options of following instructions to praise the general concept of the amendments, silence or veiled opposition. Most chose public silence. Media support for the amendments therefore depended largely on the televised testimonials of "experts" chosen and directed to appear on television by the Press Department; on letters to the editor, created or requested by the staff, from various worker or peasant groups; on press agency reporting of the amendments and their passage (written in a more restrained fashion); and on a few relatively unknown journalists.

What this demonstrated was not only that the Gierek regime feared the public's response to such sensitive issues as Polish-Soviet relations, the role of the Polish United Workers' Party and the natural unwillingness of a Communist regime legally to acknowledge the power of the Catholic Church, but also that this fear was very well founded. Even threats of blacklisting, and the *de facto* blacklisting of some prominent cultural and academic figures for doing no more than refusing to appear on television and making their assigned pronouncements in favor of the altered constitution, could not deliver a full roster of public support for the amendments. And, though they did not admit there was opposition to the amendments, the media could not be brought to falsify completely the reality of the opposition within the intellectual community, of which it was a part.

While this ritual process of official propaganda about the amendments and censorship of dissenting opinion was being pressed forward, behind-the-scenes opposition was being mounted by the Church hierarchy and leading intellectuals. A number of journalists and editors were in touch with, or even involved in, this opposition. It was expressed in letters to government leaders; in letters from Cardinal Stefan Wyszyński, the head of the Catholic Church in Poland, to the Polish leadership; and in threats on the Cardinal's part to bring the Church's opposition out into the open. The letters and protests were well known to many throughout Poland because Western radio stations reported them in detail and among intellectuals the rumor mill ground steadily. Party leaders responded by making concessions on the proposed amendments. These came after prolonged negotiations between Cardinal Wyszyński and Gierek himself, held, because of Gierek's fury at this opposition, with the Minister of Religious Affairs, Kazimierz Kąkol, serving as an intermediary and calling Gierek by phone with the wording that the Cardinal said he could accept to get Gierek's acceptance or alternative proposal. Yet the regime thought it could save face by keeping any hint of opposition to or concessions on the amendments out of the media. The signers of letters to government leaders were blacklisted: whether they were scholars, journalists or entertainers, their names and their work could not appear for months after the protest. Reports on the amendments and their ratification made no mention of the questions raised about them or of the changes that had been forced on the regime. The amendments were presented as the first and last drafts. And finally, when Stanisław Stomma, head of the independent group of Catholic parliamentary delegates, walked out of the Sejm chamber during ratification rather than cast his vote for the amendments (even though the Church hierarchy had won some concessions), the only media acknowledgment of his protest was the inadvertent swing of a television camera to catch his departure. The media would not risk legitimizing his action even by condemning it.

The Price Riots of June 1976

Five months later, as train tracks were ripped up and Communist party headquarters were burned in Radom and Ursus (factory towns near Warsaw) and riots began all over Poland, the press denounced the rioters as "parasitic elements, ruffians, criminals and anti-socialist elements." At the same time, it did little reporting on the events themselves or their causes. And when the leadership finally had to concede defeat in the face of workers' violent opposition to the price increases, it refused to acknowledge that fact publicly. Just as there had been no open press discussion of the possibility and level of the price increases before they were announced, so now no explanation was given for the rollback of the increases in the prices of meat and staple foods—even though two tumultuous days of panic buying and strikes had preceded it. To have explained the reasons for the price reductions would have been an acknowledgment of the extent and power of the workers' opposition.

Since it was a similar attempt to raise prices just before Christmas of 1970 that had triggered the riots and strikes that brought down Władysław Gomułka, the Gierek leadership had tried to prepare itself to get the public to accept the increases. According to Mieczysław Rakowski in his book *The Republic on the Edge of the Eighties*, published after Gierek was ousted in 1980, leading editors and party activists were called together for a discussion under the guidance of the head of party propaganda, Jerzy Łukaszewicz, about how best to handle the matter. Yet, ironically, even these top party officials and editors were not told the whole story. They were given the task of preparing their propaganda without being themselves informed what the price increases would be—days before the stores were to be closed and new price charts put up.

According to Tomasz Strzyżewski, the strikes that subsequently erupted were considered so critical that instead of allowing censors to rely on telegraphed instructions or on their individual judgment, top officials from the censors' office met with every group of censors to personally explain what they should know about what had happened and to lay down the guidelines for appropriate coverage. As a result, we have no precise record of the instructions drawn up in the heat of the events, although there was probably little to censor: most journalists reported that it was almost impossible to get into Radom or Ursus, and even more difficult to make contact with officials or rioters. So, at first, journalists had little to report. In addition, all realized from the start that little of the truth could be published.

In their meetings with supervisors, lower-level censors thorughout the country were provided with information on the economic situation and on the riots themselves—information that was simply not available to most journalists and to the public. The censors were then expected to use this in their assessments of materials on the rioting and the price increases. When *Polityka* dared submit an article on the strikes, it was immediately clear to the censors and to the *Polityka* staff, well-established and savvy writers who knew the limits of the media and simply served initially as reporters for their colleagues and friends, that it was unacceptable. Those who did get in had to decide whether to argue their case further. The strikers were presented in too positive a light to even have the cuts reprinted in *Report on Materials Censored,* since these were distributed not only to censors but also to party and government officials. Instead, the objectionable passages and the changes that had been requested were reported in a purely internal note to the censors. Here is an excerpt:

In addition, the editors of *Polityka,* sharing our concern, made appropriate changes in four more items.

We cite an excerpt from a note that was presented for publication in the column "In This Country":

"People taking part in the demonstration in Radom stated, 'We will do everything to win trust through creative effort and by honestly acquitting ourselves of our basic civic responsibilities.' The president of the town reported that the incidents were begun on Friday, June 25, by a group of employees from department P-6 of the 'Walter' plant. Employees of other departments and, later, from other Radom enterprises joined the group. They went to the building of the voivodship party committee, where attempts to enter into discussion proved unsuccessful. Swarming in, they damaged several rooms and set fire to the building. In addition, 24 cars, trucks, buses, tractors and fire engines on their way to put out the fire were set on fire. Shops were vandalized."

Because the above text leads the reader to assume that only "Walter" employees took part in the incidents, the editors, acting on our suggestion, supplemented the text by noting the participation of "parasitic elements, ruffians, criminals and anti-socialist elements." (Informative Note No. 55, July 9, 1976)

The silence continued and spread. Writers and journalists who had supported the striking workers or had helped to organize the intelligentsia-based Workers' Defense Committee, established at first so that intellectuals would have a channel through which to aid arrested workers and their families, were blacklisted (just as those who had opposed the constitutional amendments had been). Some of their names did not appear in publications again until 1980. Others were blacklisted for shorter periods of time. Even official events dealing with the strikes and their aftermath were kept out of the mass media or were allowed to be reported only within carefully prescribed limits. Although public meetings on the state of the economy were held to give the appearance of the kind of public consultation demanded by the workers, they were not public and were, in fact, closely controlled:

> 140. All material from the consultation meetings may be published in the central press only through the intermediary of PAP, and in the regional press only on the approval of the voivodship committee of the PZPR. (June 25, 1976; canceled October 16, 1976)

On June 24, 1976, the day the strikes broke out, the following order was issued:

> Information on the subject matter and date of the next session of the Sejm may be permitted only after a PAP communiqué has been issued. (June 24, 1976; canceled September 16, 1976)

It was at this session, of course, that the decision to rescind the price increases and to ration sugar was taken. It was also at this session that the actions of the police were roundly condemned by the same Catholic intellectual group from which the delegate who refused to vote for the constitutional amendments had come. All these events were reported in the Western press, broadcast by Polish-language radio stations in the West and discussed in Poland. They could not be mentioned in the Polish press or on radio and television until September, when the regulations against them were canceled and they were no longer news.

The orchestration of information continued as the trials of the several hundred workers arrested during the riots began. Regulation No. 142, dated July 16, 1976, soon after the start of the trials, stated:

> Materials on the trials of the participants in the incidents in Radom and Ursus may be permitted only through the intermediary of PAP.
>
> Any materials prepared by individual publications must have the approval of the Department of Press, Radio and Television of the Central Committee of the PZPR.

Following the trials, there was no further mention in censorship regulations of the issues related to the Radom and Ursus strikes, not because they could be openly discussed, but because journalists, editors and censors knew from the verdicts and the censorship during the strikes and their aftermath that these subjects were off limits. As late as 1979, during the discussions preceding the Eighth Party Congress in December of that year, the price increases and strikes continued to be nonevents, even in the Party Congress's own reviewing of events during its term of office. When one member of the planning commission pushed for some evaluation of the strikes and their handling, at least in the internal documents of the congress, he was told to keep quiet. And so the PZPR never faced up to the reality of a critical political turning point even though that turning point was being discussed openly in the pages of dissident publications that circulated widely in major intellectual centers.

The press silence on the 1976 riots and the events that followed continued and came to color all other reporting, until the workers' strikes of August 1980 broke the grip of the Gierek press managers in the Press Department and the Main Office for Control. As conditions worsened, party leaders—looking like glorified statues—and policy discussions disappeared almost completely from the media. The tendency toward "nonevents" rather than "pseudo-events," begun between 1974 and 1976, continued to grow. Increasingly, Polish censorship was creating monochromatic mass media that presented the world party leaders wanted to see rather than the world that was.

Providing alternatives to the timid and well-laundered mass media came to be the chief aim of the opposition, which formed originally to provide assistance to the workers jailed for participation in the strikes of 1976. The silence of the official press merely increased the impact of the dissident movement. The silence on political and economic issues also increasingly alienated the workers from their leaders. They realized something that the Gierek leadership did not: political propaganda must be based on real information and open discussion. The media policy of denying certain events and orchestrating others, intended to protect the leadership, contributed to its downfall.

4 / REWRITING

WORLD POLITICS

OREIGN AFFAIRS presented the censors and their Central Committee Press Department bosses with myriad subjects and issues about which the political leadership needed to know and about which the public was hungry for information. Moreover, by the mid-seventies, Poland's domestic difficulties and the Gierek regime's courtship of the West made foreign affairs reporting more useful and palatable fare than reports on the internal situation in Poland. At the same time, however, foreign affairs materials confronted the censors with a world whose events seldom proved Marxist theory right, a world where Poland was a significant—if not independent—actor in its own right. Adding to the difficulty, foreign affairs reporting was not just for domestic consumption. Western, Soviet bloc and even some Third World countries reviewed the Polish press and reacted to its comments as though they were official statements. Even if foreign officials did not actually review the press, Polish press officials and many journalists and editors assumed they would. Finally, criticism and descriptions of events abroad were used by journalists as vehicles for veiled criticism of events at home. As a result of all these different uses, foreign affairs reporting was the area in which the censors appear to have been most sensitive to subtleties in phraseology as well as to inappropriate criticism.

Out of these contradictory pressures developed a multilayered system of information and interpretation of foreign affairs. For example, the most sensitive information from Western press reports, Western broadcasts into Poland, and Polish foreign correspondents' own reports was published in a number of limited-circulation bulletins. Little of this information was available in the mass media, but some did reach a larger audience through public off-the-record talks by journalists and other foreign affairs experts, and through private exchanges of interesting information and hard-to-obtain reading matter.

In this respect Poland was unique among the Soviet bloc countries. Far more information on events and conditions elsewhere was available to Poles from a variety of sources over which censorship officials had virtually no control. Gierek's policy in the seventies was to allow almost anyone who applied to travel abroad to go. Thus more Poles went abroad annually than any other Eastern Europeans, and naturally these travelers brought back impressions of the rest of the world over which the media and censors had no influence. In addition, while there were restrictions on the kinds of foreign journals that could be received and while records were kept of who received what, large numbers of individual Poles subscribed to such foreign journals as *Le Monde, Der Spiegel, Time* and *Newsweek.* Those who did not have their own subscriptions could read many Western as well as East bloc periodicals at the International Press Clubs and foreign-press stores located throughout Poland. Translations of Western wire-service copy on less sensitive issues were circulated widely to journalists as background information. Other more sensitive information was frequently passed on by politically prominent editors to staff members for their information. So, even though Western journals with reports on internal Polish events and criticisms of the Soviet Union and other Communist states did not appear openly on the shelves, some Poles who could read another language, or with a "need to know," had access to Western sources of information.

Of even greater concern to the Polish leadership was the influence of Radio Free Europe and other West-sponsored Polish-language radio broadcasts and, to a lesser degree, publications. The jamming stations had been dismantled as a result of the liberalization of the "Polish October" in 1956 and were only partially reactivated under Gierek. Both the Gomułka and Gierek leaderships continually pressed journalists to combat these Western influences and to keep readers satiated with Polish media. Their concern was further reflected in the circulation, in an extremely limited edition, of transcripts of all Western commentary broadcast into Poland. These were apparently closely read by the leadership and given to leading editors and foreign affairs commentators to aid them in structuring responses.

(Whether such transcripts were really necessary is an open question, since the unpublished transcripts of meetings of the journalists' association and conversations with many professionals in the seventies indicated that they listened to and relied on Western broadcasts, especially in times of crisis.)

All of this made foreign affairs writing in the mass media far more complicated than it would have been had information been truly controlled. It also prevents us from judging by what was censored or censorable how much was actually known by the Polish leadership and people about the outside world. At best, the censorship guidelines provide a clear indication of what Polish leaders considered safe reporting. Such determinations were made with a number of very different but equally important audiences in mind: Polish readers, the Soviet monitors of the Polish press and the many foreign powers who might use the Polish press as an indicator of official positions.

Information from abroad comes to the Polish media through a number of channels. For most of the media, the majority of reports about the outside world come from the Polish Press Agency and its sister agency, Interpress. Each has correspondents abroad and makes use of all the major Western news agencies as well as the Soviet and East European agencies in preparing news and feature stories for the Polish media. Some major organs, such as the central party daily *(Trybuna Ludu)* and the Warsaw daily *(Życie Warszawy),* also station their own correspondents in major foreign capitals. Some, like *Perspektywy, Polityka, Kultura* and other sociopolitical weeklies, made use of special funds in the seventies to pay for trips abroad by individual journalists, or used "exclusive" articles by correspondents in major foreign capitals or by individuals going abroad on personal trips. Finally, most print media that have any foreign affairs coverage employ writers who specialize in foreign affairs analysis. These journalists use party documents, Western media sources, internal bulletins and their own political sense as the basis for their individual analyses.

The guidelines for appropriate coverage were often unclear, even for journalists writing from Poland. The American Bicentennial and the Helsinki Conference on Peace and Security in Europe are the only two foreign events between 1974 and 1976 for which detailed directives are available. Other equally sensitive events, such as the civil war in Angola, the unfolding of the Watergate crisis before the final hearings on whether to impeach Richard Nixon and the transformation of U.S.-Chinese relations do not appear in the regulations. These areas were so *clearly* problematic that censors could be left to use their own judgment, as they were on other less sensitive subjects. And, given journalists' own awareness that much here was unlikely to be publishable, the censors had little sensitive foreign affairs copy to review—journalists kept away from these subjects. Those who wrote on foreign affairs simply knew policy and publishability better than the censors. Even the foreign affairs analysis in the party theoretical monthly, *Nowe Drogi,* was discretionary: the editors decided on what to publish, who would write it and how it would be presented. Seldom, if ever, did high-level party leaders make suggestions or interventions.

Foreign correspondents normally got little guidance about what to report unless there was a special event. In part, this was clearly to ensure the most complete coverage possible for the benefit of the leadership: the censors or press agency editors could always sift through and remove materials unsuitable for public consumption. In part, the lack of guidance on most subjects and on most periods also reflected the general disinterest of the leadership in most aspects of foreign affairs reporting and their feeling that they should be able to trust the judgment of men who had been selected through the Communist Party's appointment system, which requires all jobs on the *nomenklatura* list (including editor and correspondent) to be filled by individuals approved by the party organ responsible. Correspondents were all people approved as trustworthy by the Central Committee Press Department, and so were counted on to act responsibly.

Journalists who had worked abroad in the sixties and early seventies reported that normally they selected subjects on the basis of what they, as trusted and experienced reporters, felt would "sell" to their audience of editors and readers. In general, journalists who worked for the press agencies reported on "hard news events," and those working for other papers, radio and television provided features and commentaries. Journalists reported in interviews that when their post was involved in a major crisis they could call their editors to get instructions on what to provide. Usually journalists were simply asked to give the most extensive factual information possible or were left to their own devices, unless special pro-Polish propaganda needed to be generated, as, for example to make Americans look pro-Gierek during Gierek's visit to the United States in 1974. Even those working in the Soviet Union were left alone to such an extent that one journalist who had worked there in the sixties reported that he was recalled at the request of the Soviet authorities because of a story he had written six months earlier without criticism from any Polish official. What correspondents wrote from the Third World and middle- and small-sized European countries and what they got published depended almost entirely on their skill and on the interest of Poles in developments there. One specialist on the Third World reported that his main concern in self-censorship was not the Polish authorities—he was their expert—but the sensitivities of the nations about which he wrote and to which he hoped to return.

That the reaction of other countries, especially in the Soviet bloc, was a legitimate concern of the Polish authorities is clear from the responses to stories that appeared in the Polish press. The Soviets were by far the most active and critical foreign observer of the Polish press. The Soviet embassy in Warsaw had a large press section in the seventies that read even small regional newspapers and contacted journalists from known and obscure journals all over Poland to tell them not to continue to raise specific issues. In the mid-seventies, according to interviews with journalists, Soviet embassy officials went directly to the censors and offending journals to register their complaints. When he was still a censor in Kraków, Tomasz Strzyżewski was provided by the Soviets, as were all Polish censors, with lists of events and individuals in the Soviet Union that were not to be discussed in the Polish press. These lists were kept in separate notebooks on the censors' desks.

Other governments were also sensitive to the Polish press. A story on poverty in India, for example, earned the Polish Foreign Ministry a strong rebuke from the Indian embassy. Similarly, many Western governments and scholars used the Polish media to measure Polish foreign policy. As a result of all this outside attention, care was taken not to offend other states. Thus the first censorship regulation applied to reporting about foreign countries was as follows:

1. No personal attacks should be permitted against heads of states (presidents, monarchs) with which Poland maintains diplomatic relations.

This regulation covered not just editorial attacks, but even the reporting of internationally discussed events and scandals. The most obvious of these from the mid-seventies was the Watergate crisis. In this case, for the Poles and Soviets alike, questions raised were far more sensitive than the possibility of offending a powerful leader whom they had courted. It was difficult to admit that their partner in détente had abused his power. Nor was it acceptable to them to have their populations draw parallels between what Nixon had done and his accountability and what they were doing without being accountable. Just prior to the Nixon hearings, the censors emphasized what Polish journalists now say was standard policy from the beginning of the crisis:

> 8. Until further notice, no material written by staff members should be published concerning the Watergate Affair in the United States. Any exceptions to this rule (information or commentary not from PAP) must be referred to the GUKPPiW administration.
>
> Approval to print such exceptional items in a given publication and any subsequent permission to reprint them in others will be decided on an individual basis. (August 7, 1974; canceled November 23, 1974)

This regulation was only canceled three months after Nixon's resignation and after the post-Watergate Congressional elections had been held. By then, reports on Watergate were outdated. One censor (incorrectly, according to his supervisors) even went so far as to interpret this regulation as a reason to prohibit criticism of Nixon's rhetorical style as "the product of anachronistic, false, demogogical rhetoric to which politicians are drawn and from which they cannot tear themselves away" in a review of recent American literary writing.* Although the review did make a connection between this rhetoric and Vice-President Spiro Agnew's "difficulties and Nixon's problems," the directors of the GUKPPiW criticized the decision of the censor to remove this entire reference. In their explanation, they sought to clarify the original intent of the regulation:

> This intervention demonstrates a misunderstanding of the basis for evaluating materials on R. Nixon. The text in question is not an attack in the sense of the regulation protecting heads of state, nor does it discredit Nixon's policy. The author is simply indicating the anachronistic principles of the political rhetoric employed by professional American politicians, and this should not call forth any objections on the part of the censor. (*Instructional Materials*, No. 1, February 1974)

*Intended to appear in *Nowe Książki,* Issue No. 23.

Other regulations were even more specific in guaranteeing positive press coverage of Third World nations with which Poland and the Soviet Union had diplomatic and, more importantly, real or potential trade relations, but about which censors could be expected to have little real knowledge:

> Do not use the term "military dictatorship" or other terms, such as "guerrilla" or "military junta," to refer to states with which we maintain diplomatic relations. This prohibition does not apply to Chile, Paraguay, Guatemala or the Dominican Republic.

Other states were granted specific protection from criticism because of their importance for Polish trade. Thus, since Amin's Uganda was one of Poland's major trading partners in Africa,

> Pending verification of information concerning the speech of Gen. Amin, President of Uganda, in which, among other things, he announced plans to erect a monument to Adolf Hitler in Uganda, no materials on this subject are to be permitted. Materials presented should be referred to the GUKPPiW administration. (April 30, 1975; canceled September 12, 1975)

Iran was even more important as a trading partner because it supplied critical energy resources. Poland's dependence on Iran for oil resulted not only in the Shah's being treated as an honored guest in Poland (where he and his wife were presented with honorary degrees by the Jagiellonian University in Kraków in 1978), but also in a number of repetitive regulations guaranteeing special treatment for the Shah in the media:

> All material (including the slightest mention, photographs, etc.) relating to the past and present condition of Iran and the Shah, his family and persons connected with the Shah should be approved by the GUKPPiW administration. This prohibition does not apply to PAP materials. (April 22, 1975; canceled January 12, 1976)

Censors working in this period said that the application of this regulation was sweeping enough to prevent any public announcement honoring the Shah. According to one journalist, the censors even blocked the publication, in a small provincial journal, of a photograph of a prizewinning cow named Szachy. (The name literally means "chess" in Polish, but its close resemblance to the word for "shah"—*szach*—was apparently too much for the censorship authorities.)

Reporting on Friends: The Soviet Bloc

Polish coverage of the Communist world was more closely monitored than that of any other area. Journalists dealing with the Soviet Union itself had little to report. Information was simply not available. And, when it was, journalists, editors and the censors themselves closely monitored their own decisions. In fact, most journalists interviewed in Poland in the seventies admitted that they really didn't even consider doing stories on the Soviet Union. In the case of Soviet bloc news of any import to the West, either the chief censors reviewed the information or the carefully controlled news agencies were the only approved source. Accordingly, the second permanent regulation listed for censors dealing with foreign affairs articles read as follows:

> Any information on diplomatic steps or initiatives by countries of the socialist community (especially Poland and the Soviet Union) may appear only after appropriate official communiqués have been issued by PAP or TASS, and simultaneously with them. In no case may the publisher's own information precede the official news or conflict with its content.

But in addition, for example:

> 126. All material (information, communiqués, etc.) concerning the undertaking of obligations to salute the 25th Congress of the Communist Party of the Soviet Union should be referred to the GUKPPiW leadership before permission is granted. (February 13–April 12, 1976)

Regulations such as the above forbade publication of information that might suggest involvement in any kind of cooperation that could be construed as aid to the Soviet Union, even if this information was published by TASS, the official Soviet agency. Any information that might support Poles' well-ingrained assumptions that the Soviet Union was exploiting Poland economically and was responsible for Poland's problems was also blocked:

> 92. Until a final decision has been made, no information indicating which section of the Orenburg pipeline in the Soviet Union will be built by Poland should be permitted. (May 28, 1975; canceled June 18, 1975)

A number of other regulations were drafted as part of this effort not to publicize evidence of Polish animosity or even coolness toward the Soviet Union, or to encourage that animosity. One, for example, prohibited information on the construction of a Polish-Soviet Friendship House. This was apparently deemed necessary because of the fear that any report on its construction or on the fund-raising campaign for it might serve as a reminder of the forced payments made by Poles for the construction of the much resented Palace of Culture in Warsaw during the Stalinist period, or, if only a small sum was collected from private contributors, might serve as a symbol of the real weakness of Soviet-Polish friendship. Even the granting of awards by the Polish-Soviet Friendship Society was an event Polish participants were not anxious to publicize. It, too, stood as a reminder of the absence of close relations. Thus:

> 33. No information concerning the awarding of state decorations at the Main Board of the Polish-Soviet Friendship Society should be permitted. Only the weekly *Przyjaźń* will provide information about these awards.

In both this case and that of the construction of the new Friendship Society Building, Soviet interests in having the events covered were served by the specific provision for the publication of information in *Przyjaźń*, the organ of the Friendship Society. At the same time, the fact that this journal's circulation was likely to be limited to persons friendly to the Soviets minimized the negative effects that broader publicity might have provoked.

Polish censors also proceeded cautiously in dealing with reports on events in the Soviet Union. Issues that were sensitive to the Soviets were carefully controlled in the Polish press. Only official press agency and Soviet statements were allowed in the limited and highly official announcements of problematic events:

> 112. The PAP communiqué and TASS commentary concerning the award of the Nobel Prize to the Soviet physicist Andrei Sakharov were

intended for publication only in *Trybuna Ludu* and *Życie Warszawy* on October 13, 1975.

No reprints or discussions of the above-mentioned communiqué and commentary and no information about the award should be permitted in the rest of the mass media. (October 13, 1975; canceled January 22, 1976)

The somewhat controversial reputation of the poet Evgenii Evtushenko, famous for, among other things, his sporadic criticism of Soviet policy, prompted Polish censorship to attempt to minimize his celebrity status when he came to Poland as part of an official Soviet delegation in 1975:

> 83. Evgenii Evtushenko is a member of the official Soviet delegation that has come to Poland in connection with Soviet Culture Days.
>
> Materials and information in the mass media should treat him as a normal member of the delegation, without any special emphasis on him. Furthermore, all interviews with him or articles about him or his work may be published only with the approval of the Department of Propaganda, Press and Publishing of the Central Committee of the Polish United Workers' Party.
>
> This instruction is intended only for the information of censorship groups. (April 18, 1975; canceled June 10, 1975)

The most telling indication of the Poles' conformity to Soviet desires —both expressed and presumed—was the regulation that appeared in August 1974 after Polish journals had begun to report on the popular attraction of an exhibit of Polish products put on by Poland in the Soviet Union. Their articles had stressed—implicitly, at least—the qualitative difference between Polish and Soviet consumer goods. In doing this, they made Polish products appear to be enviable successes for the Soviets. But as the censors were told:

> In accounts of the Polish exhibit set up in Moscow on the occasion of the 30th anniversary of the Polish People's Republic, excessive excitement over the success of individual exhibits—which might suggest to the reader that certain Polish items were creating a great furor among Moscow residents and were hitherto unknown on the Soviet market—should be avoided.
>
> An example of such an exaggerated account about the "record-breaking" exhibit in Moscow was the account of the correspondent for *Express Wieczorny,* published on August 5 of this year.
>
> Unofficial information concerning the possible extension of our ex-

hibit in Moscow should also not be permitted. (August 7, 1974; canceled October 17, 1974)

Polish censors also blocked more direct information about economic problems in the Sovet Union during the seventies:

> In Issue No. 29 of *Forum,* in an article entitled "The Confusion of Concepts" (a reprint from *Neue Zürcher Zeitung*), concerning "economic relations between East and West," a statement was challenged which reported that "some voices in the West express the opinion that Moscow is committing itself to the policy of détente mainly because it expects that in this way—thanks to imports of capitalist technology—it will be able to effectively overcome its internal technological and economic problems. So the Kremlin's desire for détente is motivated primarily by economic imperatives."

> Issue No. 29 of *Życie Gospodarcze* ran an article entitled "The International Economic Situation—on Money Markets, on Commodity Markets," which reported, *inter alia*, on the "very serious increase" in grain prices:

> ". . . This price increase was caused by rumors concerning the possibility that the *Soviet Union* might be importing large quantities of grain. These rumors are based on the following assumptions: the drought will damage spring grain crops in Western Kazakhstan, the Urals and the Volga Basin, which might lead to a reduction of original harvest estimates by 5 million tons; July 31 is the expiration date for a 750-million-dollar credit that was granted to the USSR by the USA three years ago to finance grain purchases and that up to this point has only been partially utilized; the USSR is ordering large tonnages for shipment from North American ports to ports in the USSR; reports from Switzerland indicate that the Soviet Union is selling gold, and the USSR Bank of Foreign Trade has taken out a medium-term credit on the Euromarket amounting to 250 million dollars. The amount of grain to be purchased by the Soviets this year is estimated at around 10 million tons, of which 7 million tons are to be purchased in the USA and 3 million tons in Canada (by way of comparison, it is worth noting that in 1972 the USSR bought 19 million tons of grain from the USA. . . ." (*Report on Materials Censored*, July 16–31, 1975)

Polish censors also followed the Soviet lead by downplaying the subject of Soviet military growth and investment, whatever the source or context:

We questioned an excerpt discussing "Schlesinger's Report," reprinted from the Associated Press in *Tygodnik Demokratyczny* (No. 13):

"... in his annual report to the Congress, numbering 237 pages, Defense Secretary James Schlesinger criticized as insufficient the means undertaken by the NATO governments for the defense of the forward-lying regions. . . . <u>Justifying the need for research aimed at substantial progress in the development of American weaponry unless SALT agreements are reached, Schlesinger referred to Soviet research on new rockets and multiple warheads. 'We want to begin to reduce strategic strength through mutual agreement and on the basis of equality. . . . But we are disturbed by the rapid development of Soviet arms, and we cannot ignore the possibility that there will be a deepening of the degree of inequality between the two great nuclear powers.' He said recent Soviet testing indicated a broad application of new military technology and techniques."</u> (*Report on Materials Censored,* March 16–31, 1974)

Coverage of other bloc countries was just as closely monitored. As in the case of reporting on the Soviet Union, articles on Poland's other allies had to suggest that all was basically well with them. At the same time, however, writers had to be careful not to suggest that conditions there were better in any respect than they were in Poland.

References to political crises elsewhere in the bloc and all parallels drawn between current leaders and Stalinist leaders, even if they were only passing references, were removed from texts. In addition, criticism or negative reports about these countries' policies—for example, preferential admissions policies of Czechoslovak universities—were blocked by the censors even when they were quoted directly from the print media of these other socialist countries. Such criticisms not only represented an attack on an ally; they also could be taken as veiled criticism of similar Polish policies:

In Issue No. 50 of *Polityka,* an article entitled "The CSSR: Should Working-Class Youth Receive Preferential Treatment?" gave an account of the debate currently underway on the pages of the weekly organ of the Czech Communist Party Central Committee, *Tribuna,* over "the proper role of working-class origin in the evaluation of candidates for admission to universities." Acknowledging our objections, the editors deleted the following passage from this article:

"... The polemic was opened by a secondary-school teacher, Dr. Bretislav Dejdar, who . . . expressed the belief that 'the preferential treatment of working-class children,' which was appropriate immediately following the victory of February 1948, is now an 'atavism' and 'anachronism.' He expressed the view that a well-rounded school can educate all children in a socialist spirit, even if that is contrary to the wishes of their parents. On the other hand, if teachers do not do their jobs properly, even the children of working-class and peasant families will not become useful members of society. According to Dejdar, this was borne out by the crisis years of 1968–69 in Czechoslovakia.

"In this connection, the author recalls that working-class children were the ones who received preferential treatment immediately after February 1948, and that, in the 1960s, fifteen- to seventeen-year-olds had already been brought up almost entirely under socialism and the future intelligentsia that was supposed to be completely dedicated to socialism was already studying at the university level. But things turned out differently.

"We read further that 'we ought to conclude that the formal categorization of children according to unrealistic criteria accomplishes nothing in the absence of effective, conscious and informal teaching methods. What good does it do us when we drag the best pupils out of trade schools and push them into liberal arts schools in order to turn the majority of them into average or below-average civil servants and technicians? And, on the other hand, we are wasting outstanding talents simply because of their non-working-class origins and, above all, because we are unable to mold them into first-rate and, at the same time, politically conscious specialists. What we ought to be working on right now is the ideological and professional training of future Lenins, and not future Dubčeks [Dubček was of working-class origin].' "
(*Report on Materials Censored*, December 1–15, 1975)

Any mention of Stalinist repression was unprintable even if it had been attacked openly before. It was unacceptable even to translate a Western commentary listing prerevolutionary and Stalinist leaders together with the present-day Soviet leadership:

In Issue No. 49 of *Forum*, in an article by J. B. Duroselle entitled "It Started in 1924," which dealt with the history of Franco-Soviet relations, we read, among other things:

". . . What does 1974 have in store for us? Two circumstances have always greatly complicated Franco-Soviet relations: a regime that has completely turned its back on the practices and spirit of liberal democracy, and the French Communist Party. . . . But everything appears to indicate that the French and Russian peoples are destined to enjoy a certain distant and discreet friendship, marked, from time to time, by outbursts of enthusiasm. Is this a function of geography, of tradition, of a certain mutual intellectual sympathy? The regime may be tsarist,

Stalinist, Khrushchevist or Brezhnevist, and the majority of French-men may take an unsympathetic attitude toward it, but it would seem that some sort of irresistible friendship is constantly maintained." (*Report on Materials Censored,* December 1–15, 1974)

Even the mention of Polish citizens working in Czechoslovakia and East Germany to fill gaps caused by those countries' labor shortages was too sensitive. Polish journalists explained this prohibition as a result of Poland's reluctance to admit that Poland was a poor supplier of workers, and its fear that such information would encourage Poles to try to go to these economically better-off states at a time Poland needed its qualified workers.

Coverage of intra-bloc relations was also closely monitored by the censors, who sought to prevent any unplanned revelations on meetings between Communist parties—revelations that might provide outsiders with more information than was intended to be released. On October 30, 1974, for instance, it was announced that "any information concerning the consulting session of the European Communist and workers' parties must be approved by the Main Office leadership." Even vacations by other Soviet bloc leaders in Poland were often carefully concealed.

One of the most basic concerns expressed in censorship regulations was preventing any appearance of conflict within the Soviet bloc. Mention of quiescent border difficulties, such as the long-standing dispute between Yugoslavia and Bulgaria over Macedonia, were to be monitored at the level of the top directors of censorship according to the regulation given the censors:

> 4. The Macedonian problem is the subject of a permanent dispute between Yugoslavia and Bulgaria.
>
> Great care should be taken in publications on this subject not to provide grounds for intervention by one side or the other.
>
> In doubtful situations, the leadership of the GUKPPiW should be consulted.

In one case, even criticism of changes in the public regulations for private travel between socialist countries—regulations that were often changed to reflect the subtle changes in relations between bloc states and the pressure of citizens of a given country for access to other Communist states—was removed.

"Żuk," author of the feuilleton "Mój Piętnastak" in *Słowo Powszechne*, in criticizing the information booklet *Passportless Vacations* (published by "Światowid"), ridiculed the "too frequently changing" regulations concerning private trips to socialist countries. (*Report on Materials Censored*, May 16–31, 1974)

The Other Communists

Reporting on other Communist states outside the Soviet bloc presented the censors with obvious dilemmas. Any reporting that was too positive would reflect negatively on the Soviet Union and the Soviet model, while too critical reporting would frustrate Poland's attempts to maintain its own political and economic ties with those states. Generally, control was exercised by limiting coverage to PAP releases or by requiring that all commentary be specially monitored. In the case of reporting on China, the rules were very strict and even the PAP correspondent cabled many reports that never appeared. This, even though:

> 149 All *information* concerning the current political situation in the PRC [following the death of Mao Tse-tung] may be published only through the intermediary of PAP.
> *Non-PAP commentaries* on this subject are permitted only if the editors have had the content approved by the Department of Press, Radio and Television of the Central Committee of the PZPR. (October 10, 1976; new version, October 22, 1976)

Coverage of Rumania and Yugoslavia was less tightly monitored, but was still watched carefully by the censors. For example, Polish connections with Yugoslavia, the traditional apostate from the Soviet bloc, were deliberately downplayed:

> 30. Information concerning the visit of First Secretary Edward Gierek to Yugoslavia may be published in the mass media *only* through PAP. (July 5, 1974; canceled July 27, 1974)

In the case of Rumania, there was a clear attempt to ignore its post-sixties behavior as the foreign relations maverick from the Soviet bloc:

96. No information on Rumania's effort to be included in the group of nonaligned nations should be permitted. (June 26, 1975; canceled July 27, 1975)

One report of a journalist's trip to Rumania was censored for suggesting that greater political independence had brought with it living standards better than those in Poland. At the same time, however, the censors blocked references to internal political struggles in Rumania —references that would have offended the Ceausescu regime:

A "Report from the Athenae-Palace in Bucharest" entitled "Toasts" was disapproved for publication in Issue No. 49 of *ITD.* The author, K. Mroziewicz, describing his impressions from a visit to Rumania with a delegation of the Polish Socialist Students' Union, included references to the history of and current conditions in Rumania. He wrote, *inter alia,* about "factional conflicts" in the Rumanian Communist Party during the time when S. Foris was its general secretary, about the productivity of Rumanian agriculture which, like the well-stocked meat shops in that country, "arouses feelings of envy in Poles" and about industrial development: "For the past ten years Rumania has led in world statistics." (*Report on Materials Censored,* December 1–15, 1974)

The possibility of comparisons with the Polish situation was enough to prevent the publication of information on Yugoslav students' freedom to protest academic decisions, which a student journal in Poland had tried to report:

In *Student* (No. 12) the following note in the column entitled "The Observer" was questioned:

YUGOSLAVIA

Omladinske Novine (a young people's publication) printed sections of a resolution passed by representatives of a group of students of philosophy at the universities of Ljubljana, Zagreb and Belgrade. The resolution is a protest against the removal of professors of the Department of Philosophy from their chairmanships, which the students see as a threat to creative Marxism. (*Report on Materials Censored,* March 16–31, 1974)

The Two Germanies

Of all the issues relating to international affairs and the Communist bloc, the problem of the two Germanies presented Polish censors with some of their greatest difficulties. For Poles, the German issue continues to be much more than the problem of a nation divided between the Eastern and Western blocs, a dramatic comparison of the successes and failures of each system. It is also an issue that summons up memories of the suffering and destruction caused by the German occupation during World War II, the subsequent loss of Polish eastern lands to the Soviet Union, and the shift of Poland's borders some 100 miles into formerly German lands at the war's end.

The wartime agreements for this shifting of Poland's boundaries westward and for dividing the supervision of postwar Germany among the wartime allies (the United States, France, Great Britain and the Soviet Union), as well as the East-West tensions that developed after World War II, left Poland and West Germany in conflict with one another. The postwar boundaries remained unrecognized by the Western states since this would have involved a recognition of the permanent partition of Germany. Nor were many Germans—particularly those displaced by the ceding of their lands to Poland—willing to accept the boundaries.

Memories of the war and fears of German revanchism were fanned in the sixties by the leadership's fixation on the German threat as the *raison d'être* for Poland's close ties with the Soviet Union. The issue remained sensitive even after Polish–West German agreements were signed in 1970 and 1972, recognizing Poland's western boundaries, establishing diplomatic relations, opening economic and cultural exchanges, making travel possible and obligating West Germany to pay reparations for World War II and to compensate the Polish government for any of its ethnic Germans who wished to emigrate to West Germany. At the same time, the Soviets and East Germans were anxious to ensure that Polish–West German relations did not become too warm. The Poles, despite continuing fears and memories of the "German threat," were interested in developing good economic relations with the West Germans and taking advantage of Willy Brandt's overture for détente with Eastern Europe.

Before the signing of the first postwar Polish–West German agreements, Polish-German relations were one of the few media issues of real concern to the Gomułka leadership. As a result, the terminology and interpretations employed in media discussions of the two Germanies was closely monitored while Gomułka was in power. In the Gierek period, the problem had become even more complex: Poland had to maintain positive political relations with West Germany in order to get the economic aid it needed from the Bonn regime. At the same time, it had to make it clear that East Germany was its chief ally. The two could not be treated in a comparative fashion since West Germany would appear in more positive colors than the German Democratic Republic. Therefore:

> 135. All in-house publications (including correspondence from the FRG) and reprints from the foreign press concerning relations between the Polish People's Republic and the Federal Republic of Germany, or concerning internal affairs in the latter country, should, until further notice, be held up for consultation with the GUKPPiW administration.
>
> All PAP publications, brief in-house information bulletins of a chronicle type (without political implications) and information on sports may appear without consultation. (May 3, 1976; canceled June 23, 1976)

It was also the responsibility of the censors to make sure that the media, in pursuing these goals, never made the Federal Republic of Germany and the German Democratic Republic sound like parts of the same nation. To this end, the censors were instructed to make sure the titles used for West Germany made it clear that it was only a part of Germany—and not the primary part. So West Germany had a less grandiose title than East Germany, and the name "Berlin" was reserved for East Berlin. The following basic regulations for dealing with the two Germanies spelled out the terminology to be used:

> 3. Given the existence of two German states, the following rules of nomenclature are to be binding for all publications.
>
> a. There should be strict adherence to the proper nomenclature for the Zgorzelec Pact of July 6, 1950, the official name of which is: "The Pact Between the Polish Republic and the German Democratic Republic Concerning the Established, Existing Polish-German National Border";

b. The terms given below may be used to designate our western border:

—the border on the Oder and the Niesse

—the border between Poland and the GDR

—the Polish-GDR border but this term should not be used: Polish-German border;

c. Proper nomenclature for institutions, organizations, sports unions and so on of the German Democratic Republic and the Federal Republic of Germany should be observed, and the adjective "German" should not be used but should be replaced instead by the more precise terms "GDR" and "FRG," or "East German" and "West German," respectively;

d. The term "German" should not be used to refer (in the context of the present day) to the territory or state of the GDR, FRG or West Berlin;

e. In mentioning the capital of the GDR, the term "Berlin" should be used, to differentiate it from "West Berlin." (See Informative Note No. 43/73)

Although these regulations, like others used by the censors, were not made public, the terminology they called for came to be fairly standard—so standard, in fact, that deviation from it was viewed as a political statement on the part of a writer. Despite these instructions, "improper" terms sometimes slipped through, and this was drawn to the attention of all the censors in their in-house Informative Notes:

In the two preceding issues of Informative Notes (Nos. 4 and 5) the use of improper nomenclature for the German states was pointed out. Unfortunately, this is still encountered in the press. In *Tygodnik Powszechny* (1/74), in the report of Kisiel from Paris entitled "About the Province," an incorrect form of the name of the capital of the GDR —"East Berlin"—was allowed to appear. (*Instructional Materials*, No. 1, February 1974)

Just as with other bloc countries, the censors were careful not to allow any negative views of East Germany:

Over a dozen deletions were made from J. Skibiński's book *Two German States* (PWN, 8,000 copies). For example, we deleted extensive excerpts describing the difficult domestic situation and the policy of the leadership in the GDR in the months preceding the June *putsch* of reactionary forces in Berlin in 1953. We questioned a statement about the Council on Mutual Economic Assistance's lack of faith in the GDR as a result of the "benefits" the latter receives from "association with the Common Market." (*Report on Materials Censored,* March 16–31, 1974)

The "Guillaume Affair," in which a member of Willy Brandt's immediate circle proved to be a spy for East Germany, was a virtual nonevent in the Polish press. Not only was it uncomfortable to criticize Willy Brandt, the first West German leader to promote a rapprochement with Poland, but spying is not something to be revealed and publicly discussed in Communist states. Censors' regulations specified that "only the general term 'espionage activity' should be used, without revealing the connection with the GDR." Censorship reports show that discussions of the affair and the subsequent political upheaval in West Germany were ordered excised:

> In keeping with the guidelines, we questioned J. Nowakowski's article "West of the Elbe River: Hunting for Agents" (*WTK,* No. 19), which discussed the situation in the FRG following Brandt's resignation. Information about the "Guillaume Affair" was also eliminated from *Tygodnik Powszechny* (No. 19), *ITD* (No. 19) and *Gazeta Białostocka.* (*Report on Materials Censored,* May 1–15, 1974)

The Polish–West German accords themselves, once they were signed, were not matters to be questioned. The battles that preceded them, and the role played by the Catholic Church in initiating the negotiations, were not matters to be discussed in print. Nor were these agreements to be treated with less than total seriousness. Furthermore, the Polish leadership was unwilling to admit the existence of opposition to the treaties within Germany. Even though such information would have made the Germans look bad, it might have also led to questions about the wisdom and permanence of the accords. When J. Turowicz, one of Poland's leading critical columnists and editor of the Catholic intellectual weekly *Tygodnik Powszechny,* spoke of the opposition within Germany and the German Church to détente with Poland, his statements drew objections from the censors. Also deleted were mentions of the letter of Polish bishops to their German counterparts in 1965, which, well in advance of any similar overture on the part of the Polish government, had invited German bishops to join the Polish hierarchy in the celebration of Poland's Millennium in 1966. (This occurred at a time when there were still no diplomatic ties between Poland and West Germany, the West Germans had still not recognized Poland's western boundaries and the former German territories were still under the jurisdiction of temporary ecclesiastical authorities. So, in the mid-sixties, this Church action had been attacked by the party authorities.)

In Issue No. 50 of *Tygodnik Powszechny,* in an article entitled "Reconciliation and Normalization," written on the occasion of the fifth anniversary of the signing of the treaty normalizing relations between the Polish People's Republic and the Federal Republic of Germany, J. Turowicz criticized the attitude of the Christian Democratic Union/Christian Socialist Union and the Episcopate of the FRG toward Poland. Noting, *inter alia,* that at the present time "a violent campaign is being waged on the political stage of the Bundesrepublik against ratification of the new Polish-German accords drawn up in Helsinki ... a campaign that is being led by the Christian Democratic parties, the CDU and the CSU," Turowicz went on to write:

"... A few days ago we marked the tenth anniversary of the publication of two documents concerning Polish-German relations, i.e., the memorandum of the Evangelical Church of the FRG (October 1965) and the exchange of letters between the Episcopates of Poland and the FRG (December 1965). ... The Evangelical memorandum courageously addressed the issue of displaced persons and issued an unequivocal demand for the recognition of the Oder-Neisse border. The exchange of letters was the result of a bold and laudable initiative on the part of the Polish Episcopate that was launched during the last days of Vatican II. The letter from the Episcopate of Poland was answered by the letter of the Episcopate of West Germany. These letters produced a strong impact on public opinion, including public opinion in Poland as well. For the first time since the end of the war, the churches of both countries had initiated a public and official Christian dialogue on the subject of reconciliation. But let us remember, in all candor, that the reply of the German bishops created a certain amount of disillusionment in Poland. ...

"We certainly do not mean to say that the Catholic Church in the FRG does not desire reconciliation with Poland. We know that it does desire this. This Church and its Episcopate have given proof of this on more than one occasion. ... Unfortunately, this does not alter the fact that the Episcopate of the FRG as a whole feels strangely restricted when it comes to taking a stand on the concrete political problems that exist between Poland and the FRG. ...

"I would not like to close this article on a pessimistic note. I personally believe that the recent accords between Poland and the FRG [mean] . . . the possibilities for reconciliation between both nations will increase. And it will then be necessary to take this action a step further and, through the common efforts of men who believe in the brotherhood of nations, to uncover the underlying causes of the difficulties and setbacks that have beset us, so that people will be able to relate to one another <u>without regard for transitory political gambits or ideological confrontations.</u>" (*Report on Materials Censored,* December 1–15, 1975)

Modulating Western News

Like coverage of West Germany, treatment of any of the states in the West had to be carefully monitored. While direct attacks on national leaders were forbidden by Rule 1 of the censors' regulations relating to international affairs, the documents available indicate that too positive or too extensive coverage of Western governments was equally unacceptable. At the same time, censors, journalists and party bosses all knew that Western news was of far more interest to Poles than anything else they might publish or broadcast, and that they had to use Western news to draw readers in. This made the tone of an article a critical issue for the censors.

They were instructed that even coverage of neutral Sweden was to be "moderate" in tone and should not indicate in any way that Sweden was not a partner for Poland and other East European states.

> 13. In connection with Comrade Edward Gierek's impending visit to Sweden, care should be taken to see that material characterizing the domestic and foreign policy of the government of Sweden and the portrayal of its premier, Olof Palme, are factual, calm, sedate and noneuphoric in tone. In addition, any information concerning the recent polemics between O. Palme and G. Husak should be eliminated. (New version, May 28, 1975; canceled July 10, 1975)

At the same time, the Polish authorities attempted to ensure that Polish coverage of Western leaders did not alienate those whose economic support they needed. Reporters covering the American presidential elections in 1976 and 1980, for example, could not write negatively about either candidate. And before Gierek's visit to the United States in 1974 censorship regulations specified that

40. Each time a publication issues its own commentary concerning Comrade Edward Gierek's upcoming official visit to the United States (PAP communiqué of August 29, 1974) the GUKPPiW leadership should be consulted.

The same applies to commentaries on Poland's relations (political, economic, cultural, etc.) with the United States, or on various aspects of the domestic situation in the United States.

On the other hand, all publications concerning the program planned for Comrade Gierek's visit *may be published only according to PAP*. (See Informative Notes Nos. 31/74, 35/74 and 38/74) (September 27, 1974; canceled November 23, 1974)

Gerald Ford's visit to Poland and the opportunities it provided for greater coverage of the United States prompted explicit directions calling for neutral coverage and limiting any individualized reporting by different journals:

99. In-house materials concerning the visit of U.S. President Gerald Ford to Poland, their range of subject matter and their formulation should be consistent with the information provided by PAP and *Trybuna Ludu.*

Care should be taken that material on the situation in the United States and the policies of the U.S. government that is published during G. Ford's visit be presented in a factual, sedate tone. (July 25, 1975; canceled September 2, 1975)

Related feature articles, often based on translated Western journal material from special bulletins published by the Polish Press Agency as background data for journalists and editors, were monitored for much more than simple conformity to the regulations. One article on White House domestic life was removed from *Słowo Powszechne* in 1975, even though it came from an American publication, because it violated a number of basic tenets of Polish journalism: it reported on the private life of a leader, something Poles regard as being in poor taste; it also presented the Ford family in less than glamorous terms by showing their efforts to economize on hospitality; and finally, it offered readers an opportunity to draw parallels with their own standards of living and to speculate about Polish leaders' life styles and how little they knew about them.

An article entitled "In the White House" was deleted from *Słowo Powszechne*. The article was based on one published in *U.S. News & World Report*. It contained detailed information about the private residence of President Ford and the living conditions of the U.S. "First Family." A few excerpts, quoted below, illustrate the content of this article, which was submitted for approval on the occasion of President Ford's visit to the Polish People's Republic:

". . . The President and his family are entitled to the use of a furnished residence, but he must cover certain living expenses. Food is one of these. Ford must reimburse the government for the cost of all food and beverages consumed by members of his family and private guests.

"In the Ford home, as in many American homes, the wife is responsible for the family budget. It is said that Mrs. Ford is very strict about these matters. Working with Rex Scouten, she is constantly checking to see which expenses have to be paid by the President out of his own pocket and which can be paid for out of the White House budget. Mrs. Ford has asked the household staff to be just as cost-conscious when doing White House shopping as when they are shopping for their own families.

"The annual White House budget appropriates 130,000 dollars for official receptions. Of this sum, 55,000 dollars are reimbursed in part by the State Department, for receptions arranged for foreign dignitaries, and in part by the Ford family, which pays for its own meals on such occasions. The other 75,000 dollars goes for the entertainment of members of Congress, various public figures and so on. . . .

"Inflation in the U.S. has made it necessary to cut down on such official functions. Mrs. Ford has reduced the number of official receptions. She has also announced that this year she will not entertain the wives of Congressmen with the traditional evening dinner but, instead, with a light brunch served in the White House garden.

"On the menus for official dinners, fish dishes have been replaced with soups, domestic wines are being served instead of foreign wines, and vegetable dishes are selected from vegetables that happen to be in season." (*Report on Materials Censored*, July 16–31, 1975)

The desire for détente made it a mistake to associate Brezhnev and Nixon with the Vietnam war: as the censors were told in an instructional memo from the first quarter of 1974:

In the previous issue of *Report on Materials Censored*, we described a photograph from the First Conference of the PZPR that had been overlooked. At this time, we would like to draw attention to the unfavorable effect of a group of photographs that were allowed to appear in the 52nd number of *ITD*. The editors, in the last issue for 1973, published a nine-column photomontage to illustrate the most important events in the world during the past year. One-half of the first column consisted of pictures of victims of the Vietnam war, while among the photographs completing that column one is struck by a photograph of L. Brezhnev and R. Nixon greeting the public from the balcony of the White House. Such a positioning of photographs could lead the reader to undesirable reflections.

In drawing attention to this example, we wish, once again, to draw attention to the need for a penetrating evaluation of illustrations. It is sometimes the case that an examination of the reproduced copy provided us does not indicate details that would have a harmful effect. In such cases, it is necessary to ask for the original illustration.

Reporting on Jimmy Carter's election was treated cautiously by the Poles. Their desire to control the coverage and to limit its scope reflected their uncertainty about Carter and how he and his Polish-born national security adviser, Zbigniew Brzezinski, would deal with Poland. Since Brzezinski had long been treated by Polish regimes as an adversary, it was feared that his policy toward Poland would not be friendly and that Polish coverage might influence his actions. To speak positively about Carter might, on the other hand, raise false expectations, while to speak negatively might complicate the prospects for good relations. Therefore, coverage was sharply restricted:

> 153. The following principles should be adhered to in censoring materials on the subject of J. Carter's election to the Presidency of the United States:
> 1) All information may be released only through the intermediary of PAP.
> 2) All editors' own materials, commentaries and so forth may be released only with the approval of the Department of Press, Radio and Television of the Central Committee of the PZPR.
> 3) Photographs of J. Carter may appear only in illustrated weeklies (the so-called "colored publications") and on television.

On broader issues, the censors, with no specific instructions, sought to provide equal coverage to Western and Soviet bloc achievements. This applied not only to mass-circulation publications, but also to such limited-circulation publications as a religious monograph of research done in the archdiocese of Wrocław:

There was substantial intervention in a joint work entitled *Colloquium Salutis,* submitted by the Wrocławska Księgarnia Archidiecezjalna (1,000 copies). For example, we did not permit the printing of a long essay, "The Genesis and Development of Empirical Peace Research," discussing the historical development of peace research and the foundations and institutions engaged in it and examining the state of such research today. The author used only Western literature and discussed only the contribution of capitalist countries—the United States, FRG, England, Canada, Norway and Sweden—ignoring and passing over entirely the activities and contributions of socialist countries. (*Report on Materials Censored,* March 16–31, 1974)

Even the reporting of foreign social experiments such as flexible work scheduling, then under discussion in Poland as a possible means of helping women to combine the responsibilities of home and work, touched a nerve in Poland, where more and more people were beginning to realize that the economic program of the early seventies had failed and that there was little coming to them from the system. Discussion that reflected too positively on the West, with no reference to the Soviet Union, had to be censored:

An article by A. Barański entitled "Flextime Scheduling. No More Rigid Working Hours" was disapproved for publication in Issue No. 30 of *Tygodnik Demokratyczny.* In an uncritical and one-sided fashion, the author highlighted some of the experiences of Western countries in the introduction of "various new working methods as a result of flextime scheduling" of productive and administrative activities. The author wrote, *inter alia,* that:

—the flextime work scheduling system—also known as self-supervision—is increasing labor productivity and efficiency and, at the same time, "displays humanitarian concerns" since "self-supervision . . . helps the employee derive satisfaction from his job and is even tending to bring about a change in life style";

—in the West the "self-supervision" system has been introduced in "more than 6,000 enterprises of various types," thereby abolishing "the static management model," which "is characterized by . . . a rigid hierarchy," "a purely *pro forma* style of management" and "the total subordination of the employee's needs to the needs of the work system";

—"changes in working methods have led to . . . structural changes in organization," positions formerly occupied by chief directors have been taken over by executive committees . . . and separate levels of management have been replaced by planning teams";

—"another result of these changes is that worker teams are allowed to evaluate their own performance, to organize their own work . . . and to influence changes in the organizational structure of the whole enterprise";

—in the FRG, "by the end of 1975 the eight-hour working day will have been abolished in 50 percent of the total number of business enterprises. Even now, 1.5 million workers can . . . freely decide what time they want to start and finish their working days";

—"a characteristic feature of the flextime system" is that the employee can independently determine how his personal life is going to interact with his working life without having to seek management permission." (*Report on Materials Censored,* July 16–31, 1975)

The internal directives for chief editors and censors on the American Bicentennial reflected a similar concern over too positive or too extensive coverage of developments in the West:

80 As protection against an uncontrolled avalanche of publications concerning the 200th anniversary of the United States and the popularization of various sorts of spontaneous presentations organized "in honor of" or "on the occasion of [the Bicentennial]," the following censorship guidelines have been laid down:

1) Information concerning ceremonials and performances and other forms of commemoration of the Bicentennial being observed in the United States, foreign countries or our country may be reported only through the intermediary of PAP. Information on this subject from other sources should be eliminated.

2) Any sort of author's remarks (mentions, references) about this anniversary are permissible in those publications where such mentions are absolutely essential to the discussion (e.g., in contexts such as: what influence on the preelection atmosphere in the United States is exerted by the fact that the elections are being held on the 200th anniversary; what has remained of the values for which the struggle was waged, now that 200 years have elapsed; and so on).

3) Mentions of and references to the anniversary are also permissible in publications popularizing the role of Poles in the revolution, history and modern-day life of the United States and in historical articles that contrast the progressive nature of those past events with current U.S. socioeconomic problems.

4) All other publications referring to the Bicentennial but not mentioned here should be referred to the GUKPPiW leadership. (February 21, 1976; canceled October 16, 1976)

Good relations between Poland and Western nations were not necessarily good news. Since Poland was far more tied to the West than other Soviet bloc nations, any emphasis on this made Poland's allies uncomfortable, as it was seen as encouraging Poles to turn to the West. In the spring of 1976 even such events as the establishment of new societies for Polish friendship with Western nations became non-news. Information about the involvement of Western firms in the Polish economy, something long sought by Poland's leaders, was also relegated to the status of non-news. So was information about Western contributions and aid in the construction of hospitals and public health facilities in Poland (at the time of the construction of the American-funded children's hospital in Kraków). In part, these regulations were simply attempts to make Poland look no more pro-Western than any other member of the Soviet bloc. In part, they appear to have been designed to avoid the appearance, as Poland's economic situation worsened, that any gains were the result of Western help or to raise people's hopes with talk of aid from the West. Therefore, the Gierek regime took steps to increase its Western contacts and aid without allowing its own citizens to know what they had gained from the West. Such censorship of information was extended to cover even basic travel agreements much desired by Polish citizens, which in the West symbolized the beginning of a reintegration of Poland into the West, but in Poland signaled easy access to jobs paying in Western currencies, necessary to get goods desired in Poland but available only abroad:

16. The texts of agreements concerning the introduction of non-visa border traffic (the elimination of visas) between Poland and Austria, Finland and Sweden, as published in *Dziennik Ustaw,* should not be reprinted in whole or in part, nor should more extensive comment and discussion of the details of these agreements be permitted.

The mass media may indicate the signing of the above-mentioned agreements *only* in the form of short informational notes. (Canceled October 17, 1974)

Bad news about Western countries was also not always acceptable. Accusations made against foreign diplomats stationed in Poland were sensitive enough to require approval by the security police. This allowed the police to pursue investigations of such individuals with a minimum of interference and also to monitor leaks on this subject. It also reduced the occasions for making inferences about Polish diplomats abroad (from attacks on Western ones), and kept Poland from offending the home countries of those accused of spying. This regulation, however, appeared more as a final safety screen than as a necessary protection. Leaking information or writing about spying and intelligence work was not something journalists and their editors would even consider without high-level direction during a time of crisis.

> 12. In material pertaining to the activities of enemy agents in Poland (spy rings of foreign intelligence services), do not permit any mention of the connection between these agents and the diplomatic representatives of foreign countries (this does not apply to PAP information). Materials (with the exception of PAP communiqués) concerning violations of Polish law (e.g., economic crimes, smuggling, violations of law and order, etc.) committed by representatives of foreign states should also be held up for clarification.
>
> Because the work of the Security Service of the Ministry of Internal Affairs may be impeded by the premature revelation of certain data concerning the activity of persons convicted of spying or of other acts violating state security or by the premature revelations of information of a related nature, it is recommended that chief representatives refer all material of this sort to the First Deputies for Security Affairs of the Voivodship Headquarters of the Citizens' Militia.

Ideological Friends and Enemies

Gierek's foreign policy in the mid-seventies did draw fine distinctions between Poland's friends and enemies. While the basic premises of Soviet foreign policy were never actively challenged, Poland moved to expand détente far beyond the limits of Soviet-American relations. It also sought quietly to reinforce its position as an autonomous nation. For the mass media, this meant that the political left in Western Europe, international organizations and Communist states outside the Soviet bloc were sensitive issues.

A number of articles described in the censorship documents dealt with leftist movements in Western Europe. They were censored because of their political tone. One article had sections censored whenever it indicated that Euro-Communist parties were hardly revolutionary or independent forces. By the censors' rules, a translation of Western comments that one of these parties was a servant of the Soviet Union was objectionable not because it bespoke of Soviet influence but, first and foremost, because it was a critical remark:

> Critical remarks about the French Communist Party, which "is neither nationalist nor internationalist, but foreign-nationalist" and which has "always accepted uncritically" Soviet foreign policy, were deleted from the article "Ill-Fated 1976?" reprinted from the British publication *The Economist* (*Forum*, No. 13), in which France was assessed critically as a partner and ally of England. (*Report on Materials Censored*, March 16–31, 1974)

Similarly, this passage from an interview showing that the left was neither strong nor revolutionary even in the context of its acceptance and participation in daily government was barred from publication:

> " 'I see a fairly bright future for parliamentarism in France. It is more promising under Giscard than under de Gaulle, who most assuredly disliked parliament and regarded it as a necessary evil.' 'What about the Union of the Left in France?' 'I do not have much faith in its reputation. Besides, in France the Communists are a normal political party—in the towns and departments which they control, they are not carrying out any reforms, but are simply performing administrative duties—they are doing a good job of administration. The same thing is going on in Italy. . . .' " (*Report on Materials Censored*, March 16–31, 1974)

Polish coverage of Communist states outside the Soviet bloc was regulated to stay well within the limits of what was acceptable to the Soviet Union while avoiding a tone so strident and Soviet-like as to displease Western nations with which Poland was seeking closer relations. Regulations required any mention of Albania be cleared at the highest levels of the GUKPPiW. They also specified the precise terms to be used in referring to the Communist and non-Communist sections of Korea and China. These terms ascribed less legitimacy to the non-Communist than to the Communist governments. The censors were even sensitive to making China seem too important or culturally developed in comparison to the other neutral or Communist states in East Asia. In one case, a writer reported that her Chinese cookbook was sent back to her by the censors, who ordered that it be enlarged to include foods from other less controversial states in Asia.

Poland's relations with Third World states also required careful handling. The contradiction of ideological claims by economic or other interests meant the removal of media information that might hurt Poland's economic goals by revealing the weaknesses of the products they were selling or that did not conform to Soviet policy statements. Thus Poland's contacts with states with which it did not have formal diplomatic relations and against which it and the Soviet Union had waged press campaigns were not reportable. In fact, even the regulation specifying this was hidden from journalists and editors, for they might have argued against it or gotten the idea that Poland's dealings with these nations were extensive:

> 11. No information may be published which suggests the existence of any sort of contacts (commercial, cultural, scientific, athletic, tourist or any other) between Poland and the regimes of South Korea, Taiwan, South Africa or Rhodesia—which are not recognized by our country —or enterprises of citizens of these lands. This prohibition also applies to all information which might imply that any sort of efforts are being made by these regimes to establish such contacts. Any doubtful material should be referred to the GUKPPiW leadership.
>
> This prohibition is intended solely for the information of censorship groups. (September 8, 1974)
>
> c. All information concerning the participation of representatives of Israel at congresses, international conferences, or performances organized by Poland should be cleared with the GUKPPiW leadership.

Similar blind spots were required in covering events in key parts of the Third World, where Polish support did not always go hand in hand with political stability or pro-Communist domestic policies. Censoring passages allowed Poland, like other Soviet bloc states, to shroud expedient policies toward what it considered vilifiable states or enemies of nations Poland held as allies, and also to "double-support" both governments and their leftist opposition forces "in accordance with the principles of foreign policy toward the Third World":

> g. Do not permit the publication of information about meetings and rallies of Arab and African young people and students temporarily in Poland if the gatherings are used to attack the regimes of Arab and African countries.

i. Do not permit the publication of information about the possibility of visits to Poland by representatives of opposition organizations from Arab and African countries.

d. Do not permit the publication of information concerning possible limitations of the freedom of movement of political activists or Communist parties in the Arab Republic of Egypt, Algeria, the Sudan, Iraq, Libya or Syria.

In dealing with Third World disputes, Poland sought not to alienate any potential allies and to this end maintained a position of absolute neutrality in its media reports:

e. In publications concerning the Palestinian resistance movement, no favor should be shown to specific organizations. Only the Palestinian Liberation Organization expresses the interests of the whole Palestinian resistance movement. As a body of the operative leadership of the Palestinian organizations under the auspices of the Palestinian Liberation Organization, the Central Committee of the Palestinian Resistance Movement, created in 1970, should be regarded as equally representative.

f. In view of the inter-Arab polemics which have been growing since August 1970 between advocates of political means for solving the Middle Eastern crisis and supporters of extremist positions, be very careful in using verbatim quotations from the statements of Arab commentators and politicians on these subjects.

International Forums

In the mid-seventies, the Helsinki Conference and the United Nations were considered by Poland's leaders to be important forums on which the country's international position could be established. One aspect of the Helsinki Agreement signed by the United States, Canada and the nations of Western and Eastern Europe was a recognition of Europe's postwar boundaries, a matter of greatest concern to Poland, and the promise to move toward the kind of European disarmament for which Poland—the major battleground for past wars in Europe —had long been the Soviet bloc's chief spokesman. Helsinki also encouraged the kind of economic and technical cooperation that Gierek's Poland needed. On the other hand, the Helsinki Agreement's Basket Three provisions for increased interchange threatened Gierek's ability to keep a tight hold on his population while maintaining close ties with the West. They also required signatories to publicize the provisions of the agreement. The Press Department laid down clear guidelines for the coverage of this event, which reflected Polish needs and concerns far more than compliance with the provisions requiring publication of information on the accords:

GUIDELINES ON THE PRESENTATION OF THE PROBLEMS OF THE CONFERENCE ON SECURITY AND COOPERATION IN EUROPE

We are treating the idea of the all-European security and cooperation conference as the logical concretization of the Leninist principle of peaceful coexistence among nations with different sociopolitical systems. Its assumption: the transformation of Europe, in which destructive world wars began twice, into a continent of lasting peace and equal, mutually beneficial cooperation, is a permanent, strategic assumption, and it cannot be treated by anyone as a temporary, tactical achievement.

A key issue will be its implementation by all the participants in the conference. The agreements open up a new state of relations in Europe and create possibilities for the resolution of many problems of cooperation on the European continent.

The unprecedented nature of the drafting should be emphasized. It took entirely equal effort on the part of all participating countries (East and West, large and small) to draft the principles for relations between countries concerning all aspects of growing international cooperation.

It should be particularly pointed out that the CSCE and the agreements reached are a [joint success] of the socialist countries and the political forces, governments, political circles, and personalities based on the principles of peaceful coexistence. In the West attempts are being made to distort information on the agreements to ignore the course of the Phase II work. Efforts are being made to advance the hypothesis that, under pressure from the West, the socialist countries have backed down from their principled positions and only this has made it possible to finalize the work. Without going into the polemics on the various formulations negotiated, we should emphasize that it was possible to finalize the work because jointly agreed upon, optimal, feasible solutions were reached.

Poland is vitally interested in implementing the CSCE resolutions to bolster security in Europe and serve the cause of the development of international economic cooperation and, in the area of culture, information and interpersonal contacts, helping to make détente permanent on the European continent.

In the period between the second and third phases (between the drafting of the agreements and their signing by national leaders) we should not go into the details of the agreements, putting their significance into a hierarchy or the like, in order to avoid, before the signing of the documents, any arguments that might lead to making interpretive statements on the documetns of the CSCE in the third phase. This follows, for example, from the unclear nature of the CSCE documents up to the point they are signed, in keeping with the CSCE procedure adopted by the foreign affairs ministers during the first phase (July 1973) (Final Recommendations). This makes it possible to write very positively about the completion of the work and its general significance without creating the impression that issues and problems are being avoided.

With reference to the various "baskets," the following should appear in the media:

A catalog of the principles of particular significance to security and cooperation in Europe, as recognized in the multilateral document as the basis for relations between European countries;

Adoption of principles that should be used as a basis for mutually beneficial economic cooperation serving to break down the divisions in Europe, creating the infrastructure for a system of security and representing the lasting quality and irreversibility of the processes of détente and cooperation;

Definition of the directions, goals, principles and areas of cooperation in the realm of culture, education and interpersonal contacts and information, on the basis of mutuality, which creates the circumstances for making equal the imbalances so unfavorable to us in this exchange.

Second Point: Cooperation in the Realm of the Economy, Science and Technology, and Environmental Protection
No attempt should be made to make any distinction between those resolutions which are more advantageous to us and those which are less so, but the fact that the resolutions coincide with our long-range economic interest and existing regulations and practice in our country should be emphasized.

Cooperation in the Area of Trade*
Industrial Cooperation
The agreements create the framework for the development of industrial cooperation and are an expression of the countries' readiness to create conditions favorable to its expansion.

Of great importance to the development of general European cooperation are the provisions concerning, among other things, the improve-

---

*For brevity's sake, some descriptive passages have been omitted.

ment and acceleration of the circulation of information on industrial cooperation.

Scientific and Technical Cooperation

It will be of the essence to improve cooperation and to eliminate the existing barriers by: improving conditions for the exchange and dissemination of scientific and technical information, upgrading the organization and programming of visits by scientists, as well as making broader use of trade channels in the realm of applied research and the transfer of the results, while ensuring the proper protection of intellectual and industrial property.

Cooperation in the Realm of Environmental Protection

The agreements help to increase the effectiveness of national and international environmental protection measures.

The following are among the important means for accomplishing cooperation between countries in the area of protection of the environment: unification of norms and standards of environmental protection and the exchange of scientific and technical information, documentation and results of research.

Cooperation in Other Areas
Transport
Economic Cooperation in the Realm of Tourism

Poland is vitally interested in the development of tourism. From the economic point of view, serving tourists from abroad is a part of export.

Cooperation in the Realm of Staff Training

Third Point: Cooperation in Humanitarian and Other Areas

We should present the recommendations that show the constructive possibilities for the broad development of general European cooperation, particularly the expansion of exchange in the realm of culture and education. In this connection, the broad scope of cultural-educational cooperation between Poland and Western European countries and the high level of the dissemination of the cultural contribution of many Western countries in Poland should be emphasized. Particular attention should be given to the principle of mutuality.

In the area of interpersonal contacts, the dynamic development of tourism between Poland and other countries should be shown.

(The problems of uniting families should not be taken up.)

The problem of the counterbalancing of information and cultural exchange in connection with proposals that are not beneficial to us may be undertaken using concrete examples.

Contacts Between People
Information

There is a serious imbalance—to our detriment—in the level of mutual knowledge and information. We expect the CSCE agreements to help the societies of the Western countries to become informed about Poland to the same extent that the Polish society is informed about their countries. (June 1975)

For the journalists who were selected to attend the conference, Polish policy was well defined. For others, the accords were virtually inaccessible, so little analysis could be done. Only the censors had a clear set of detailed guidelines to follow. These specified Polish leaders' policy statements as the definitions of tone—something done naturally in most cases by censors and journalists alike.

101. In censoring publications on the results of the Conference on Security and Cooperation in Europe and the bilateral talks between our leaders and the delegations of other countries (especially the Federal Republic of Germany), the following principles should be observed:

1) The general tone of our materials should be consistent with the content and spirit of the Final Document of the CSCE signed in Helsinki (*Trybuna Ludu*, August 2–3 of this year), and all assessments "from the Polish point of view" should be consistent with the address of Comrade E. Gierek, head of our delegation (*Trybuna Ludu*, August 1), the communiqué issued by the Politburo of the PZPR Central Committee (*Trybuna Ludu*, August 5) and the commentary printed in *Trybuna Ludu* on August 6.

2) Comrade Brezhnev's address, published in *Trybuna Ludu* on August 1, states the position of the USSR.

3) Any "in-house" speculations or assessments or uncritical inclusions of the opinions and views of "others" that would tend to undermine the historic significance of this conference and its results should be eliminated. On the other hand, such opinions (e.g., from the foreign press) may be quoted in a polemical context.

4) . . . in our publications (including polemical ones) what should be emphasized is the unanimity of all the signatories to the resolution, reflecting the attitudes and aspirations of whole nations, and the improving moral-political atmosphere of international relations under conditions of détente. . . .

It is in this context that the abbreviated names [for the accords]— "Great Charter of Peace" and "Peace Agreement" [*Pokojowe Porozumienie*]—should be promoted and popularized. (August 7, 1975; canceled September 12, 1975)

According to the available censors' reports, much of the deleted material on Helsinki made use of comments by Westerners, whose observations were phrased differently from Polish statements. One such case involved a translation of comments by French political observer Raymond Aron, on the value of the accords, that appeared in *Forum*, a journal featuring translations from the foreign press. Aron focused on the existence of political and economic blocs in Europe, noting the relative weakness of Western Europe as a bloc and the continued existence of dissatisfaction with the state of Europe that existed even with the accords. His conclusion that Europe was "doomed to be insecure" was too negative to be reprinted, given Gierek's desire to glorify the conference as the "Peace Agreement":

> The text of an article by Raymond Aron entitled "Negation" (a reprint from *Le Figaro*) was disapproved for publication in Issue No. 39 of *Forum*. Commenting on the Conference on Security and Cooperation in Europe, the author belittled the value of the Helsinki accords, stating *inter alia,* that:
>
> —"the territorial status quo . . . which was recognized by the Helsinki Conference is based, at the same time, on the existing balance of forces and ideological conflicts." The USSR occupies the dominant position in East Europe, and "has its troops in the GDR." The Western countries "accept the status quo because they cannot change it. . . ." "They insisted on the presence of the USA and Canada at the conference, since Western Europe . . . otherwise would have felt that it was at the mercy of Moscow."
>
> —the situation in Europe is "abnormal," since "regardless of whether the Russians are talking about détente or a cold war, the difference between the two Europes still exists."
>
> —"The Soviet Union is militarily too strong, and Western Europe is too divided and weak in a moral sense for peaceful coexistence to be able to ensure true security for both large and small countries. Liberal Europe is doomed to live in insecurity." (*Report on Materials Censored,* September 16–30, 1975)

The United Nations has traditionally been considered an important permanent forum for Polish foreign policy. Two Polish correspondents are regularly assigned there. Poland has played an important role in various negotiations and peacekeeping forces organized by the UN. Participation in these activities was seen as crucial for establishing Poland as an international actor in the eyes of its own population and those of other nations. No matter what problems Polish soldiers encountered on their peacekeeping missions, there could be no negative reports about their work:

> 11. Reporting, correspondence and other material discussing the service of Polish soldiers in the Middle East should have any information eliminated from it that might indicate a lack of true cooperation, a bad atmosphere or various sorts of incidents occurring between soldiers of other states making up the UN emergency forces. (See Informative Note No. 5/74) (New version, January 12, 1976)

The deference shown to the United Nations was so great, in fact, that even experienced and trusted Polish journalists, whose work was rarely questioned, were often judged to have crossed the lines of the permissible when the subject was the UN. Wiesław Górnicki, Poland's chief UN correspondent in the mid-sixties (he was recalled in 1968 for criticizing Poland's anti-Semitism and was a leading press spokesman for the martial law government) managed to break many of the unspoken taboos. His book, *High Society,* containing his observations as a UN correspondent, was censored in a number of places not only for expressing a less than positive view of the work of the United Nations as a whole, but also for the tone of its remarks about Soviet, American and Polish participation. These censored passages illustrate the conflict between an experienced journalist's sense of the proper balance between critical statements and deference to the censorship, and the official censors' sense of the absolute outer limits. Reporting on the voting system of the UN, for example, Górnicki noted that:

> ". . . until 1955 the first delegation in alphabetical order always sat in the front left corner of the hall and the last in the right rear. As fate would have it, the first delegation was Afghanistan, and after it came Albania. Because the order of voting in those days went according to the order of seating in the hall, the poor Albanian delegation always had to be the first ones in the socialist camp to cast their vote. I don't know if you realize what a terrible difficulty it is when they call for a vote and you haven't the slightest idea how to vote. If Australia had been the first country to declare its vote, then the decision would have been easy. One could simply have voted the opposite way from the Australians. However, Afghanistan is a neutral country, and in those days it preferred to abstain rather than offend anyone. We, on the other hand, never hide in the corner—if someone has to be taught a lesson,

they have to be. The Albanian delegation asked so often for a five-minute recess (basicaly, three minutes is sufficient to jump up from one's chair, run to make a friendly consultation, and return) that in the end everyone grew tired of it.

"Anyway, there were several lamentable occasions on which, through inattention or lack of insight, the Albanian delegation voted for entirely inappropriate resolutions or, conversely, torpedoed resolutions on the most vital issues under the sun. So the principle was adopted whereby the seating arrangements of countries in the General Assembly would be subject to annual rotation. . . .

"I do not mean to say by this that absolutely every country in the General Assembly now knows exactly how it is going to vote on any given issue. There are still countries like the Maldive Islands, which refuse to vote for anything until they have had a chance to confer with their former colonial master, or countries like Madagascar, which will not cast a vote until they know for sure what the majority intends to do. . . . I suppose you would like to know whether it ever happens that countries which belong to large and cohesive voting blocs cast contradictory votes. Of course they do. Such votes are cast. I remember a case where the Netherlands voted differently from the United States. . . ."
(*Report on Materials Censored*, December 1–15, 1975)

This passage, like so much of the material censored, broke no specific regulations. Nor did it directly attack the legitimacy of the UN or the behavior of the Soviet Union. Through its references, tone and juxtaposition of comments, however, it reminded Poles that Albania had once been a loyal Soviet ally, that bloc politics and actions were not always well coordinated and that independent voting occurred more often in the Western bloc than in the Soviet bloc. None of this was acceptable. The same was true of Górnicki's comments about Soviet and American delegates and the historical parallels drawn by the passages quoted below. Even though the Soviet delegate in question and Khrushchev had both fallen from favor, and Górnicki's comments about their successors were complimentary while his comments on the American ambassador to the UN under Eisenhower were negative, his attacks on former Soviet officials were construed as a broader criticism of Soviet policy. The following passage was seen as a veiled attack on the Soviet Union itself. And the passing comments about the suitability of publication "at the present time" and about the dead silence with which some events were treated were undoubtedly seen as far too open a reference to censorship.

—an appraisal of the Soviet ambassador to the United Nations, Andrei Yanuarievich Vyshinsky:

". . . a lot could be said about the late Andrei Vyshinsky, a lot of things that are not very complimentary. However, he had one quality that not even his most stubborn enemies could dispute—oratorical talent.

". . . Vyshinsky never smiled. His stern, tense face was always full of such obvious disdain and animosity for the enemies of socialism, real and imagined (it was Vyshinsky who called Jawaharlal Nehru 'a lackey of the British imperialists'), that hardly anyone in the UN would engage him in conversation for pleasure. It is no secret that the employees of the Soviet mission and the representatives of the other socialist countries were simply frightened of this tall, gloomy man. . . .

". . . I think that in spite of his undeniable talents, this man did a poor job of serving the cause of his country and the interests of socialism. Fortunately, all of this is now nothing more than a distant, fading memory. The team of outstanding diplomats that has since represented the Soviet Union in the UN has succeeded in totally erasing the unfavorable memory of Vyshinsky and has enhanced the genuine prestige of its country. . . ."

—the participation of Nikita Sergeevich Khrushchev at the 25th session of the United Nations:

". . . True, there are some unusually colorful personalities at the UN who appear to have no use at all for the regulations dictated by protocol. They are few and far between, but they are there nonetheless. . . .

"Certainly, one such figure was the former Soviet head of state, Nikita Khrushchev, whose unrestrained temperament, gruff sense of humor and self-confidence gave rise to an unusually large number of UN anecdotes. Not all of the numerous—very numerous—incidents, utterances and altercations that are associated with Khrushchev's visit to the 25th session in 1960 are suitable for publication at the present time, but there is one anecdote that is mentionable even now.

"The Americans, who have generally been fortunate in their choice of representatives to the UN and usually have no reason to be embarrassed over their behavior, did commit an indiscretion by appointing a certain Henry Wadsworth as ambassador to the UN at this critical juncture. This was somebody that Eisenhower had dug out of one of the dusty inner recesses of the Republican Party machine, who was totally unqualified for the job and, moreover, endowed with an unusually churlish disposition. Like Khrushchev, he was of short stature and considerably overweight, and at moments he betrayed the unmistakable signs of an imminent attack of apoplexy. The old hands in the corridors of the UN, for whom nothing is sacred, called Khrushchev and Wadsworth 'the fat ones.' The clashes between these two politicians at the 25th session were characterized by an unusual degree of liveliness and an especially colorful vocabulary. . . ."

Sections were also cut out that revealed expedient but not ideologically pure Polish actions and presented Polish UN representatives as less than perfect:

". . . Professor Lachs, a first-rate lawyer with an international reputation, adviser to several Polish ministers of foreign affairs and a member of the Polish delegation to practically every session of the United Nations General Assembly, is a well-known and highly popular man in diplomatic circles, but it is difficult to relate any gossip about him. As an experienced lawyer, he has never yet uttered a single superfluous word, nor has he ever expressed a single inappropriate opinion. But there is one incident in his professional career that is hard to believe. Namely, though this may not seem so terribly exciting to the average reader of the press, he induced the International Tribunal of Justice, an essentially infallible institution, to repeal its own verdict on Southwest Africa (awarding it to South Africa). This is more or less the same thing as if the Pope had sheepishly declared that he had made an error in his own encyclical. . . .

"Finally, it has not often happened that we have had a good Polish chairman sitting on the International Tribunal of Justice. There have been some chairmen, to be sure, but they have sometimes done more harm than good. The venerable Professor Winiarski, who presided over the Tribunal once as our representative, cast his vote in favor of the above-mentioned verdict on Southwest Africa, which recognized the mandate of the Republic of South Africa over this territory. Despite the many good services that he performed, Winiarski left something of a mess behind him in the International Tribunal of Justice, something of which I am all too painfully aware since on many occasions I have had to explain to my colleagues from Africa and Asia that I am not the one who is responsible for awarding Namibia to those barbarians in Johannesburg. Incidentally, I do not really understand why this unfortunate case was passed over in complete silence by our press. In Poland it is either 'a great success of Polish diplomacy' or dead silence. . . ."

References to less than dedicated Polish diplomatic representatives clearly caught the censor's eye:

". . . Satis. Since instead of spreading malicious gossip I am winding up saying a votive mass, I would like to close this chapter about Poles in the United Nations with something on the order of a dedication.

"Namely, I dedicate it to all of those Polish diplomats who do not begrudge their country sleepless nights and interrupted Sundays, whose talents, skills and experience truly bring us credit in the eyes of the world and ensure that no one will shrug his shoulders when mention is made of our country.

"But at the same time I am writing this to express my disapproval of those artful dodgers who have turned diplomacy into an impenetrable screen to protect them from the labor of life and from anything that would test their ability to do anything else.

"Let these lazy ones, convinced that they can take care of various things in Poland (especially journalists, since that is always easiest), be convinced that there is something no one can arrange for another: a good name among people who are very particular about that. . . ."
(*Report on Materials Censored,* December 1–15, 1975)

Even after the censors had purified the foreign news with respect to its potential effect on Poles' perceptions of their own country and of foreign countries, far more was available than appeared in most other East European and Soviet media. But it hardly satisfied the Polish population. As the seventies wore on and Poland entangled itself more and more in international obligations, journalists saw more and more of what interested them and what their readers sought red-penciled out by the censors. The news that was left was a curious amalgam of rosy images of life elsewhere—even in the West, which Gierek hoped would make his regime look pro-Western and deserving of more economic help—and constant reminders that life was either better still in Poland or at least not so different from life in the West. The contradictions of this amalgam left Polish journalists in a constant quandary as to what was reportable and what had to be ignored. The quandary grew in the last years of the seventies as the economic situation in Poland grew blacker and it was harder to publish domestic news. Foreign reports seemed a safe alternative for writing interesting and critical articles, but little from abroad could be written about without offending Poland's diverse friends or making the Polish situation look worse.

5 / MAKING SOCIAL

PROBLEMS NONPROBLEMS

THE POLAND of the Polish media that the Gierek regime tried to mold was a joyous haven. There was virtually no crime, and no preventable accidents, no alcoholism, no serious or contagious disease. The cities and countryside were clean and well maintained. There was no pollution. Factory and farm workers worked happily for good wages under ideal conditions. Women workers had no difficulty holding down a job and caring for their families at the same time. Food and consumer goods were plentiful at uninflated prices whenever and wherever they were needed. No one, including political leaders and celebrities, lived better than anyone else. Sportsmen were model citizens. The young were well educated. Families were well provided for; the elderly, adequately cared for. Even discussions of the flu were not allowed to darken the media's image of Polish life, regardless of how widespread the disease became. And naturally, no one sought to leave this perfect society.

This image, which the Polish leadership sought to create for its public, reflected little of the reality of everyday life in Poland—reality that was filtered out at the censor's desk. Journalists who attempted to represent reality, to expose social problems or to advocate the interests of various groups found themselves more and more often thwarted as the unspoken "social contract" on which Gierek based his authority—work and political support in exchange for better living conditions—increasingly collapsed.

Some of the censorship regulations and reports on censorship of social issues provide specific reasons for the restrictions. Implicit in them is the assumption that the media not only can report on behavior but can shape it as well. The media came to be the regime's instrument for the creation of the new socialist man: as the possibilities for providing material rewards for loyalty and obedience began to dwindle, it presented Poles continually with evidence that they lived in a perfect society so that they would in turn see problems as being of their own making. Conversely, it was assumed that the media could help to shape proper attitudes and behavior by presenting a perfectly positive image—just as it could also, by reporting on social problems, encourage their spread. Hence the following regulations used by the censors for all or part of the mid-seventies:

> In order to combat any tendency of our professional athletes to play for foreign teams, no material (statements, opinions, suggestions) by either journalists or contestants on this subject should be permitted for publication. (Valid July 15, 1974–March 19, 1975)

> No material concerning the hippie movement in Poland may be permitted for publication if it expresses approval or tolerance, does not take the question seriously and so on. Only unequivocally critical material may be published.
> Material that favorably assesses the activities of this movement in other countries, particularly in the West, should be referred to the GUKPPiW administration.

> Material that might aid or encourage the spread of the use of narcotics in this country should not be permitted to appear in the mass media. Publications on this subject should be devoid of sensationalism and unilaterally critical. The following should be eliminated completely from materials permitted for publication:
> Names of habit-forming substances and narcotics and methods of use, or information on places where such substances can be acquired or where addicts can meet.
> This prohibition does not apply to works published in purely scientific periodicals.

> All descriptions of an instructive nature should be eliminated from materials on theft, burglary, airplane hijacking and other acts of violence and terror. It is a matter here of avoiding the popularization of methods for committing crimes, means used by criminals to avoid detection, ways of destroying evidence and so on. This directive also applies to excessively detailed information concerning strikes (various forms and methods of organization).

This prohibition applies to domestic materials and reprints from the foreign press.

Reporting on Polish society was also shaped by the leadership's concern with foreign trade and economic support. Discussions of problems, accidents, industrial failures, or plant and animal diseases might—in the perception of the Polish leadership—discourage foreign investment and support. Likewise, it was feared that reports of shoddy workmanship and poor-quality goods might discourage foreign buyers and dull the image of the new modern Poland the leadership claimed to be building in the seventies:

> 4. All publications presenting general, compiled numerical data for divisions, branches and sectors of the economy, enterprises and the country as a whole pertaining to the occupational health and safety situation or to occupational diseases should be held up.
>
> Such information should not appear in the press, on the radio or television, or in other publications. There is still some possibility of publishing figures on the rate of accidents in the public materials of the Main Statistical Office, the Planning Commission of the Council of Ministers, and the ministries. (Decisions on these matters will be handled on a case-by-case basis by the GUKPPiW administration.)
>
> Information about work-related accidents in particular plants may also be permitted for publication. (New version added November 14, 1975)

Equally important to the Gierek regime was the search for support from Polish émigrés. Gierek tried to court Polish communities abroad. Efforts to contact Poles abroad were greatly expanded. Only those Poles who left for political reasons after the Communist takeover or who attacked the regime from abroad were excluded from this campaign. The royal castle in Warsaw, destroyed by the Germans during World War II, was rebuilt with money donated in large part by Poles living abroad. To support these efforts, the censors were instructed to check all publications for material that might be unnecessarily offensive to the Polish emigration. So far did these efforts go that the official title of one of the men in charge of relations with the emigration was made a closely guarded secret:

> Because of the fact that certain groups of émigré Poles are sensitive to contacts with official representatives of our country, in publishing the

name of Comrade Wiesław Adamski, only his social function, i.e., Secretary-General of the "Polonia" Society, should be given. In every case, his title of Deputy Minister (Undersecretary of State) should be eliminated. This regulation should be kept completely secret.

At the same time, however, the government was not anxious to encourage further emigration from Poland. Information about the emigration that did occur was kept out of the media: the regulations and statistics were all but state secrets, and censors were instructed to eliminate references to almost all famous Poles living abroad and to the successes of recent émigrés. This regulation was followed by the provision that it "should be kept completely secret," lest the deception and prohibitions become known either at home or abroad.

Other regulations reveal that where there were conflicts between the goals of industrialization and social welfare or environmental protection, it was industrialization that was given priority. The media were forced to cooperate in this effort. Finally, it is clear from the reports of the censors and from the instructions given to them that the media were not to aggravate complaints and social tensions by making them appear to be broad issues. Thus, as discontent about inflation (camouflaged by new packaging and product names), shortages, poor working conditions and housing problems increased, so did the prohibitions against discussing it. The leadership clearly hoped people would see their problems as unique and as their own fault—and not as problems shared by everyone.

Ironically, it was the Gierek leadership, and not the Polish people, who ultimately lost any sense of social problems and the tensions they had created. All the issues raised by striking workers in the shipyards of Gdańsk and elsewhere in August 1980 had been noted in the mid-seventies by journalists whose articles had been blocked. This criticism and discussion were usually cut in the hope that the population would not notice the pervasiveness of the crisis. As a Central Committee Press Department director explained to a gathering of journalists, "until we say it is bad, it is good." Whatever the regime's insistence that black was white, the population did notice and in the end rose up as much against the unwillingness of the regime to tell the truth as against the problems themselves.

Living conditions in Poland were difficult. As a group of prominent establishment intellectuals observed in 1979 in an unpublishable survey of intellectual opinion on "Experience and the Future of Poland":

In 1960, nearly one-third of national investment went into "nonproductive" areas of the economy like education, health care, social services, recreation and athletics. Now the proportion has fallen to 19 percent.*

The resulting decline in social services was dramatic. Higher education was subjected to severe cutbacks. Not only were fewer resources now available for education, but there were fewer places for qualified students than ever before in the postwar period. As a result, getting admitted to a university came to depend much more on one's connections than on one's academic or even political qualifications.

Despite a growing demand for housing, construction declined and apartments grew more expensive. Young adults were forced to continue living with their parents or to rent apartments "off the books" for much more than an average salary could cover while waiting, often for more than ten years, for an apartment of their own. This meant taking on extra private work to meet living expenses.

Basic necessities, like furniture and telephones, were in increasingly short supply. Even medical care was hard to come by. Medicines were often not available or available only for hard currency. In an attempt to save energy, regularly scheduled planes and trains were often canceled and electricity was cut off in entire regions for hours at a time. The result of this overall situation was a disintegration of respect for governmental authority and a rise in frustration and low-level violence. Poland was, in the view of many leading journalists and intellectuals, becoming a country in decay.

By the mid-seventies, the standard of living as measured by wages, prices and shortages was the critical social issue. The Gierek regime, realizing that there was little more it could promise and deliver, shifted its media from the visions of a bright future on every front that had characterized the propaganda of the early seventies to a policy of increasing silence. So, by 1974, little could be published that promised any improvements. Only occasionally were long-term plans and proposals permitted in the press. At the same time, the Gierek regime was unwilling to allow a public discussion of policy problems or alternatives. Instead, when the Party Congress of 1975 (see page 81) made some review necessary, it was turned, despite the growing crisis, into a celebration of the triumphs of the regime. The moratorium on

*Experience and the Future Discussion Group, *Poland Today* (Armonk, N.Y.: M. E. Sharpe, 1981), p. 56.

discussions about the future represented much more than an attempt to make problems go away by not recognizing their existence. By keeping the public in the dark about the national situation, the authorities hoped to deal with social groups separately, buying them off with concessions while preventing any comparison of their situation with that of other groups. In this way, the regime hoped to avoid having to concede to costly demands from the entire society at once.

Not only were wage scales and wage increases banned from open discussion, but details of fringe benefits provided for employees in various industries were also not allowed to be reported. Nor could there be any discussion of work hours, special vacation provisions or extra pay used to induce workers to come to new industrial sites or to go into difficult or dangerous occupations:

Section VII: Wages, Prices, Pensions, Health Services, Social Security
1.a. No information concerning *wage regulations in preparation or already enacted,* or changes in the wage systems of particular sectors or vocational groups may be permitted until the issuing of an official PAP communiqué. (This also applies to cases where decisions have already been made.)

This principle does not apply to an enterprise's in-house press, which may publish information concerning wage scales that have been decided upon for that enterprise (even in advance of the PAP communiqué).

b. No commentary, discussion, interviews or the like concerning an increase in mean earnings throughout the socialized sector of the economy, or an increase in pensions, retirement pay or other social benefits that have been adopted or promised by the Seventh Party Congress may go beyond what is contained in those congress documents.

The only wage indices that may be used are those contained in official Main Statistical Office communiqués. (According to the communiqué issued by that office on January 21, 1976, the nominal net monthly wage in the socialized sector of the economy was 3,537 złotys in 1975, 352 złotys higher than in 1974. This represents an increase of 11.1 percent. In the industrial sector, the increase was 438 złotys, or 13.3 percent. The cost-of-living index for the average employee's family was 102.9 percent of that of 1974.

No criticism of wage decisions or current social policy should be permitted. Demands for more wages should also be eliminated. This also applies to calls for increased social benefits of various types: pensions, retirement pay, vacations, medical care, scholarships and so on.

c. Information concerning the adoption of a five-day workweek by various enterprises should be removed from all publications (except the specialized media) discussing *working time,* regardless of whether such a change is in preparation or has already been carried out. Nor should such enterprises be held up as an example worth following. This does not apply to the decision concerning free Saturdays in 1976 handed down by the December 17, 1975, resolution of the Council of Ministers.

The in-house press distributed exclusively within a given enterprise may publish information on decisions concerning the organization of work within that enterprise, including a reduction of the number of hours in the workweek, which have been or will be put into effect.

d. Calls for the introduction of *free Saturdays in the schools* should be eliminated from all publications. (June 18, 1976; subpoint canceled December 27, 1975)

2. All announcements made in the mass media by factories, firms, construction enterprises and so on seeking employees or recruiting applicants for vocational schools run by the Ministry of Education or other ministries should have eliminated from them data on the earnings and salaries being offered to employees and apprentices, as well as on other perquisites of employment or study such as the possibility of obtaining an apartment, free working apparel, a driver's license and so on.

Only phrases like "earnings to be discussed" and information of a social nature, such as the availability of cafeterias, workers' hotels and so on, may be permitted. The above criteria do not apply to the comprehensive information supplied in the posters or information manuals produced annually by voivodship departments of employment or social services, school superintendents' offices, work establishments or volunteer work teams. (New version, April 6, 1976)

3. No demands for an immediate reduction in the taxes paid on salaries and/or earnings by craftsmen, farmers and others should be permitted for publication.

On the other hand, considerations and proposals for changes in the methods for computing taxes and the scale according to which they are levied, in the context of long-range future changes, are permitted.

4. Do not permit publication of information concerning the awarding of special pensions to various persons by the Premier. Information on special pensions may appear, but without any indication of who awarded them.

5. No information should be permitted on the subject of special allowances awarded on an individual basis by the Premier to certain families with many (more than six) children. . . .

7. No information concerning reductions or increases in the price of any kind of consumer goods or durable goods should be permitted without the approval of the ministry [in question], a deputy premier or the chairman of the State Price Commission. This applies to all publications. Official PAP information on these matters should also be approved by the persons mentioned above.

All information concerning local price changes (on the voivodship level) should be confirmed by the chairman of the voivodship price commission and party bodies before it may be allowed to appear. This prohibition also applies to all changes in fees charged for services by state and municipal institutions. In materials concerning so-called *"new market items,"* opinions generally critical of the prices of or the price policy concerning new products should be stricken. . . .

12. In discussions of the increase in average earnings thoroughout the socialized sector between 1971 and 1975, only the indices contained in the "Instructions of the Central Committee at the Seventh Party Congress" may be used: i.e., increase in mean earnings from 2,235 to 3,500 złotys, mean annual rise in the cost of living of 2–3 percent, level of real earnings in 1975 about 40 percent higher than in 1970. (September 11, 1975; canceled January 22, 1976)

Even the gradual introduction of periodic five-day workweeks was kept out of the media until just before the regime was ready to give occasional "free Saturdays" to all enterprises and institutions. This censorship policy hampered the efforts of enterprises to hire workers, since neither articles nor advertisements could include information about wages, fringe benefits and working conditions (though it could be specified in posters published and posted by local industries, service centers and government institutions). Similarly, the potential propaganda benefit of awards for meritorious work or large families was limited because these awards usually involved additional sums of money for the individuals involved, and their granting therefore could not be mentioned in the mass media since the leadership was committed to claims of equality even as it pursued policies of deliberate inequality to reward themselves and those who served their interests.

Even reports of the much sought-after increased productivity stimulated by introducing five-day workweeks in various industries could not appear:

On the basis of the relevant regulation, an article by K. Gąsiorowska and A. Sikorski entitled "Doing a Good Job Was the Decisive Factor"

(*Życie Gospodarcze*, No. 22) was challenged. The article reported on the way in which the "July 22" Plant of the Sugar Industry Association introduced a free Saturday once a month. In Issue No. 22 of *Za i Przeciw*, the following passage was deleted from the reply of a reader to the survey "How I Spend My Weekends," in which there was a comment about the way in which a certain unspecified institution in Warsaw rotates free Saturdays:

". . . I am employed by an institution where several of us, working in a common room, are able to enjoy free Saturdays on a rotating basis. Our wise and understanding director simply agreed to assign only certain workers to be on duty each Saturday, since there was no need for all of us to be there every Saturday. In this way, I have practically every other Saturday off, and it often works out that I work only one Saturday a month. Moreover, our labor productivity has increased sharply, something which naturally has not escaped the notice of our superiors." (*Report on Materials Censored*, May 16–31, 1974)

Living Standards

By 1976 unannounced price increases had reached a point where journalists felt compelled to write about the failure of wages to keep up with the cost of living. The dramatic drop in the purchasing power of wages was so clearly spelled out in an article written by Marta Wesołowska for the July 10, 1976, issue of *Polityka* that even though the powerful editorial board of that journal tried, it could not muster enough support to force the censor's hand. Ironically, this censored article reflected the very same tensions that had boiled over so dramatically and publicly only one month earlier, when workers in Radom and Ursus rioted over increases in basic food prices (see page 104). And, the solutions this workers' family was said to propose—ration coupons for scarce food and changes in prices—were solutions the Gierek regime had begun to try to implement. These problems of rising costs and a falling standard of living, as well as growing dissatisfaction with the system, were to be increasingly censored in the years that followed, until in August 1980 they exploded once again into the open, in Gdańsk.

Main Office for Control of Press,
Publications and Public Performances
No. ZI-Pf-050/153/76

Warsaw, July 9, 1976
5 Mysia Street
Telephone: 28-32-61
C O N F I D E N T I A L
Copy No. 35

Informative Note No. 55 concerning current intervention

On July 8, there was intervention in 41 pieces of material.

After consultation with the Department of Press, Radio and Television of the PZPR Central Committee, the editors of *Polityka* withdrew M. Wesołowska's "There Is Enough Sun" from Issue No. 28 of the journal. In this article, which required reediting, the author presented a Warsaw working family of four in order to examine, among other things, living conditions under Bierut ("furniture was cheap," "the state provided an apartment free of charge," and you could buy leather shoes "that didn't wear out" for 150 złotys) and "under Gomułka" (you had to pay a "deposit" of 7,500 złotys for a room with a kitchen window). "They have not gone on a vacation for 25 years, since how much would a vacation for four people cost?" The father works to support the family ("he gets 5,000–6,000" at the Kasprzak Radio Enterprises) along with the eldest son (railroad employee, "he gets 1,870"), but after "analyzing the budget" their mother is also going to get a job. She will work as a clerk in a clothing store, although "something went wrong with her abdomen, and she cannot stand for long periods of time." It has become "traditional" to borrow 10,000–13,000 złotys each May for "major expenses—they cannot imagine living without loans." Here are some excerpts of what the author wrote in the article:

" 'This year, too, May was the nicest. In fact, the best thing to do would be to compare May purchases with those in, let's say, January. In January—searching through our notes, we find our income was 5,088 złotys and expenditures came to 5,029 złotys, which means that 59 złotys were left over. Ulung tea [a very cheap brand], Sport cigarettes [the cheapest brand], *Express Wieczorny* [a newspaper], milk, lard, instant soup powder, buckwheat groats, orange drink, blood sausage, ordinary sausage [the cheapest variety], apples, beans, laundry were 70 złotys—the January records are monotonous, modest. But in May, even though income from work wasn't much greater, there was the loan! Now, just see how we let ourselves go: 20 decagrams of chocolate for 19 złotys, slacks for 450, two pairs of men's slippers (I bought them for both sons, because their toes were beginning to stick out of the old ones), men's shirt (for Mietek), extension cord, deluxe sour cream, select coffee, one visit to the dentists' cooperative, foot salts, hand cream, hair dye (I was dark, but I'm getting terribly gray), panty hose, and Nivea cream. Twelve narcissus. Three movie tickets for 24 złotys total. Tulips (we were going to visit somebody on their name day), real honey for 130 złotys (it's very good for your heart), tulips again, five of them for 15 złotys (no, not for anybody's name day, for the vase on the table), paper tablecloth for 7.50, 10 decagrams of pâté, *Dookoła Świata, Przyjaciółka* [weekly magazines]. . . .

" 'Yes, it is a real joy just to read the notes for May. And it was nice writing them down. . . .' "

Further on, we read, among other things:

"Her older son, Edek, and her husband like ham and good-quality cold meats in general. Of course, they do eat pâté, black pudding and blood sausage, but Józef blurts out, 'What are you giving me? Animal feed?' and recalls the black pudding of another time. So if she wants to do something nice for him—and the atmosphere at home is, after all, the most important thing—she takes the train to Polna market [a private farmers' market] or to a butcher not far from home. She often gets up at 5:00 A.M.; but, unfortunately, it sometimes happens that she can't get anything. She sees various people who have been standing in front of the shop since 3:00 and 4:00 in the morning. People buy up whole sides of meat and lots of hams and, later, they sell them at a higher price in the market places. If somebody needs it for a sick person or a small child, he can always get it. But she says, 'I would rather pay 20 or 30 złotys more for meat in a state store just so things like that wouldn't happen.' Mr. Siekierski breaks in with his own idea for solving the meat problem. He is aware of the problem. If agriculture can't feed the population and the peasant still buys things in town, everybody could be given a coupon: once or twice a week he could buy such-and-such a quantity of good-quality meat. But at the same time a lot of fish, vegetables and processed foods should also be put on the market. And they would be even more of a bargain than the meat. Just so long as they were available everywhere. 'Eh!' protests Mrs. Siekierska. 'You're talking nonsense! Ration coupons after 30 years of People's Poland? And besides, don't you realize that it would just increase the number of speculators?'

"Mrs. Siekierska also sees the bread problem clearly: 'How much lies wasted in the garbage dumps, and how many rural folks buy it as fodder for their cattle?' After all, she has eyes and can see! And she would not be particularly unhappy if bread cost, say, 6 złotys instead of 4, just as long as it wasn't sour or a swindle, but tasted good, just the way it does at the WSS bakery on Aleja Niepodległości [a special bakery], the one Hortex [an independent chain of restaurants run for profit] is taking over, so that there would be the same sort of bread for other areas as there is for that nice district.

"All right, and what should we do about sugar? 'We can raise the price,' Mrs. Siekierska says, looking at her notes, 'but not too much. All I can give for a kilogram of sugar is 15 złotys. After all, June was so beautiful and July began so nicely, sugar beets ought to be plentiful since there is plenty of sun. Fruits, vegetables, too, Butter I understand. It's a problem, like meat, but how much can you pay for a package of butter? Twenty-five złotys?'

" 'Oh dear, we got into politics, and after all this was supposed to be about something pleasant.'

"Besides May, however, the summer is the time when the nicest things are bought. That is, ice cream and the swimming pool at Glinki (they go in on the free side, but all the same a person wants to buy the cream, oils, orange drink and beer), the Mokotów Fields. . . . They were out at the Fields today. 'It's so beautiful there that you don't want to go outside of Warsaw: roses, sun, water. Only it's terribly expensive. A bottle of beer is 11.50 with the deposit, and a soft drink costs 3.90. In what is supposed to be a state-owned booth they sell a 2.50-złoty ice cream for 4 złotys. But maybe it's the pretty view you have to pay extra for. So what? Sometimes a person has to allow himself something crazy, a nice view, or even ice cream for 4 złotys. You can't be so thrifty that you sit in a dark corner and eat old potatoes all the time.' " . . .

The censors' reports on material deleted from articles dealing with wage problems present the same alarming picture of the decline in the standard of living for most groups in the society. Journalists pointed out in mid-1974 that the centrally planned economy had created visible and illogical inequalities in wages. It was noted, for example, that the minimum wage in locally sponsored industries, especially the construction industry, was 38 percent lower than the average wage in light industry, even though light industry normally had the lowest wage scale of any of the centrally funded industries.

Journalists were concerned with their own position. One of the key points they raised, according to the censors' reports, was that "policy in our country is all but programmed to put the intellectual occupations in second place [financially]." One article in a Silesian Catholic weekly documented this, pointing out that the prewar tradition of completing only the minimal amount of required education and then going to work continued in People's Poland because there was no financial incentive to get more education. The censors' rules did not allow the educational opportunities promised to Poles to appear hollow. So they censored all the passages shown below:

> "... The sooner you begin to work, the sooner you can earn a nice little house with a blue-tiled bathroom, sliding doors, super furniture, super television and your own car, and laugh at those who have spent many years studying. Workers look down on technicians since they earn more than the technicians do, even though the latter had to go to school two years longer.
>
> "A bricklayer told me, 'I make more than my engineer, who graduated from a technical college. And a painter, plasterer or roofer also earn more than he does.'
>
> "They're right: a driver earns more than an engineer at an automobile plant, a welder more than a researcher at the Welding Institute, an electrician more than an electrical engineer. Especially when you talk about specialists who are just starting out. Before a teacher, engineer or scientist can earn a four-room apartment, furniture, a television or a little Syrena [automobile], an industrious worker already has these things, and ones of better quality, too.
>
> "The population of Silesia is unusually practical, a quality which is popularly characterized as "materialistic," as a drive to achieve nothing except material goods. Docent Kutyma sees it differently:
>
> " 'The most important reason why the stereotype "You've finished your basic schooling, now go get a job" still lives on is that there is often no relationship between education and amount of earnings. I, after all, am a classic example of this. As an employee at the Silesian Institute, after years of higher education I earn less than an excavator operator employed in the construction of the electric power at Czarnowasy, who needed to have only seven years of schooling and a suitable course.' "
> (_Report on Materials Censored,_ May 1–15, 1974)

Journalists drew implicit comparisons of wage levels for their readers. They reported on the high wages and fringe benefits promised to newly recruited miners. This was considered especially objectionable by the censors because miners came from Gierek's region: the one he led before he became the leader of the entire Polish Party. Mining had, after all, been a favored occupation. Its prosperity made Gierek's reputation as the "workers' man" and an economic modernizer. Thus, an article on miners, their wages and their problems suggesting the need to make high offers to induce men into the mines violated the spirit of a 1974 regulation:

> 11. In connection with the need to intensify the mining of coal and the mining of iron, copper, zinc and lead ore, a number of decisions have been made regarding wages and fringe benefits in order to make mining work, and especially work underground, more attractive. These decisions apply to miners and certain other groups of mining and mine-construction workers. Information about the wage and fringe-benefit privileges (without information about monthly wages) may be permitted *only in announcements and other materials* specifically intended for use in the hiring of personnel. (New version, October 31, 1974; canceled November 23, 1974)

One *Polityka* article, however, rather than glorifying the high wages of the miners, suggested that the wage package, however high it was for some, was disadvantageous to most miners and that conditions in the mines and the towns built for their workers were not good enough to encourage workers to remain there:

> In a report entitled "Above and Below Ground" (*Polityka*, No. 49), J. Fabirkiewicz, describing "everyday mining routine" on the basis of the Staszic Mine, stressed that "coal is now the prima donna of modern Poland." Our observations concerning his article have to do with passages evaluating wage scales and the methods used to recruit new employees at the Staszic Mine. The editors, after appealing to the Department of Propaganda, Press and Publishing of the PZPR Central Committee, acceded to our objections to the passages below:
>
> ". . . Miners working below ground are entitled to double bonuses, which are paid once a month (not once a quarter as was hitherto the case), provided they do not miss a single working day for any reason whatsoever. A double [bonus] 'thirteenth' [month] salary (they call it a 'fourteenth' salary) is awarded on the same conditions. It does not pay to get sick or to go to a sanatorium. . . .
>
> "This is an attractive benefit for those who are young and healthy, as well as hard-working. As of November, of the 5,000 men working at the Staszic Mine, seven were earning wages in the 20,000-złoty category, and quite a few in the 10–15,000 category. (This, of course, only refers to men who are actually working with coal.) The older, less adroit and less healthy miners and middle- and upper-level supervisors are less enthusiastic about the new wage and benefit package. The mine

is constantly trying to recruit new workers. Given the overall man-power shortages, these efforts are not very effective; in Lublin Voivod-ship there have been few results, though some small encouragement is offered by the prospect of cooperation with the leadership of the Union of Socialist Rural Youth of Warsaw Voivodship. . . . It would seem that, given this situation, there is a need to reorganize the system of recruiting so that it is based not on simple canvassing (which has proven so ineffective in the face of a declining surplus labor force), but mainly on the recruitment of graduates of trade schools, who are, of course, young and hence more readily adaptable to this admittedly strenuous occupation in the course of a three-year apprenticeship.

"It appears that in the present situation, which is, moreover, particu-larly difficult in Silesia, where the mines must compete for workers with the Bielsko Automotive Plant and the Katowice Steel Works, there is a need for a rational plan to handle fluctuations [in the labor force] and to solve recruitment problems. It is certainly crucial to introduce a permanent system of high wages for miners, based on clear principles. There is also a need to resolve the problem of vacation time and free Saturdays, no matter how difficult it may be. This year's provision of one free Saturday a month for the miners should not be used again next year, when most people will have 12 free Saturdays.

"A program is already underway to build a large number of housing units. It may not produce the expected results, however, if, as is the case at the Staszic Mine, the planners forget to construct a network of support facilities and create entire little towns of apartment buildings in the middle of nowhere with almost no stores, restaurants, bars, cafés or clubs nearby. And, moreover, with very few links to the outside world (no mass transit on Sundays!).

"It would seem that these problems ought to be investigated by an appropriate team of sociologists and psychologists familiar with the work and special conditions in the mines, as well as with the whole complex of interpersonal relations peculiar to the mining industry. These are the cause of most conflicts, especially between older and younger miners. The younger workers, raised under new and different conditions, do not find the kinds of behavior that were approved of in earlier years to be acceptable anymore, even when their older col-leagues are motivated by the most noble of intentions. This applies equally to unskilled recruits, graduates of ZSG, and technicians and trainees from mining and metallurgical academies." (*Report on Materi-als Censored*, December 1–15, 1974)

Shortages of personnel and poor-quality work in a number of indus-trial sectors were blamed on insufficient rewards. This kind of criticism was excised even when it appeared in newspapers written and published by workers in individual plants and dealt with tiny groups of people:

An article entitled "Vocational Instructor or Foreman" (*Technika + Ekonomika + Organizacja = Postęp*, No. 23, published by the Automated Industrial Equipment Plant in Ostrów Wielkopolski), analyzing the causes of the inferior quality of vocational education, read in part as follows:

". . . A workshop director in one of the country's better trade schools came right to the point and said, 'Who is going to give up a job in industry for a career in education? What kind of good skilled worker is going to leave his industry when salary scales are organized in such a strange way?'

" 'The Teachers' Charter of Rights' spells out quite clearly the conditions under which teachers are to be employed. But what is good for a mathematics teacher or a Polish-language teacher does not necessarily prove satisfactory for a metalworker.'

"Succinctly put, teachers' salaries are determined on the basis of their level of education and the length of their service in a particular trade. . . .

"But the only thing is that a master's or engineer's degree is not at all necessary for a vocational instructor. A good craftsman does not have to rely on diplomas to establish his credentials. His concrete and demonstrated practical knowledge is of greater importance.

"At the same time, a master craftsman who switches to a career in education faces reduced earnings. And who can afford that?

"Not just anyone is qualified to be a good vocational instructor. And yet appeals and promises of pedagogical satisfaction are not enough to attract first-class craftsmen to the teaching profession.

"And the fact of the matter is that the prompt resolution of this dilemma should be 'taken to heart' by those officially responsible for the educational system. Because industry cannot afford to wait. . . ."

(*Report on Materials Censored*, December 1–15, 1975)

Criticisms of low wages in some occupations were also related to problems affecting public safety:

A passage discussing the excessively low wages paid to firefighters as a reason for the aging of the personnel employed in plant fire brigades was deleted from an article by A. Sikorski entitled "Learning to Show Wisdom Before Things Go Wrong, Before Things Start Burning."

(*Prawo i Życie,* No. 50) (*Report on Materials Censored,* December 1–15, 1975)

As early as 1974 the *Report on Materials Censored* for March 16–31 noted that "there was far-reaching criticism of wage regulations recently introduced for certain vocational groups." Much of this discussion took place in low-circulation journals published for specific professions or in very limited circulation publications. Here, too, the underlying theme was that some of the intelligentsia had either been overlooked in the 1973 wage regulations or simply were always underpaid. Professional journals presented their groups' demands for higher pay and their feelings about being overworked and underappreciated. Poor working conditions and low pay were specifically blamed for the chronic shortages of personnel in such professions as education and medicine. The censors almost always deleted these protests.

One example of such impermissible discontent was an article in a journal produced by medical students and trainees. The author of "The Provinces—Light and Dark Spots" (*Nowy Medyk,* No. 6) was negative in his assessment of the working conditions and earnings of provincial physicians when compared with the situation of physicians in Western countries, and called for a change in Polish practices. The following passages were deleted from the article to remove these negative images and transform the thrust of the article:

"... The health service finds itself on the threshold of an increasingly crucial and welcome reform. A first step toward reform has already been taken. This was the creation of the National Health Service Fund. <u>Unfortunately, as a matter of fact, no one knows what the next step should be.</u> The needs are tremendous. ...

"... Our present health system is, given present needs, outdated. It served its purpose perfectly when there was a need to create a universal, free health care system. It is high time for us to do away with the halfway measures <u>heralded as 'reforms'</u> (I have in mind chiefly the creation of the Health Care Enterprises), and to create a new public health care system from the ground up. ... <u>The most serious shortcoming in the provinces is the low pay. A physician here earns 2,000–2,700 złotys (after 25 years of study).</u> Theoretically, this is pay for a six-hour [day], but in practical terms, if we add three extra hours of volunteer work (for example, in a specialization) in a hospital, the work often lasts nine to ten hours on a so-called full rotation. ... Sometimes, after seeing 40 to 50 patients, he has to make eight to ten house calls.

... If a physician involves himself in his work, makes careful examinations and really concerns himself with the care of his patients, he will have more and more patients and less and less time, but his pay will be the same. . . . In France, a physician sees from five to ten patients a day. . . .

". . . The physician leaving the clinic at five or seven in the evening can no longer get anything for dinner. He can't eat at a cafeteria because there aren't any. . . . He does not get paid for the time he spends traveling to make house calls (and especially not for the time spent walking up and down stairs), and does not and will not receive a thirteenth month's salary the way his colleague, the industrial physician, does. He has to buy his own soap to wash his hands, and he does not get a 'tea allotment' unless somebody in the administration treats him. He cannot even get free medication as military personnel, miners, railway workers and others do.

". . . In talks with dozens of physicians in clinics, one idea kept coming up again and again: a desire for change (we should add, for the better) in the payment system and in the system of administration. . . . I think that the regional clinic is the most important treatment facility, and should be given high priority. The raising of salaries to two or three times their present levels and an insistence on more highly qualified personnel than in other parts of the health care system are essential. . . ." (*Report on Materials Censored,* March 16–31, 1974)

Although there was a serious campaign to encourage greater respect for government administrators, journalists were not allowed to reveal that the administrators, often suspected by the population of living better than anyone else, earned far less than the industrial managers who worked under their direction:

In an article entitled "A Non-Apostolic Epistle, Effort and Its Equivalent" (*Barwy,* No. 12), H. Gaworski noted that there is a widespread belief that "in the world of work, in the broadest sense, the ration of remuneration to actual merit is not always what it should be." Gaworski added:

". . . Everyone is aware, for example, of the degree of responsibility for the overall conditions of life in a given region that is borne by the *gmina* authorities, particularly the *gmina* manager. . . . For doing a good job in the performance of his duties, the chairman of a *gmina* cooperative receives appropriate bonuses and rewards, while the *gmina* manager receives nothing extra for doing his job well. And it therefore often happens—not at all rarely—that the chairman of a *gmina* cooperative, even though he shoulders far less responsibility than the *gmina* manager, who has jurisdiction over the cooperative and many other institutions within the *gmina,* earns a much higher salary than the *gmina* manager, his nominal superior. . . . A similar situation exists in the case of principals of consolidated *gmina* schools, the directors of certain cultural centers, plant directors and so on. . . . I have used the *gmina* to illustrate this problem, but it is also a problem in higher-level organizations and institutions. It is said that the people expect appropriate action to be taken to correct these problems." (*Report on Materials Censored,* December 1–15, 1974)

As it became apparent that broad attacks on the wage structure were not going to be allowed, journalists increasingly focused on questions of benefits and the specific wage needs of their constituencies. These kinds of suggestions were deleted, even from trade and factory-produced journals. Examples include calls for:

—an increase in average wages in the construction industry (*Budownictwo—Zeszyt Naukowy,* No. 28, published by the Engineering and Agricultural Academy in Bydgoszcz);

—"The reevaluation of wage scales and an increase in bonuses paid for working under conditions harmful to health" in the Chemarz Plant in Kielce *(Słowo Ludu);*

—"an earlier retirement option for workers with thirty years of service in the industry is one of the fundamental questions that remains to be resolved in the coke industry and, for that matter, in the metallurgical industry as a whole" (*Koksochemik Wałbrzyski,* No. 22, published by the Wałbrzych Coking Plant). (*Report on Materials Censored,* December 1–15, 1975)

A number of these critiques of benefits reflected causes and constituencies long championed by individual journalists who had become specialists in a particular area. To strengthen their arguments, journalists referred to the obstacles that inadequate benefits created in achieving the social goals Gierek supposedly championed. This subjected articles dealing, for example, with the problems that faced young families, to dual causes for censorship: raising the issue of wages and discussing the social problems exacerbated by wage problems. The censors were unwilling to allow the bleak picture of life in Poland and of the state's provisions for its citizens this kind of information drew.

The disproportionality of wages, benefits and expenses and the existence of poverty in Poland were so clear from the statistics presented in one scholarly work entitled *Minimum Standards for Social Benefits*—the first study to set forth the concept and exact data on subsistence-level income in Poland—that the book was released in an edition of just 1,000 copies (a number that essentially kept it off the market). This interference in the dissemination of scholarly research on social needs was attacked in a scholarly journal produced for economists. The censors noted that:

> A remark was deleted from J. Rosner's review of A. Tymowski's *Minimum Standards for Social Benefits: A Methodology and Attempt to Define the Problem* (PWN: 1973), which was carried in the bimonthly *Ekonomista* (No. 6), stating that "the 'basket' of goods and services put together by the Central Statistical Office to determine the cost of living and the fluctuations in real wages has not been disclosed to the public." A statement was also deleted which expressed the opinion that "the publication of this work, which discussed issues of vital importance to the lives of each of our 33 million fellow citizens, in an edition of just 1,000 copies surely indicates that our publications policy fails to take the minimum requirements of society into account." (*Report on Materials Censored,* December 1–15, 1974)

Criticism of the book itself was heavily censored in another review that appeared in *Sociological Studies,* the major scholarly journal of sociological research:

> In his review of A. Tymowski's *Minimum Standards for Social Benefits,* in *Studia Socjologiczne,* No. 2, J. Strzelecki commented on the table proposed by Tymowski as a basis for the " 'basket' of monthly personal expenditures encompassed by this 'social minimum' ":

EXPENDITURE CATEGORIES (IN ZŁOTYS)

TYPE OF NEED	SINGLE	RETIRED	MARRIED
Food	682	546	2,110
Clothing and Shoes	252	218	833
Housing	234	151	405
Heat and Light	93	90	216
Hygiene and Health Care	60	45	192
Culture and Education	60	62	117
Transportation and Communication	54	25	125
Miscellaneous	72	57	122
TOTAL	1,515	1,202	4,210

N.B. These statistics are taken from the original documents.

"These minimum standards are supposed to be normative in character, i.e., the result of a properly implemented social policy should be that 'every citizen in the country should be able to satisfy' at least the minimum needs drawn up by that policy. However, it seems that the amounts indicated by Tymowski's book are not pegged high enough to encourage a more active policy in this regard, and they also do not correspond fully to socially conditioned needs. The figures compiled by A. Tymowski—and even more, his table of categorized expenditures, which has a more vivid impact on our imaginations—seems to me to come disturbingly close to what I would characterize as a 'social vegetative minimum.' In other words, I believe that the range of needs covered by the category 'culture and education' is too narrow and limited, at least in comparison with the needs 'recognized as socially justified' at this stage of our country's economic development. Giving broader scope to this category in any definition of minimum social welfare standards would seem to be one of the fundamental prerequisites for any cultural policy that is to be implemented in a truly socialist manner, i.e., a policy based on the mass availability of 'works of the spirit.' . . ." (*Report on Materials Censored,* July 16–31, 1975)

The Cost of Living

The attacks on wages and social benefits that appeared in the mid-seventies were not the result of a wage freeze. In fact, part of Gierek's economic program was an effort to increase worker productivity by increasing living standards. What this created, however, was a rapid increase in the demand for goods that remained in short supply. To control the demand, and to pay for the costs of imports and the increasing costs of subsidized food production and industrialization, store prices had to be increased. But since price increases in 1956 and 1970 had been a major factor in bringing down party leaders, Gierek was initially unwilling to deal with this problem openly. Instead, old products were given new names (and new, higher prices), imported goods were given artificially high list prices and then marked down slightly for sale, and prices for some services and nonessential goods were simply increased. Throughout, as one censored quip in a plant newspaper put it, "Most changes in price are shrouded in silence." The result was not the blind acceptance and social peace that had been hoped for: on June 24, 1976, the first public announcement of open increases in food prices triggered widespread rioting.

The consumer gains of the earlier seventies had in fact brought some popular satisfaction, but this rapidly ebbed away as consumers (and journalists) saw through the sham of price maneuvers. As the censors pointed out in their midyear report in 1974:

> During the last quarter there was a decline in the number of publications containing criticism of the price level and price system. The problem of higher prices for "new" products, which has figured prominently in interventions over the past dozen or so months, was important only at the beginning of this quarter. People writing on this question suggested that such increases in prices were justified neither by an improved assortment of items nor by an upgrading of the quality of the products in question. Examples of such "novelty pricing" were also cited, such as the new prices for footwear and some clothing. The following trade practice noted by some authors also aroused criticism: "in Bydgoszcz shops you often buy an item with a price that has been crossed out and replaced by one in pencil. . . . Practices of this sort annoy consumers. . . . Why are price increases imposed secretly [so that they] come as a surprise to the customer?" *(Szpilki)*
>
> In most cases, the material questioned contained criticism of the level of prices on particular goods and services. For example, opinions about the high cost of camping equipment, sailboats, yachts, footwear, imported Greek textiles, float pumps, furniture, books, fruit and bus fares were eliminated. (*Bulletin of Themes of Materials Censored*, Second Quarter, 1974)

Innovations that resulted in increased prices for food products did not go unnoticed, though they did go unpublished. One such case involved the imported concept of packaging milk in foil pouches:

> J. Doliński's "Bag of Milk" (*Wiadomości,* No. 11), commented in a critical manner on the Wrocław Dairy Cooperative's introduction of the sale of "select homogenized milk with 3.2 percent butterfat content at 5.50 złotys per liter, packaged in foil bags." We proposed that the item be reedited, but the editors rejected the entire text. The following passage particularly aroused our objections:
>
> ". . . The new milk was greeted with applause by the mass media. Appreciating its value, I do not want to close my eyes to the negative social implications of the new technology. Besides the virtues listed, the nutritive value of the homogenized milk remains the same. And it is a rare mass consumption food product whose new packaging increases its retail price by a whole 25 percent! No commentary is needed.

Assuming the average bottle can be refilled 30 times, packaging in foil is four times as expensive. . . ." (*Report on Materials Censored*, March 16–31, 1974)

Other financial maneuvers were also noted by writers. In one case, the censors reported that in a specialized volume on banking they had not been willing to allow a passing reference to the fact that payments on apartments as yet unbuilt were used to fund other projects rather than to cover the costs of building the apartments. The problem of criticism and discussion of various price manipulations was, in fact, so serious that an entire memo for the censors was devoted to "errors" in this area in 1974. In more popular journals, poking fun at advertised sale prices was taboo:

On the other hand, the following information was removed from the "Taken from Life" column:

"A low-price sale of furniture was announced with a great deal of excitement by the Szczecin Platan Furniture Store. Spanish furniture was on sale. At the reduced price, a Granada suite cost 84,440 złotys, instead of the former 86,120 złotys. 'Toledo' was reduced to 111,570 złotys from 112,700. The price of Spanish furniture was reduced on the average by 2 percent. People who previously could not afford, let us say, a dining room set for 112,700 złotys were now offered the marvelous possibility of buying it for the accessible price of 111,570 złotys." (Informative Note No. 55)

Likewise it was impermissible to note that imported goods were sold at inflated złoty prices:

In a *Gazeta Handlowa* article by E. Gajo entitled "Not All Knit Goods Are of Equal Quality," a remark to the effect that prices of imported Greek knit goods "are too high, at least by 50 percent," was expurgated.

In Issue No. 6 of the monthly *Sad Nowoczesny,* a remark to the effect that the high price of the insecticide "Benlate" (for sale in Pewex stores [State stores where goods are sold only for hard currency]) "makes the use of this agent totally unprofitable for fruit-growers" was deleted from an editorial reply. (Informative Note No. 55)

Restaurant prices came in for some attack in the Polish press after a national reclassification of restaurants raised prices in better-quality establishments. An article submitted by the weekly *Literatura* broke far more taboos than that on discussions of price increases. It openly attacked the difference in quality between the restaurants catering to foreigners and the wealthy and those catering to the rest of the population—a difference that occurred in most other areas of life:

In an article entitled "Light and Shadow in the Restaurant Industry" (*Literatura*, No. 12), K. Jagiełło was critical in her assessment of the prevailing situation in the restaurant industry. In her opinion, the industry is bent on making profits from the sale of monopoly items and gives priority to foreign tourists, continuing to be a "stepmother" to ordinary citizens, for whom it is a problem to obtain an inexpensive, tasty, nonalcoholic meal. The article contains indirect attacks on recent decisions (increasing profit margins) that have not, in the author's opinion, corrected the situation. The following passages were deleted from the text:

". . . New profit margins for eating establishments were introduced as of February 1. The categories of existing facilities have also been changed. Category I restaurants have now become too expensive for the pockets of the average citizen. Category II facilities have also become too expensive for those who must eat dinner out. Category III and Category IV restaurants are within the range of the average person's possibilities. In popular language, they are referred to as 'dives.' This is an insulting expression and since customers call most of the popular restaurants in our country by that name, you can see that they do not have a very fond opinion of them. It would be worthwhile to think about restaurants and, in general, about what the restaurant industry is offering its patrons today, when any chance of eating a somewhat more expensive dinner under better circumstances is gone. Hence the average Pole is condemned to school and worker cafeterias. What is that like? The song written after the war that began with the words 'Cafeteria, cafeteria, you are a dirty word' could be popular today, too. . . . It is my firm belief that plant cafeterias should be run not only by professionals, but by the best professionals. The proper meal can restore the strength that an individual has expended at work, can even increase his strength, and can help to give him a feeling of satisfaction about the hours he passes on the job. Why are popular taverns and restaurants for foreign tourists considered to be proper matters for the attention of the food service industry, while school and plant cafeterias are not?

"Probably because when we talk about the food service industry in this country, we think only in terms of enterprise income. . . . Now we are arguing about basic differences in profit margins. Restaurants can be freer in setting the size of their profit margin and have more ready access to the profit gained from them than they used to. Sound reasoning should therefore make them more interested in their customers, who can be enticed with better service.

"Maybe somebody wants to operate that way, but I personally do not believe that the situation in our food service industry has changed in any basic way as a result of this measure. If only because few restaurants complained about a shortage of money or profits in the past. . . . There was once a plan to make a poultry restaurant in the main floor of Junior [Department Store in Warsaw], where the You and I Café is. There was also a proposal to have a dining room in the Caucasus Restaurant, which is a nightspot and is unused during the day. Somehow all these projects fell through, even though carrying them out did not require any particular expenditures. It is clearly not a question of money. It is a question of conception—the conception of the development of the restaurant industry. I am in favor of an industry that first of all seeks to meet the needs of the citizen. At present, we have managed to create a deepening gulf between the best and the worst restaurants, providing some sort of opportunity for foreign tourists and our wealthiest citizens and practically none at all for Polish tourists or average mortals who need to eat dinner once a day." . . .

After changes were made in the text three times, a fourth version of the above article entitled "Dinner Polish Style" was accepted for publication. (*Report on Materials Censored,* March 16–31, 1974)

Even criticism of prices for services used only by the affluent—yachting, for example, or automobile servicing in a nation of nearly five million cars—were removed from various articles. However irrelevant boat ownership might have been for most workers, a trade union newspaper was not allowed to criticize high prices in this area —it implied an unequality of opportunity for ownership that did not go with an ideology of vacation luxuries being made available for all.

In an article by J. Iwaszkiewicz entitled "Yachts for Everyone," published in *Głos Pracy,* references to the "excessively stiff" prices of racing and touring gear for boats were challenged, and a statement that "the high prices of this gear are retarding the growth of boat ownership" was deleted.

Criticism of the price list for services rendered by the Polish Motorists' Association was stricken from an article entitled "Touristic Monstrosities" *(Tempo)*:

". . . Increases in the prices for services were all out of proportion.

For example, for every kilometer that an emergency repair truck travels in haste to the aid of a damaged car or motorcycle, eight złotys must be paid during the daytime and even more at night. The costs of towing the vehicle are not included.

"We should fear that, with prices calculated in this way, a useful service will go to waste, since, contrary to the opinion of the experts who determine these prices, it is not easy to find millionaires among the automobile drivers and motorcyclists traveling on the highways." (*Report on Materials Censored,* March 16–31, 1974)

Quantity and quality of goods and services became even more sensitive issues than price. It had become increasingly clear as the seventies passed that little of worth could be bought at any price. One writer in the weekly economic supplement of Warsaw's leading daily accused "socialist economies" of limiting production for their own benefit while simultaneously attacking "capitalist states" for doing the same:

In his article "In Whose Interest?" (*Życie i Nowoczesność*), J. Chłopecki questioned the assumption that "the primary goal of the socialist producer is the satisfaction of social needs." The following passages were deleted:

"Several years ago in our country there was talk of overproduction of radios, despite the fact that we were far from the point where every family had a radio and in terms of number per 1,000 households we were in one of the last places in Europe, because it can be more profitable for producers, even under socialism, to limit production in order to maintain a high price for the items they produce, or else to create an artificial demand for a pseudo-novelty.

"It is worth pointing out that even the greatest fads in fashion— which incline women to buy white stockings one time, those with seams another, ones without seams, or with dots, and so on—would not ensure the producers a profit if the stockings did not run. The production of durable stockings is by no means beyond the capacity of modern technology, but slowly, discreetly, the durability of stockings has been reduced both by capitalist and by socialist producers. The former are concerned with making (at least) their planned profits, while the latter are interested in achieving the planned indices of increased productivity. . . ." (*Report on Materials Censored,* March 16–31, 1974)

Most criticism, however, was far from theoretical. One of the main topics of concern for both censors and journalists was the meat shortage. The problem was attacked from many angles, tying meat prices and supplies to broader promises of the Gierek regime.

1) Nutrition

In Issue No. 50 of *Kierunki,* in the column "Elsewhere in the Press," in an article taking issue with the arguments advanced by Z. Jurkiewicz on the food crisis in *Dookoła Świata,* a statement in which the author noted that "more than 10 percent" of our population "is less than well fed" was challenged. (*Report on Materials Censored,* December 1–15, 1974)

2) Family Welfare

In an article entitled "Christmas Eve Dinner" (*Stolica,* No. 50–51), M. Sadzewicz claimed, *inter alia,* that "the gradual extinction of close-knit family life is, in part, the result of the destruction of the tradition whereby families take their meals together at a common table." A statement in which Sadzewicz remarked that "if there is no meat in the stores, while it continues to be available in the cafeterias, a final blow is dealt to the traditional gathering of the family around the dinner table" [was deleted]. (*Report on Materials Censored,* December 1–15, 1974)

3) Misadministration

It was recommended that the following passage in a report by A. Zię- ba, filed from Płock, entitled "A City's Second Childhood" (*ITD,* No. 50), be rewritten:

"Meat is on sale twice a day, at eight o'clock in the morning and at four o'clock in the afternoon, so that people getting off work can buy what they need. But this is rarely possible, since nonworking grand-mothers start queueing up at five o'clock in the morning and wait in line until noon, and if the line is unusually long or the meat shipment delivered to the shops is unusually skimpy, the customer who just drops in will have to buy smoked mackerel or chicken loaf at 130 złotys a kilo, or cheese, which is always in plentiful supply. Nobody knows why meat-eaters are having such a hard time, since every month the Munici-pal Administration distributes 1,000 tons of meat products to all the stores, which comes out to about 10 kilos per capita per month. So, either some people are buying more than they need, or the above estimates are invalidated by purchases made by people passing through town, or too much meat is being sold to cafeterias and restaurants, of which there are still not all that many, or else some undetected evil-minded gnome is at work here, the same one who is creating so much mischief in Konin, Słupsk and several other places. . . ." (*Report on Materials Censored,* December 1–15, 1974)

Censors also prevented attention from being drawn to informal systems of rationing, especially when it implied that the rational reasoning behind the rationing was as much for political manipulation as for seeing to it that those truly in need received goods that were in short supply. In the following article, cuts not only blunted the attack on rationing but also changed the sense of the argument:

In a feature article entitled "To Each According to His Merit" (*ITD*, No. 20), we read:

". . . The time has come when, in order to buy a couch on the installment plan—or, to put it more elegantly, to obtain a couch on the installment plan—one has to show a marriage certificate. This is, after all, completely justified. . . . I would go even further with the regulation and would not sell any couches to single people at all. I think that in this way we could take care of many social problems in a manner beneficial to the state. For example, we could sell birthcontrol pills only to families corresponding to the ideal model of two plus three, and television sets only to people with technical college diplomas. Not only would the latter relieve much of the burden of the ZURT [radio and television repair] outlets, but it also could not fail to have a good effect on the intellectual life of the rest of the nation.

"Items in short supply could be sold only to those who met particularly difficult preconditions. Sell ham only to people with yellow bathing caps, and fashionable suits only to heroes of labor. Moreover, we could say that this represents a special distinction for the very best [people], and not a burden imposed on everybody else." (*Report on Materials Censored*, May 1–15, 1974)

When workers rioted in June 1976 over the suddenly announced food price increases, objecting to the increases and demanding real information and consultation before such measures were taken, the response was not to open the media to discussion, but to impose an even deeper silence. Panic buying brought on by rumors of price increases on sugar depleted the supplies of that commodity. Thus the regime was forced to import sugar, a product that Poland had exported during the interwar period. As panic buying of other foodstuffs and consumer goods caused temporary shortages and serious overbuying, the regime responded by issuing the following order to ban information that might encourage hoarding of goods that might be rationed:

155. All material calling for or suggesting (directly or indirectly) the extension of the coupon system to commodities other than sugar should be eliminated. (August 14, 1976)

Local government attempts to deal with the meat crisis by selling workers meat at their place of work—a tactic that was later to be employed all over Poland—could not be discussed. The unwillingness of government leaders to allow broader discussion of the meat problem and efforts to solve it was a sign of their fear that demand for such measures might spread to so large a group and raise expectations to such a degree that even special distribution measures could not satisfy them:

161. This December *Gazeta Robotnicza* and *Słowo Polskie* published a communiqué of the Department of Trade of the Wrocław Voivodship administration concerning the sale of ham and high-quality processed meats by enterprises and institutions.

No material on the Wrocław initiative or attempts to promote similar initiatives in other voivodships should be permitted.

All materials on other forms of regulated sale of meat should also be eliminated.

Materials of an official nature (for example, communiqués of the *województwo* departments of trade) should be held up and referred to the GUKPPiW administration.

This instruction is intended solely for the information of censors. (December 16, 1976)

Even information about the achievement of the much touted promise to produce color television sets on an RCA license proved too sensitive to publish. In part, this was because the sets were exorbitantly priced and basically unavailable:

163. Until further notice, no information (articles, mentions) of the price and conditions of sale of the new Polish color television sets should be permitted. This prohibition also applies to possible reprints of *Monitor Polski* No. 3/1977 or *Kurier Polski* from February 16 of this year, where the price and conditions of prepayment for future buyers of Polish color television were discussed. (February 19, 1977. This instruction also applies to any commentary related to the government presidium's repeal of Council of Ministers' Resolution No. 8, dated January 1974. Information on this subject was published by the Polish Press Agency on February 18, 1977.)

The ultimate result of the protests in 1976 and of the emerging economic crisis enveloping Poland was not an open discussion of the achievements and shortcomings of the economy, but a final shutdown of all discussion of living standards in Poland. The following order, put out after the Workers' Defense Committee had begun to talk about the dire conditions under which the nation's workers lived and worked, was considered of such great significance that it was delivered first verbally and then as a written, encoded regulation signed by the Vice-Chairman of the Main Office instead of remaining unsigned, as was customary:

> 170. Information on monthly nationwide indices of earnings, prices, labor productivity and employment may be permitted for publication only in official communiqués, which will be provided to PAP by a government press spokesman.
>
> Vice-Chairman E. Adamiak
> (Cryptogram, March 2, 1977)

Family Life

The growing economic crisis in Poland cut sharply into most areas of national life. One key area of decline was in basic and expected social services like education, health care and social welfare. Journalists did try to report on this decline, but much of what they had to say appeared only in the censors' reports.

Among the issues on which journalists and scholars focused their attention was the complex of problems related to family life in Poland. Many of these problems, it was suggested, were either created by or could be alleviated by changes in government policy. And although some of this discussion was allowed to appear in the press and specialized journals, much was removed by the censors. A great deal of the discussion was centered on the need for greater investment in social welfare. Other critics pointed out the failure of central planning to provide a viable environment for healthy family life, especially for families with two working parents.

The bulletin of materials censored in the second quarter of 1974 summarized many of the basic issues raised, all reflecting the realization that Gierek's investment policies would not bring real prosperity to the population unless priorities were reevaluated:

One of the key areas of intervention was the problem of state family policy. In the items questioned, this policy was judged to be unsatisfactory, and there were demands that it be made more dynamic. For example, people wrote about the threat posed to national population growth by "the adverse influence of the contemporary family's material living conditions." It was stated that "at least half of the elderly, about 1.5 million people, live in difficult circumstances in Poland" *(Chrześcijanin w Świecie)*. Another item pointed out that the family is left largely on its own in its "investment" or "input" function (the support and upbringing of future workers). At the same time it called for the state to increase social assistance.

The materials questioned also contained very specific proposals for meeting the problems of working mothers and women raising children. It was pointed out that the free maternity leave provided in the past is inadequate and there was a call for various sorts of leave with pay.

It was proposed that a pro-birth policy be instituted, for example, through the "creation of child-care benefits for working women who stop working at their jobs during their child's infancy and nursery school period," "raising the family allowance for nonworking mothers" or else "raising the size of benefits in accordance with the number of children" from the present 11 to 25 percent of gross average wages to 30 and 50 percent of wages *(Chrześcijanin w Świecie)*. ("The Part-time Employment of Women"—Proceedings of a PAX symposium)

In other publications it was suggested that "family allowances paid in the past for children should be paid for a nonworking mother caring for three or four children," and that retirement pay "should be provided for every woman who has raised at least two children." It was also stated that the benefit for the third child of a nonworking mother "should be at least 1,000 złotys." There was a call to reduce, or at least limit, night work for women. Czechoslovakia, Hungary and Great Britain were cited as examples. *(Słowo Powszechne, Odgłosy, Chrześcijanin w Świecie)*

The impact of the regime's pro-birth policies on the one hand and the economic exigencies forcing women into the marketplace on the other were a real concern to many journalists writing about social issues. In general terms, articles tended to point out that, despite its policy statements, the regime was not acting either to encourage women to have children by making child care manageable or to give enough support to families to enable women to work. In 1974, for example, one lay Catholic journal published an article listing a number of the social policies meant to encourage women to have more children, policies that were advocated by various government leaders as "pro-family"—the stance supported ostensibly by Gierek. The article was censored, however, since the regime was unwilling to have these policies spelled out so explicitly and thereby raise expectations for real new gains for women with children:

> In over a dozen texts, critical judgments concerning family policy and the material and social environment created for the family and various social and vocational groups were challenged.
>
> *Chrześcijanin w Świecie* (No. 27) presented an article by Z. Droźdek entitled "The Family and Economic Life," from which extensive passages criticizing our family policy, particularly "benefits outside the wage system," were eliminated. . . .
>
> In another item presented for this issue of *Chrześcijanin w Świecie,* T. Zembrzuski's "Social and Legal Measures for the Protection of Motherhood and the Family: Results of a Symposium of the Institute of Labor and Social Affairs," we questioned the following passages, among others:
>
> "Economic measures include: cash benefits during maternity leave, monthly benefits (supplements) for families with children, lump-sum benefits paid on the birth of a child, monthly benefits for nonworking mothers raising children, relief provided by the state to families with children (income tax credits, reductions in rent, priority in obtaining housing and so on), other benefits for children, such as free school equipment, clothing and meals, discounts on transportation and so on. . . .
>
> "The legal instruments of pro-birth policy include, for example, laws forbidding abortion. . . . The question of families with a large number of children should be considered only in the context of social policy, not demographic policy. On the other hand, demographic policy should be aimed at reducing the number of childless or one-child families. Family benefits paid in the past for children should be paid for nonworking mothers caring for three or four children.
>
> "A significant increase in the size of the aid to families with children, depending on the number of children, is recommended. At present, for example, benefits for a three-child family constitute 11.6 to 17.4 percent of average gross earnings, and 17.9 to 25.5 percent for a four-child family. As a result of the proposed increases in benefits, these percentages would become 30 and 50, respectively.
>
> "We should also create child-care benefits for those working mothers who interrupt their careers for the first three years of their first child's

life. . . . Measures in the interest of the family should be undertaken as part of an immediate general program. The immediate program—for example, the five-year plan—should attack the most critical needs. . . .

". . . It is necessary to build up modern social assistance machinery. . . . Social assistance should operate not only directly but also through other social resources, such as pensions and retirement pay, medical care, housing policy and so forth.

"There is a call to take up, during the first five-year period, the cases of especially underprivileged children, to raise pensions and introduce an automatic pension escalator to at least maintain the real value of the money, to introduce cash benefits and services for families caring for the elderly, to modernize housing for the elderly . . . to expand children's homes, to increase the number of places in nurseries and pre-schools, to introduce free school lunches for all, and to expand the child-care services of elementary schools.

"In addition, the principle is advanced that women should have a free choice as to whether to get a job or stay at home after the birth of a child. It might be helpful here to have an appropriate system of benefits, since one of the most frequent reasons for a woman's taking a job is an economic one. . . . It is considered desirable to make it easier to obtain and collect family pensions, for instance, by eliminating the possibility that family pensions can be suspended after work-related accidents and by ensuring the right of distant relatives who were supported by the deceased to a pension as a dependent. . . ." (*Report on Materials Censored*, May 1–15, 1974)

At the same time, articles aimed at bettering women's position in the workplace were also blocked. Such discussions not only reflected badly on working conditions in general, but also pointed to the need to balance the needs of industry against human needs:

In an article entitled "The Social Aspects of Shorter Working Days" (*Studia Socjologiczne*, No. 2) J. Penc presented the results of research conducted among the workers of 11 light industrial enterprises in Łódź [where the textile industry is concentrated and women constitute the majority of the work force]. This research sought to evaluate various alternative means of shortening the working day that would be feasible under the socioeconomic conditions of our country. The following material was deleted from the article:

—the opinion that "the multiple shift schedule is especially arduous" and that "for social reasons it would be advisable in the near future to abolish the third shift, especially where women are concerned";

—the statement that working women "work, on the average, 17 hours a day, and the majority find it difficult to get enough sleep (on the average, especially among women textile workers, they lose about six hours of sleep [a week]). They do not have very much time to devote to raising their children, and they have no time at all for active recreation." A lengthening of the working day "could lead to a critical situation in many areas of life." (*Report on Materials Censored*, July 16–31, 1975)

Two other articles removed from leading national weeklies offer dramatic evidence of the poor conditions under which manual laborers had to work in areas that were almost entirely dominated by women. In both cases, the articles dealt with areas and problems that had already been recognized by the leadership. There had been a long, officially sponsored campaign to encourage more courteous service by bureaucrats and store personnel (most of whom were in low-salary positions), yet:

In *Życie Gospodarcze* (No. 28), in an article entitled "Both Sides of the Counter," D. Zagrodzka wrote about the causes of the frequent conflicts between salespeople and customers. It was recommended that the following passages be reedited:

"Analyzing the socioorganizational conditioning of the vocational role of women employed in trade . . . Marzena Mokryszewska and Teresa Przewłocka of the Institute of Domestic Trade stated that women working in shops, especially food stores, usually work out of economic need, not out of any personal desire. They would give up their jobs if only they had the possibility to do so. What is more, their families and husbands by no means consider women working to be a natural thing, and the women themselves are convinced that their work is not accepted in the family. . . .

"The attitude toward women's work in general, in conjunction with the real disadvantages of such work (overtiredness, an excessive burden of vocational and household duties) give rise, in the opinion of the authors, to a negative attitude that results not so much in a woman's deciding not to work—since she has to work—as in the development of bad attitudes that are bound to reflect on work quality." (Informative Note No. 55)

There had also been official acknowledgment of archaic working conditions in the textile industry in Łódź (where the bulk of the work force was women). In 1971, when women of the Łódź factories went on strike, Gierek had even met with them, acknowledged their difficulties and promised improvements. In 1974, director Andrzej Wajda made a film on the horrors of industrialization, *The Promised Land*, based on a nineteenth-century classic Polish novel set in the factories of Łódź. In an interview published in *Polityka* in 1975, he said he had made the film when he did because the nineteenth-century factory buildings and equipment were slated for modernization in the late seventies and he wanted to use them as authentic sets before that happened. But even though conditions in Łódź were a matter of public knowledge, and there were no objections to printing Wajda's comments in *Polityka*'s "cultural affairs section," an article appearing at the same time in *Zorza* that dealt specifically with contemporary working conditions and the delays in building and renovation at the plants was heavily censored:

> Interventions were made in several reports on working conditions in various plants.
>
> In an article entitled "Heavy Work—Light Industry. *Zorza* Pays a Visit to Milanówek" (*Zorza*, No. 51), D. Kosiarska described working conditions at the Milanówek Natural Silk Plant. The following statements were among those challenged:
>
> "... We go back to the weaving plant, where the outsider's first reflex is ... to run as far away from the place as possible! Bent figures stand over the looms clad in smocks and protective scarves. ... And the tempo! They keep up the same tempo for eight hours a day, working in a din that shakes and rattles the old walls down to their foundations. Their condition alone attests to the need for the plant's immediate demolition.
>
> "There are other rooms, nooks and crannies, and sections in Milanówek whose appearance and working conditions are reminiscent of old-fashioned factories. Well, let's at least take a look at the silk reeling frame operation. ... I walk into the middle of a large room and am overwhelmed by the sickening stench of scalded silkworm cocoons. ... The movements of the women working on the frame are quick, skillful, almost automatic. 'Washed out' from being constantly immersed in water, their hands show signs here and there—despite special protective lotions—of mycosis between the fingers, and the finger joints of the older women are deformed by arthritis. ...
>
> "The plant doctor, Dr. Alicja Dickson, knows the plant very well. She has been working here for nine years, and her parents were also associated with the plant. ... To a great extent, the employees are old and tired out from long years of work. Dr. Dickson says that 'most of

the women, my patients, came to work at Milanówek when they were still very young. Some of them were still in their teens. So it is hardly surprising that they are exhausted <u>and worn out.</u> And it is hard to classify all the occupational diseases, <u>among which I might mention hearing disorders, bronchitis, allergies, high blood pressure, neuroses.</u> . . . The outpatient group consists of 120 people. . . .

"In keeping with the principle that 'the plant is the people' [a Gierek-era slogan stressing popular labor as the critical element of production], <u>it is high time to finally give the go-ahead for the construction and modernization of a new Milanówek.</u> The technical designs and budget for the <u>construction of a new weaving plant and silk reel frame operation,</u> which would bring about a radical improvement in working conditions, and for the replacement of old machinery were approved by the Executive Director of the Association on July 31, 1974, and *should not* be permitted to lie around any longer in somebody's desk drawer, but should be translated into action. . . ." (*Report on Materials Censored,* December 1–15, 1975)

Education

The subject of education presented the Polish censors with another complex of problems. A part of the promise of Communist societies has been that all would have equal opportunity for education and that social mobility would depend on individual achievement rather than on family background or personal connections. Schools were also to be prime instruments in creating the new socialist man and, further, were presented as important tools for the modernization of Poland, the means by which Poland would attain equal footing with more developed countries.

But while regime propaganda trumpeted the glories of Polish education and the achievements of the new, highly educated younger generations, the reality was quite different. Not everyone could get into universities and technical schools—places were limited and were distributed on the basis of test scores or personal connections. Worker and peasant youth, who were not as well prepared academically as the children of the intelligentsia, were awarded special additional points that enabled them to attend the universities even if they did not score well on the entrance examinations. This was not only resented by those who could not get into university programs because they did not get the extra points, but, finally, did not even guarantee poor peasant and worker youth an education—they were given neither the funds necessary to live on nor the remedial aid that would have allowed them to complete their studies successfully. Other students got positions through their parents' connections and power, and, occasionally, their own political activities. For them, there were special points for political activity and also rector's seats given out at his discretion. At the same time, though many positions required a university or technical school education, many of the most educated in the society were paid far less than skilled workers. This gave the promise of social mobility through education a hollow ring.

Polish schools, from grade schools to universities, were also far from their propaganda images. As political instruments, they hardly met their goals. Most teachers in grade school and high school were not committed to communism.* Nor were they well trained. Until the reforms carried out by Gierek, grade school teachers did not need to have a full university degree. The result was that Polish education was not rigorous or consistent. It further failed to meet its stated goals of equality because the best teachers stayed in the major cities and the least qualified and committed went to the rural and worker schools, so some schools were far better than others.

At the university level, academic rank carried with it a great deal of prestige and status. And despite the injection of Marxist politics into the curriculum and the political constraints under which Polish academics had to work, university life was carried on far more independently than life in many other segments of society. University admissions were influenced by concerns about the requisite class balance, but those who remained in most programs tended to be well trained. Research was carried out in the humanities and in technical fields under the guidance of leading academics, and not merely as political work. In many fields, Polish academics and their work were respected internationally.

The Gierek era brought with it attempts to modernize the educational system and make it a more efficient producer of useful citizens for a mobilized and industrialized Poland. This involved the centralization of rural schools into larger consolidated schools, the introduction of a requirement for all grade school teachers but those who were near retirement to get master's degrees, and a redesigning of grade

---

*Joseph R. Fiszman, *Revolution and Tradition in People's Poland: Education and Socialization* (Princeton, N.J.: Princeton University Press, 1972.)

school and high school curricula to increase the amount of technical education and actual work experience students were given—at the expense of training in the humanities, especially in the Polish language and literature.

At the university and technical school level, the Gierek regime attempted in the mid-seventies to place scholarly research under its control. A national research plan was set up, projects were tied to central plans for funding and, more than ever before in postwar Poland, research projects were expected to have a sponsor and serve that sponsor's interests. At the same time, however, and just as the crest of the postwar baby boom was ready for college, Poland's growing economic problems brought with them a drop in educational funding. Even with quotas, workers and peasants and those with no personal clout had a harder and harder time getting places in the university, especially in the more prestigious programs. And those who were able to get accepted found that the state did not provide enough scholarship support to allow them to survive, much less live as their wealthier colleagues did. Finally, as journalists were trying to point out, by the mid-seventies, the academic world was becoming corrupted: places were kept aside for students with "pull," and faculty ranks and professorships were increasingly dependent not only on achievement but also on personal ties and, in some fields, political reliability.

For those who wrote about the educational system and for the censors who monitored what they wrote, the problems and the changes were difficult to handle. It was clear from the moment the educational reforms were announced that intellectuals, parents and students did not support them. At the same time, there were few who thought there was no need for change and modernization in an educational system that developed on its own in the fifties and sixties.

Even as the regime was making known its intention to reform radically some of the existing Polish educational practices, the censors forbade broad-scale attacks on the old system. The attacks themselves, even when they indicated the need for reform, provided evidence that neither the students nor the teachers were committed to the political rules of Marxism-Leninism—and, by extension, that the Polish population itself was not committed to those rules. Furthermore, they criticized something that reforms would not change, namely, the premium placed by educational institutions on conformity, the fact that schools taught students that they had to play by the rules—regardless of how hollow their commitment to those rules was. Under the old educational system, and even more under Gierek's reforms, students were expected to learn facts—not learn to think on their own or to question the system. So, when the weekly of Warsaw Technical University tried to publish the following essay criticizing a world that the students knew all too well, the bleak picture of the past it painted was—even with the reforms being carried out at the same time—all too applicable to the present to be permitted to appear. In addition, attacks on institutions and authorities even at far lower levels were too suggestive of problems that pervaded every level of the system and of the contempt in which the society held its political leaders to be allowed. Nor could this essay's unabashedly explicit attack on the meaninglessness and frustration of party membership be tolerated in any media, much less in a press for students the party wanted to recruit. The entire essay was cut:

"A Letter to Father. Before We Lose the Second Round," in *Politech-nik* (No. 37), was challenged. The author, a student in the fourth year (22 years old), looking back over his life, was critical of the methods, content and atmosphere of his schooling ("round one") and his higher education ("round two") as well as of the activity of youth organiza-tions. Below are portions of the "letter."

". . . I am 22 years old. I am a student in the fourth year. I belong to the first well-fed and well-raised 'generation,' a quick and skeptical generation, which grew up faster than its predecessors and began ear-lier to ask the teachers difficult questions. What did I learn from my school, a school with renown and traditions, named in honor of the Red Castellan?

"I learned that there's no sense in asking questions. I learned hypoc-risy, petty opportunism, laziness and bootlicking. I got my first lesson in how to work for show, how to write an effective report, how to copy and to cite, how to study for grades, and finally, what to do in order to have peace, a good reputation and a good report card. And since, as I've noted, I belong to a clever generation, I learned to do all of this quickly and effectively.

"Naturally, I wrote essays about the hero I would like to imitate, but in reality I had no ideal. History and literature were full of words and facts, but not people. There were no living, real people.

"Do you have any idea, O honored Super-zealots, how you are succeeding in making us feel revulsion for the characters in whom we ought to believe, whom we are supposed 'to love'? When will you learn that success in this field does not depend on the quantity of words, on the learning of biographies by heart? Don't the words 'must' and 'should' too often take the place of arguments, of attempts to convince?

"In the lyceum I lived through two great lectures on contemporary history. They came at a most crucial period, the one in which I was beginning to form my own opinions, my own view of the world, a period when every young person feels a sudden need to compare what he studies in school with life.

"I lost my first 'school' round. It is amazing how my teachers succeeded, in the course of two months, in changing my views. What had once been white suddenly became black. An avoidance of questions, an avoidance of discussion—my teachers did not manage to be partners.

"Nor did my school organization manage to be a partner. [Extracurricular organizations ranging from the scouts to Communist youth organizations were virtually required activities for Polish students. These groups, which became more politicized in upper grades, were controlled and directed by teachers or professional youth organization directors, some of whom used their positions to make political careers.] It was a parody—people were not too sure what it was they were saying, but they repeated it. (I pass in silence over the relation between membership in the organization and one's grade in physics. The sponsor was the physics teacher.)

"Nor did my parents succeed in being partners. Their 'examples from life' sowed even more confusion in the world of youthful conviction than they enlightened or gave perspective.

"But at the same time I became convinced that it is possible to teach and be raised in another fashion. I had a teacher who was fascinated by knowledge and erudition. She was a supporter of genuine truth, not an affected and superficial truth.

"She always said that the only source of satisfaction is an active life, a creative life. That's the way she lived. And as a matter of fact, she didn't keep her place warm for too long in my school. She was followed by 'a normal Polish teacher.'

"I also lost the first 'school' round with myself. I let myself be led by the hand, wore my school emblem, went to the barber and dressed in navy blue. I was obedient and obsequious. The kind of pupil that my teachers wanted to see.

"I began my higher education. I believed that one stage could come to an end, and that everything could start anew. . . .

"Reality provided a rather cold shower. On the one hand, I allowed myself to be frightened all too easily by a grade of "two," by a flunked exam, by the attendance register. On the other hand, I succeeded, with unusual speed, in adjusting, in being absorbed into the sleep-inducing mechanism of 'higher studies.' I quickly learned the secrets of success, the secrets of getting a high rank and, often, of cribbing.

"It turned out that I had adjusted well. I was able to get a respectable rank. I have a high average and, from time to time, receive university president's awards. I know that I am not, nor have I ever been, a good student. I have never managed to look for causes and connections—and, for that matter, nobody ever demanded that of me. I am simply a well-adapted student, although my grades say something different about me.

"My teachers. During the last three years: two excellent, four good, and the rest ... At times I have the impression that a large part of them don't want and don't try to teach me anything, that in their eyes I am a kind of intruder in the school. Contacts with the authorities? A lecture for 200 people, a written examination administered by a teaching assistant, a signature in the register—that is the only souvenir. That's all.

"Sometimes, my fathers, I am envious of you, of your universities. . . .

"Sometimes, my successors, I am envious of you, and of your options, about which we can only dream today. We can only dream. . . .

"In the Organization [apparently a reference to membership in a Communist youth organization] I sought everything that the school had not managed to give me—satisfaction. Here, too, I wanted to start all over again, to forget about my old experiences and premonitions.

"The magic of reports, my discouragement, small and great departmental diplomacy, all of these came with a torrent of words about how to involve the so-called 'gray' student blessed with less understanding than those in the Organization. And in the end [we were] marching in place or going down the wrong road. With time, routine and organizational eloquence and phraseology take hold. And everything was just as official and just as obsequious. . . . After weeks of work, attempts to escape [from the regimentation] and then weeks of inertia, I couldn't take it, and so I came back, each time with more doubt and less of a choice. Until finally, the last time, I didn't come back. I never thought about turning in my Organization membership card—although I should have done it. Now I pay my dues once a semester, when necessary, have my membership verified, when necessary, vote and elect. I am among the 76 percent of the students in my department who belong to the Organization.

"On the advice of the school hygienist, I ate a great deal of phosphate as a child and, as a result, have an excellent memory. For this reason, I no longer go to plenary sessions of the department council or the university council or to meetings with the dean. I know what they will talk about and I know how they will present their conclusions later. The discussion will be conducted according to the proposed outline of discussion; the discussants will emphasize, limit themselves, draw attention to, and pass from the quantitative to the qualitative stage of development while defining the essence and taking into consideration changing circumstances. It was the same last year. It will be the same a year from now. And two years from now.

"Squandering words, we are nonetheless amazed that they come to mean less and less, and that those using them often have something completely different in mind. Great things, involvement, dedication, work, activity, success, satisfaction, tradition. But perhaps we should begin with an elucidation of basic concepts. Perhaps we should find what their significance is today—that's right, today—and not add to their number or alter them by circumstance. . . .

"Isn't that a little too easy? But wait, everything in its place. At times I envy you, fathers, if you were really the kind of men you sing about in your poetry. . . . At times I envy you, my predecessors, if you were really the way you recall yourselves today. I envy you your beliefs and impulses, your full clubs and your discussions.

"But is it my fault if the armor of indifference grows ever thicker, that it is more and more difficult for me to carry on a real discussion today? What can I do about the fact that I find less and less for myself in the organization? Your advice doesn't help us much here. We simply differ from you. We're different!

"Once, the power went out at the discothèque. It suddenly grew silent. In the clouds of smoke, half-deaf, lifeless, alien figures hovered, people who could not even manage to talk to one another. *The Wedding, Ashes and Diamonds, Salto*: has the time come for our—undescribed—dance of the straw men?

"Honored announcers! You are nothing but skilled craftsmen changing records. You are not the masters of our souls.

"But answer me, you, honored disc jockeys of student ideology. Honored agitators, honored editors of the student press, why are you so rarely the rulers of our souls? Aren't you a bit too often nothing more than skilled craftsmen, changing records?

"I am twenty-two years old. In a year and a half I will finish my studies." (*Report on Materials Censored*, December 1–15, 1974)

Other articles tackled more specific topics, such as vacation schedules for schools. Using readers' letters for support, popular journals tried to campaign to have grade school and high school vacations coordinated so that families could be together. But even though they parroted the words of Gierek's policy to encourage a healthy family life, their arguments were not allowed to appear:

> In Issue No. 22 of *Tygodnik Powszechny,* a letter from a reader and the ensuing editorial commentary printed in the "Family Advice" column were challenged:
> "I have read the new order concerning the scheduling of vacations during the upcoming school year. As a mother, I am shocked by it. One of my children attends elementary school, while the other is in secondary school. With this new system of staggered school holidays, what is going to become of our joint family vacation plans? Summer camps are not the answer for everyone, especially for those parents who want to be involved in the upbringing of their children—at least during the vacation season. A year of full-time work does nothing to help cement family relationships. It is only possible to give one's full attention to this task during leisure time. Unfortunately, the new rules on school holidays will not help matters in this regard."
> Editorial reply: This letter alerts us to a problem that was probably not taken into account when the decision was made to reschedule school vacations. There is still time to reconsider this decision, since we have three full months until the start of the new school year. The reader's arguments seem to be compelling, and in any event the well-being of the family is important to all of us. By the same token, the ability to retract ill-advised plans can only attest to the responsibility of the social planners. (*Report on Materials Censored,* May 16–31, 1974)

Many Poles saw the educational reforms carried out in the seventies as no better, and perhaps worse, than the old system. Censors were directed to keep criticism and information about problems created by the reforms out of the public eye. After all, opposition to the reforms was based on a concern that some of them were little more than attempts to transform primarily Polish school programs to primarily Communist programs. For many, this was a major threat. In addition, as was true of so many other projects undertaken by the Gierek regime, even the simplest reforms were carried out without adequate funding and planning. So the censors not only had to remove attacks on the increase in the ideological character of education, but also had to filter out everything that so much as implied that the programs were poorly established and doomed to fail.

One of the earliest reforms was the centralization of rural schools so that, in theory, a higher-quality education could be provided to peasant youth and the children of workers from the factory towns built in the countryside during the seventies' industrialization push. Of all the reforms, this seemed the most acceptable, but its enactment still brought with it problems for all involved. When local journalists talked about what needed to be done to make the reform work, and about the need for a greater commitment on the part of local officials to finding solutions for these problems, the censors refused to allow descriptions of the poor conditions in the schools (conditions that were certainly known to the parents involved, and discussions that might have forced local élites to act). For ultimately these problems required a commitment of funds to build new schools and repair old ones—something the Gierek regime was unwilling to do. The censored commentary below avoided these issues and made quite a different point:

In a radio program hosted by W. Bąk entitled "The *Obstacle* in the Way of Future Progress" (carried by the Radio Broadcasting Center of the city and *powiat* of Rzeszów), describing working conditions at Elementary School No. 1 in the *gmina* of Lubeń, which serves as the *gmina* school, the underlined portion of the program title was challenged, as was a description of the school facilities (e.g., "ramshackle" lecture rooms, "dank cellars" for laboratories), and the following passages of the program text were prohibited:

"The reform of the school system aimed at the centralization of teaching and the educational process in consolidated school districts with a solid base of support and highly skilled teaching personnel caught the *gmina* of Lubeń unprepared.

"The *gmina* center, the village of Lubeń, has one school building with a small number of classrooms, built in 1910. Moreover, it is in a very poor state of repair. . . . The local teachers and pupils have overcome a great deal of resistance and obstacles raised by a conservative mentality and lack of belief in the possibility of success, but what has been accomplished is, unfortunately, all that can be done. The human potential has not been exhausted, since the teaching staff and pupils are capable of doing much more. Rather, it is a question of the limited physical potential of five ramshackle classrooms, which are a barrier to the future progress of education not only in the village of Lubeń, but for the entire *gmina* as well. The problem of building a school for Lubeń was already overgrown with legend when plans were hatched for the establishment of *gmina* schools. These plans fill some people with righteous indignation, while others are filled with disgust and given to ironic smiles. Few people are actually trying to carry out the plans. Blueprints were brought in and approved, land was purchased with public funds, a well was dug. The implementation of the architects' design has not proved too successful, and what has been done so far has not aroused too much enthusiasm among sensible people. The future development of education in the *gmina* remains problematical. Many barriers standing in the way of progress can be overcome by hard work, enthusiasm and a sense of commitment. However, the barriers raised by the lack of a supporting infrastructure and the need to build a building that could truly serve the entire *gmina* exceeds local capabilities and will have to be overcome by action on a higher level. The fate of education in a region of more than 7,000 inhabitants, a region for which education represents an important opportunity, ought to be worth an emergency appropriation of several million złotys." . . . (*Report on Materials Censored*, December 1–15, 1974)

Another aspect of the regime's attempts at reform drew attacks not for its intent but for its faculty planning. Like the centralization of rural schools, raising grade school teachers' educational level from a mere two-year teaching certificate to a university degree was not considered a bad idea. But the implementation of the plan was nearly impossible, since teachers were expected to teach and, simultaneously, to do their university course work. Journalists championed their cause, and censors cut the articles since not only did they attack an important element of the program Gierek was claiming would upgrade the schools, but they also suggested that the reforms were rendering that educational system less than high in quality. In one censored article, entitled "Marginal Notes on the System of Advanced Teacher Training" (*Tygodnik Powszechny*, No. 50), the censors reported, "N. Jaskiewicz expressed his admiration for teachers who agree to combine teaching duties with advanced studies, and he noted that this requires "above-average abilities, a well-rounded character and a highly developed set of general intellectual skills." He continued:

". . . I must confess that during the latter half of the interwar period when, in certain respects, conditions were more advantageous than they are now, I could not handle extracurricular advanced studies while carrying a normal teaching load at school. I had to take a leave with pay (after reimbursing the school for the cost of hiring substitute teachers). My application for a leave was accepted without too much difficulty, since the separate salaries made two people very happy, and each of them was satisfied in his own way. . . . Many years of experience have shown that a great many teachers go to work in the secondary school system right after earning their basic teaching certificate. They have done their work without faltering in the least and, in many cases, they have worked even harder than their colleagues who already had master's degrees. . . .

"Taking advantage of the fact that most elementary school teachers have already completed a two-year course of teacher's education, it would be possible, by granting leave without pay, to organize annual courses for them, preceded by an entrance examination. The final exam for a given course would, at the same time, be equivalent to a basic certification exam for secondary school teachers. In any event, the organizational problems of advanced teacher training could be solved in a number of ways.

"But if the university wants to preserve its good reputation, and if teachers want to maintain the prestige that they are used to and that they still enjoy in society, extramural advanced teacher training on a massive scale at the university level does not appear to be feasible."

(*Report on Materials Censored,* December 1–15, 1974)

Other aspects of the educational reform announced in the mid-seventies and put into effect beginning in 1978 were, in the eyes of many journalists and intellectuals, far more threatening to the quality and tenor of Polish education and its traditions. Of prime concern to them was the shift from a liberal arts–oriented curriculum, with a strong emphasis, at least in time allocations, on Polish language and culture, to one with far fewer hours of training in the humanities and far more emphasis on technical education, work experience and political training than had been the case in Polish schools. In meetings of professional associations and intellectuals with government officials, as well as in newspaper articles, critics of the reforms repeatedly expressed the view that the reforms were not a modernization of the curriculum but a denationalization, which would only serve to further reduce young people's social and moral standards as well as the educational level of the generations coming of age.

The plan to have students do a set number of hours a week of physical labor encountered enough opposition in the mass media for the censors to report in their quarterly *Bulletin* that this proposal had been subjected to far-reaching criticism. A number of different kinds of journals were reported to have tried to criticize the introduction of required labor into the schools and also the "requirement" that students carry out their own voluntary projects, like cleaning park land, planting trees and cleaning parts of their school buildings. Not only was it said that these projects were seldom initiated by students, being planned instead by their teachers, but:

> "Skill at getting out of ill-fated projects," *Tygodnik Powszechny* commented with respect to the same directive, "can only be good testimony to the social responsibility of the planners of the project." The introduction of the work requirement into school curricula was considered to have been a mistake. "In this connection, the status and importance of volunteer work has been greatly degraded," it was said. "In this situation it is hard to speak of any sort of benefit, economic or moral" *(Politechnik)*. In another item, an author wrote about "the bad reputation of volunteer projects" and the protests of families rebelling, "since we cannot even spend one day a week with our children" *(Słowo Powszechne, Literatura)*. (*Bulletin of Themes of Materials Censored, Second Quarter, 1974*)

An even more serious concern of the Polish intelligentsia in this period was the downplaying of an education in the humanities, particularly Polish language and literature. One of the most extensive critical discussions of this problem that the censors reported having blocked was a round-table discussion organized by *Literatura*'s editorial board for the purpose of allowing those involved in Polish education to publicly air their views on educational policy. The discussion was not supportive of the new school program, even though all the participants had prominent positions in the educational establishment. They did make reassuring references to other Soviet bloc countries' programs to justify their contention that under the new plan the Polish language would be undertaught. They tied their discussion to an earlier critical article that had been published, and they used that article as a pretext for the discussion. This veiling, however, hardly covered the fact that the participants believed traditional Polish values and culture were taking second place to the needs of unpopular "political education" in Marxism-Leninism, that the changes proposed were not universally supported by specialists in education and that in fact there was a great deal of controversy about them (something the Gierek regime was unwilling to admit existed about any of its proposals). The discussion was so totally unacceptable that it could not be published even with cuts. So the educational specialists and intellectuals who did not support the reform went unseen, although their comments were certainly brought to the attention of Ministry of Education officials:

> Permission was denied for the publication of an editorial discussion in *Literatura* (No. 38) on the projected program for teaching the Polish language in the basic ten-year school of the future. In the introduction to the discussion, we read the following:
>
> "We are on the eve of the gradual introduction of a program for the general school, which has been expanded to become a ten-year school. This program is to begin functioning in 1978, beginning with the first grade. The Institute of School Programs has, for some time, been working out the precise guidelines for this new program. The meager information that has reached the public concerning this matter has given rise to a certain uneasiness among groups interested in that work. This concern has been expressed, among others, by Stanisław Bortnowski, a journalist for *Życie Literackie*. In an article entitled "It Is Time to Break the Silence," published in Issue No. 24 of that journal, he briefly described the ideas of the Institute of School Programs concerning the teaching of Polish language and literature in the future ten-year school. According to this scheme, "in the fourth grade, six hours a week (hitherto eight) will be spent on the Polish language; in the fifth grade, six (six); in the sixth grade, four (six); in the seventh, three (five); in the eighth, three (five); and in the ninth and tenth, two, i.e., half the time hitherto devoted to this subject! On a comparative chart of the number of hours spent studying national language and literature in all socialist countries, we would be—the author indicates—in last place. The number of hours of instruction in national language and literature in the USSR, the GDR, Czechoslovakia, Bulgaria and Hungary would be almost twice as many as in our country.
>
> "A special concern, it appears, has been aroused by the decrease in the number of hours of instruction in Polish language and literature in the ninth and tenth grades, for students aged fifteen and sixteen, who are for the most part finishing their general education and ending their contact with this subject.
>
> "Alarmed by S. Bortnowski's article and by the information reaching us, the members of our editorial board have decided to take up this question and to begin a discussion of it, in the belief that a public discussion at a moment when certain projects are still under consideration and can conceivably still be altered may exercise a positive social role. The participants in the discussion, which took place in our editorial offices, included: Prof. Maria Janion (Institute of Literary Research

of the Polish Academy of Sciences), Bożena Knapska (a teacher in the general lyceum in Zgierz), Prof. Zdzisław Libera (Department of Polish Philology of the University of Warsaw), Prof. Józef Werle (Institute of Theoretical Physics of the University of Warsaw) and, from the editorial board of *Literatura,* Janusz Maciejewski, Ryszard Matuszewski and Piotr Wierzbicki. The participants were welcomed by the Associate Chief Editor of *Literatura,* Jan Koprowski.

"We present the following excerpts from the discussion:

"*Ryszard Matuszewski:* 'Before deciding to organize this meeting, we considered it our responsibility to check the sources of information in S. Bortnowski's article. Minister Jezierski received me as a representative of the editorial board of *Literatura* and had an extensive conversation with me about the first tentative decisions concerning the teaching of Polish language and literature in the projected ten-year school. The decisions taken do not yet deal with the distribution of hours, and the minister expressed his view that a discussion would be premature at this stage of the process. In his opinion, only on the completion of a program of instruction based on a definite schedule of hours, a project now in preparation, would a substantive exchange of opinions be possible. I conveyed this view to my colleagues, but it was met with decided opposition. They are of the opinion that if questions are already being raised about the time schedule on which the program of instruction will be based, then the working out more developed provisions on the basis of that schedule should arouse even greater concern. . . .

" 'The issue rests for the moment precisely on the decisions concerning the distribution of hours, which in fact does call for a decrease in the number of hours of Polish language instruction in the last two grades to two hours a week. At the same time, however, a new course is to be introduced into these two grades, entitled "Contemporary Culture," and it appears that the teacher of this course (which is also to be given for two hours each week) would take over some of the functions of the Polish language and literature teacher, discussing literature as one of the elements of cultural life. Another new subject is also to be introduced into these two grades, designated for the time being with the title "Family Life." Two hours a week are also reserved for this course. It is difficult at the moment to indicate precisely just what problems of social ethics or hygiene would be the subject of instruction here. We should add that a similar allotment of time would be given to the two obligatory foreign languages, and three hours a week are reserved for the study of the political and administrative foundations of our government. As can be seen, the study of Polish language and literature does not occupy, in this program, the special place it has hitherto occupied in the general education of young Poles. It is difficult not to notice that, given such a formulation of the matter, a certain canon of humanistic culture, traditionally linked with the study of the national language, appears to be seriously threatened. . . .'

"*Maria Janion:* 'The article of S. Bortnowski made an enormous impression on Polish language and literature circles in the universities. Even more, the announced projects have caused a great uproar. I am of the opinion that we need to talk about this, to debate it.

" '. . . Everyone who has studied in school knows how much the role and significance of a given course depends on the number of hours allotted to it. And so, we are dealing here with a very real threat to that traditional canon which—in our culture, at least—has assigned an undoubted primacy to the literary content conveyed by the Polish language and literature teacher.

" 'Such is the nature of our national culture. We must recognize that the assumptions of these reformers are aimed at changing that canon and as a result at bringing about an equally fundamental change in the nature of our culture. . . .

" 'I would pose the problem this way: Are we really anxious to change the traditional nature of our culture, in which—as a result of specific historical circumstances—there is a preponderance of humanistic attitudes that would require a great deal of effort to substantively change? I do not think it is appropriate that the school, of all things, should be saddled with the task of weakening the bond between society and its traditional values—values that are in fact humanistic. Obviously, in response to this, various polemicists of the type of Mr. Bratkowski [a leading journalist and critic who was blacklisted in the mid-seventies], with whom I have had to lock horns a couple of times, would say that this is all the claptrap of some crazy *literati,* the delusions of their exuberant imaginations, when what we need most of all are trained technical specialists and good workers. I, on the other hand, believe that what we need are honest working people with imagination, and imagination is supplied by the humanities and by humanistic attitudes. Having one of the most outstanding traditions of romantic poetry in Europe, we ought to know how to take advantage of that, even if only in the manner of previous generations, who were able to realize "the miracle of independence," thanks to, among other things, the romantic point of view.

" 'What is to prevent us from realizing the "miracle" of a modern industrial society thanks to romanticism? I do not see any contradiction between a modern industrial society and Polish romanticism. For it is precisely romanticism that can furnish us with the energy and imagination it would be hard to find anywhere else in art or literature.

" 'Turning to the question of those two hours planned for the teaching of Polish in the upper grades of the ten-year school, I would like to express my fear that they will, of necessity, be spent in the study of language rather than literature. . . .

" '. . . But here we are faced with the problem of whether it is possible to teach a national language in isolation from literature. . . .

" 'For literary language is the spiritual space of a given society. Not the language of the newspapers, or the language of advertisements. If we educate a person without that spiritual space, the results could be shocking. . . .'

"*Zdzisław Libera:* 'I want above all else to defend literary values and the teaching of literature as part of the educational and upbringing process. . . .

" 'I would now like to deal with the question of a historical approach to the study of literature in the school. I understand and appreciate the arguments of the opponents to the historical presentation of literary facts as part of school education. However, it seems to me that a greater evil than the one that results from a historical point of view is the absence of a historical point of view. I believe that young people from a very early age should study historical thinking. It is well known that a knowledge of history aids in an understanding of the present. I envision a program of literary studies in which, for the first seven or eight years, the subject would be approached in terms of general problems, but in the last two or three years a historical approach would be obligatory. In this case, the student would finish school with a synthetic historical-literary consciousness, based on a knowledge of selected works and a general knowledge of the history of Polish literature as an aspect of general cultural history. . . .

" '. . . The knowledge that a student gains in school is often the chief basis of his education in the humanities and is not supplemented or deepened by many students afterwards. This would provide support for the demand that the projected program of the ten-year school ensure a sufficient amount of time for the study of the Polish language.'

"*Bożena Knapska:* 'The planned reduction of instruction in the national language and problems of contemporary culture for the last two grades of the ten-year school is very disturbing to me as a teacher of Polish language and literature. It is clear to me that the two hours allotted for national language in the ninth and tenth grades will have to be completely devoted to the practice of speaking and writing—to descriptive grammar, which is always in need of improvement. There will certainly be no time for literature here, although I cannot imagine the study of the national language without knowledge about literature and its development. Without recourse to the classics of literature, the teacher of Polish will not be in a position to realize his task. I do not even want to consider the possibility of giving up the teaching of literature, but the very possibility of a radical limitation of the material covered essentially undermines the educational role of this subject. A teacher is well aware what two hours a week means in practical terms: how many of these hours will be lost as a result of holidays and various unexpected interruptions? What is a young person going to read after he has finished school if no time had been taken to awaken his intellectual interest or to give him practice in the independent interpretation of literary works? He will be spiritually impoverished.'

"*Piotr Wierzbicki:* 'I have not added my voice to the appeals for an increase in the number of hours of Polish language. In the course of the last thirty years, a number of changes of an ideological character have been made in school programs. Other than that, everything has remained in place: when you compare the programs of thirty years ago with those of today, you see that nothing essential has changed.

" 'In the discussion that has been going on in the pages of *Literatura* during the past year, we have proposed something very substantive: a transformation of the structure of the humanities courses in school and the introduction into them of a serious approach to ethical, sociological and psychological questions. Meanwhile, the Institute of School Programs has proposed a meager compromise: instead of a transformation of the entire system, the addition, in the last grades, of three general "integrative" courses—the foundations of the policy of the party and state, the study of the family, and the study of culture. . . . I propose that we struggle for the common goal of an essential change in the course schedule and educational values. . . .'

"*Janusz Maciejewski:* 'It seems to me that the educational authorities, in considering the question of the program for the ten-year school, have committed a basic error, consulting briefly with scholars and perhaps selected teachers and not carrying on any basic research into what teaching is like in a concrete sense or into the tendencies that are visible in the schools. Concrete reality is often overlooked and a program is formulated from above, not taking into consideration the interests of, and trends among, young people. The opportunity that following spontaneous interests [of young people] would afford is missed. There is also an apparent danger that the program will elevate courses which practical experience in school would discredit or at least question to a privileged position. If submitted to such a test [in reality], half the courses would have their program reduced incredibly and it would not even be clear what to do with the other half.'

"*Józef Werle:* 'I am a member of the consultative commission created by the ministry. Our work has involved one meeting at which we were able to express our individual complaints. Since then, various officials of the ministry, in meetings with teachers, have cited our names as individuals who allegedly agreed with the conceptions of the ministry.'

"*Maria Janion:* 'I would like to make one more point. If we do not teach young people to understand culture as a whole (and this goal is achieved, among other things, by acquainting the student with literary works), then we may bring about the phenomenon of functional illiteracy, that is, a situation in which an individual understands individual words but cannot understand the sentence. In such a situation, it is not possible even to train highly qualified workers, who need to understand the instructions for caring for machinery—instructions that are rather complicated and composed of many sentences, instructions that one must be able to understand as a whole.'

"*Ryszard Matuszewski:* 'It also seems to me that one needs to retain in school the practice of literary interpretation as an opportunity for discussing nonliterary—moral, philosophical and political—issues with the students. In practice, this is often a much more suitable setting for such discussions than the one provided by the teacher of courses like "family life" or "civic education." In this sense, the teaching of literature in school would not be limited to linguistic and merely technical issues, but would continue, in line with our tradition, to be a window on the world of ideas and values. And if this is the case, the window must be open wide, and it is not right to begrudge a place in school to the teaching of national language and literature.' " (*Report on Materials Censored,* September 16–30, 1975)

Ironically, during this same period, the censors would not permit the publication of an article demonstrating that teachers of Polish language and literature were overworked and unable to manage the number of class hours that they had to teach under the old system. Though from one perspective it would have shown that the hours spent on language and literature were not quality hours, such an article would also have shown the failure of the Gierek system to provide decent working conditions and expectations for its teachers:

In Issue No. 49 of *Życie Literackie,* E. Najwer wrote about the working conditions of Polish language teachers in general secondary schools in an article entitled "Learning Our Native Language: This Is How the Reform Will Work." According to the author, Polish language teachers were carrying too heavy a teaching load (21 hours of class per week) when the change in class scheduling on May 1, 1972, made it even heavier (22 hours a week). A statement expressing the opinion that this change "proved to be disadvantageous to Polish language teachers" was deleted, and cuts were made, *inter alia,* in the following passages:

". . . In order to enable the Polish language teacher to carry out his teaching duties properly, the number of classes he has to teach should be reduced, not increased. This is because he must read constantly and systematically, take advanced classes, keep up with what is going on in the cultural world and attend theatrical performances if he is to do his job competently.

"Nor was any thought given to reducing the teaching load even for instructors teaching at the university level, even though this kind of work requires a conscientious effort to take advanced courses in history and the social sciences, to keep up with current trends in the graphic arts, film and drama, and to attend, privately or in the company of students, extramural lectures and performances. . . . The secondary school teacher works, in fact, not 22 hours, but 28 to 30 hours a week performing teaching-related duties. This means that he devotes 25 to 36 percent more time to teaching than he did a year ago, and this means an increased expenditure of effort. A similar situation exists in the elementary schools, with the sole difference being that the basic class load is even greater. Thus what is supposed to be an upper limit to the teaching load is merely an underappreciated minimum." (*Report on Materials Censored,* December 1–15, 1974)

Educational issues raised by journalists and specialists also touched on the question of the flow of information. The history texts used in elementary schools were criticized. The censors were unwilling to allow *Tygodnik Powszechny* to state that history books were written in "a dull and lifeless style" or that "history and tradition are constantly being manipulated and used for purposes that are not always apparent."

The running of higher education programs was equally troubling to journalists and censors. Discussions of admissions, faculty, student aid and the funding of research were attempted by journalists and scuttled by the censors. Underlying many of these discussions were the issues of equality and freedom of inquiry, both of which were highly sensitive subjects.

The subject of equality was raised in a number of guises and on a number of levels. The prime target was the admissions system, which, though based on an entrance examination for each program and the ranking of students according to their scores on that examination, still did not guarantee equal access. Not only were peasant and worker students given extra points on their examination scores to compensate for their more deprived family and school background, but other students were given points for their political activities. The real irritant, however, was the so-called "rector's positions" in each department. These positions were set aside for the dean to give out at his discretion. The recipients were the children of party and state officials —individuals with enough pull to get their children admitted no matter what their scores or skills. All of this took on greater significance as the number of candidates seeking admission to universities increased and the number of openings remained the same or dropped because the Gierek regime failed to invest substantively in education. The censors were unwilling to allow any criticism of this system even when such criticism supported changes advocated by Gierek's men:

> In an article entitled "Introduction to . . ." (*ITD*, No. 30), Z. Pietra- sik assessed the current rules and procedures governing admission to the universities. Several minor deletions were made in the article, elimi- nating descriptions of the system as "unfair" and "discriminatory," and the following statement of opinion was deleted:
> "As long as the number of applicants continues to exceed the number of spaces available in institutions of higher learning, entrance exams will continue to be the most important means of thinning out the number of applicants competing for places. No one needs to be per- suaded any longer that this is hardly the best way to go about this. The view expressed by Professor Szczepański, the greatest expert on this question, that a lottery would accomplish pretty much the same thing as the present system of entrance examinations has gained almost universal acceptance. So, if the present system is defective, and every- one is aware of this, perhaps one could expect that it will be changed in the not too distant future." (*Report on Materials Censored*, July 16–31, 1975)

The censors' preoccupation with matters of educational equality extended far beyond articles about admissions. Items such as an- nouncements of benefits for students attending vocational schools also had to be watched for and eliminated. Likewise, censors were ordered to eliminate from the advertising sections of daily papers any mention of private tutoring services that provided those who could afford them with advantages on entrance examinations or in their schoolwork.

This regulation also clearly reflected an effort to keep education under government control as much as possible, but it hardly cut down on these services that were so necessary for most students to pass the admissions examinations in competitive departments:

> 5. No publication of offers (announcements) concerning educational services conducted without the approval of the Ministry of Education (preparation for entrance examinations to secondary schools or institutions of higher education, preparatory classes, preparatory courses for institutions of higher education, foreign language courses, various vocational courses and so on) should be permitted. (Detailed information in Informative Note No. 14/74)

What went on during the university admissions process also went on in the awarding of the much prized academic titles. In the seventies, professorships came increasingly to be awarded not only for academic merit and achievement but also for political connections and activities. All of this was rumored throughout the intellectual community, but little could be said about it publicly. Some journalists did attempt to question the validity of these practices, but their statements were eliminated by the censors since they were simply too critical of established social institutions as well as of those who were awarded the undeserved titles and who often held "honored" and powerful political positions or connections:

> Intervention proved necessary in a number of items raising questions about problems of Polish science and academic life.
> In *Kurier Polski, Z.* Płochocki wrote about "the personnel policy" of Polish science, and was critical of its "inconsistencies" and the ways in which scholarly degrees and titles are awarded:
> ". . . Right after the war, the most capable assistants and adjuncts were raised to the status of independent [tenured] scholars. However, the war ended nearly thirty years ago and, since we continue to employ extraordinary criteria, the number of exceptions continues to be <u>massive</u>. If we consider the habilitation [the required 'second doctorate' for tenure] process to be a demonstration that one has matured to the point of being an independent scholar, <u>why do we appoint as docents [associate professors]</u> individuals who have not yet managed to complete their <u>habilitation work? (The legal basis for this is one paragraph of a certain</u> <u>law, and people who receive their titles this way are known,</u> for short, as '<u>docents</u> from the paragraph.' The argument that we need to have

a sufficient number of docents is a fallacious one. After all, when scmeone is named a docent by the scholarly council, his scholarly qualifications do not automatically increase. . . . There should be uniform criteria for all fields and institutions, criteria that do not allow situations where all one person needs to obtain the position of an independent scholar is a position, while another has to work his way up the ladder of academic degrees. . . . If, at the present time, a significant number of scholars have made their way into the system on the basis of special dispensations, then before we know it we will find that these undereducated 'exceptions' dominate Polish academic life. . . ." (*Report on Materials Censored,* March 16–31, 1974)

Questions of equality and quality were also part of the discussion about the unrealistically low stipends provided for students who could not affcrd to support themselves while in school. The censors were adamant in their refusal to permit the publication of articles in student periodicals demonstrating that the stipends and food allotments provided did not begin to cover even the most basic of expenses. Nor would they allow any suggestion that students who received stipends were forced to work at menial jobs in order to survive while in school. Such material was eliminated even though the situation it described was an everyday reality for a large number of students—a reality they were well aware they faced as a group, since most lived together in dormitcries and thus were quite familiar with one another's problems. The cersors' refusal to permit publication reflected the belief of Gierek's press watchdogs that airing of complaints gave them legitimacy:

In Issue No. 21 of *ITD,* a letter from a first-year student at the University of Poznań entitled "How I Squandered My Stipend on the Good Life" was challenged. The student, who in accordance with the new regulations receives the maximum monthly stipend of 1,200 złotys, provided a detailed "accounting" of his living expenses, which indicates that his stipend is sufficient for only 19 days of very frugal living. The student's "accounting" was as follows:

    3.50 zł—Half-liter of milk, roll and butter

    27.35 zł—two rolls, butter and egg; trolley ticket good for 20 trips (student rate, naturally); half a stick of Palma margarine; three lemons

    32.60 zł—raspberry jam, but, as it later turned out, second-class (sour); two small packages of Georgian tea and two of oolong; sugar

38.20 zł—eight rolls; greeting cards for Women's Day (without stamps); black pudding for 7.40 zł

26.00 zł—milk, bread; textbook of Esperanto for Ela; small glass of tea

24.50 zł—Polo-cola drunk alone; stamps for yesterday's cards; watery *bigos* [hunter's stew] with bread in the park; half a loaf of dark rye bread, recommended by the doctor

170.30 zł—payment for dorm room; film with Luis de Funes; half-kilo of apples; socks

9.10 zł—two Pola-colas with Długi and two teas

22.60 zł—*ITD;* milk; Mazurian cheese; rolls

353.20 zł—cafeteria dinners for the month; *The Daily Telegraph;* half a loaf of bread

29.70 zł—Bobo Shampoo for Children (for me); frozen *pierogi;* half a bar of Export Butter

38.40 zł—three razor blades; ticket to afternoon dance; *Radar;* eau de cologne; certified letter

280.20 zł—very pretty checked shirt; class dues for Women's Day celebration; milk; stuffed cabbage

56.90 zł—trip home; taxi

27.50 zł—canned meat; sugar; bread; three eggs

42.30 zł—shaving cream; potted plant for room; newspapers; batteries for radio; letter to uncle; kefir

17.70 zł—letter home; bread; jam; half bar of butter
_____
1,200.05 zł

After 19 days of "riotous" living on 1,200 złotys, I have a debt of five groszy. (*Report on Materials Censored,* May 16–31, 1974)

In an article entitled "The Academic Race for Good Health" (*Politechnik,* No. 21), A. Światecki discussed "current conditions affecting the health of the academic community." In the section entitled "Nutrition," he wrote, among other things, that "the current daily spending limit on food used to prepare each meal in ordinary cafeterias (and most of them are in this category) is 22 złotys." The following statement was deleted: "In order to prepare meals that meet requisite standards in terms of grams per meal, it would be necessary to make a daily expenditure of 27.22 złotys per meal. Consequently, the current spending limit is dragging student cafeterias down to Category D, i.e., substandard." (*Report on Materials Censored,* May 16–31, 1974)

Discussions of Polish higher education also pointed to problems in the institutions themselves. Among those that the censors did not allow to be fully broached was the inability of scholars to write honestly about certain questions. This issue was raised in the following censored passage from *Kwartalnik Historyczny,* a historical quarterly, quoting a statement made by a professor participating in a discussion on academic work:

> The Polish reader is critical and able to make a choice. It is clear that he selects what seems most correct to his way of thinking, what seems closer to the traditions of his family or political group. Nor should we forget that forbidden fruit has a better taste. A reader indisposed to overly specialized historical research or disappointed by the work of domestic journalists is eager to get his hands on émigré writing or to listen to historical accounts broadcast by foreign radio stations. The sensational atmosphere in which these sources reveal facts that we have allegedly overlooked or that are completely false is extremely unhealthy. (*Report on Materials Censored,* May 16–31, 1976)

The Gierek regime's policy of making it difficult for academics and researchers to hold more than one position limited the earning potential of academics. Ultimately, it meant that students were not exposed to many of the best minds in Polish academia who were involved in full-time research and under this policy could not supplement their salaries by taking on extra teaching or research responsibilities. In a few cases when researchers were working in areas that could not be openly taught at the university, or when scholars could not get permission from their directors at the Academy of Sciences and the university to work at both institutions, they were forced as a result of this policy to hold special private seminars for their assistants or students in their field. This was, of course, officially unacceptable:

> The following passage from J. Tazbir's statement was eliminated:
> "The system of permitting scholars to occupy only one position, a policy that has been rigidly enforced for several years, has deprived many famous specialists of an opportunity to conduct university classes, and in practice has become one more source of unnecessary tension between the Polish Academy of Sciences and institutions of higher education. As a result, these specialists often conduct seminars with a small group of students in their own homes on an illegal, surreptitious basis. We should make it possible for them to conduct

such classes in a legal manner at the university (in the form of a lump-sum, part-time position, or something of the sort)." (*Report on Materials Censored,* March 16–31, 1974)

Journalists also criticized what was considered an excessive regulation of funds allocated for research in the social sciences. The problems resulted in part from the regime's refusal to commit the kinds of funds that were necessary to conduct quality social science research in a sustained fashion, and not simply on a commissioned project-by-project basis. In part, too, they were an outgrowth of the mechanics of the research funding system. The regime had set up a comprehensive national research program with specific priority topics. Directors of the program were given power over the funds for each research topic, and it was left to them to distribute the funds to various existing research institutions. This provided for far greater control over topic selection and direction of research since money was given on a project basis to established experts rather than to university and research institutes to use for funding their own staffs' individual work.

In *Literatura* (No. 18), in "Unexploited Possibilities: The Effectiveness of Scientific Development," J. Krzemiński wrote about conditions for the intensive development of the social sciences, including sociology. We intervened in the following passages:

". . . I find it paradoxical that funds awarded rather lavishly for research are accompanied by a regulation that makes it practically impossible to create new positions and hire people to carry out the projects funded. As a result, all major research is done on a contract basis, at least in the field of sociology. . . .

"The selection of scientific personnel is a complex affair, but I think that two issues are of particular importance: . . . the question of officially adopted criteria that a scientific worker must satisfy. In theory, the criteria used at present seem to consider talent, skill and knowledge on the one hand, and so-called social commitment or sociopolitical attitude on the other. Personally, it seems to me that in practice the latter criterion is too often applied and the former passed over too lightly. It seems to me that the criterion of sociopolitical attitude is sometimes used, without sufficient reason, to eliminate the most gifted candidates." (*Report on Materials Censored,* May 1–15, 1974)

Health

In the world construed by the Polish censors, mention of even the most common flu epidemic was considered a critical comment on society. The risk of exacerbating an epidemic by not warning people to avoid exposure or urging them to get inoculations was, it seems, a risk that even the Ministry of Health and Social Welfare was willing to take. In large part, the purpose of censorship regulations controlling discussions of health issues appears to have been to avoid popular panic over an epidemic or a safety hazard by presenting such problems as involving isolated individuals rather than whole segments of the population. In addition, the regulations seem to have been aimed at cleansing Poland's image of the slightest blemish, including the existence of health and safety hazards—problems that were often the result of insufficient safety precautions and rapid industrialization:

8. All information concerning the following:
   1) mass poisonings and illness (regardless of cause) affecting large groups of the population or enterprises of particular importance to our country;
   2) mass food poisoning in cafeterias of places of employment, vacation centers, summer camps and so on (including poisoning resulting from the consumption of food contaminated by pesticides);
   3) occurrences of particular serious diseases (such as smallpox, cholera, etc.);
   4) occurrences of epidemics of contagious diseases in this country, including influenza; and
   5) concrete threats of epidemic diseases being introduced into this country

may be published in the mass media only upon approval of the Ministry of Health and Social Welfare or the Chief Sanitary Inspector, Deputy Minister R. Brzozowski.

Approval is not necessary for general articles or statements by representatives of the health service concerning preventive measures against poisoning or contagious diseases or demonstrating achievements in this area with the aid of positive examples.

Approval is also unnecessary for information concerning specific cases of flagrant public health violations resulting from the carelessness of specific individuals or enterprises of local significance.

9. Information on direct threats to life or health caused by industry or chemical agents used in agriculture, or threats to the natural environment in Poland, should be eliminated from works on environmental protection.

This prohibition applies to specific examples of air, water and soil pollution and impurities in food that are an endangerment to life or health.

This prohibition covers information on contamination caused by pesticides as well.

All materials and information concerning endangerment of the health of employees engaged in the production of polyvinyl chloride (PVC) and the dangers stemming from its use (in construction, for example) or from introducing these products of the chemical industry onto the market should be eliminated.

Critical materials concerning the adverse effect on the natural environment resulting from the location of industrial installations (existing or planned) should be referred to the GUKPPiW administration. (See Informative Note No. 32c/73 and Nos. 9/74 and 4/76) (October 18, 1974)

10. Absolutely all compiled statistical data concerning the following should be eliminated from PAP, the press, radio and television: highway accidents, fires, drownings. Excessively alarmist publications on these subjects should also be toned down. This prohibition does not apply to descriptions and accounts of a specific accident or to materials concerning preventive activities (without detailed numerical data). (November 14, 1975)

The reporting of catastrophes occurring in Poland was carefully limited by censorship regulations. Airplane crashes, for example, happened only in other countries:

16. Information concerning crashes of PLL "Lot" aircraft, as well as public health aircraft (air ambulances) or so-called "available" aircraft (serving, for example, foreign and domestic delegations and the directors of industrial associations) may be published in the mass media only through the intermediary of PAP.

All publications' internally generated materials on this subject must be cleared with the GUKPPiW administration. (August 27, 1974)

Some regulations, like the following, were designed to keep information on accidents (regardless of their significance) limited to local papers:

118. On January 3, 1976, as an exception, a communiqué appeared in *Słowo Ludu* concerning an accident in Kielce in which two persons were killed and two others suffered bodily injury.

No reprinting or discussion of or any kind of information related to this communiqué or accident should be permitted. (January 5, 1976; canceled March 31, 1976)

85. No information concerning the accident in Słubice that resulted in the death of two soldiers, a teacher and a student, and in injuries to 14 other students should be permitted.

This instruction does not apply to *Gazeta Zielonogórska*. (May 5, 1975; canceled July 13, 1975)

Human error in public health services was not to receive public attention. In this way, it was hoped, deaths and injuries would always appear to those affected to be individual, freak occurrences, rather than the result of shortcomings of the health system in general:

68. No materials concerning the tragic deaths of three persons as a result of poisoning with contaminated barium sulfate in the Białystok X-ray clinic should be permitted for publication. (February 15, 1975; canceled June 10, 1975)

Traffic accidents, accidents at work or school, and fires were likewise not matters for discussion in the media if they were examined collectively rather than as isolated events. Censorship rules blocked information that illustrated, for example,

the number of school accidents caused by "carelessness, laxity and lack of imagination." During the school year 1972–73, "about 72,000 pupils were victims of accidents suffered in classrooms or on the playground. About 67,000 of the students injured were permanently incapacitated by their injuries, and 1,210 of them died." (*Report on Materials Censored*, March 16–31, 1974)

This attitude also prevented magazines oriented toward parents from dramatizing the danger of traffic to their children:

The following was also eliminated:
—Information on highway accidents in which children were the victims: "On the average the number of children killed on Polish roads each year is equal to the number of children in an average school," and

"for each 10,000 children under the age of 14, the number killed was 0.42 in 1968, and 0.54 in 1974. The indices for those injured was 2.86 and 5.99, respectively." (*Magazyn Rodzinny*, No. 9) (Informative Note No. 55)

During the mid-seventies alcoholism, Poland's most critical health problem, was at what would have been considered a crisis level in most countries. Industrial safety and labor productivity suffered greatly as a result. So, too, did child health and family life in general. Strict laws were passed to punish drunk drivers and to protect the children of alcoholic parents. But the state continued to derive large profits from the distillation and sale of alcohol. And the media, rather than being pressed into a public education campaign against alcohol abuse, was systematically cleansed of all discussions of what was a highly visible social problem:

> 10. Numerical data on the nationwide increase in alcoholism should not be permitted for publication. Such data may be permitted to appear only in serious specialized publications, such as medical publications, *Problemy Alkoholizmu* and so on.

The ban on discussion of alcoholism extended far beyond any possible sensationalization of the problem by the mass media. Despite the above regulation, local ecclesiastical reports as well as medical texts were also affected. Not only did the ban prevent publication of statistical data on the dimensions of the problem, but it also forbade dramatic statements, such as those below, about its seriousness:

> In Issue No. 1 of *Kronika Diecezji Przemyskiej*, in "Instructions to Priests Engaged in Temperance Work in the Diocese of Przemyśl," we challenged statements that "drunkenness is our national weakness," and that it "has now taken on the dimensions of a national disaster," so that "every effort should be made to vanquish the scourge of drunkenness, to rescue the nation from biological extinction, and to lift it up out of its moral degradation." (*Report on Materials Censored*, May 16–31, 1974)

Simple but damning statistics were removed from another Church publication. The figures indicated not only the great scope of the problem, but also its notable increase since the Communist takeover:

The following data illustrating the scope of alcoholism in Poland were deleted from the "Appeal of the Episcopate's Temperance Committee" in *Kronika Diecezji Sandomierskiej,* Nos. 1–2.

"About 150,000,000 liters of alcohol (reckoned in terms of pure spirits), worth 51 billion złotys, are currently consumed in Poland, not counting privately produced alcohol, the amount of which is difficult to determine.

"In our country there are about 2 million people with alcohol abuse problems, including about 1.5 million alcoholics (completely addicted).

"Statistics indicate that each day in Poland as many as 800,000 citizens become intoxicated (including, alongside alcoholics, people who become intoxicated occasionally)!

"The consumption of alcohol is continually on the increase. Take the following example: From 1933 to 1937, about 1 liter of alcohol was consumed per person in this country; already in 1945, 1.5 liters; in 1950, 3 liters; in 1957, more than 4 liters; in 1969, 5.3 liters; and in 1971, 5.5 liters per person (including children)." (*Report on Materials Censored,* March 16–31, 1974)

Even short reports on incidents of public drunkenness among workers and the fact that they, if not their superiors, had been severely punished were not permitted to appear in local newspapers. For example:

A brief item entitled "Railroad Cocktail Party," scheduled for publication in *Wieczór Wrocławia,* was challenged. The article described the "exploits" of an engineer and his assistant on the Kołobrzeg–Koszalin express. "The intoxicated engine crew accidentally engaged the safety valve activating the train's emergency brakes," and "the train, full of passengers," came to a halt somewhere between Kołobrzeg and Koszalin. Jumping down from the engine cab to investigate the cause of the sudden stop, the engineer sprained his ankle, but "instead of calling for help, he lay down on the ground and fell asleep. The drunken assistant went off in search of his boss." The passengers were "miraculously saved" by a militiaman who happened to pass by. The report concludes as follows:

"The railwaymen were subjected to disciplinary proceedings and immediately fired from their jobs. Naturally, criminal proceedings have not been ruled out. The dispatchers also failed to fulfill their duties. Seeing that the train crew was completely intoxicated, they nonetheless gave permission for the train to leave the station. It may eventually be necessary for passengers to take it upon themselves to make a predeparture check at the train station to determine the level of alcohol in the bloodstream of the engineer and his assistant, as well as to make sure that they are not carrying a portable bar in the engine cabin." (*Report on Materials Censored,* May 16–31, 1974)

The reason for avoiding any public discussion of alcoholism appears to have been far more than a desire to conceal the problems of Polish society. A discussion of alcoholism might well have led to a broader discussion of social malaise, but, even more importantly, alcoholism could not be discussed because the state, despite all the losses resulting from alcohol abuse, was ultimately unwilling to take serious action to wipe it out. The government, after all, made a substantial profit from the sale of alcohol. And though alcohol was the cause of industrial accidents and social problems, it was also a palliative for popular dissatisfaction. Two articles censored in the last two weeks of June 1974 illustrate the scope of the problem and the nature of the regime's attitude toward it. Both came from books addressed directly to the problem: a trade union anti-alcoholism tract and a medical tract.

Several deletions were made from J. Malec's *They Do Not Have to Be Criminals* (Publications Institute of the Central Council of Trade Unions, edition of 10,000 copies), in which the author discussed, among other things, the scope of socially deviant behavior. A statement that in Poland there are "2 million people who drink to excess," including "1.6 million drunkards" and 400,000 alcoholics, of whom "at least 50,000 require hospitalization," was deleted, as was the statement that "the number of dipsomaniacs addicted to alcohol runs as high as 15,000." The following statements of opinion were also deleted:

". . . We are all aware of the dangers that drunkenness and alcoholism pose for the physical and mental health of the nation. <u>Nonetheless, embarrassingly little is being done to limit this menace.</u>

"Some countries, such as Rumania, have higher rates of alcohol consumption than Poland. . . . While most of the alcohol consumed in those countries is in the form of wine, in Poland it is mostly in the form of vodka. Vodka accounts for more or less two-thirds of all the alcohol consumed in Poland (expressed in terms of pure spirits), while wine accounts for 14 percent and beer for slightly more than 23 percent. <u>If vodka alone is considered, Poland is first in Europe in per capita consumption (of those countries that publish statistics of this kind).</u> . . .

"The role of alcohol as a cause of crime can be substantiated by the percentage of suspects who committed crimes while in an intoxicated state. . . . <u>Recently, the traffic control authorities have recorded an</u>

annual number of more than 100,000 vehicles driven by persons under the influence of alcohol. . . .

"Recent records show that approximately 220,000 heavily intoxicated individuals are detained each year in sobriety centers alone (of which there are 27). Over 2 million individuals were so detained from the establishment of these centers in 1956 up until 1971."

More than a dozen interventions were made in a book by T. Bilikiewicz entitled *Psychiatry* (State Medical Publishing House, edition of 10,000 copies). Challenged material included, among other things, statistical data illustrating the incidence of alcoholism in Poland, the reasons for alleged delays in waging an effective battle against alcoholism, and critical remarks about social legislation, particularly anti-alcoholism laws. Below are some excerpts of that text:

"The passage of appropriate laws is the only possible way of combating the social abuse of toxic substances, which in Poland is primarily a question of alcoholism. Current Polish legislation in this area has proven incapable of controlling this sociobiological disaster, or even of preventing its spread.

"The war against alcoholism does not always appear to have been waged in a consistent manner. One reason for this might be the apparent profits that are realized by the sale of alcoholic beverages. Every year our society spends 50 billion złotys on alcoholic beverages. The costs involved in the production and sale of alcohol are negligible compared to its selling price, so almost all of the sum noted above represents pure profit. However, it will be easier for us to gain some sense of its dimensions if we express it in terms of certain other material goods. Fifty billion złotys is roughly equivalent to the value of 500,000 passenger autos, 250,000 housing units or 150,000 modern hospital beds with a full range of support equipment. These figures could be cited by those who are opposed to the passage of laws against alcoholism, and it would appear that they are being used in certain circles. However, it should be taken into account that this is only a superficial profit.

"Generally speaking, it can be said that widespread alcoholism and drunkenness can lead to the biological and moral destruction of a nation. This truth was recognized by Hitler's occupation forces. This is the reason for their lenient attitude toward persons manufacturing alcoholic beverages and helping to keep society in a drunken stupor, while other economic 'crimes' were punished with the most barbaric and brutal of sentences. In addition to the misconception that the sale of alcohol is profitable, there is still another point of view hindering the war against alcoholism. When making proposals that call at least for substantial restrictions of the sale of alcohol for personal consumption, we often meet with the response: 'What will we put on the market in its place?' This, too, is the result of a misconception. There can be no doubt that the growth in output of goods and services that would result from a restriction of alcohol consumption would more than compensate for the unsatisfiedisfied demand created by these restrictions. . . ." (*Report on Materials Censored,* May 16–31, 1974)

The high consumption of cigarettes was likewise recognized to be a serious health problem. Discussion of the hazards involved or of measures the government could take to reduce cigarette smoking was also censored, as this, too, touched on national pricing policies and the profits made by the government from cigarette sales, as well as on the failure of the government to use its power to encourage better health habits:

> The following sentences were deleted from an article by J. Czyż entitled "Daily Poison" (*Polityka,* No. 30), on the subject of the "smoking plague": ". . . In Czechoslovakia and Bulgaria, where a number of limitations have been imposed on the production and distribution of cigarettes, tobacco consumption has declined by several percentage points over the past few years. In Poland, however, the increase in the number of lung cancer cases is planned for in much the same way as plans are made for an increase in the number of vacuum cleaners. As if there were nothing that could be done to make the curve turn downward.
>
> "A minor, say, 12 percent increase in the price of tobacco products would not help matters any. . . . Only a price increase on the order of 100 percent for the cheapest cigarettes and 50 percent for the more expensive brands would be effective in reducing the scope of nicotine addiction. Even then, cigarettes in Poland would still be relatively cheaper than in the countries of Western Europe or in the GDR. If this kind of price increase could be offset by an increase in wages, the standard of living would not be reduced, and instead people would be encouraged to buy other kinds of goods instead of costly cigarettes. And the state would not suffer any economic hardship. . . ." (*Report on Materials Censored,* July 16–31, 1975)

Environmental Pollution

The rapid industrialization of Poland in the seventies and the spread of factories into rural areas created serious environmental hazards.

Pointing out these problems, however, was read by the press authorities as questioning the government's policy of industrialization. Responding fully to such criticism would have involved costly modifications of industrial plants in order to filter out harmful wastes. Such safety mechanisms had been viewed as an unnecessary investment expense by the Gierek leadership when the plants were being built, and by 1975 they were simply beyond Poland's already overextended capacities. In the minds of the censorship authorities, moreover, reports that suggested food or environmental contamination not only might give rise to panic among the population, but might also discourage foreign buyers and tourists. So reports of this kind were not only kept from appearing in the media, but were also ignored by a leadership committed to immediate industrial success rather than to the long-term preservation of Poland's natural resources and the protection of the population against serious health hazards. Regulations such as the following were issued:

> 88. No materials should be permitted that provide information about the current level of pollution or the increasing pollution of the Polish sections of rivers flowing from Czechoslovakia that results from industrial activities in this country.
>
> On the other hand, information on pollution in these rivers caused by industrial activity in Czechoslovakia may be permitted. (July 16, 1975; canceled February 4, 1976)

Another regulation prohibiting any mention of a health problem in a certain school demonstrates that the censors were concerned about the possibility of a single event being taken as evidence of far broader problems:

> 110. It was discovered that harmful substances were being emitted from material used to seal the windows in School No. 80 in Gdańsk. Classes have been suspended in that school.
>
> Absolutely no information on this subject should be permitted. (September 23, 1975; canceled January 22, 1976)

When part of a forest area in Warsaw was cut down for the construction of a recreation area, the media were not permitted to report what was clearly visible to all who passed by this popular recreation area just outside Warsaw:

71. No materials critical of the fact that part of the Anin Forest located within the Warsaw city limits has been cut down should be permitted. Recreation facilities are to be put up there. (March 5, 1975; canceled December 19, 1975)

The articles to which the censors objected provide ample evidence of the destruction wrought by industrialization and carelessness. The fact that journalists could write these articles indicates that such information was available and that enough questions were being raised by specialists and by the people affected for these developments to become real issues. And, clearly, local leaders and national policy makers chose to continue the pattern of industrialization that had prevailed despite the difficulties it caused.

The material cited in *Report on Materials Censored* between March 16 and 31, 1974 tells a tragic tale of the environmental havoc wrought by industrialization, by Poland's neighbors and by a simple lack of basic investment. It also serves as clear testimony to the ineffectiveness of the published criticism that had appeared. The great number of articles cited in the *Report* on this topic further indicates that environmental pollution was coming to be a matter of great concern:

This period was characterized by an unprecedented and heavy concentration of interventions. They were made in materials dealing with the problem of environmental protection. Interventions were made in 16 texts, and a great deal was eliminated, including information—much of it pessimistic in tone—about the level of atmospheric, soil and water pollution, about the ongoing devastation of the environment, about the irreversibility of certain damage, about the poor location of many industrial enterprises, which resulted in an increase in pollution, and about immediate threats to human health.

We include examples of interventions made in several texts:

"Concentration of Production or Concentration of Pollution?" was the title of an article reporting on an editorial discussion organized by *Życie Warszawy,* with participation by specialists on the environmental impact of the concentration of industrial production. We intervened in the following passages, among others:

". . . J. Jacyna: 'Industrial development cannot take place without having some effect on the natural environment. Along with the growth of industry and its concentration in a given terrain, we can witness the growth—not always proportionately but, more often than not, explosively—of pollution and, underlying it, a degradation of the environment. . . . Biźle Zagłębie—the cement plant near Kielce—represents a vast concentration of industry, and an even vaster concentration of pollution. Nonetheless, new heavily polluting enterprises continue to be located in that terrain, which is, in the opinion of many specialists, already overloaded.'

"Docent St. M. Zawadzki: 'We have outgrown the doctrine of concentration. For a certain time now, one can note a fascination with the processes of concentration. . . . In fact, there are already very few places where electric power plants may be built without radical changes in technology, using the same fuel as before without a reduction in its sulfur content. The emissions of electric power plants may, by the year 1990, cover 313,000 square kilometers, or the total area of our country.

" 'We cannot locate any more heavy industrial enterprises in the Upper Silesian Industrial Region, because the environmental limits have already been reached. It is not even a question of atmospheric pollution; the population can survive that somehow. It is a question of a lack of water. How many billions would need to be expended—and it is an open question whether such an undertaking will ever be possible —to overcome the shortage of water in the Upper Silesian Industrial Region?'

"J. Jacyna: 'And yet large water-consuming enterprises are still being located there. . . .

" 'No one in Puławy expected such an outcome, no one was aware of the dangers. Some very optimistic statements were made about the situation there, yet Professor Siuta has spent several years of his life replanting the desert that grew up around the enterprise in Puławy. Today it is clear that locating such an enormous enterprise there, in the forest, was an unsound decision. We went one step further there than we should have. Perhaps the application of new technology, a rebuilding of the factory, and intensive recultivation will succeed in stopping the pollution process. We were also not aware that the heavy industry in Nowa Huta would cause the stucco in Kraków to deteriorate. . . . It is essential that we work out what might be termed environmental operating principles for all branches of industry. Building an enterprise, we should be aware of what will result from its operation.

" 'Docent Zawadzki referred to the effects of the power industry. It appears that by the year 2000, 50 percent of the country will be endangered by power industry, specifically by the emission of sulfur dioxide. In the event of unfavorable meteorological conditions, half the country could suffer serious damage. Taking into account the development of other branches of industry—the chemical industry and heavy industry, as well as small-scale power production, heating and so forth—it may be said that somewhere around the year 2000 the entire country will be faced with the problem of the contamination of the natural environment. . . . In 20 years, the enterprises that are being planned today will have to have a different kind of technology. Otherwise, we will be faced with the kind of situation that presently exists in Silesia. Silesia is at present the only region where the environmental pollution limit has been reached. Here it is already impossible to build new industry; because there is a lack of a few cubic meters of water per second, it is impossible to build drains, transportation routes are becoming clogged, and so forth. And if we encumber Silesia with still more intense motor traffic on a massive scale, there will also be a shortage of breathable air, a shortage which, for that matter, already exists. . . .' "

A prominent science writer, M. Iłowiecki, published a book, *New, Not Too Wonderful World* (Wiedza Powszechna, 20,000 copies), on the destruction and pollution of the natural environment. From it, the following passages were reported censored:

". . . On the coast of France, one sees more and more people swimming in the shallow coastal sea in skindivers' outfits, which do not let in water.

"We like to make fun of the French and Belgians, so we should give them something to laugh about, too. When Poles swim in the Baltic, they are swimming in the largest basin of waste water in the world.

"Every year 10,000 tons of phosphates (the concentration has tripled in the last 15 years) and several tens of thousands of tons of other types of poisonous chemical substances are drained into the Baltic.

"In 1971 the Vistula River alone supplied the Baltic with 2,475,000 tons of lime, 1,734,000 tons of chlorides, 1,731,000 tons of sulfates, 918 tons of soda, 353,000 tons of potash, 48,000 tons of nitrogen (in inorganic compounds) and 5,000 tons of phosphorus (also inorganic). True, the situation along the Swedish and Finnish coasts is even worse, but that is little comfort. . . .

"The oxygen content of our sea water is systematically declining. Hydrogen sulfide is appearing, which rises, unoxygenated, from the bottom, leaving an 'aquatic desert' behind, a lifeless, poisonous expanse. According to some specialists, the Baltic at a level below 100 to 120 meters is already a dead zone.

"Baltic seals have ten times as much DDT in their bodies as North Sea seals. Certain species of fish have already ceased to multiply, and the concentration of mercury in the bodies of other species along the coast of Sweden has forced the Swedish government to ban their harvest.

". . . Tanks of German poison gas from the time of the war have begun to break open—the English obviously preferred to dump them in the Baltic rather than someplace closer to the British Isles. For the time being, containers of several thousand tons of potassium cyanide, dumped at another time by the Swedes, are still holding together.

"Too often, thoughtless 'technocratic' decisions are made in this country. The nitrate plant in Puławy is our pride and joy, a symbol of our modernity and our industriousness, but we are now aware that it should not have been built in the midst of a pine forest. We now realize that 700 hectares of forest have been irreversibly destroyed there, while another 10,000 hectares are severely endangered: the forestry industry alone around Puławy has suffered a loss of approximately 60 million złotys. Even higher are the costs that cannot be measured, the harmful effect of the pollution on people. The regions around Puławy, Kazimierz and Nałęczów have lost much of their value as recreation areas. Great effort and enormous cost are now being expended to remove the cause of the damage and to try to counteract its effects. Perhaps the harmful effects of locating the nitrate works in this region could not have been foreseen: in any case, we have learned a good lesson for the future. How carefully and thoroughly we must now analyze the plans for technological undertakings and the location of factories! And yet here we have built a vast electric power plant in Kozienice, in the midst of a forest, the last one remaining in this region. Roads and paths for the high-tension lines must be cut through the forest. Very little of the forest will remain.

"In 1970, 300,000 hectares of forest were damaged by industrial pollution in Poland. Every year the losses sustained by agriculture, horticulture and forestry as a result of air pollution cost us 10 billion złotys. Architectural monuments like the Wawel [the castle of the first kings in Poland] are threatened as well.

"There does not appear to be a lack of places where industry could be built without serious damage to the environment. I even think that sometimes it is worth giving up various illusory savings (which we must then pay back several times over). But there's no point in moaning. The electric power plant in Kozienice is already built. One more lesson . . .

"In 1971 several weeklies and daily papers carried on a fierce struggle against the building of a silicate factory in the Augustów Forest: the forest was cleared and building began all the faster—obviously, a delay might have caused losses.

"At that time, an interview appeared in *Życie Warszawy* with Deputy Premier Zdzisław Tomal concerning that Augustów silicate plant. The Deputy Premier, who at that time was responsible for environmental protection, said that the decision to locate the plant there had been a bad one, but owing to the lateness of the alarm and the advanced stage of the construction work it had to be approved. Nonetheless, the appropriate institutions were charged with trying to limit the adverse effects on the environment.

"*Życie Warszawy* expressed its satisfaction that 'instead of 120 hectares, only 30 hectares of forest would be destroyed. Of course, the factory will destroy much more than that, since it will upset the biological balance in a fundamental way, changing the water balance and various other elements. . . .

"All too rarely do we hear in this country about the interdiction of some idiotic location decision. All too rarely are obligatory environmental standards and regulations adhered to."

In an article by J. Weiss entitled "The Baltic Can Be Saved" *(Słowo Powszechne)*, sections of a statement by a scientist at the Maritime Fisheries Institute concerning the extent of damage to the flora and fauna of the Baltic were challenged:

" 'The research conducted by Prof. Rusiecki and me,' said Dr. Dubrawski, 'indicates that Baltic seals have, on the average, 150 milligrams of DDT per kilogram of fat. The amount of DDT in the yolks of seabird eggs is as much as 2,000 milligrams, as compared to 14 milligrams per statistical inhabitant of Poland. Such fish as flounder find their food more saturated with harmful substances. The same is true for dab, plaice, turbot, halibut and others.' . . . In our country, certain innovations, to put it mildly, should be introduced. For example, it is a fact that pesticides accumulate mainly where there is a lot of fat. Hence, insofar as fish are concerned, in the livers. Dr. Dubrawski is convinced that fish livers should not be consumed. Fish-liver oil is also a problem. Baltic fish-liver oil is 40 times as polluted as Atlantic fish-liver oil. Just how harmful is the effect of various chemical compounds that find their way into the sea and later into living organisms? We still do not know, in many cases. Of course, the laboratory is doing intensive research in this area as well. In our biological testing, a plankton crustacean dies in a DDT bath of the concentration found during certain seasons in the Bay of Gdańsk. Another example: a 40-fold concentration of water from the Vistula or a 20-fold concentration from the Odra will kill 50 percent of our experimental animals within 24 hours." *(Report on Materials Censored,* March 16–31, 1974)

An item by R. Jarocki entitled "How Much Time Do We Have Left?" *(Argumenty,* No. 11) reported on an interdisciplinary scientific gathering at the University of Warsaw devoted to the protection and shaping of man's environment. The following passages were deleted:

". . . It is known, for example, that the Ojców National Park cannot be saved, due to the location nearby of industry using a technology that has had a destructive effect on the flora of that special area. This, even though it had been thought that the industry was relatively far away, and ought not to pollute the air above the park. It is also known that the level of pollution in our two major rivers, the Vistula and the Odra, exceeds any kind of norm. . . .

". . . As far as the legal guarantees of environmental protection go . . . it is worth nothing two matters emphasized by various authors. First of all, that it is difficult to demand of the Ministries of Forestry and the Lumber Industry that, on one hand, they carry out the economic plan for the harvest of timber and, on the other, acting in the role of Cato, defend our forest resources, because this conflict will always be decided—perhaps with an aching heart—in favor of the current plan. It is similarly difficult to demand that the agency for Regional Economic Management and Environmental Protection be an effective force in this area. . . .

"Lawyers from Jagiellonian University have appropriately called for a supra-agency organ, acting on behalf of the Government Presidium and closely linked with the Planning Commission, which could take the interests of the state as a whole into account. Such an organ not only would be able to authoritatively call all agencies and central institutions to order, but, what is more important, could direct a long-range strategy for the development of the country with the aim of harmonizing the needs for environmental protection with general development plans. I would add, on my own behalf, my belief that this organ should be supported in its activity by a special statute passed by the Sejm, and that the Chairman of the Council of Ministers should be obliged to report to the Sejm on its activities."

There was also intervention in other items dealing with environmental protection. For example, a critical assessment of the location of the Nitrate Plant and the Zazamcze housing settlement nearby was eliminated from *Echo Celulozy*; passages about the Turow electric power plant's pollution of the Nysa Kużycka were deleted from an article by E. Popczyńska entitled "Rain Falls in Turoszów," in No. 12 of *Życie Literackie*; information about the amount of chemicals emitted by the Polfa plant in Pabianice was removed from *Głos Robotniczy*; and data concerning the excessive concentrations of pollutants in the immediate vicinity of the Głogów Copper Plant were removed from *Stilon Gorzowski* [a factory paper].

There was similar intervention in "The Life of a Ball-Bearing Factory" (*Kraśnik Fabryczny*), *IKP, Literatura* (No. 13), *Kultura* (No. 13), *Pobrzeże* (No. 62) and Polish Radio's *Channel 74 Reports*. (*Report on Materials Censored*, March 16–31, 1974)

Later that year the compilation of censored passages indicated that the high level of concern among journalists and experts about industrial poisons continued. It was an issue being raised all over the world, but one that no Communist regime was willing to face:

Interventions were also made in several items concerned with threats to human health.

An article entitled "New Proof of the Carcinogenic Effects of Vinyl Chlorides" was disapproved for publication in Issue No. 12 of *Przemysł Chemiczny*. Excerpts from the text of the article are reproduced below:

"A causal relation between vinyl chloride and angiosarcoma, an extremely rare form of liver cancer, can no longer be doubted. The connection was demonstrated by research conducted by Professor C. Maltoni, director of the Oncological Institute in Bologna, at the request of four leading European chemical firms—Montedison, Rhone-Progil, Solvaya and ICI.

"The announcement of the unquestionable results of this research came as a great shock to the producers of PVC. . . .

"Recently, in the United States, two further cases of angiosarcoma have been detected, in this instance in two workers employed in an enterprise manufacturing PVC. These are the first cases of this type, and, in the opinion of experts, they may be simply the result of coincidence. Nonetheless, Ch. Levison, Secretary General of the International Federation of Chemical Workers' Unions, has stated that 'there exist, at present, sufficient grounds to call for a decisive preventive program in order to curb and eliminate the risk of angiosarcoma, not only as a result of the production of PVC, but also as a result of the processing and use of items made of PVC.'

"The discovery of the relationship between contact with vinyl chloride and cancer of the liver has inclined industry to sharpen its monitoring of concentrations of this chemical in production areas. In Great Britain, for example, a system for the continuous monitoring of the concentration of vinyl chloride has been introduced.

". . . The chemical workers' union in the FRG has worked out guidelines on means to avoid risk of illness as a result of working with vinyl chloride. They impose, for example, an obligation on enterprises producing vinyl chloride to measure continuously its concentration in work areas, call for the mechanical cleaning of polymerizing autoclaves, and the introduction of a system of regular medical examinations for those employed in a given enterprise. . . ."

In a report entitled "The Daily Routine of the Łęczyca Health Service" *(Zielony Sztandar),* filed after the reporter attended a plenary session of the *powiat* organization of the United Peasant Party, K. Popielecki called attention to the appearance of a "dangerous phenomenon" in that region: "frequent stillbirths." He went on to say [in a passage that was censored]:

"It is hard to say what the reasons for this problem are. Observations suggest that stillbirths are being suffered by women frequently exposed to chemical agents for the protection of plants. This is a question to which the health service should address itself, and not just in Łęczyca Powiat. . . ."

In his book *The Kraków-Wieluń Highlands* (Wiedza Powzechna, edition of 10,000 copies), S. Michalik wrote about, among other things, "the incalculable effects of man's interference with the natural environment." To substantiate his contention, Michalik cited a case in which "approximately 30 liters of a substance used to impregnate railroad ties was dumped out onto the track bed by workers during the construction of a section of track leading to the quarry in Zalasie near Krzeszowice in 1972" and "subsequently seeped into the nearby Sanok River." A statement that "the dissolved substance passed through an entire complicated water filtration system at Bielany and greatly contaminated drinking water at the Kraków area waterworks" was deleted. (*Report on Materials Censored*, December 1–15, 1974)

Crime

The unwillingness of the Polish authorities to admit to imperfection went far beyond concern over criticism of the system or of the leadership's policies. The authorities were by and large unwilling even to admit that certain individuals fell short of the socialist ideal. In the world they tried to create in the media, crime did not exist. All personal decisions were made with the interests of society in mind. Rules were obeyed without coercion.

Censorship documents prove that Poland was not a crime-free society. Nonetheless, the censors sought to maintain the image that Poland was a land where violent crimes did not occur. Regulations were continually issued banning the publication of information about a whole series of sensational crimes:

4. Until the beginning of the trial of the arrested "Katowice vampire," no information on this subject should be permitted. (See Informative Notes 6/74, 15/74, 16/74, 30/74 and 32/74) (Canceled 1975)

24. No information should be permitted concerning the murder of an infant by its mother, a student at the Silesian Medical Academy in Katowice. (Canceled November 23, 1974)

44. No materials (information, references, etc.) should be permitted concerning the youth who lived in Niegłowo, Wołomin Powiat, at one time suspected of having caused crippling injury to an officer of the Citizens' Militia at the railroad station in Wyszoków and now charged with other criminal activity. (See Informative Note No. 29/74) (September 5, 1974; canceled November 23, 1974) [Soon after this was withdrawn, Andrzej K. Wróblewski, one of *Polityka*'s leading writers, "forced through" a story challenging the accusation that the boy pushed a policeman under the train. This was allowed after much argument and appealing of the censors' initial rejection.]

63. With the exception of items in the local Lublin press, all information concerning the rape and murder committed on January 21 of this year in Ostrówek, Lubartów Powiat, should be eliminated. (January 27, 1975; canceled March 19, 1975)

The Polish criminal justice system was to be presented as egalitarian and humane. The statement in one Catholic monthly that "our criminal justice system is one of the harshest in Europe" was deleted.

When laws were broken by officials, when lawbreakers were aided by officials or when crime and criminals had a political cast, even the most mundane of crimes became unacceptably sensationalist. A docu-novel based on a trial of a doctor and party insider in the late sixties could not make even passing reference to contacts between criminals and party officials—even former party officials. The book was also censorable because it implied that there had been patronage and bribery in People's Poland:

Shortly after the trial of Abram Icek Kierbel, alias Marian Kargul, in 1968, A. Rowiński undertook a detailed investigation of the "Kargul Affair," checking out the truthfulness of Kargul's testimony and statements in order to shed more light on the personality of the accused and to explain the underlying motivations for his crimes. In the resulting book, *In Better Company* (Czytelnik, edition of 30,000 copies), Rowiński used statements made during the trial and in conversations with Kargul in Wronki prison after the trial, and a comparison of the statements of the accused with documents from foreign archives and the testimony of persons cited by Kargul. Several deletions were made from this book, including:

—passages containing generalized opinions about the conditions in our society that were conducive to the criminal acts perpetrated by Kargul: "the belief of the naïve, defenseless and guileless that it is possible to buy judicial verdicts and admission to universities and hospitals, and to buy professors, doctors, judges, militiamen and officials. . . . The sins of the years when there was never enough of anything are made manifest, culminating in the institutions of bribery and patronage."

—passages containing extensive quotations from articles by R. Gontarz [a leading spokesman of the anti-Semitic faction in the PZPR whose activity in 1968 as a leader in the Moczarite campaign made him an unpublishable embarrassment to the Gierek regime] (among them, "Justice Sandomierz-Style" and "Officials and Pickpockets," published in *Polityka*), which deal with anti-Semitism in Poland": "In Sandomierz . . . the worn-out, ugly slogan 'Beat up a Jew!' echoes as loudly today as 20 years ago" ("Justice Sandomierz-Style"); "For many years [since the 1968 campaign] Dr. Maria K. has been the object of incessant attacks, ugly slander and petty harassment. The sole reason for this campaign is the fact that 'she lives with a Jew' " ("Officials and Pickpockets").

—passages discussing Kargul's contacts with representatives of "the highest circles of authority in Poland," including Zambrowski, Ochab and Starewicz [former party leaders of Jewish origin], and with "other highly placed persons," including directors of departments in the ministries of health and finance. (*Report on Materials Censored,* December 1–15, 1974)

Another article was removed because it seemed to make a single incident representative of a larger criminal tendency. The censors were also unwilling to permit statements that a youthful hooligan had been freed because of "official protection." This, after all, implied a kind of inequality and official tolerance of crime that simply did not exist in the world the Polish officials tried to portray:

Several interventions had to be made in material describing the dimensions of certain social problems in an overdrawn manner (which might have unduly excited public opinion).

In Issue No. 21 of *Stolica,* an article entitled "Satisfaction" was challenged, in which M. Sadzewicz recounted an assault on one of his colleagues employed by the same weekly, artist-photographer K. Jarochowski. Jarochowski was assaulted late one night on the street in Warsaw by a young hooligan . . . who "was unable to provide any explanation for the assault. He was not drunk. He does not want to go to school or get a job. He continues to be supported by his family, which is well off and . . . even well connected." After attacking Jarochowski, [he] "testified that he was bored with life and wanted to get himself sent to prison." The case was supposed to go to court immediately, in accordance with regulations for the handling of cases of hooliganism, since "this was indeed a classic case." But "a telephone call was received from a certain ministry concerning this very matter," and things turned out otherwise. The accused "is now free. He can go on bashing people's heads in. The case against him will peter out in deadlines, stays and appeals." At the end of the article, Sadzewicz wrote: "A hooligan can murder someone, and if he has official protection they will let him go. That's what people believe." (*Report on Materials Censored,* May 16–31, 1974)

Another censored article suggested that the police force was incompetent. Not only did the criminal justice system have to be portrayed as absolutely fair; it had to be portrayed as absolutely unerring as well:

In an article entitled "Damages for False Arrest" (*Polityka,* No. 49), Wanda Falkowska described the false arrest of a resident of Warsaw Voivodship who went to court "to sue for damages amounting to 10,000 złotys for false arrest and distress suffered in the process." She reported further that the Voivodship Court in Warsaw "fully acknowledged the material claims lodged by Citizen B., noting that "this is an unusual case." In accordance with our suggestion, the editors deleted the author's remark that "incidents of precipitate or not completely justified arrests are unfortunately less unusual." (*Report on Materials Censored,* December 1–15, 1974)

Sports

Sports reporting was carefully controlled as well. Even though the country's supposedly amateur sports clubs competed actively for team members and engaged in all sorts of chicanery to get outstanding athletes, sports reporters had to turn a blind eye:

Issue No. 21 of *ITD* ran the second installment of the memoirs of J. Makowski, entitled "I Was a Coach," in which the author described his experiences as a member of the Sports Club of the town of N. while "building a champion soccer team." Deleted portions included discussions of the "business deals" made by athletic clubs, the "buying" and "selling" of athletes, the current "prices" of athletes (20,000 to 120,000 zł) and the existence of "slush funds" "which are indispensable for closing player trades." At the conclusion of this installment, a statement that "these kinds of practices are not confined to N." was deleted.

Nor were the authorities willing to have it suggested even in cabaret performances that Poland's "amateur" athletes (many of whom participated as such in international competitions for amateurs) were not really amateurs at all. It was explained to the censors that such statements represented an "exaggerated view of reality":

We intervened in over a dozen texts that presented an exaggerated view of the dimensions of socially harmful phenomena.

The following example was eliminated from a feature entitled "Poachers" *(Sztandar Młodych)*, in which the author wrote about the pirating of young sportsmen.

"A certain Silesian club at the top of the First Division sent a man to Warsaw for the express purpose of enticing basketball player P. to join it. The traveler had all the arguments necessary for this encounter, namely, a blank card for study at the university in the field of one's choice. All that was necessary was to write in the name. He made the offer along with the promise of a good apartment and a job paying 5,500 zł a month. There was only one condition: the conversation was never to go any farther than the room where it took place. . . ."

The cabaret program "Hurdy-Gurdy" had deleted from it a skit by J. Mulewicz entitled "The Master Craftsman," which made fun of the fictitious jobs of "amateur" sportsmen with well-paid positions in various enterprises (some even on the level of director). (*Report on Materials Censored*, May 1–15, 1974)

On the other hand, Polish censors were also unwilling to allow articles that pointed to the poor quality of the training facilities available to athletes, even though this information would have made Poles appear to be "amateurs" to the rest of the world. Such criticism would have upset many in this sports-conscious society:

In an article entitled "The Magic of Soccer" (*Literatura*, No. 50), which discussed the scoring records of players in the Stal-Mielec Club,

T. Zalewski quoted several team members. The following statements were challenged:

"Krzysztof Rześny, guard, former representative of Poland in international matches: 'How did I get into sports? . . . I like the game, and I was impressed by all the famous names. I graduated from the School of Economics, but I have never worked in my field. I've never had a chance to find out what it is like to work in this field. . . . Everybody thinks that we lead wonderfully prosperous lives. But it's not true. Our salaries are not all that bad for Poland, but they are all out of proportion when you consider the amount of strain placed on the health of athletes in this country in comparison to other countries. In the West an athlete can go to a reconditioning room and regain 60 percent of his lost strength right away. . . . But here in Poland we only have unsophisticated equipment. . . . Furthermore, in this country you are only a supposed amateur, and, as a matter of fact, they trade you back and forth like a commodity. I ought to be able to take off and join another club if I don't like the one I happen to be playing for. But at the present time, the Polish athlete does not have the right to make decisions about his own career. And the clubs do not care about or respect their players. You don't have the right to jump around wherever you please. . . . When you give it up and get a regular job, it's all over. . . . And all of us are afraid of going to work in a regular job, and we worry about what will become of us later in life. . . . After all, what do we know about leading a normal life?'

"Wiesław Siewierski, goalie: 'We have a good life, we get to travel a lot. But it is too late for some of us to go on to study or to get a skilled job. They say that the club will help us out, but who knows for sure what will happen? . . . All of us dread the fate of ordinary mortals.' "
(*Report on Materials Censored,* December 1–15, 1975)

Another concern for the censors in respect to athletes (and other prominent figures in Polish society) was the fact that many of them did not stay in Poland but emigrated to the West. The authorities made it clear to the censors that publicizing these defections or making them appear to have improved the lives of those who left would be setting a bad example—as though the only contact between the two worlds of those who remained and those who left was the mass media. Obviously, the Olympic fencer who was accused of spying on the Soviets for West Germany dropped out of all press discussions of the past and present of the sport, without his trial ever being mentioned, but the censors were also told that:

All information concerning the Polish track and field athlete Andrzej Badeński, who extended his stay in the Federal Republic of Germany without permission, may be given only through PAP.

The authorities clearly hoped that the following regulation would help to discourage similar defections:

17. In order to combat the tendency for our athletes to play on foreign teams, no material (statements, opinions, suggestions) by either athletes or journalists should be permitted on this subject. (August 15, 1974; canceled March 19, 1975)

The issue was, however, a real one, as revealed in a student newspaper article:

In *ITD* (No. 50), Z. Pietrasik, in an article entitled "Everything for Sale," examined, among other things, the controversial problem of "Polish athletes" joining foreign sports clubs. Deletions were made in the following passage:

". . . The prospect of legal emigration to join a foreign sports club —the mere mention of which would have sounded totally incredible until recently—presages the advent of a small revolution on the domestic sports scene. After all, in the past any such excursion was regarded with suspicion, as something morally ambiguous, something that should not be spread around. Instead of press reports, there were rumors, which, in this case, were very often true.

"If we were to mention the names of all the Polish athletes who are now working abroad, it would be a rather long list. And there is nothing at all strange about this. . . .

"It would be a highly amusing project to draw up a complete list of all the official explanations for emigration of some of our professional athletes and coaches. Zygmunt Hanusik, a cyclist, whom we have forgotten all too quickly, is living in France, where he is undergoing 'special training.' As for Lubański, *Przegląd Sportowy* recently wrote that he left the country to play with the Lockeren Club, where he is doing his part to strengthen ties of friendship and cooperation between Poland and Belgium. No one has written anything about Joachim Marks, since there has not been enough time. On October 26 of this year Marks played against Italy at the Tenth Anniversary Stadium, and was unable to sneak anything past the Italian goalie, but just one week later he scored as many as three goals, this time for a French club, Lens.

"Nonetheless, I am amazed by the silence on the subject of the former Ruch [soccer team] player, since his emigration was in fact legal and had the official approval of the Polish Soccer Union. Marks is over 30 years old, and the Polish Soccer Union adopted a resolution years ago according to which a soccer player may leave the country once he has turned 30. . . ." (*Report on Materials Censored,* December 1–15, 1975)

Emigration

The concern of the Polish authorities that coverage of émigré athletes might serve as an example for others was paralleled in the censors' treatment of members of the cultural intelligentsia who had stayed abroad after World War II or who had emigrated since the war. Even as Poland sought to bring in hard currency by appealing for aid from Polish émigrés, the authorities were unwilling to encourage citizens to hope to leave Poland. To this end, censors were instructed to allow a minimum amount of information so Poles would not be sure of the rules and would therefore not know if they were eligible or how they could become eligible to leave.

Section VIII: Emigration

1. Permission should not be given to publish any information about the possibility of emigration to the United States by Polish citizens registered with the U.S. embassy for that purpose, or any announcement of the embassy on that subject.

2. No favorable view of the Association of Polish Veterans should be permitted. The association is a reactionary organization. This does not apply to general information about émigré veterans' groups, veterans and so on.

3. No comprehensive, extensive publications concerning the current operation of Polish émigré organizations in the Federal Republic of Germany, particularly those relating to Polish émigré gifts and contributions to Poland, or relating to the scope of the rights and political freedoms of these organizations in the FRG should be permitted.

In publications dealing with the tendencies toward consolidation among the Polish emigration in the FRG, an evenhanded approach should be taken in assessing the "Zgoda" Union of Poles and the Union of Poles in Germany.

Please refer any possible problems to the GUKPPiW administration.

4. Care should be exercised to see that materials discussing progressive changes in Polish émigré organizations toward greater cooperation with Poland maintain objectivity and a calm, moderate tone. These developments should be treated as a matter of course. Any excessive, exaggerated reporting on the work of émigré activists favorably inclined toward us could supply hostile circles with additional arguments for campaigns against them.

To further discourage emigration, the censors were instructed to tread a thin line between making the Polish leadership look like promoters of worldwide Polish culture and denying the successes of Poles who had left their homeland. All of this resulted in émigré leaders and prominent members of the Polish intellectual community abroad disappearing from the Polish media. Among the instructions given to censors for controlling discussions of cultural matters were blacklists of individuals whose names were simply not to be mentioned in the media. For these lists, see Chapter 9, "Culture: The Final Conundrum."

All the attempts by Polish censors to create a better world in the mass media than the one that actually existed did nothing to convince or calm the Polish population. In fact, the social problems were apparent to everyone. Denying not only information about policies and problems for which the mass media were the sole source of information, but also reports on the mundane and universal elements of life, fueled the fires of an explosion in the strikes of 1980. The media did not reflect reality, problems were ignored, and the people of Poland knew only that the leaders did not seem to recognize their world.

6 / **CENSORING ECONOMICS**

Rewriting the Tally Sheets

B Y 1974 Poland's economic picture had begun to darken. Even before consumer goods began disappearing from the marketplace and Poland had to turn to high-interest loans from the West to cover its existing loans, Polish officials, specialists and journalists realized that Gierek's promises of an economic miracle were empty. Party and economics officials at all levels reacted to failure by imposing a veil of silence over everything relating to problems. No plant manager or economic planner was willing to expose himself and his work to public criticism by providing journalists with information that might point up his ineffectiveness. Nor were such individuals any more willing to admit their shortcomings to their superiors; instead, they often supplied them with falsified statistics. The consequence of this fear of providing information and the new inability of journalists to get most of their economic criticism published was a decline in the number of articles written on economic affairs. Thus one of the major sources once used by the leadership to double-check official statistics given them by those responsible about the real state of the economy was no longer available to them.

Even when journalists managed to get information for their economic reporting, less and less could appear in the press, on the radio or on television as the crisis progressed. To a far greater degree than most of the political reporting attempted by journalists, economic reporting involved what by the mid-seventies came to be state secrets. By that time the Polish authorities wanted to protect their ties with the West, to be sure they could continue to sell what they could and borrow to keep their sinking economy afloat. They would therefore not permit reports in any journal that could in any way discourage Western buyers. Nor did they want Western nations or their own public to know how dependent they had become on the economies of the West. As a result, it was only after the Gdańsk strike in 1980 that the Polish population and even many Polish trade specialists became aware of just how much had been borrowed overall from the West and how poorly Poland was faring on the international market. On the other hand, this information policy also made it impossible for the Gierek regime to make excuses for its failings: it could hardly point to the recession in the West as at least partly responsible for Poland's difficulties as long as it refused to admit that any difficulties existed or that Poland was deeply in debt. Polish workers resorted to wild speculations to explain to themselves why their standard of living did not appear to be even maintaining itself. Such speculations usually placed the blame on the leadership.

The government's information policy sought to deny the existence of problems that the population was forced to confront on a daily basis. So, while Poles had to stand in line for bread, detergent, soap, shoe polish, paint, shoes and so on, and while policy makers and party officials took note, the discussion of daily shortages and the deteriorating quality of goods was excluded from the media, as were the problems of various factories—problems that were clearly apparent to factory workers. (Ironically, this ban on the discussion of production problems prevented reporting on the positive results of experiments designed to deal with them.) The media thereby lost their credibility. They also lost their value as a source of information and a link between groups in the population. The media could not make life any easier for Poles or serve as means to mobilize them. Nor could the media serve as a monitor of the work that was going on in the country. And so the Polish economy careened unchecked toward the disaster of a twenty-seven-billion-dollar debt to the West, a negative growth rate, the collapse of the economy and the disappearance of almost all basic necessities from store shelves in 1980 and 1981. Economic difficulties, most of which were not unique to Poland, turned into a crisis of confidence that gave rise to demands not for gradual economic change, but for a full-scale political transformation.

By the mid-seventies, economic mismanagement and overcentralization were clearly paralyzing industrial development. But the Gierek regime, as it increasingly centralized political control, was unwilling to consider the need for or possibility of economic decentralization. Hence management problems could not be discussed. Nor could the tie-ups and blockages caused by mismanagement: congestion in the ports, lack of adequate labor and raw material supplies at points where they were needed, and the shortcomings of the transportation system. Foreign trade decisions were not always well made, but they were always beyond criticism. The shortcomings, as well as the technology and products Poland was committed to buying or producing, were nonsubjects. Trade between Soviet bloc countries was, as always, a secret. Information on the extent of Polish trade and of Soviet aid to Poland could not be provided. Agriculture was the neglected stepchild of the Gierek industrialization drive, and it, too, could not be openly discussed. Even the reporting of economic successes was a sensitive issue, since they might raise hopes and expectations with which the regime did not want to and could not cope. Consumer industries and housing construction were, by the mid-seventies, falling behind promised rates of production. But the failures in these industries, obvious though they were, could not be discussed in the media. Nor could articles be published advising consumers on how to deal with the problems they faced.

In the review of materials censored during the second quarter of 1974, all these problems were raised. The criticisms the censors kept out of the press in 1974 were the same as those that would be made by intellectuals against the Gierek regime in the late seventies, and they were the same as those that remained to be resolved after the Gdańsk strike in 1980. These doubts and criticisms were raised even before the mid-seventies when Poland had entered into the dizzying spiral of borrowing to pay back previous debts and stave off the collapse of the domestic market. But despite statements by economists and journalists and the reports produced from them by the censors for internal distribution, these problems were not considered publicly by the party leadership nor were they resolved in the seventies. Instead, it took workers' strikes to force the political and economic leadership to even admit that there were problems.

2. Intervention in the Area of Economic Problems

The items challenged often involved negative assessments of the planning methods and socioeconomic mechanisms operating in our country, or one-sided criticism of negative phenomena in various areas of the economy. Intervention in this area was somewhat more frequent than in preceding quarters. A characteristic feature of the passages questioned was, in addition to doubts about the wisdom of aspects of our current economic strategy, an effort to find the causes of economic failures in the models adopted by our economy over the course of the three decades since the war.

As before, one of the accusations made concerned the inadequacy of the recent economic reforms, illustrated most often by a critical analysis of the principles of the new financing system used by so-called "initiating units." In the view of one author, "the principles of the new system appear, in theory, to comply with most of the demands," but "the specific provisions adopted do not create the special conditions necessary for developing grass-roots initiative" and carry with them "a real danger of deforming the original principles [of the reform]." B. Kolibowska's article "Innovative Processes in the Management System of Initiating Units," questioned in its entirety, was devoted to an analysis of the "negative aspects" of this system. Assessing its provisions, the author made use of such phrases as: "oversight," "causes reservations," "strong counterincentive," "raises doubts," "moot principle," "difficult to agree with in principle," etc.

Without going into the details of the discussion, it is worth noting its final summary assessment: "the new management principles for initiating units have been implemented too rapidly. The central planning machinery has still not been adapted to it, and all of its elements and parameters have not yet been completely thought through. The problem of setting prices has not been resolved. We cannot expect that all of the virtues and defects of this new system will be apparent by the end of this five-year plan, since its operation will be limited by the influence of principles adopted earlier. It has affected only one level of the economic administration—the industrial associations. For this reason, the real danger is that the original principles [of the reform] will be distorted, grass-roots initiative will be further hampered and there will be no mechanisms by which industry can take advantage of innovations." The final suggestion [of the article] was: "In the near future, the problems in the operation at other levels of administration must be resolved."

In another item, it was stated that the new system "creates pressure to raise the price of goods. But this increase is made under the guise of introducing so-called 'new products' to the market." Similar accusations, this time formulated more categorically, were found in a book by M. Nasiłowski, *Analiza Czynników Rozwoju Gospodarczego PRL* [Analysis of Factors in the Economic Development of the Polish People's Republic]. The book points out that the economic decisions made at the beginning of the 1970s did in fact reverse adverse trends and activate economic growth factors but only "to the extent that was observed in Poland in the latter half of the 1950s." In this situation, according to the author, "it is difficult to determine whether this tendency is a permanent one or is merely the result of market factors, that is, fleeting factors associated with the exploitation of economic reserves fairly close to the surface." Elsewhere the author wrote, "The reliance on criteria for the evaluation of the effective operation of enterprises that concentrate on the extent to which the indices outlined in the annual economic plan are met continues to encourage the trend toward increasing production by exploiting already existing conditions of growth, expanding production that is not properly adapted to the needs of the consumer and counting on the detection of untapped reserves within an enterprise." He also pointed out that there is still "no effective economic mechanism to bring pressure so that all sorts of technological and organizational innovations can be introduced into the production process."

In the view of another author, "the problem of eventual temporary employment is a burning one [for Poland] in light of the engagement of the entire labor force in traditional industry, the absence of any gradual transition to automation (which is taking place elsewhere) and difficulties of shifting the labor force." In this situation, he notes, it is essential, "beginning now . . . to prepare for a group of people to live without work" (*Człowiek i Światopogląd*).

More general statements about "the low level of management and the defects in its organizational structure" were deleted from several other items dealing with investment problems. For example, there was a revival of the tendency to undermine the authority of the regulations in this area. A. Mozołowski wrote in *Tygodnik Kulturalny* that the record-breaking rate of construction at the North Port was "the result of the incessant violation of all kinds of regulations."

Among those with criticisms were some individuals involved in various sectors of the economy who have significant professional achievements and successes to their credit. Deleted from one item was a section of a statement by the director of construction for the Łazienki Highway [in Warsaw], who said, "if we had operated in accordance with the regulations in force at the beginning of this project, we would be barely in the initial phases of the construction today." Another article noted that the "bureaucratic system of pay in the construction industry does not encourage any increase in productivity." The existing regulations were judged to be "outmoded and rigid." It was pointed out that the director of construction, "who has hundreds of millions of złotys to work with, does not have even 500 złotys to use in rewarding people who deserve it, because the Supreme Chamber of Control is sitting on his back" (*Polityka* and *Głos Pracy*).

Similar problems were raised in a challenged interview with Architect-Engineer M. Budzyński, chief designer of Ursynów [a new Warsaw housing development] *(Literatura).* In evaluating the working conditions for the design team, he noted that there was a lack of coordination among the individual investors ("the general lack of confidence the parties [involved] have toward one another is striking; you have to do everything you can to cheat your partner at all costs"), that work was based on inaccurate data ("but maybe someday it will be known how much earth was dug up for nothing"), that there was a great deal of just marching in place ("we are doing a tremendous amount of work and getting nowhere") and that tension was created by the authorities' constant change of mind. "We realize that we are being watched. All around us are people who are never in a hurry, who shift from one foot to the other and wait. If something works out for us, it will mean that we aren't such dopes, that we can be put to the test. That is why it is very important for us to make even one forward step." This was the closing observation. (*Bulletin of Themes of Materials Censored,* Second Quarter, 1974)

Not only were journalists not free to discuss evident failings in the marketplace, but even scholarly discussions were limited.

In the second edition of a collective work entitled *Poland's Social Development in Forecasts* (Książka i Wiedza [the PZPR publishing house], 5,000 copies), we intervened in the following passage:
'. . . We cannot expect the technological gap separating us from very advanced industrial countries to be closed in the 1970s. Nor will it be closed by an increase in the number of people with a technical education. In this regard, we are ahead of many very advanced countries in Western Europe. But this large number of engineers does not produce the effect that has been achieved in many other countries. This is the result of the relatively low level of education of those engineers, the administrative organization that makes it difficult to utilize people properly, the low level of economic administration and errors in organizational structure, a faulty system of pay and bonuses, and so on." (*Report on Materials Censored,* May 1–15, 1974)

In 1974 journalists also pointed to the insufficient cooperation and coordination between ministries and agencies supposedly guided by the decisions of the Planning Commission. One article specifically discussed the fact that a number of projects were simply canceled without good reason after the groundwork had been laid, and also charged that transport prices were set with no logic to them:

In an article entitled "Cheaply and Effectively" (*Perspektywy*, No. 51), H. Boruciński evaluated the extent of waterway utilization and discussed the prospects for the development of water transport in Poland. He wrote:

"... It will be difficult to regulat rates schedules in our transportation industry, since they are closely connected to our internal fiscal and economic system. But as long as transport costs are still not based on real costs, then anything is possible when it comes to rates schedules. It can even prove cheapest to ship goods by truck.

"The most important thing that ought to be done is to simply start doing something: In the meantime, investment projects like the construction of a port facility at Ścinawa, which was supposed to serve the Górażdże cement works, or the dam site at Różanka on the Oder River have been canceled. Were these cancellations necessary? The investment projects mentioned above are very well provided for in terms of both technical documentation and the processing capacities of the enterprise charged with carrying them out, the Inland Waterways Shipping Association, which had included these projects in its plan for this year. . . ." (*Report on Materials Censored*, December 1–15, 1975)

One of the ironic aspects of Polish economic management, an aspect pointed out again and again by Polish journalists in 1974 and the period that followed, was that the dollar had become the currency of the Polish government. Already in 1974, in an effort to place a real value on domestic production and to provide various areas of the economy with disposable hard currency, Polish institutions began to transfer goods and services to each other not by barter or by using złoty values to account for sales and purchases, but by placing a dollar value on each transfer and having institutions pay each other in dollars. This process was termed "domestic export" and occurred at all levels in the economy, from individual citizens' purchases at hard currency stores to cases like the one from an article by A. Bat entitled "Autosan Export Plans" (*Podkarpacie*, No. 18):

"Twenty out of 50 cars produced last year were sold as part of the so-called 'domestic export.' For the ordinary bread eater, domestic export appears to be an entirely unfathomable creature, for how can one imagine, for example, that the Polish Ministry of the Machine Industry sells Polish buses to the Polish Ministry of Culture and Art for foreign currency? It is true that if the transaction had not taken place, the Ministry of Culture and Art would have had to import them for foreign currency, but what we have here is a classic case of shifting money from the right pocket to the left. Why else do we produce something at home than so that we will not have to buy it somewhere else?" (*Report on Materials Censored,* May 1–15, 1974)

Journalists also tried to point out that even with Gierek's attempts to centralize everything and eliminate regional power, the old regional rivalries created problems for the economy. Such observations were eliminated:

"For example, mention was made of the 'unhealthy rivalry between the electronics centers of Warsaw and Wrocław, and in reference to this it was stated: 'This is still one more evidence of poorly conceived centralization. If something appears in the provinces that is not in the capital, then somebody or something has to be brought to Warsaw right away, or at least the existence [of the provincial product] must not be made any easier' " *(Głos Glinika).* (*Bulletin of Themes of Materials Censored,* Second Quarter, 1974)

Transport

By 1974 the strategy of developing the economy through rapid industrialization based on the import of new technology and selected consumer goods and the export of finished products to pay for the imports was beginning to take effect. But as journalists began pointing out in 1974, there was not sufficient infrastructure to cope with this added industrial load. The problem was critical in the area of transportation, especially in the case of facilities such as the Baltic port system. As the pace of imports and exports increased in the early seventies, the development of the ports not only failed to keep pace, but added to the costs of Poland's international trade. Censors' regulations explicitly forbade most discussion of this issue:

6. No articles or information discussing in a critical manner the service provided for foreign contractual partners in our ports may be published. This pertains in particular to the following: the number of foreign ships waiting for a place in the port, the holding up of foreign ships, shortages of workers, cargo, railway cars or warehouse space for ships and foreign shipowners, and so forth. In doubtful cases, the GUKPPiW should be consulted.

For journalists and their editors, however, the failure of the Baltic port system was a symbol of the failures in the economy as a whole, and, according to the censors' bulletin issued in the second quarter of 1974, it became a major subject of discussion and attack:

> A new phenomenon in press journalism during the last quarter was the appearance of opinions critical of the situation in the maritime industry. Several of the items we challenged contained information and evaluations that all but disqualified the achievements and present status of this entire branch of the economy. Individuals not only wrote about the poor performance of the seaports and the losses incurred as a result, but also tried to spread the view that [our ports] have a bad reputation with foreign customers and users. In a report on the port of Szczecin, for example, it was stated: "The situation is dramatic. There is no coal. . . . The cranes stand motionless. As far as the eye can see, the whole port is moving sluggishly" *(Walka Młodych)*. It was argued that "goods are loaded and unloaded in our country more slowly than in the ports of other countries," and "container ships that sail to Gdynia for cargo must wait at the port, because only one ship can be moored in the temporary base" *(Życie Warszawy)*. *Tygodnik Morski* wrote: "It is no secret that pilots coming into the Danish straits on ships bound for Poland tell their crews: 'You are going to a port where nobody will tell you the day or the hour when you will set out to sea.' " In *Głos Wybrzeża* "the poor performance of the ports" was said to be a "shameful and costly game." It was indicated that last year we paid shipowners more than four million dollars in contract fines for holding up numerous ships in port, and fodder and grain imports "cost us even more due to the fact that foreign shipowners, aware of the situation in our ports, demanded shipping charges that were several cents a ton higher." There was also the expression of alarm that "the situation in the ports has become clearly worse this year." It was estimated that it will be "absolutely impossible" for our shipbuilding industry to maintain its competitive position in the near future "if too many agencies are involved in making decisions about implementing modern technology and the scientific and technical support working on behalf of the the shipbuilding industry continues to be so modest." *(Bulletin of Themes of Materials Censored,* Second Quarter, 1974)

Other material on the situation in the ports and the maritime industry that the censors questioned would have revealed, had it been allowed to be published without the censorship of specific passages, the unbalanced character of industrialization in the early Gierek years and the inefficiency and waste that resulted in the ports alone would have made dramatic news. For the censors, the details of the problems in the ports were simply too sensitive to appear even in local port city journals that were read almost exclusively by shipyard workers, their families and friends who saw these problems, and more, daily:

> In an article entitled "A Container Full of Questions" *(Życie War-szawy),* J. Redlich wrote about the need for the rapid development of containerization in Poland. The author observed that for several years "we have been forced to rely on a single, temporary transshipment facility at the port of Gdynia, one that is equipped with a single crane for the servicing of large container ships" and that is "overburdened":
>
> "Last year this modest facility of ours was called upon to handle nearly 144,000 tons of container cargoes, or approximately 30,000 tons more than its nominal capacity.
>
> "All of these containers have to go somewhere. And so they are now being stacked up outside of the facility, under primitive conditions, along the shoulders of access roads. The container ships that call at Gdynia to pick up cargoes have to wait in line, since the dock of the temporary facility can only accommodate one ship at a time. And it often happens that two or three ships will come into port at the same time."
>
> In an article entitled "Freight Trains Loaded with Air" *(Głos Wy-brzeża),* B. Thoma described current conditions in the port facilities of the Tri-City area. According to the author, "through no fault of their own, the ports of the Tri-City area are proving to be an obstacle restricting the flow of goods in international trade" because:
>
> ". . . the situation in our ports has worsened considerably during the current year. During the first quarter of this year the Polish State Railways barely managed to send 34.9 percent of the coal cars ordered to the docks (during the first quarter of last year 85 percent of the coal car orders were filled, but in April deliveries dropped to 26.5 percent. During the same month the ports were hit by work stoppages of cargo-handling crews and the tie-up of mechanical installations. . . . While fully appreciating the efforts being made by our railroad workers, who are rapidly making up for long years of neglected capital spending, it is still difficult to be reconciled to the fact that this rolling stock, which is in such short supply, often carries nothing more than a load of fresh air. . . . So, a paradoxical situation is emerging where, on the one hand, due to a shortage of boxcars the transshipment facilities of the ports are idled and ships are forced to endure costly layovers in port, while, on the other hand, empty box-

cars roll around the country or decorate the tracks leading into the ports. . . ."

In an article entitled "Looking Down on the Checkerboard Landscape of the Macro region" (*Kierunki,* No. 50), devoted to a discussion of regional planning, J. Zaleski wrote, *inter alia*:

"Increasingly, views are being expressed on a number of different occasions to the effect that regional planning in Poland is presently in the throes of a profound crisis. Is this not perhaps due to the fact that the status of what is—for lack of a more precise term—referred to as a 'region' has become rather uncertain? . . . Theoretically the maritime macroregion encompasses an area composed of three voivodships. However, what we are talking about here is the regional nature of coastal population patterns and the effects of that population's close proximity to the sea, manifested, for example, in the unusual transport system of the coastal communities. As a result, population and manufacturing centers located outside the territorial jurisdiction of the three above-mentioned voivodships are also included in the macroregion's orbit of interests. As integrative processes continue in the future, other areas are also bound to enter this orbit: the Bydgoszcz-Toruń conurbation along the Włocławek-Świecie-Grudziądz axis, the Gorzów Kostrzyn urban chain along the lower Warta, the Piła transportation center, and the Braniewo and Pasłęk *powiaty* of Olsztyn Voivodship, which lie within the Elbląg metropolitan service district. . . . Not without reason the development of maritime transportation services is proving to be a factor closely related to the feasibility of rapidly reforming Poland's unfavorable regional industrial investment structure. . . . The growth in demand for maritime transport services may prove to be a salutary stimulus, which will contribute to the rapid restructuring of what is perhaps the most backward component of our economy, the transportation network. This is an issue of key importance both to our system of domestic interregional transportation links and to the integration of the Polish transport system on an equal basis into the international transportation network, thereby filling the gap that exists at the very center of the European transportation system.

"What proportion of the tens of thousands of automobiles with Swedish and Finnish registrations bound for Yugoslavia and Italy during the tourist season travel along Polish highways? Why is it that the freight tonnage of goods transshipped from south to north on the ferry routes linking us with Scandinavia is 35 times the amount moving in the opposite direction? Why is it that such a large amount of Czechoslovakia's small-scale transit trade passes through Hamburg? Why is it that the containerized freight traffic by sea, rail and truck from Western Europe to Japan carefully avoids Poland, while a large part of it does pass through the GDR and almost all of it passes through the USSR? Knowledgeable experts (including Professor M. Madey-ski, in his address to the National Regional Economic Development Committee) do not deny that our underdeveloped transportation capacity may pose <u>as serious a threat</u> to the national economy as the <u>scarcity</u> of water resources and the energy <u>shortage</u>." (*Report on Materials Censored*, December 1–15, 1974)

Revelations of work stoppages or of the increased pressure on the ports and freight shipping facilities, as in the passages above, even when bracketed by information about the increase in imports and efforts to catch up after the low rate of investment during the Gomułka years, were simply not permitted. The failure of the railroad industry to meet the demand created by the new industrialization was obvious to all, but it, too, could not be discussed. Nor could the mismanagement of the railroad cars which Poland did possess, a problem of even more critical importance. The prohibitions went so far as to ban the mention of new railroad construction that might indirectly imply that the existing system was inadequate or might indicate where investment would be concentrated. Ironically, military restrictions in this area gave way to the desire of the military to improve its image as a positive force in national life.

> 20. It should not be revealed that a second track is being constructed along the railroad line from Wrocław to Zielona Góra, Szczecin and Świnoujście (sometimes referred to as the "Main Odra line," "the main line from Lower Silesia to port," "the main coal line" and so on).
>
> On the other hand, information about the modernization of this railroad line may be provided, along with the news that the army is participating in this work. (Canceled November 19, 1975)

Foreign Trade

The question of foreign trade was an especially sensitive one for the Polish leadership. Much as their hopes for Poland's modernization were based on buying technology so the economy could skip ahead, and much as everyone knew that things Western were of much greater value than things produced in Poland and other Soviet bloc states, they did not wish to be presented as being indebted to the West for the progress Poland had made. As they instructed the censors:

6. Information on the licenses that Poland has bought from capitalist countries should be eliminated from the mass media. This prohibition applies both to licenses already introduced and to newly signed licensing agreements and all calls for the purchase of licenses. Only brief mention of such generally known licensed products as Leyland engines, Jones cranes, Fiat automobiles, Berliet buses or Grundig tape recorders, already in production, may be permitted, and information about any expansion of the scope of such licensing should be eliminated.

This prohibition is dictated by the need to avoid an excess of material concerning the purchase of licenses in capitalist countries. A mass of such information might lead the average reader to conclude that the basic way to modernize our economy is to purchase licenses from advanced capitalist countries. The prohibition does not apply to technical publications, specialized publications, advertising intended for foreign consumption or in-house periodicals of plants carrying on production of licensed goods (provided such material does not violate any other directive). (See Informative Note No. 3, 1975) (Canceled September 12, 1975)

Among the regulations available to us are prohibitions against the discussion of most of Poland's major purchases abroad and of their broader implications:

7. All material (deliberations, suggestions, proposals, etc.) on the subject of agreements currently being made with foreign parties for the purchase of licenses and technical assistance for our tractor industry should be eliminated from the mass media. Nor should any information about the purchase of tractor production licenses be permitted for publication.

7.a. All material providing an overall assessment of our policy concerning the placing of orders at foreign shipyards and imports of merchant ships from foreign countries should be held up for consultation with the GUKPPiW administration.
  b. No information concerning Poland's signing or carrying out of trade contracts for the sale or delivery of ships to member countries of the Common Market or to U.S. shipowners should be permitted for publication. (December 15, 1976)

17. Until further notice, all information concerning Poland's purchase of an American license to produce television sets should be eliminated. (April 9, 1976; canceled August 2, 1976)

18. No information concerning intended or completed ship deliveries to France should be permitted for publication. (December 10, 1976; canceled December 17, 1976)

The censors were provided with a special and revealing explanation for the reasons behind the limits on the reporting of major purchases from the West. The purchase of a license to produce DuPont's synthetic leather, Corfam, was hardly unassailable. Poland had bought the technology and exclusive rights to produce this and other products that had failed in Western markets and did not serve the needs of either their population or export markets. Since this transaction had been heralded as a major purchase, the GUKPPiW used the subject as a case study of the need to exercise care in approving articles:

Main Office for Control of Press,
    Publications and Public Performances
Instruction, Evaluation and Control Group

Warsaw, May 26, 1976
CONFIDENTIAL
Copy No. 29
[Handwritten note:] Canceled December 27, 1976

Informative Note No. 7

In connection with Regulation No. 136, forbidding the publication of materials critical of Polcorfam, we provide the following clarification.

Kurier Polski (No. 112, May 18) published an article entitled "We Cannot Afford It—Inadequate Effects," in which the author, Z. Ró-szański, raised the issue of the inadequate quality of certain market goods, often ones produced on the basis of expensive modern technology purchased with foreign currency. The journalist used as an example Polcorfam, which is produced in the United States. Although there was at that time no concrete censorship directive, the following underlined passages were quite correctly challenged (these passages were presented as an example of proper intervention in *Report on Materials Censored,* No. 15):

"In the allocation of foreign currency for pressing needs (refineries and textile), the synthetic materials industry—particularly the manufacture of synthetics—has always ranked low on the list of investment priorities. So when the expansion of the synthetic leather production unit at the Synthetic Substances Plant in Pionki was announced, it appeared that this problem was at last going to be solved.

Problems with Quality

"Failure in this area came far more quickly than expected, however. Instead of the promised technical 'miracle,' the bales of Polcorfam from Pionki remind us more of variegated fabric than raw material for men's and women's shoes, jackets, etc. Bubbles, cracks, holes, several colors on a single piece of 'hide,' and varying thickness and stains account for the fact that, for example, the Alka Leather Plant in Słupsk sends about 60 percent of its supply of Polcorfam back to the producer. The reason: the raw material is not suitable for the production of shoes.

"The difficulties with Polcorfam are not just limited to quality, however. A square meter of Polcorfam costs from 420 to 425 złotys, while the price of top-grade natural leather is 417. Furthermore, research done by the Central Shoe Laboratory in Kraków indicates that Polcorfam is not suitable for the manufacture of shoes for children, the elderly or individuals with sensitive feet.

"The case of Polcorfam—all the more irritating because three million foreign-exchange złotys in hard currency had to be spent to set the production of this material in motion—is just a more dramatic example of the general quality of production in the chemical industry. It is alarming that the building machinery and road machinery industries have far more seals of quality on their products than does the chemical industry, despite the fact that the latter clearly turns out many more products for the market."

We wish to point out that in connection with the intention of Regulation No. 136 (which has been in effect since May 25), somewhat broader deletions from the above material would need to be made, in order to remove the sentences concerning the price of Polcorfam as well as the underlined passages below, taken from the conclusion to the article.

"As a result of such substantial foreign purchases, Polish industry has been greatly expanded and modernized. There is therefore every reason to expect rapid production results from industry in proportion to the money spent for its expansion.

"But is this cardinal principle being remembered everywhere? The case of Polcorfam proves that foreign currency spent to purchase new machinery and equipment does not always produce the anticipated results. And this situation needs to be changed. We cannot afford to use imported machinery and equipment to turn out goods of poor quality."

Let us point out that, in keeping with the intent of the regulation, materials critical of various kinds of goods made of Polcorfam (shoes, ready-to-wear clothing, etc.) should also not be permitted for publication, if the context indicates that the poor quality or unsuitability of the product is the result of some characteristic of the raw material used—i.e., Polcorfam.

On the other hand, permission may be granted without hesitation for criticisms of the quality of particular products if this poor quality is the result, for example, of poor finishing work or the use of a type of Polcorfam contrary to the producer's recommendations.

In doubtful cases, please consult the GUKPPiW administration.

Vice-Chairman
Edward Adamiak

Copies made: 96
Distributed according to the list

In addition to foreign licenses, other aspects of Poland's burgeoning Western trade were kept out of the mass media—even in the first half of the seventies, when imports were viewed as a positive step. This left the population incapable of judging trade decisions made by the leadership. It also prevented them from getting any perspective on the relative value of Poland's exports and imports:

13. Information about intentions to make a specific foreign transaction, particularly to import, and data concerning the products and conditions involved in import, export or cooperation contracts should not be published *while such agreements are being negotiated* or before they are signed. After the signing of a contract, too, data of this type permitted for publication should be limited to the most important elements concerning the product involved, the date of delivery and the technical or utilitarian features of the commodities. It is neither necessary nor justifiable to provide other *details* of the contract, such as *conditions of payment.*

This applies in particular to so-called binding transactions and to barter agreements providing for payment by deliveries from the Polish side for deliveries of specific commodities from the trading partner. Data concerning such transactions should not be published (except from PAP communiqués). (See Informative Note No. 84, 1973)

Even more significant in understanding the state of affairs that helped to fuel the events of August 1980 is the fact that the value and implications of Poland's foreign debt were hidden from the population and even from trade negotiators. As the debt leapt from five billion dollars in 1974 to more than 25 billion in 1980, the regulation below was more and more strictly enforced. The decision was simply an automatic "no" to any information about the foreign debt until the August strikes forced the government to reveal the extent of the financial catastrophe as an explanation for the economy's failure and a response to citizens' demands for the truth.

> 14. All materials and notes concerning foreign credits and loans to Poland and all information on the subject of claims of foreign governments or private parties stemming from the nationalization by the government of the Polish People's Republic [in the years after World War II] should be referred to the GUKPPiW administration for approval.

Another prohibition, intended to protect Poland's foreign trade options, could be used effectively to prevent criticism of almost any industry, since all industries had foreign trade implications:

> 1. In the interests of our foreign trade, no information discrediting specific export commodities in the eyes of foreign customers may be published.
>
> On the other hand, it is permissible to publish materials in the press discussing shortcomings in technical and scientific infrastructure, work organization, delays in technological progress and the like, as well as material discussing the efforts of factory workers to raise production quality and technical standards.

These general prohibitions were accompanied by more detailed directives. Some, like those prohibiting discussions of the financial details of foreign trade, made all governmental policy decisions in this area secret. For example, the following regulation was put into effect in 1976, when the spiraling process of borrowing to pay interest on earlier loans was already underway and, publicly, trade problems were being admitted to as "temporary phenomena" that were part of Gierek's "economic maneuver." Along with other similar regulations, it prevented any analysis or criticism of Poland's international economic relations. The information was simply not made available to anyone outside of an increasingly small leadership circle. Such restrictions on information made it harder for foreign lenders and Polish regulators to make informed judgments about the situation in Poland. Polish citizens were never made fully aware as to the nature of Poland's credit decisions or varying exchange rates for different kinds of trade. These limits on information left Polish experts far more prepared to discuss trade theory than to address and contribute to the development of ongoing Polish trade policies. They also allowed ministries and industries to buy on the whim of their directors without considering where their needs stood in the larger picture or coordinating their purchases with those who handled other stages of production.

> 4. No materials (mentions, suggestions, etc.) should be permitted for publication that concern the new regulations (in effect for Polish foreign trade as of January 1, 1976). These regulations define the principles for financial reckoning in import and export, and involve:
> a. in import: compensatory charges, compensatory surcharges, turnover taxes, subsidies
> b. in export: lump-sum return of accumulations, return of indirect accumulations, raw materials tax, export tax and other types of financial reckoning
> Absolutely all information (both general and detailed) should be eliminated that concerns legal documents (confidential or for internal use only) which imply that the above-mentioned forms of financial accounting are or were used in Polish foreign trade. This pertains in particular to the *confidential* Council of Ministers Resolution No. 191/75, dated October 10, 1975, on the system of financial accounting in import and export, and to Resolution No. 170/70 (October 23, 1970), Resolution No. 309/71 (December 29, 1971), Resolution No. 269/72 (October 13, 1972) and Ordinance No. 85 issued by the Chairman of the Council of Ministers (October 23, 1970).
> In addition, information should not be published concerning the use, in domestic calculations on foreign trade, of different rates of currency exchange (border rates, permissible rates) for the three different payment areas, nor any indication that a given rate of exchange is in force for a given payment area.
> On the other hand, in publications of a scientific nature and other *theoretical* works (scripts, textbooks), permission may be granted for the publication of such concepts (terms) as rates of exchange, liability, grants-in-aid and subsidies, along with explanatory definitions and an indication of how they operate in foreign trade, provided that such matters are not connected with Polish foreign trade. (October 18, 1974; canceled February 4, 1976)

This rule effectively subsumed a more limited prohibition that had been in effect since 1974 to minimize publicity about "domestic export" and the multiple values assigned to the złoty, depending on whether it was used in individual currency exchanges by tourists or Polish citizens, or for governmental exchange:

> 5. Information on the use, in domestic foreign trade calculations, of different rates of exchange (border rates, permissible rates) in the three payment areas should not be permitted for publication, nor should information showing that a given exchange rate is used in a given payment area. (October 18, 1974; canceled February 4, 1976)

Only one example of censorship involving the inconsistencies in the value of the złoty in comparison to Western hard currencies was provided in the censors' reports smuggled out by Strzyżewski. A plant newspaper had submitted an article which included a statement that, as of the end of 1975,

> "our active foreign-trade balance for the five-year plan now coming to a close amounts to 21 billion foreign-exchange złotys, while our foreign trade debt amounts to approximately 20 billion foreign-exchange złotys." (*Report on Materials Censored,* December 1–15, 1975)

The passage was deleted.

The case of the Polish Fiat Model 76/77 provides the most ironic example of noninformation about sought-after production. Despite the high demand for automobiles in Poland and the investment made by the state to help fill at least a small part of that demand, the censors were instructed that:

> 11. No information, mentions, photographs or the like concerning the so-called Model 76/77 Polish Fiat [a Polish automobile with a completely different body designed by the Italian firm] should be published. This model will begin to be produced in 1976 or 1977. (April 8, 1975) (See Informative Note No. 12, 1975)

In the summer of 1974 Prime Minister Piotr Jaroszewicz, a close ally of Gierek, visited the Żerań automobile factory with an entourage of journalists to publicize his visit. The journalists were also to be shown a display of new models of these large, expensive cars. Both the visit and the display would normally have called for major press coverage; however, for reasons not given in the regulations, journalists were taken on the tour but not allowed to publicize the production of the new élite-model car.

12. On July 13, 1974, Piotr Jaroszewicz, Chairman of the Council of Ministers, will visit the Żerań Passenger Automobile Plant.

During the visit, there will be a display of new automobile models including the so-called "Model 75." Journalists present will be informed by the organizers about the prohibition on taking photographs or publishing restricted information about the new models. In the event that journalists ignore this directive (or in the event of other leaks), all information, mentions, photographs and so on concerning "Model 75" should be eliminated without exception. (July 12, 1974; canceled)

A similar policy is reflected in the restrictions on discussions of detailed aspects of Poland's fishing industry. An event that could have been heralded as an economic achievement thus went unreported—as happened often in other cases. In this instance, fear of having information used by competitors was the reason given for keeping reports on major Polish fishing expeditions out of the news:

16. In connection with the second Polish fishing expedition in the waters of the Antarctic, now underway, it is necessary to eliminate information that might be of interest to competing fishing fleets and those conducting economic espionage. Because of this, no material (press, radio, etc.) should be permitted concerning the following:
   Specific fishing sites
   Types of marine life caught by ships of the Polish Expedition
   Productivity of fishing
   Processing methods
Please refer all doubtful material to the GUKPPiW administration. (February 17, 1977)

8. Materials concerning the following aspects of the Polish deep-sea fishing industry should be held up: the number and type of ships operating in various fishing grounds and the quantitative results of their work; the amount of fish meal produced at sea and on land; detailed information about continued bilateral cooperation between Poland and other nations in the catching, processing and marketing of fish or about the formation of joint enterprises of a corporate nature and Poland's involvement in them; the results of research on the biological resources of the sea conducted by Polish scientific and exploratory ships or facts concerning the undertaking of a "fishery reconnaissance" in search of new fishing grounds (this prohibition does not apply to the research conducted by the research ship *Professor Siedlecki*, built in accordance with a Polish-FAO-UNDP agreement; the results of research conducted by this ship are turned over

to the FAO in keeping with Poland's obligations); the production of protein and jelly from fish according to Polish methods (canceled September 12, 1975). Publication of this type of information is exploited within the international fishing organization to the detriment of new socioeconomic undertakings. Please consult with the GUKP-PiW administration concerning any doubtful matters.

Polish exploration for gas and oil and Polish efforts to develop a process for converting coal into oil and gas were also not to be publicized in the media. These efforts and their potential impact during a period of international energy crisis were considered to be a state secret, even though they could have been used in the media as a demonstration of the vitality of Polish science and the country's future economic potential:

> 5. Until further notice, no information about Polish exploration for oil and natural gas as well as any discoveries made in Poland or long-range prospects in this area should be permitted in the mass media. This prohibition does not apply to scientific works (scientific periodicals and nonserial publications), which are bound by current regulations on the preservation of state secrets.

> 14. All information about the Polish method of producing liquid and gas fuels from hard coal, a method protected by the regulations on state secrets, should be eliminated. Until further notice, to avoid the drawing of implications, all information concerning the method of processing coal to produce gas and oil currently in use at the Carbochemistry Institute at Wyry near Katowice should also be eliminated. (February 13, 1976)

Both Poland's trade with the West and its trade with other members of the CMEA (Council for Mutual Economic Assistance) were sensitive issues, the latter even more sensitive than the former. To begin with, Poland, as a member of CMEA, was responsible for seeing to it that the "secrets" of intra-bloc trade were not revealed. The restrictions were partly designed to allow the Soviet bloc to present an undivided image to the outside world, and partly to avoid providing the West with any information it could use to weaken the bloc and its international position:

> Section IV. Council for Mutual Economic Assistance
> 1. In information concerning CMEA, no material questioning the appropriateness or the principles of economic cooperation among the

socialist countries, or revealing differences between individual countries or critical of their individual positions, should be permitted for publication.

2. No data on the defense capabilities of CMEA countries should be permitted for publication in information about CMEA.

3. No compiled data on raw material shortages in CMEA countries should be permitted for publication in information on CMEA.

4. No information about the existence of a CMEA commission coordinating cooperation between CMEA countries and the developing countries should be permitted for publication in materials on CMEA. This prohibition does not apply to official communiqués issued through PAP.

Economic relations between Soviet bloc states were likewise to be kept secret. Even basic information necessary to encourage citizens to travel within the bloc was not recorded in the media. While the exchange values for Eastern bloc currencies were posted at banks, they were not to appear in the mass media and could not easily, therefore, be compared with previous years or with other Soviet bloc states' policies, nor were they of use to anyone who did not have a reason to go to the bank with hard currency.

6. The rates of exchange and coefficients for the national currencies of the CMEA countries (Bulgaria, Czechoslovakia, Cuba, Mongolia, German Democratic Republic, Poland, Rumania, Hungary, the USSR) or Yugoslavia, expressed in terms of the common currency—i.e., the transfer ruble—or in terms of the direct exchange should not be permitted for publication. It is likewise forbidden to publish statistical data about the amounts of currency exchanged at these rates. The content of this prohibition is not to be made known outside of the censors' office.

Soviet products imported into Poland were to be beyond reproach. So seriously was this principle taken that instances of extensive criticism of Soviet products were to be called to the attention of the chief censorship authorities. Interestingly, efforts also were made to reassure the censors themselves of the quality of Soviet products:

8. Criticism of Soviet-produced drilling equipment used in geological exploration in Poland should not be permitted, nor should any calls for the purchase of drilling equipment from other foreign sources. The

utility of the Soviet equipment imported by us does not differ from that of equipment produced by Western firms. We shall therefore continue to import Soviet equipment, but unjustified criticism could lead to a delay in delivery by the Soviet side. All minor criticism should be deleted without exception, and more extensive materials should be referred to the GUKPPiW administration.

Nor were the censors to permit the admission that Western goods were better than Soviet goods. Trade in basic commodities between Poland and other members of the bloc was plagued by periodic shortages of basic commodities, and the public was constantly suspicious that commodities in short supply at home were being sold to other Soviet bloc countries as other East Europeans suspected that their shortages were a result of exports to Poland and the rest of the bloc. The Polish authorities were unwilling to allow any material that might increase such suspicions to appear in the press. So deep was this concern that reports of East German meat exports to Poland were not to appear in the Polish press, lest this information be picked up by East German readers who faced shortages of meat in their own markets:

> 10. No information or data concerning the import of meat or meat products from the German Democratic Republic should be permitted for publication. On the other hand, both general information on meat imports and data concerning specific importation agreements that have already been made (except with the GDR) may appear, provided they do not violate other censorship regulations.

> 12. No information concerning Poland's export of meat to the USSR should be permitted. This prohibition is intended solely for the benefit of the censorship teams.

Polish regulations also prohibited most material on the nature of Polish-Soviet trade. In at least one case, prohibitions made it impossible to draw attention even to a Soviet technological contribution to Poland:

> 1. Do not permit any sort of information concerning the USSR's transfer to Poland of documentation concerning liquid self-hardening substances used in the founding industry or concerning our founding industry's use of this technology. (Canceled October 9, 1974)

Nor could there be any mention of the rail line built to fit Soviet wide-gauge trains which were to carry steel and iron ore from the new steel plant in Katowice to the Soviet Union until eighteen months after its construction. The regulation was partly an attempt to prevent feeding the suspicions of the Polish population that Polish resources were being siphoned off by the Soviet Union. But it reflected far more than simply an attempt to keep an economic secret and an acknowledgment of Polish anti-Soviet feeling; it also reflected the Soviets' and Poles' concern about revealing possible military targets:

> 65. No information should be permitted on the subject of the construction of a second (wide-gauge) railroad track along the route between Hrubieszów and Katowice via Biłgoraj. (January 31, 1975; canceled May 31, 1976)

The food situation in Poland was already a sensitive issue in 1974. According to one of the regulations available to us, journals were prohibited from providing any reportage of their own concerning the importation of grain, itself a sign of grave economic failure since, before the Communist takeover, Poland was a major grain exporter. Given the problems with food in the seventies, the following regulation was probably designed to prevent speculation about the failure of the yearly grain harvest. It was a hedge against raising popular expectations:

> 9 Journals' *own* information concerning the foreign grain import negotiations should not be permitted.
> Figures on the size of individual purchases should not be published either, nor should forecasts for coming years be provided. This does not apply to official communiqués from PAP.

Another sensitive subject related to the import of food was Poland's apparent role as a purchasing agent of basic supplies for other countries, supplies Poland itself was lacking:

> 11. Information about annual national coffee consumption should not be provided, to make it impossible to determine the amount of coffee that is reexported.

Productivity

Polish industry was of real concern to journalists (and to the censors who monitored them). Gierek's original economic program had hinged on increasing plant and worker productivity. In the early seventies, the plan was that a combination of higher salaries, a greater supply of consumer goods, and new factories would transform the Polish economy. But as censored materials make clear, this was never achieved. Many areas of the economy suffered from serious labor shortages, which in large part resulted from the dramatic decline in the birthrate and the massive population losses that Poland suffered during the war. There were simply few stable, middle-aged workers available. And as the postwar baby-boom generation came of age, it saw itself as too well educated to take low-status, low-salary jobs in the service sector. As a result, in the mid-seventies many stores were so short of clerks that they had to close for days at a time. Even better-paying factory jobs, which the decentralization plans required be concentrated outside of major cities, often went unfilled, since few young skilled workers were willing to relocate. They knew that since construction plans were seldom if ever realized, housing, stores and goods would not be available in new industrial areas for years. As a result, factory directors were forced into cutthroat competition for a scarce supply of workers who would relocate, or had to count on absences and transfers from one factory to another.

Propaganda aimed at mobilizing workers was not successful in raising labor productivity. Poles simply had no incentives to compete on the job market. Anyone who wanted to work was guaranteed a job and a base salary, but the salaries were never sufficient to inspire workers to be productive or to bring young women with working husbands to the work force when they had young children. Poland's consumer industries, a frequent target for journalists' criticism, often did not produce the kinds and quality of goods the public wanted. Nor did the centralized economy facilitate reasonable pricing in relation to earnings. It was clear, too, that corruption, the manipulation of statistics and management inefficiency were pervasive.

Labor problems were a matter of primary concern to the Gierek leadership. As new factories were built, the traditional problem of low productivity became almost secondary to that of the supply of labor. For three months, censors were instructed to keep all discussion of these shortages and their implications out of the media:

> 12 (Supplement). Articles and information about the supposed general shortage of factory personnel as a major cause for the fact that investment and production plans are not always fully realized should be removed from the mass media. (October 18, 1974; canceled January 31, 1975)

Censored passages from articles dealing with this problem while the regulation was in effect bear witness to the serious nature of the labor shortage and to some of the unorthodox methods used by state factories to compete with other state factories to obtain workers:

> A statement was challenged in a report from the Nizan Construction Enterprise entitled "Nizan Construction Workers" (*Konfrontacje,* No. 11). It expressed the opinion that the local area was overrun with wildcat labor brokers from all over Poland, to whom some people are willing to pay appropriate fees for " 'producing' a new worker."

> The following deletions, among others, were made in this article by L. Pracki entitled "The Jobs Have Been Filled" *(Głos Pracy),* on the manpower situation in the Okęcie Transportation Equipment Plant:
> "The Transportation Equipment Plant in Okęcie needs several dozen more people in order to have a fully staffed plant. The biggest labor shortage is in the manual labor category. A similar situation exists in many other plants. This is why personnel managers are literally grasping for people wherever they can find them. It does no good to try to forbid this kind of activity, since the incentives motivating personnel managers to outbid each other in buying workers are much stronger than the force of any official injunctions. The failure to fulfill plan targets and the lack of bonuses for workers can be a lot more costly to a plant director than the evasion of regulations restricting manpower transfers. Equipment is certainly important, but personnel is most important of all. In the meantime, in the machinery department, conditions and even the level of cleanliness (due to a shortage of cleaning ladies) leave much to be desired despite the improvements that have been made. The range between the highest and lowest wages is narrowest in the internal transport department and in other auxiliary sections. This hinders the possibility of wage increases and makes high turnover a foregone conclusion. The latter is a serious problem in this department, which is several dozen persons short of being fully staffed. Engi-

neer Bogdan Żywica says that it is high time to get rid of brooms and shovels and to proceed with more rapid mechanization of those jobs that are simple, strenuous and mostly low-paying. He adds that it is also high time to adopt the principle that every job well done can be more profitable than one that is done poorly or any old way.

"This would amount to a first step in the direction of curtailing excessive employee turnover. The second step ought to involve a greater concern for working conditions, work safety and hygiene, as well as for social services. According to the plant director, more attention should also be devoted to devising a better system of encouraging workers to take a personal interest in plant affairs, <u>for example, by granting earlier bonuses for the completion of worker training periods in one and the same plant.</u> . . ." (*Report on Materials Censored,* December 1–15, 1974)

Housing

Workers' lives were complicated by the problems of daily life in Poland. None of the promises of the Gierek regime to provide readily available good housing and high-quality consumer goods were being fulfilled by the mid-seventies. Housing was the most critical area. The problems seemed so irresolvable to journalists that they rarely tried to intervene or to comment on them. When they did deal with housing, they were barred from pointing out, for example, that construction plans were not being fulfilled and that statistics were being doctored to cover up that fact:

In *Walka Młodych* (No. 12) we questioned the following item by A. Zieliński entitled "No," accusing construction enterprises of providing false information about their implementation of the 1973 plan. Here is the text:

"Official communiqués were optimistic. In housing construction the 1973 plan had been carried out. At first, everyone rejoiced. Only later did the people for whom there were no apartments despite the earlier findings begin to do a detailed count. Calculations indicate that 2,314 apartments were missing from the category of general housing cooperative construction. Which count was correct: that of the Ministry of Construction or that of the housing cooperatives? We began to examine the problem in a different way. Why was it that the plan was reported to be 100 percent fulfilled, when last year several thousand apartments were completed under the special program known as 'youth patronage construction"? I emphasize the fact that these apartments were constructed outside the framework of the plan. The construction enterprises were not playing fair. A whole 3 percent of the apartments (2,314) included in the statistics as apartments completed within the framework of the plan were actually built under the 'patronage' program. The construction enterprises claimed someone else's work as their own. Therefore, to set the record straight, it should be stated that the cooperative housing construction plan was not carried out. But other questions still remain. Why were the apartments constructed by the young people included in the housing construction report (when they should have been reported as construction in excess of what was planned), thereby leading people astray? Will this year's cooperative construction plan be exceeded by 2,314 apartments, i.e., by the number that were not completed in 1973? And finally the last question, or rather a reflection: In 1974 it is expected that, in addition to the plan, the young people will construct 3,300 apartments under the 'patronage' program. Perhaps this will provide even more of a percentage cover for the official plan. Does this mean that still more dishonest enterprises will be discovered?" (*Report on Materials Censored,* March 16–31, 1974)

Nor could they draw attention to the all too visible allocation of the housing on an ad hoc basis, at best, most often to those who had pull or could offer the best bribes.

A. Paszyński also discussed the country's current housing situation in an article entitled "On the Threshold and Beyond" (*Wektory,* No. 12). The author was primarily concerned with calling attention to "several problems that call for immediate corrective action." Certain statements and arguments made by the author, including the passages marked below, were either challenged or recommended for rewriting.

"The subordination of housing distribution policy, at a time of general housing shortage, to ad hoc goals, or as it is more elegantly characterized, to 'general social considerations,' has meant, in practice, that the quota of housing allocated to enterprises [for their employees] has grown at the expense of that allotted to cooperatives and people's councils. Thus people waiting in line for an apartment, who keep close tabs on the allocation of housing units, are bound to become agitated, especially since they are not familiar with the working of the allocation machinery, only with its results.

"Given this situation, it would seem to be necessary to submit an urgent request calling for a reexamination of current practices governing the distribution of housing units.

"A decision needs to be made between two alternatives. Namely, either to agree that enterprises are to have access to an increased quota of apartments and, at the same time, to require them to draw up a waiting list covering all employees, both those on the general community waiting list and those who expect to receive an apartment out of the allotment assigned to the enterprise, or—and this option is probably more consistent with a sense of social justice—to make available to the cooperatives the entire allotment of housing units constructed by them, while setting aside a certain percentage of this housing, to be determined in agreement with local authorities, to meet the needs of factories undergoing expansion. . . ." (*Report on Materials Censored,* December 1–15, 1974)

Even when there was new housing to write about, journalists could not draw attention to its quality since much of the housing being produced was shoddy:

"The time is certainly drawing near, however slowly, when the vision of having a roof of one's own overhead will not be as remote as it once was, when it will become feasible to make a real choice about the form, type and even the size of the housing unit that one desires. When that time comes, will anyone be interested in the kind of housing that we have to offer nowadays? However you look at it, I do not think that anyone will be interested. The kind of housing that proves acceptable under conditions of a housing 'emergency' is bound to be rejected when things are different.

Nor were the problems posed by the lack of shops and services to be admitted to in print, even though readers coped with these problems every day and knew them well:

"Next on our list of demands is the question of trade and services. One can't really complain about the services, since there simply aren't any. You could run all over half of Warsaw and not find a shoemaker. To say nothing of plumbers, carpenters or tailors. What about retail trade? Generally speaking, there are a few well-stocked stores, but they are as crowded as the open-air market in Nowy Targ. As for the rest?

"You ought to try just stopping off at a small store in a housing project after work to buy some cream or fresh butter! Another common problem is the signs hanging in store windows that read: 'Closed due to illness or lack of staff.' You have to go back downtown for a loaf of bread." (*Report on Materials Censored,* December 1–15, 1975)

Consumer Goods

The failure of the Gierek promise to provide Poles with an array of consumer goods was evident in daily Polish life. But, as the censors were instructed, articles like those *Życie Gospodarcze* was able to run (over the censors' objections) on the poor quality of basic consumer goods and on the serious shortcomings of the consumer goods industries, were not to be tolerated. The issues they raised were certain to touch raw nerves in a public constantly in search of usable consumer goods:

> Main Office for Control of Press,
>   Publications and Public Performances
> Instruction, Evaluation and Control Group
> No. ZT-PF-134a/2/76
>
> > Warsaw, July 6, 1976
> > CONFIDENTIAL
> > Copy No. 48
>
> Instructive Note No. 2

Życie Gospodarcze, No. 5 (July 1976), published two articles in its "Industry-Trade-Consumers" section that were very critical in their assessment of the market situation in Poland, of the supply of ready-made clothing and of the quality and prices of the goods available: A. Szymańska, " 'Czesia' for 360 Złotys," and Z. Długosz, "Raisin Bread."

In her article, A. Szymańska wrote that the overwhelming majority of goods offered in shops selling ready-made clothing are what we refer to as "junk," and on top of that they often come with a ticket proclaiming them to be something new.

In addition to its one-sided criticism of market supply, this article made extensive generalizations about the policy of introducing doubtful "novelties" onto the market. It was also very pessimistic in its note that despite enormous outlays in the knitwear industry, the situation in this field nationwide is becoming worse.

In the second article, entitled "Raisin Bread," A. Długosz likewise discussed the supply of clothing in the stores. In her opinion, most of the items offered are unfashionable or of poor quality. The stores rarely get goods that the customers like, and therefore, when they do, such items are eagerly snapped up. According to the author, this situation reflects the fact that industry is largely concerned with its own advantage and convenience. At the same time, Długosz offers the example of some Hong Kong shirts eagerly bought up by shoppers because of their attractive appearance and low price, and asks how it is that a capitalist can produce attractive, inexpensive goods while we cannot. One of the reasons she suggests is that "there are elements that hinder an improved adaptation of the supply of goods to demand."

The depressing tone of these articles is accentuated by the addition of an unfavorable comparison between the paralysis of our "key" investments and the efficiency of local and foreign "private businessmen."

In this context, the collection of photographs included also should have been evaluated: those on the first, second and third pages ("our junk") were compared with the photograph of two models on the fourth page ("Between Warsaw and New York").

Although this publication also contains some positive statements and points of view, on the whole a negative tone predominates.

The controversial items from *Życie Gospodarcze* discussed here concerned very important, difficult socioeconomic problems, and should have been assessed with great care both by the editorial board and by the representative of our office.

It was the censors' rejection of all open critical discussion of the consumer goods industry, coupled with their refusal to permit any discussion of shortages, that probably most galled the public. This, more than any other aspect of economic reporting, created a crisis of confidence. Restrictions on other types of economic journalism cut out so much information in the middle and late Gierek years that the people were left with no real sense of either the shortcomings or achievements of Poland's industrialization effort and its foreign economic involvement. But the disaster that was the consumer goods and housing industry was painfully apparent to everyone except the few who could shop in special party and government stores.

Agriculture

Although industrialization was given the highest priority by Gierek's economic policy and its coverage was therefore strictly monitored, agriculture presented Polish journalists with even more perplexing problems. In ideological terms, private agriculture is an anathema to a Communist state; in reality, the bulk of Poland's agricultural land was cultivated by private peasant farmers who provided most of the country's foodstuffs. For the media, this conflict between ideology and reality presented a serious problem made worse in the mid-seventies by the decreasing productivity of the entire agricultural sector, Poland's increasing reliance on agricultural exports to pay its foreign debt and the continuing failure of the leadership to create a balanced and effective agricultural policy.

The ramifications of the agricultural crisis were far broader in the mid-seventies than they were earlier, when food shortages affected only part of the population. Gierek's promises of a better life had increased popular expectations, and his failing industrial projects forced the government to take Polish food off the market and ship it abroad to earn hard currency. All of this meant that virtually no one was untouched by the dramatic shortages in food and by the constant search for something to buy and the waiting in line required to feed a family. Rather than explain the reason for Poland's reliance on agricultural exports to the West and for shortages on the domestic market, censors were instructed to keep information on potential shortages and supply problems out of the media:

> 36. No information about or mention of the failure of the wholesale centers to purchase the expected number of cattle and hogs from the farmers should be permitted for publication. (March 19, 1975; canceled June 10, 1975)

At the same time they sought to screen out information on successful harvests that might raise expectations for a good supply of foodstuffs:

> 148. In addition to the ban on reporting data from this year's harvest of the four basic grains and of root crops and data on the wholesale purchase of these products (see *Rules and Recommendations*, p. 129, 1 and 2), no *percentages* indicating the status of the ongoing wholesale purchasing process or information about its full realization should be permitted for publication.
>
> Information (assessments, statements) tending to imply that yields, harvests or wholesale purchases (on a nationwide or voivodship scale) this year were better than those of previous years should also be eliminated. (See Informative Note No. 12/76) (September 26, 1976; canceled November 20, 1976)

Main Office for Control of Press,
    Publications and Public Performances
Instruction, Evaluation and Control Group
No. ZI.Pf-131/12/76

> Warsaw, September 25, 1976
> C O N F I D E N T I A L
> Copy No. 29

Informative Note No. 12

In connection with Regulation No. 148, we wish to further explain that
the purpose of this censorship directive is to avoid the publication of
material that might lead the reader to mistakenly conclude that grain
yields this year in our country are better than last year or in previous
years. As everyone knows, this year the climate varied greatly from one
region of the country to another. (Among other things, losses in yields
due to drought in the commodity-oriented western voivodships were
surely not compensated for by better yields in others.)

For this reason, even such general formulations as those in an article
entitled "Holiday for Thrifty People" (*Gazeta Olsztyńska,* No. 208,
September 13) should be eliminated:

"Today every Olsztyn farmer can boldly say, with satisfaction and
pride, that all the work done in the voivodship was done efficiently and
the yields obtained are higher than in past years."

In connection with the fact that large foreign grain purchases are
anticipated, such exaggeratedly optimistic assessments of this year's
yields are not warranted. In addition, various sorts of official statements clearly reveal that the past three years have not been the best for
Polish agriculture.

Thus, for example, we read the following in the text of the information presented by [Prime Minister] Piotr Jaroszewicz to the Sejm on
September 22 of this year.

"Current difficulties are chiefly the result of three bad years in a row
for agriculture. The preliminary estimate of the losses that agriculture
suffered in 1974–1976 in comparison to annual plans places the amount
at 63 billion złotys in terms of final production. We have fallen short
by more than 6 million tons of grain, nearly 15 million tons of potatoes
and about 300,000 tons of meat during the past three years of poor
crops.

"This year alone we will be about 4 million tons of grain short of
planned targets, approximately the amount that is collected by government wholesale-purchasing points each year. Harvests of hay and other
fodder were inadequate. Everyone knows that plantings of potatoes,

sugar beets and some other vegetables also suffered adverse effects from the weather in the spring and summer.

"In this situation, the government decided on substantial imports of grain and fodder. In fiscal 1975–1976 they reached the equivalent of 7 million tons of grain. This has eased but not eliminated the shortage of fodder.

"Difficulties with fodder were responsible, particularly on peasant farms, for slowed growth and then decline in the number of livestock. We are now 1 million head of cattle and 2.5 million hogs short of the goals of the 1976 plan.

"These are the consequences of three years of poor harvests, which, it is true, have affected different parts of the country from one year to the next, but which altogether have had a serious impact on crop and livestock production and, as a result, on the general market situation and the economy as a whole."

Hence it is the aim of Regulation No. 148 to prevent the mass media from publishing information that might unintentionally mislead the reader.

> Vice-Chairman
> Edward Adamiak

Copies made: 96
Distributed according to the list

The censors were also instructed to prevent the publication of information indicating that scarce basic agricultural commodities might be exported to earn increasingly desperately needed foreign currency:

47. Information that might reveal (directly or indirectly) the size of production plans or the amount of sugar produced during this year's sugar campaign should not be published. This applies both to the sugar industry as a whole and to individual sugar refineries.

Nor should any information be provided on the size of sugar reserves from past years. No information should be permitted on the possibility that our foreign trade might take advantage of the favorable export market for sugar due to a world shortage. (This includes any indication of export trends, the possibility of increasing export or obtaining a higher price, etc.)

On the other hand, it is permissible to allow information on the unsatisfied demand for sugar in various countries, the adoption of conservation and "protective" measures there and the establishment of prices of this product in the commodities market. (November 20, 1974; canceled March 8, 1975)

Another subject not to be discussed was the incidence of various agricultural diseases and pests, on the grounds that such information might cause panic in Poland or discourage Western buyers. Farmers who had to combat these threatened epidemics were therefore also left with virtually no information:

2. In view of the incidence in this country of certain agricultural diseases and pests, and in view of the possibility that it might be difficult to export agricultural products if these diseases or pests were revealed, no information concerning the incidence, distribution or level, on either a nationwide or a regional scale, of the following diseases and pests should be permitted to appear:
   1. Corynebacterium sepedonicum
   2. Urocistis cepulea
   3. Heterodera rostachiensis
   4. Prunus virus 7
   5. Corynebacterium michiganense
   6. Synchytrium endobioticum
   7. Dytylenchus dipsaci
   8. Dytylenchus estructor
   9. Quadraspidictus perniciozus
   10. Edwinia amylovora

3. In certain regions of the country there may occur cases of diseases of cattle, hogs and horses which, if revealed, could cause Poland to suffer problems in the export of livestock and raw and processed animal products. In this connection, no information (in the daily press, radio, television or periodicals) concerning occurrences of the following animal diseases in our country should be permitted for publication:
   1. hoof-and-mouth disease (Aphta epizootica)
   2. vesicular disease of swine (SVD)
   3. brucellosis
   4. leukosis
   5. equine influenza
   6. glanders
   7. swine plague (pestis suum)
General statements about the incidence of epidemic diseases of cattle and hogs in certain regions of the country should also be eliminated.

On the other hand, there should be no interference in statements about disease prevention campaigns, or in propaganda to encourage the vaccination of cattle, hogs and other livestock.

Nor should popular scientific articles in professional journals and the daily press discussing the above-mentioned diseases in a theoretical manner (i.e., not indicating their occurrence in Poland) be questioned.

The publication of materials describing the efforts and achievements of the veterinary service in combating the above-mentioned diseases may also be permitted once the occurrence of the disease has become public knowledge or once it has been announced to the International Office of Animal Health.

In doubtful cases, consult the GUKPPiW administration.

Discussions of general agricultural policy problems were kept circumspect. Although 90 percent of Polish agriculture was privately owned and run, its advantages and successes were not allowed to be discussed in print. To do so would, after all, not only prove Marxism wrong but also encourage private farmers and their children to hang on to their small farms and not relinquish them to the state when they grew too old to farm or moved to more attractive and exciting urban centers. Thus such positive statements about private agricultural production as the following, from a regional party conference, were kept out of the regional party paper:

> In an article entitled "The Peasant Is a Powerful Force, and That's That!" (*Wiadomości Zachodnie,* No. 50), J. Cieślak, made use of the conclusions of a plenum of the Koszalin Voivodship Committee of the PZPR devoted to a discussion of agriculture and offered an analysis of the current situation in this sector of the economy in the Koszalin region. The following statements of opinion were either deleted or recommended for rewriting:
>
> "I do not have much faith in figures, but these particular figures are persuasive. Private peasants in the Koszalin region farm up to 45 percent of the arable land in the entire voivodship. <u>On the other hand, they account for 66.4 percent of the region's grain production, 58 percent of the total livestock production and 64 percent of the total hog production. Private agriculture is outstripped by the performance of the socialized sector only in the production of milk and potatoes.</u> . . . At the same time, it needs to be said that this is not modern agriculture, with the exception of its acreage potential. . . . The average size of farms exceeds seven hectares, and half of them are larger than ten hectares in area. . . . <u>Thus the situation is such that, under a favorable land tenure structure, represented by large state, agricultural-circle and private farms, the private farm, owing to its high economic and commercial efficiency, has become the chief factor regulating the rate of change in agriculture as a whole.</u> . . . The better things are in this latter sector, the more abundance and tran-

quillity in the socialized sector. . . ." (*Report on Materials Censored,* December 1–15, 1975)

The impossibility of indicating the importance of private agriculture in the mass media was a cause as well as a result of the government's inability to develop an agricultural policy that would give the private sector its due. The ban on the publication of information and discussion that presented private agriculture as a viable part of Polish life left agricultural specialists and policy makers at least partially blind to its needs and potential. One area in which the censors imposed blinders was the mechanization of agriculture. The difficulties created by the government's refusal to take account of the needs of private farmers for mechanized equipment were not allowed to be discussed in the media:

> In an article entitled "Progress Is Not Made by Machines Alone" (*Plon,* No. 51–52), K. Woźnicki made the following introductory statement: "As everyone knows, the demand for tractors and farm machinery in Poland is enormous. There is talk of 100,000 farmers waiting for tractors, for which they have filed numerous applications. At present, no one really knows how many farmers are waiting for tractors. However, it is known that at an auction held in Łosice, 150 farmers submitted bids on four old tractors that were almost ready for scrapping. Although the tractors were appraised as being worth a few thousand złotys, the selling price went as high as 65,000 złotys. . . ." (*Report on Materials Censored,* December 1–15, 1975)

The censor's decision here was based on his instructions to eliminate even implicit criticism of the shortage of machinery for private farms:

> 10. Calls for the sale of new or recalled tractors to farmers working their land privately should not be permitted for publication in the mass media. Material illustrating farmer demand for tractors should also be eliminated.

Even raising the possibility of recycling used tractors was disallowed:

> In a challenged article entitled "The Simplest Solution Is to Scrap Them . . .," carried by *Słowo Ludu,* H. Bezak criticized procedures followed in arranging for the sale of used farm machinery. According to the author, the promotion of the sale of used farm machinery could

"substantially alleviate" the "shortage" of tractors and other machinery that is experienced chiefly by private-sector farmers. Stressing that "the resale of used equipment is a universal practice even in the affluent countries," and that "there are good economic reasons for this," H. Bezak wondered why "this problem is regarded in Poland—quite wrongly—as a matter of such marginal importance." (*Report on Materials Censored,* March 16–31, 1974)

Following is a graphic illustration of the chaos that resulted from a confused agricultural policy and both the inadvertent and the deliberate discrimination against private peasant farmers—the most productive agricultural sector—as well as the general corruption and the control exercised from the party leadership rather than by local populations:

The Książka i Wiedza publishing house submitted a collection entitled *A Ploughed Field, a Nice House: Reminiscences of Rural Women* (to be published in an edition of 5,000 copies). Interventions were made in the following passages, statements made by women about contemporary rural living conditions:

"Buildings are going up in the villages and towns, but it is becoming increasingly difficult for a peasant to build a good house with central heating and running water. And connection into a gas line is an unattainable dream for us. Only a few farmers are well off enough to be able to afford gas. . . .

"Things will not go well for the peasant as long as bureaucracy and bribery continue to run rampant. Some people say that the peasants should stop paying out bribes, and the officials will stop taking them. But this isn't where we should start. A peasant wants to build himself a house, but there aren't any building materials. He goes from the *gmina* cooperative to the *powiat* administration of *gmina* cooperatives. He runs around everywhere asking and begging. But if he doesn't have a liter of vodka with the chairman and doesn't dig down into both pockets, he won't accomplish anything. He will come home hungry and cold and just have to keep on waiting. I know from experience. I know for a fact that this is how it is, because my husband doesn't like to drink, and—as I wrote above—he couldn't even get a hoe from the agricultural circle when he wanted one. Most likely they said: 'If you don't drink and you're a miser, you'll just have to wait.'

"There is a lot that this institution could do to improve the efficiency of its work, too. There is a lot that we are also doing wrong in the district council and the *gmina* cooperative. In these institutions people complain that we are unfair in the way we distribute cement, wire and bricks for homebuilding: some people get their allotments right away, while others have to wait a very long time. No attention is paid to who is first on the waiting list, and there are a lot of misunderstandings because of this. So, even in the 'Peasant Self-Help' cooperative, which ought to be called 'Peasant Self-Destruction,' despite the members' good intentions, the director always manages to get the most of everything he wants before anyone else, to the great dissatisfaction of the other members. It is an unsavory business, but whenever it comes time to elect a new administration, the names of the new presidents are always brought to us in somebody's briefcase. And there is nothing we can say about it." (*Report on Materials Censored,* July 16–31, 1975)

Similar ironies were stressed in the following censored picture of the struggles in peasant life:

In Issue No. 30 of *Życie Gospodarcze,* interventions were made in a letter from a reader in Nysa who had worked and lived in the countryside for a number of years. In his letter, entitled "What Is There to Eat in the Polish Countryside?" the reader offered his views on, among other things, the subject of meat consumption in rural areas, "how rural people supposedly eat less meat."

"While I was working as an inspector, a certain farmer called my attention to the following paradoxical situation: 'One day I delivered two hogs to the procurement stockyard, each weighing between 170 and 190 kilos, and then set out for the *gmina* cooperative butcher shop to buy a half-kilo of pork. The kids asked me to get some for them, since they had helped to fatten up the pigs I'd just sold. "There might be some pork for sale around Easter, Pops," the butcher told me. So I didn't bother to fatten up my third hog, which already weighed almost 150 kilos. I just butchered it for home consumption. But I ask you, is that any way to run a farm? And this is all because the *gmina* cooperative can't manage to supply me with half a kilo of pork, even if it's only once a month. We aren't conserving meat. Instead, we're eating more than we should. . . .'

"The slaughtering of hogs for home use is also a pretty widespread custom in my own village in Opole Voivodship. The farmers don't care what the *gmina* cooperative might think about it. They just go ahead and slaughter their hogs. They make arrangements with their neighbors and give them half of the slaughtered pig as a loan. When their neighbors get around to slaughtering their own hogs, they pay back the loan in kind. I have done the same thing, since, as a pensioner, I no longer live in the city. . . ." (*Report on Materials Censored,* July 16–31, 1975)

The resolution of these difficulties on the farms, no matter how visible they were, eluded the Gierek administration, just as it had previous leaderships. The failure of policy makers to make headway in this area was so obvious that they could not permit even scholarly discussions of past agricultural policies. The censors also refused to allow discussions of the continual changes in agricultural policies:

> In an article entitled "Agriculture and the National Diet at the Seventh Congress of the Chief Technical Organization" (*Postęp w Rolnictwie,* No. 10), Professor R. Manteuffel, one of those who "took the floor" in the pre-Congress debate, wrote, among other things:
> ". . . The Role of Agricultural Engineers and Technicians. In my opinion, their primary duty consists in showing a sense of responsibility for the land placed in their care and for the natural environment in which they do their work. They must not be allowed to ruin the land's productive capacity and thereby contribute to reduced output. On the contrary, they should contribute to the economically rational maximization of production per unit of land area. They must also be prevented from contributing to or tolerating the destruction or poisoning of the natural environment inhabited by people, plants and animals. In addition to duties, they also have certain rights. The authorities must in turn be loyal to them. What I have in mind here are the various sudden and frequently unjustified reorganizations of agriculture on a massive scale, with the result that people who consciously chose careers in agriculture because of the prospects it offers and because of the nature of the work per se, are suddenly forced to take different jobs for which they may be (and frequently are) unsuited. What I am saying here is not just an expression of sentimental appreciation for their lot. These kinds of organizational changes make them unhappy in their jobs, and in the end they are inclined to give up practical agricultural work altogether in favor of pursuing different careers or purely administrative jobs." (*Report on Materials Censored*, December 1–15, 1974)

Nor would the censors allow any reference to the well-known postwar distrust between Communist party leaders and the peasantry:

> In an article by J. Poniatowski entitled "Mass Agricultural Education" (*Wieś i Rolnictwo,* No. 4), cuts were made in passages commenting on

"the underdevelopment of self-government among European farmers" and about agricultural education.

"The several generations that separate the European countryside from the age of feudalism and serfdom have not afforded enough time in which to develop widely shared political skills and to create broadly based rural political institutions. The more serious steps in this direction have usually stemmed from initiatives launched by rulers, and they have always been based on officially sanctioned plans and procedures. The well-known loyalty of the peasantry to the state is for all practical purposes a function of their helplessness in the face of the pressure and repression of the administrative apparatus. The so-called peasant revolts and food delivery strikes are important to the extent that they alarm public opinion and produce loud demands for the opening of a dialogue with governmental authorities with a view to putting an end to some intolerable state of affairs. Even the most clearly defined and undisputed self-government rights have been neglected, and since the peasants lack their own central political institutions capable of mobilizing a widely scattered rural population, these rights are quietly surrendered to the administrative authorities. They have been overshadowed by a pervasive denial of responsibility, which is so very characteristic of our own countryside. (*Report on Materials Censored,* December 1–15, 1974)

The regime's sensitivity to all matters pertaining to agricultural problems meant, ultimately, that no policy alternatives could be discussed. This was in part a measure of the total inability of the regime to deal with agricultural problems and in part a product of the authorities' fear of the peasant: to reveal any potential program for peasant lands was to risk having that policy blocked at its inception by adverse peasant reactions. Therefore, even to suggest that "the creation of suitable economic and legal conditions . . . will be conducive to the direct takeover of land from private farmers by agricultural circle centers," or to make a statement demanding that state subsidies be granted to "agricultural circles that take over the land of elderly private farmers—for the purpose of putting these lands back into production," was considered too potentially incendiary to publish, since it would alert already wary peasants that their land was not safe. This government goal was expected to, and did, make peasants— opposed as they were to the very concept of state intervention—hold on to their land even after they could no longer farm it, or when they were working in cities, just to keep it safe from the hated state. Therefore, even experts closely involved in the making of government policy had their remarks on the future options of Polish agriculture eliminated by the censors:

> The Program for the Growth of the Food Industry adopted by the 15th Plenum of the PZPR Central Committee was the subject of an interview entitled "A Program for Abundance" by M. Pisarek with Professor A. Wosiem, director of the Institute of Agricultural Economics in Warsaw (*Argumenty,* No. 49). The professor's opinion concerning "the anticipated socioeconomic reconstruction of the Polish countryside," quoted below, was deleted from the text of the interview.
>
> "Certainly, this process will take a different course in our country than in other socialist countries. I would, however, avoid the use of formulations like the 'Polish road,' first of all because there is a bit of megalomania in such an expression, and secondly because every one of the countries in our camp has resolved the agrarian question at a different rate and in accordance with existing socioeconomic and historical conditions. After all, for example, in the German Democratic Republic, Czechoslovakia or Hungary, those demographic problems that we are now experiencing in our rural areas and that are pushing us toward rather basic changes in the structure and model of our agriculture were already being experienced 15 years ago. In short, in those countries that were more advanced economically than we are, the process of intensified migration from the country to the city took place much earlier. Hence, in these countries, the conditions became ripe earlier for the transformation of the structure of agriculture. And here we must add that those countries, thanks to those changes, enjoyed important successes in production that aided the dynamic expansion of agriculture. Ultimately, we are aiming at the same goal, only more slowly and gradually. I would say that by means of the agricultural circles, which after all are nothing but the simplest form of association, and then by means of the development—especially intensified of late— of various forms of cooperative peasant ventures, we have made possible the maturation of the social consciousness of the peasantry. . . .
>
> "The next stage of the development of this peasant consciousness is cooperative associations. After all, hundreds of production cooperatives have appeared—and continue to grow—on the basis of agricultural circles and cooperative groups. On the other hand, the motive of younger peasants for joining cooperatives has increasingly been a desire to have a better life, rather than a desire to increase production or income. In the cooperative there is an eight-hour workday, so that the member has free time, can take a vacation, goes on trips, etc. On a private farm, he has to toil from dawn to dusk and is tied down year round, since even in the winter he has to take care of and feed his livestock.

"So, summing up, this is not so much a Polish road as it is the natural process of the transformation of a peasant economy into socialist agriculture." (*Report on Materials Censored,* December 1–15, 1974)

The policies for media coverage of agriculture, like those for the coverage of industry and foreign trade, reflect the concerns and confusion of the political leaders and the economic policy makers. They also reflect leadership perceptions of popular concerns and sensitivities. By the mid-seventies, the leadership was inclined to cut the risk of high expectations or popular disaffection by maintaining a silence on problems, prospects and achievements, as the economic situation grew more complicated. The irony, however, was that Poland's leaders were thereby prevented from demonstrating the gains they did achieve. They were also prevented from indicating that at least some of the failure of Gierek's policies was a result of Poland's movement into the world economy at a time when the latter was sliding into a recession. And ultimately censorship demobilized the population by depriving them of the sense that they could play any role in deciding their economic destiny or do anything more than suffer from the waste and corruption they saw around them—as long as the regime remained in power.

7 / REWRITING RELIGION

Pretending It Isn't There

C ATHOLICISM AND COMMUNISM have been forced to coexist in Poland since the Communist takeover. Neither has been strong enough to totally dominate or displace the other. At times each has even needed the other enough to cooperate implicitly or explicitly. At other times, one has served as a check on the other. The hope of the Communist Party has been to isolate the Church by denying it a mass forum or publicity. The hope of the Church has been to maintain its image as the beacon of Polish nationalism and its power as a moral and ethical force. The Church has consciously limited its political activity to moral and religious questions, in order to avoid open confrontation with the party authorities. In exchange, the party has acceded to the strength of the Church's popular support and has allowed it a far more extensive number of publications than religious organizations have elsewhere in Eastern Europe and in the Soviet Union.

In Poland, where more than 90 percent of the population is Catholic, religion and the Catholic Church are synonymous. There are other faiths in Poland—Protestant, Orthodox Christian, Jewish and even Muslim—but after World War II these faiths were overwhelmingly outnumbered by Polish Catholicism. The Jewish community was all but exterminated by the Nazis, and the redrawing of Poland's boundaries after the war resulted in Poland no longer having sovereignty over the primarily Eastern Orthodox territories and, instead, taking over formerly German territories from which most of the German (and Protestant) population had fled or been expelled. So in postwar Poland to be Polish meant, in literal as well as figurative terms, to be Catholic.

The only other religious group that played a significant role in postwar Polish political life was the Jewish community. It had been an important element in Polish culture and society for centuries before World War II. In the early nineteen hundreds, it had also been a major source of membership in the minuscule Polish Communist Party, which was seen by most of the population as being opposed to Poland's regaining its national sovereignty from Russia. After World War II some of the Polish Jews who survived kept their old traditions. Others tried to assimilate into the Polish population. For a significant number of Communist leaders in the immediate postwar years who returned after spending the war in the Soviet Union, or who had survived the death camps, the vehicle for this assimilation was the Communist Party. All this, of course, fed the strain of anti-Semitism by linking it with anti-Communist and anti-Russian sentiments.

In 1968 anti-Semitism was fanned by an intra-party struggle to unseat Gomułka. Because of their ethnic background, many Poles of Jewish origin were expelled from their positions in the party, the bureaucracy or the professions on the grounds that they were professionally incompetent and ideologically impure. To cool the popular frenzy and protect his own position, First Secretary Władysław Gomułka encouraged those being attacked to emigrate. This final wave of emigration left Poland with almost no people of Jewish background. This, coupled with the fact that Gierek's major rival in the late sixties had been Mieczysław Moczar, leader of the anti-Semitic campaign, made the "Jewish issue" a nonissue for the media of the seventies. As a result, there are virtually no articles in the *Report on Materials Censored* that deal with Jewish journals (one of which continued to publish on a weekly basis in both Yiddish and Polish throughout the seventies) or Jewish issues.

In the sixties and seventies the media and the government's ability to control what appeared in it were an important tool both in government attempts to stymie the growth of the Catholic Church and other much smaller Protestant denominations, and in the efforts of religious groups to reach their constituencies. Religious journals and even internal printed documents were treated as a special catagory in the censors' office and subjected to extremely careful scrutiny. The basic government policy was to try and cut down the Church's access to all but the faithful who attended church and to keep the Church from appearing as an equal of the government. At the same time, however, the government was unable to ignore the Catholic Church: it had to engage in continual negotiations with the Church and to concede to it on such matters as the religious education of children and the opening of new churches. But these concessions did not extend to increasing the Church's access to the mass media. No matter how often Cardinal Stefan Wyszyński (the powerful head of the Polish Catholic Church who proved a strong negotiating partner for the government throughout the postwar period, until his death in 1981) and other Church leaders demanded increased paper supplies for their publications, freedom from strict censorship on religious subjects or access to the airwaves to broadcast religious services, they were met with a total refusal. The government was firmly committed to not allowing the Church to become any stronger than it was. The failure of its policy to weaken the Church, however, was clear to all. Church attendance and the belief in God, anathema to Marxist-Leninist ideology, remained very high (information the censors tried not to allow in the media). And one of the first demands of the striking workers in the Gdańsk shipyard was the broadcast of Sunday Masses on radio and television. (This was a concession quickly granted and maintained throughout the martial law and post–martial law periods.)

To ensure a modicum of tolerance from the regime, Church officials, until the mid-seventies, avoided explicitly political stands. In sermons, public statements and articles, Church leaders and Catholic laymen concerned themselves primarily with moral training and ethical models—things, they argued, the Communist authorities were either unwilling or unable to provide. They also pressed for Catholic teaching to be reflected in policy on birth control, abortion, Sunday work hours and human rights. During the seventies, when the state was anxious to increase Poland's population, Church and state were in agreement on some of these issues. On others, like Sunday work hours and human rights, they were in direct if not public opposition. It was on the issue of human rights that the Church leadership became increasingly vocal and critical of regime politics after the formation of KOR (Workers' Defense Committee) in 1976.

Catholics in Poland were not united in their basic philosophy or their relations with Communist authorities and, consequently, the censors. The Church was divided between the highly educated and politically attuned hierarchy and the often less educated parish priests who dealt directly with parishioners' problems. On major issues, when the hierarchy sent pastoral letters to its flock, parish priests communicated the viewpoint of their superiors. The censors had the right to prohibit the publication of ecclesiastical documents, printed memoranda, conference papers, and religious books and pamphlets, so some of the general guidance from Church leaders to parish priests was sometimes limited, and as a result parish priests came to act more independently on a wide range of religious matters.

The Catholic lay community was also divided. Two organizations dominated the scene: the pro-Communist and nationalist PAX group formed after World War II as a means of winning the loyalty of the Church for the regime, and the non-Communist, independent Catholic humanists in the Znak group. Both groups, in different ways, were islands of political independence in Poland. PAX had been founded in Eastern Poland while that area was still held by the Soviets. It was to be a source of Catholic support for the regime. In time it came to be a fairly powerful and well-to-do organization, with its own book and periodical press and a number of industrial enterprises. And though in the early years PAX followed the regime line exactly, its leaders eventually went their own way on many issues—taking positions that differed not only from the Church hierarchy but also from the party leadership.

Znak was the antithesis of PAX, holding the position that Communist control had to be tolerated but not supported. While it had close ties with such religious leaders as Archbishop Karol Wojtyła of Kraków, Znak was not an organ of the Church leadership. It was made up of members of Catholic intellectual discussion groups (KIK), which published periodicals and met to discuss various moral and ethical issues. It also had a small, independent parliamentary delegation (as did PAX) that functioned essentially as a group committed to the preservation of Catholic values. Until the late seventies it went further in its public stands on human rights than the Church leadership was willing to, and its use of theology was more political in tone. As a result, the major publications coming from this group were the most censored publications in Poland.

The Ground Rules

The censorship of all religious publications was guided by a very detailed set of directives. In fact, this work was considered so technical and important that a group of censors was specially trained to handle religious publications. The basic principle underlying the regulations on the censorship of religious issues and materials was the desire to prevent religion and the Church from appearing to be more important than, or even equal to, Marxism-Leninism and the party. This was a difficult goal, because the Catholic Church had been the central force in Polish life since the state itself was founded—so much so that to be Polish meant, to many, to be Catholic. Nor could the media be allowed to reveal the Church's differences with Marxism-Leninism, or touch in any way on the importance of religion in politics. So, the names of many religious leaders out of Poland's past who were heroic national figures were kept out of the press. The censors were also instructed to see to it that Church publications did not discuss the role of the Church in community and educational work, even though it was perfectly legal. Detailed instructions prohibited coverage of various Catholic groups and movements in Poland. The position of the Church was not to be bolstered by discussions of its ties to the Vatican or even by references to the Vatican, with which Poland, like other Soviet bloc states, has no diplomatic relations. Finally, censorship limited what could be said by Catholics identified as Catholics about social problems like alcoholism and hooliganism, and about the problems of family life. These limits were even placed on discussions that followed the same line as that of the party leadership. However useful the support of the Church might have been in these cases, the censors deleted such discussions, since they were interpreted by the party leadership as implicit criticism of the secular authorities for having failed to deal effectively with such problems themselves. Regulations on religious coverage not only outlined these general themes, but also provided precise instructions for dealing with various aspects of religious and ecclesiastical life:

Section X: Religious Matters

1. All criticism of Marxism should be eliminated from religious publications. Only in the specialized periodicals listed below:
Collectanea Theologica
Roczniki Chrześcijańskiej Akademii Teologicznej
Roczniki Katolickiego Uniwersytetu Lubelskiego
Studia Philosophiae Christianae
Studia Theologica Varsaviensia
Zeszyty Naukowe Katolickiego Uniwersytetu Lubelskiego

and in specialized works of a theological-philosophical character may theoretical works containing accents critical of the Marxist conception of religion, communism and the concept of the individual in the collective be permitted.

2. The following should be eliminated from publications discussing ideological and political issues in terms of the pluralism of outlook that exists in Polish society:

a. any attempt at the political differentiation of society on the basis of religious belief or world-view;

b. suggestions that certain privileges are due the religious majority in a society;

c. hypotheses concerning the existence of a "privileged" [Communist] world-view and a [Catholic] world-view that is "discriminated against";

d. attempts to differentiate "ideology" (as a "sociopolitical category") from "world-view" (as a "philosophical-moral category");

e. the slogans "the neutrality of the world-view of the state" and "democracy of world-views";

f. slogans and views directly or indirectly attacking legal norms (e.g., the promotion of attitudes and actions contrary to existing legal regulations, demagogic criticism of the law permitting abortion, etc.);

g. calls for securing the influence of religious inspiration on sociopolitical life, for example, by "ensuring a place in public life for lay Catholics";

h. hypotheses about the theoretical inpirations or enrichment of socialism by Catholicism.

In such matters, only formulations that confirm the simple fact of the existence of different religious views and world-views may be permitted.

3. The following elements should be eliminated from publications discussing the moral and sociopolitical sources of inspiration and motivation shaping the views, transformations and attitudes of individuals and groups:

a. overt or covert disparagement of values derived from nonreligious sources (moral education programs of secular organizations and institutions);

b. any attempt to ascribe phenomena of social pathology to the curtailment or elimination of religious values, or any attempt to hold the authorities or secular institutions (publishing houses, film, radio, television) responsible for demoralization;

c. any exaggeration of the influence of religious inspiration on the shaping of morally and socially desirable actions and attitudes;

d. formulations ascribing an essential role to religion in defining the *sociopolitical* attitudes of groups of believers;

e. the promotion (directly or indirectly) of attitudes or actions bearing any trace of political opposition.

On the other hand, permission may be given for traditional religious exhortations concerning love for one's neighbor, one's duty to perform good, conscientious work, and respect for human health and public property, as well as the exhortations of Catholic social associations offering their members religious reasons for personal social commitment in keeping with the principle of the political unity of society. The term "religious inspiration" may be permitted when it concerns individual motivation or religious, cultural and artistic creativity.

4. The following should be eliminated from publications dealing with the relationship between the Polish character and Roman Catholicism:

a. identification of the Polish character with Catholicism and the related attempts to put everything that is not Catholic outside the realm of tradition and national life;

b. updating the list of the Church's contributions to the nation to include aspects of current conditions in the Polish People's Republic;

c. an extremely clericalist interpretation of the history of Poland in works dealing with the history of the Church in Poland.

5. The following may be reported solely through the intermediary of PAP communiqués:

a. information on talks between representatives of the state and representatives of the Vatican or the Episcopate;

b. information on the appointment of bishops or apostolic administrators.

The following should be referred to the GUKPPiW administration:

c. any independent attempt to interpret problems related to the status of the Church in Poland or relations between Poland and the Vatican.

d. any commentaries on statements of the Episcopate or its representatives concerning political or social matters.

e. communiqués and documents of the Vatican, the Episcopate, the press office of the Episcopate or information based thereon (discussion, commentary, notes).

Information on the appointment of parish priests may be permitted after consultation with the Office of Religious Affairs.

6. In order to limit the range of the Church's efforts to clericalize secular groups in the church or parish under the auspices of "pastoral

care," the popularization of these efforts in religious periodicals will be governed by the following principles:

A. The following may be permitted to appear solely and exclusively in official organs of the Episocopate and Curia and diocesan liturgical calendars:

a. publications indicating various forms of so-called group, vocational, family ministry and related intra-church organizational structures and personnel:

1. Mary's Helpers Groups
2. Youth Apostolic Groups or Oases
3. Youth Charity Circles
4. Catechetical Helpers Groups
5. family life instructors or counselors
6. parish guardians
7. parish catechists

b. information on the internal structure of the Church's organizational and executive apparatus for charity and temperance work (such as temperance teams, groups and instructors; parish guardians; and so on);

c. information on unconventional forms of ministry (more characteristic of secular organizations) such as performances (Sacrosong), camping and sports activities, art exhibitions, etc.;

d. in addition, purely homiletical material for communal, vocational, youth and affinity groups may be permitted in *Katecheta* and *Biblioteka Kaznodziejska*.

B. Only the following may be permitted in other Catholic publications:

a. information on Masses held for vocational and other groups and on liturgical activities, retreats and days of recollection held for affinity groups;

b. general information (without a description of organizational structure) concerning charitable work and temperance activities of the Church and concerning the activity of the Catholic Caritas association. In this context such names as "Apostles of Temperance" and "Parish Temperance Registers" may also be used.

7. All information about the intention to build, expand or rebuild churches and chapels or about efforts to open new parishes or monastic communities should be eliminated. All information about church construction in progress, the opening of a new parish or the establishment of a monastic facility should be referred to the religious affairs department of the appropriate voivodship office or to the GUKP PiW.

8. Any information on the following illegally operating educational and propaganda facilities of the Church should be deleted:

—Primatial Institute

—Jasna Góra Institute of National Vows

—Institute for Higher Religious Culture

—Jasna Góra Mariological Institute

—Papal Theological Faculties, or Theological Departments: in Kraków, Poznań and Wrocław (note: the prohibition naturally does not apply to the Theological Departments of the Catholic University of Lublin or the Catholic Theological Academy, or to the activities of these papal faculties under their legal name, which is Higher Ecclesiastical Seminaries)

—Papal Theological Institute in Warsaw

—affiliation of the Higher Ecclesiastical Seminary in Pelplin with the Papal Lateran University in Rome (note: the prohibition does not apply to information about the Pelplin Higher Ecclesiastical Seminary itself, but only to the affiliation)

—Department of Christian Culture of the Catholic Institute in Gietrzwałd

—consultation centers of the Catholic Theological Academy in Częstochowa and Ożarów (similar centers in Gorzów, Katowice, Płock and Szczecin have been legalized)

—religious knowledge centers

—clerical counseling centers, except insofar as they deal with worship activities (an exception can be made in the case of official diocesan organs and diocesan liturgical calendars, in which information may be published concerning counseling centers dealing with the problems mentioned in regulation 6 part A)

9. The following titles of ecclesiastical posts not included in the decree "On the Organization and Assignment of Ecclesiastical Positions" should be eliminated:

—vicar-steward (eliminate the word "steward")

—rector of a pastoral care branch

—rector of a pastoral care center

—vocational ministry specialist

—quasi-pastor and quasi-parish

10. Terminology suggesting that Higher Ecclesiastical Seminaries have the prerogatives of institutions of higher education should be eliminated (e.g., "academic year").

11. All material that directly or by analogy is subject to prohibitions concerning domestic religious affairs should be eliminated from reprints of foreign works or discussions of the religious situation in other countries.

12. All material critical of the religious situation in countries of the socialist community should be eliminated. Materials containing information about religious problems in socialist countries should be referred to the GUKPPiW administration.

13. All information concerning Archbishop Jan Cieplak, who died in 1925, should be eliminated.

14. In censoring materials concerning intentions and efforts to beatify or canonize Poles, the following principles should be observed:
—Materials on the subject may be permitted in all publications, providing that
    a. they do not concern people covered by other prohibitions (e.g., Archbishop Cieplak);
    b. the text of the publication does not suggest that the candidate for beatification "served with honor" or "suffered" in the struggle against the socialist or Communist movement.
—The GUKPPiW administration should be informed of proposals for the beatification of noted historical figures (leaders, politicians, scholars, etc.) and of individuals associated during some period of their life with Marxist ideology ("converted Marxists"). (December 24, 1976)

15. All information concerning the current existence in Poland of a Greek-Catholic rite and its subordination to Wyszyński [the head of the postwar Polish Catholic Church until his death in 1981] or concerning any sort of Uniate [the Ukrainian form of Catholicism] activity in this country should be eliminated.

16. All information concerning statements issued by the Episcopate forbidding priests to cooperate with the National Unity Front, social organizations, Caritas or PAX should be eliminated.

17. All claims of Church officials to church buildings currently in the possession of state institutions should be eliminated.

18. In materials dealing with the Second Synod of Bishops, the third session of which was held at the Vatican in 1974, no speculation should be permitted concerning the content of Cardinal Wyszyński's address, nor should any assessment be permitted of the role of the Polish participants or the high level of their addresses.
[Addendum to first version dated January 14, 1975—T. Strzyżewski:] In addition, Cardinal Wyszyński's term "second world," used to designate the community of socialist states, should be eliminated. (Section canceled March 1, 1976)

19. The following should be eliminated without exception from all Catholic publications (official ecclesiastical press, lay Catholic press, books, minor publications, etc.):
—All information about aid for people in economically underdevelped countries in the form of packages of clothing, food and medicines sent by institutions and Catholic social organizations or by private individuals.
—All calls and appeals to participate in the collection of gifts, including those in letters to editors. (March 1, 1976)

20. No materials concerning the pilgrimage from Poland to Rome to take place in October 1975 as part of the so-called Jubilee Year being observed by the Roman Catholic Church should be permitted. (See Informative Notes No. 10/75 and 29/75) (March 1, 1975; canceled October 30, 1975)

Censorship of Church publications and documents went far beyond these regulations and disrupted the printing of the simplest, most basic materials: affirmations of loyalty and commitment to the Church, cards for notifying parish priests if a parishioner was ill, internal parish communications, announcements of Church meetings and jobs, and hymn texts all were interfered with. None of these documents had any apparent political relevance or would have reached beyond a relatively limited circle of parishioners. Such prohibitions merely served to complicate the basic operations of parish churches and the national Church administration in making and keeping contact with believers. In reality, though, these hindrances had little or no effect on the links between the Church and believers, new and old:

Permission was denied for the publication of two leaflets submitted by the parish of Charłupia Wielka in Sieradź Powiat, to have been published in an edition of 500 copies. The leaflets announced "The Schedule of Masses" to be said in the parish during the period January 1–8, 1975, and the "Schedule of Services to Be Held During the Visitation of the Image of the Holy Virgin, January 9–10, 1975." (*Report on Materials Censored*, December 1–15, 1974)

Permission was denied for the publication of 2,000 copies of a "declaration" entitled "A Profession of Faith," which was submitted by the Bishop's Curia in Olsztyn. We cite the opening and closing passages of this declaration:
"I, ———, firmly believe and acknowledge the universal and specific truths contained in the Symbol of faith, to wit:

"I believe in one God, the almighty Father, creator of Heaven and Earth and of all things seen and unseen; and in one Lord Jesus Christ, the only Son of God, born of the Father before all time, God of God, Light of Light, true God of true God. . . .

"I also accept and earnestly abide by the universal and specific truths pertaining to faith and custom that are solemnly proclaimed by the Church or established and clarified by normal instruction as interpreted by the Church, and in particular I acknowledge and abide by those truths that pertain to the mysteries of the Holy Church of Christ and its sacraments, the sacrifice of the Holy Mass, and the primacy of the Bishop of Rome. Witnessed by ———— ———— (signature) Date ————"
(*Report on Materials Censored,* May 16–31, 1974)

Permission was denied for the printing of 300,000 "Sick-Registry Cards," submitted by the Metropolitan Curia of Warsaw. The "card" contained, *inter alia,* the following sections to be filled in:
—name, age and address of the sick person
—nature of illness
—Holy Sacraments: confession, communion
—is material assistance or relief necessary
—is the sick person able to participate in the parish day set aside to honor the sick
(*Report on Materials Censored,* December 1–15, 1974)

After consultation with the Office of Religious Affairs of the voivodship administration in Katowice, permission was denied to print 2,500 invitations with the following message:
"In the Jubilee Year of the parish (1325–1975), on September 14, 1975, at 16:30, the Church of Saints Peter and Paul at Trzebin-Szersza will be consecrated. The consecration will be performed by Cardinal Karol Wojtyła, Archbishop of Kraków. Mr. (Mrs.) ———— and his (her) family are invited to the parish celebration.
Parish Priest"
(*Report on Materials Censored,* July 16–31, 1975)

Acting in cooperation with the Office of Religious Affairs, the monastery of the Paulines in Warsaw was denied permission to make copies of the texts of five religious hymns (in a proposed edition of 1,000 copies). The copies were intended for distribution to participants in the 259th Warsaw Walking Pilgrimage to Jasna Góra, which is to set out on August 6, 1975. (*Report on Materials Censored,* July 16–31, 1975)

In conjunction with the Office of Religious Affairs, we denied permission for the publication of a tract entitled *New Statutes for Salesian*

Auxiliaries, submitted by the Inspectorate of the Salesian Society (proposed edition of 150; translated from the Italian). This work, which was mainly concerned with pedagogical matters, discussed work methods and techniques of the "Salesian Auxiliaries," including detailed discussions of "the scope of the Salesian mission," "commitment to Christianity in family life," "commitment of the community to the cause of justice," "witnessing for the Gospel through work" and "ways for the auxiliaries to collaborate with one another." At the same time, it was explained that "an auxiliary is a Salesian serving the lay community or any Christian, layman or priest who, without taking any special religious vows, makes his vocation the cause of holiness through involvement in ministering to the needs of youth and the peasantry in the spirit of Father Bosco [John Bosco, founder of the Society of St. Francis de Sales in Turin in 1859], by serving his local church and in particular by maintaining close contacts with the Salesian Order." It was also stressed that "anyone over 16 years of age can become a Salesian auxiliary." The tract goes on to discuss the "fundamental organizational rules of the auxiliary," and a great deal of space is devoted to the organizational structure "at the local level." The excerpt that follows describes the "principal areas" of activity engaged in by "Salesian auxiliaries":

". . . The principal areas in which auxiliaries, each according to his abilities and capacities, carry on their activities are as follows:

"1. Primarily among young people, especially rural youth and those young people who live beyond the pale of society and are exposed to the dangers of atheism, moral corruption, drug addiction and crime;

"2. The social, cultural and religious problems of youth in foreign lands;

"3. Problems of family life, child rearing and the preparation of youth for marriage;

"4. The identification and development of missionary vocations for laymen, priests and members of holy orders for the good of the Church and society;

"5. The teaching of catechism according to modern methods;

"6. The Christian evaluation of the mass media;

"7. Cooperation in preaching the Gospel to non-Christians and support for lay missionaries and the ecumenical work of the Church;

"8. Cooperation in support of the work and activity of the Salesians and the Daughters of the Virgin Mary, Bringer of Divine Help. . . ."
(*Report on Materials Censored*, December 1–15, 1974)

The following announcement was stricken from *Słowo Powszechne:*

"Parish of Wielichowo 64-050, small town in Poznań Voivodship, seeks a catechist, graduate of the Catholic University of Lublin or qualified graduate of another institution or even a young female high school graduate who would like to be a catechist. Possibility of catechetical studies in Poznań. Housing and good conditions. Contact *Słowo Powszechne,* Advertising Department." (Informative Note No. 55, 1976)

Similar limitations were placed on communications concerning PAX, the Catholic lay organization committed to cooperation with the government, and contacts between Vatican and state officials:

79. All information on the meetings organized by PAX between its activists and representatives of local government administrators should be eliminated. (April 4, 1975; canceled November 5, 1975)

70. No information may be published concerning the greeting extended to Bolesław Piasecki [the head of PAX] by members of the party and government on the occasion of his 60th birthday.
This prohibition is intended solely for the information of the censors. (February 19, 1975; canceled March 18, 1975)

32. A commentary on Minister Czyrek's talks with Archbishop Casaroli [the Vatican's representative] appeared by way of an exception [by a special decision of the authorities] in *Słowo Powszechne,* July 13–14, 1974.
Any reprinting or discussion of this commentary and other materials on this subject should be held up and referred to the GUKPPiW administration. (July 13, 1974; canceled August 30, 1974)

Censorship also aimed at hampering the activities of Znak and the discussion groups for intellectuals connected with it by keeping information about it out of the mass media—even though that organization was, like PAX, a legal one:

21b. All announcements of the Catholic Intelligentsia Clubs and the monthly publications *Więź* and *Znak* should be approved by the GUKPPiW administration. This does not apply to the Catholic press.

The government moved to a more frontal attack after some members of the Znak leadership came out in support of KOR. It deprived the organization of its financial base, a small industry producing religious artifacts. The censors were explicitly informed that Libella (as that enterprise had been called) was to become a nonentity immediately:

> 160. As of December 31, 1976, the *economic activity* of the Warsaw Catholic Intelligentsia Clubs, conducted by the Libella Production and Service Center, will be terminated. Any attempts to criticize this decision, to emphasize the merits of Libella, or to advertise its products by, among other things, paid advertisements in the press (including the Catholic press) should be eliminated.
> This instruction is intended solely for the information of the censors. (December 16, 1976)

The Struggle for Dominance

State attempts to weaken religion by limiting the possibilities of religious institutions to print materials for their members and to have access to the mass media were only part of the battle. The government engaged regularly in both direct and indirect attacks on religion and religious institutions, using policies designed to undermine the power and authority of the Church. For example, religious statements in published obituaries could appear only when they were written by individuals or small private groups, not when they were credited to official groups or institutions:

> 23. Religious sentiments may be expressed in obituaries only if the latter are signed by: private persons, craftsmen's guilds or circles, or associations and societies other than those of a general political or general social nature. (March 1, 1976)

Protests against government programs designed to substitute for religious occasions were regularly eliminated from the media. Satirization of state-sponsored ceremonies designed to compete with those of the Church was strictly forbidden:

> 22. Material ridiculing secular naming ceremonies [substitutes for christenings], weddings, funerals and the means employed to popularize them should not be permitted for publication. (January 27, 1976)

Media articles could not even call attention to the fact that television shows satirizing religion and religious traditions were produced, and that they were often presented at the same time as Sunday services:

> An article entitled "Overindulgence Is Unhealthy," the contents of which are reproduced below, was disapproved for publication in the column "Publikatory" in *Słowo Powszechne:*
>
> "Television viewers who happened to watch the Channel One entertainment program *Show Off, Don't Make Excuses* had a truly rare opportunity to sample a brilliant new idea conceived by the producers of Polish television.
>
> "As is well known, this program presents the recipes for various dishes, which are prepared in front of the camera. As on this particular occasion, these broadcasts are usually accompanied by performances by singers and ensembles whose repertoires are distinctly popular in character.
>
> "Last Sunday, the producers obviously felt that the program needed a little jazzing up. And was it ever!
>
> "At one point in the broadcast, viewers heard a parody of a litany of supplication, a hymn sung in churches during times of great tragedy or natural disaster, such as war, epidemics, famine, etc. Each stanza of the hymn ends 'Lord, deliver us.'
>
> "Perhaps one might go so far as to approve of one of the supplications intoned on this occasion. Namely, at one point we heard the entreaty 'Lord, deliver us from television.' Especially from unamusing gags of this kind.
>
> "Compared to the same type of program broadcast, say, by Czechoslovak or GDR television, our entertainment programming does not rank among the best in the world. We often complain about this, even though one can mention a few well-done programs. But the point here has nothing to do with objective criticism and nothing at all to do with the inferior quality of this program, which is not one of the worst that Polish television has to offer. The point here is something quite different. We probably do not need to spell out exactly what the point is. But somebody missed it.
>
> "So it would be a good idea if the management at Polish Television would [discipline] this 'somebody.' Overindulgence is unhealthy. And not just at the dinner table." (*Report on Materials Censored,* December 1–15, 1974)

Administrative difficulties imposed on parish life could also not be admitted to in the media. When permission for the construction of new churches was refused or delayed, this was not reportable. And even when permission was given, construction delays caused by special fees, design regulations, and problems with building materials were not publishable and were not to be known to parishes in other areas of Poland:

> In Rev. E. Rzeszuta's account of the ceremony of "Blessing the Cornerstone of the New Church in Łączki Brzeskie" (*Currenda*, No. 9–12), which took place on April 15, 1974, cuts were made in the following passage, which quotes from the "pastor's address."
>
> "... It has been 25 years since the residents of this small village first received permission to build a new church. In the meantime, Łączki Brzeskie became a part of the parish of Przecław, located nine kilometers from here. In 1957 the parishioners welcomed their first priest, Rev. Józef Majchrowicz. They then enlarged the chapel and turned it into a parish church. Their active faith and community solidarity would not let them rest. Together with their parish priest they are striving to continue [his work]. . . .
>
> " 'In July 1972 the parishioners received the joyous news that they had permission to build the church. Their hearts were filled with joy. . . . But this joy turned to sorrow. With their eyes they saw their priest, who for fifteen years had done everything in his power to make this church a reality, fall down dead on the foundation of the new church. . . .' " (*Report on Materials Censored*, December 1–15, 1974)

Diocese after diocese was in need of more church buildings to serve the parishioners and was prevented by the censors from even making its needs public. For instance:

> An article entitled "The Church on the Bug and Narew" (*Tygodnik Powszechny*, No. 39) included an interview of J. Susuł with Bishop Mikołaj Sasinowski of Łomża, in which the latter discussed pastoral work and the current situation and tasks of the diocese. Deleted material included the statement that the diocese "needs 28 various buildings, churches and roadside chapels," and statements concerning the various "types of ministry." . . . (*Report on Materials Censored*, September 16–31, 1975)

Even unused but historic church buildings were normally allowed to decay rather than be preserved for some other use, and regional journals could not report what was well known to those in the area:

In *Głos Wybrzeża*, a notice entitled "Knickknack in Kaczymnos" was disapproved for publication. This notice contained an appeal directed to the "authorities of Malbork Powiat" concerning:

—"fixing up the ruined little church" in Kaczymnos, dating from the 18th century, which was restored in 1960;

—"finding a tenant-patron for this project": perhaps "the prosperous local state farm? Perhaps it could remodel the church and turn it into a movie house or theater. And perhaps a way could be found to use the old relic as a tourist facility? . . . The church has a convenient location (not far from the Malbork-Elbląg highway), so it could be used, for example, as a hotel for tourists. . . ." (*Report on Materials Censored,* December 1–15, 1974)

Nor did the government provide the kind of financial support necessary to maintain either Church archives or the buildings of the Catholic University of Lublin. But the censors would not allow even internal Church publications to refer to this lack of government support and the problems that it caused:

In Issue No. 28 of the Lublin Catholic University periodical *Archiwa, Biblioteki, i Muzea Kościelne,* an article by Rev. S. Librowski entitled "The Current Accessibility of Materials Held in Church Archives" was challenged for its demand that religious archives be granted "permanent state subsidies for the modernization of facilities and the preservation of resources" and that "Church buildings currently being used by state and self-government institutions" should be restored to the Church. (*Report on Materials Censored,* May 16–31, 1974)

The following "Communiqué of the Diocesan Curia" was deleted from Issue No. 11–12 of *Kronika Diecezji Sandomierskiej:*
    "At the request of the Rector of Lublin Catholic University, a duplicate copy of the following letter is to be made public:

L.dz. 734/74,R.   October 29, 1974
The Editors
Trybuna Ludu
Plac Starynkiewicza 7
Warsaw

Dear Sirs:
    A notice entitled "Ringing in the New Academic Year at Lublin Catholic University," published in the October 22, 1974, edition of *Trybuna Ludu,* contained the following sentence: "The old buildings of the Lublin Catholic University are now undergoing a major renovation effort, thanks to substantial state subsidies."

This is an inaccurate statement. The government has indeed shown us understanding and good will as far as the construction and renovation of University buildings are concerned, but we have not received any subsidies for this purpose. When it comes to its normal day-to-day operations as well as the undertaking of capital improvements, Lublin Catholic University is supported by contributions from the general public. We would be grateful if you could print a correction to this effect.

Respectfully yours,
Secretary of the University
Rev. Dr. Henryk Rybaszyński"
(*Report on Materials Censored*, December 1–15, 1974)

Censors were instructed to keep rumors concerning "miracles," which might serve to strengthen the religious convictions of some, out of the media:

23. No information should be presented concerning the alleged "miracle" in Piotrków, Radziejów Powiat, Bydgoszcz Voivodship. A supposedly "miraculous" glow was noted over the steeple of the town church.
   The content of this prohibition is intended solely for the information of the censors. (Canceled July 27, 1974)

An effort was made to downplay the role and influence of the Church in Polish history, including the influence of religion on various national heroes of Poland's past. Concerns of this sort led to the deletion of the following article about Romuald Traugutt, a leader of the national uprising against Russia in 1863:

In *Zorza* (No. 18), we did not permit publication of an article by B. Rodziewicz entitled "Ripening Grain," which presented a portrait of Romuald Traugutt as a "candidate for the altar." The first part of the article contained information on an application for the beatification if R. Traugutt and a biographical sketch demonstrating his deep religious convictions. (*Report on Materials Censored*, May 1–15, 1974)

The activities and successes of the Catholic Church were also kept out of the public eye as much as possible. The participation of young people and professionals in Church activities appears to have been a particularly sensitive issue, even when it was dealt with in small diocesan publications:

Interventions were made in four articles carried by the monthly *Wiadomości Diecezjalne Łódzkie,* No. 7, deleting references to the participation:

—of young people "on the eve of graduation from secondary school" (in an all-night vigil of nuns from Łódź in Częstochowa)

—of "secondary school certificate candidates" in retreats ("The Eucharist as a Spring of Mortification and Sacrifice")

—of "secondary school certificate candidates" in a pilgrimage to Częstochowa "prior to the taking of their final exams" ("The Pilgrimage of Secondary School Certificate Candidates to Jasna Góra")

—of "nurses" from Łódź in prayer-day ceremonies in Niepokalanów ("Łódź Nurses in Niepokalanów") (*Report on Materials Censored,* July 16–31, 1975)

Statements noting the popularity of Church activities were not publishable even in the Church's own magazines for its members:

A notice entitled "'Living Sound' in Silesia" was disapproved for publication in the "Church Life" column of Issue No. 48 of the weekly magazine *Gość Niedzielny.* The notice reported on performances of an American vocal and instrumental ensemble, "Living Sound," in Katowice, Michałowice, Chorzów and Paniewniki-Ligota during October of 1974. It was stated that this ensemble, which "preaches the Gospel through song and music in a contemporary way that brings Christ closer not only to young people, but to adults as well," was received in Silesia "with much applause." (*Report on Materials Censored,* December 1–15, 1974)

Thirty years after the imposition of Communist rule in Poland, the Church's popularity remained very strong. This proved an embarrassment to the party leadership—adhering as it did to an ideology that pictured religion as "the opiate of the people" imposed by capitalist exploiters. Consequently, sociological reports on the level of religious affiliation in new housing settlements, among high school students and in Gierek's home province of Katowice were all disapproved for publication. Each contained specific data testifying to the high degree of at least sporadic participation in religious life in all these areas:

Interventions were made in 66 texts submitted by the publishing houses of the Episcopate and lay Catholics. Thirty-nine of those were in materials dealing with the sociopolitical activity of Catholicism; the others have already been described in preceding sections of the Report.

In the quarterly of the Polish Theological Society, *Collectanea Theologica,* No. 44, two articles in the "Research" section were not approved for publication.

One of them was a description of the doctoral dissertation of Rev. S. Karsznia entitled "Membership in a Catholic Parish in a New Large Urban Area. A Social Psychological Study of the Nowa Huta–Mogila Parish." In it, we read the following:

". . . The aim of this dissertation was to study the degree to which membership in the parish is shaped by sociopsychological factors. It is a question of membership defined as an acceptance of doctrines on faith and morals, an observance of religious practices and an identification with the parishioners, priests and the group as a whole.

"This study was based on three sources: 1) published materials dealing with Nowa Huta, 2) Church documents, and 3) materials gathered in the course of fieldwork.

"The basic material for this study was gathered in fieldwork conducted from February to November of 1970. The research was based on a representative random sampling of the population residing within the boundaries of the parish, ranging in age from 18 to 70. The residents of worker hotels and boarding schools, as well as persons registered only for temporary residence, were excluded from the population studied. . . .

". . . Of the 515 persons under examination, 84 percent considered themselves to be believers or devout believers, 10.4 percent as doubtful, indifferent or searching for the truth, and 5.3 percent as nonbelievers. The majority of the nonbelievers emphasized their attachment to the Christian tradition.

"Six criteria were used as the basis for determining an individual's sociopsychological attachment to the parish. The six were defined by E. Pin as: the external criteria of membership in the parish, such as baptism and residence in the territory of the parish; the acceptance of group values; the acceptance of the same patterns of behavior; participation in the common activities of the parish; social relations between parishioners; and the intention to belong to the parish.

"The percentage breakdown of the various categories of parishioners in the population under study is as follows:

" 'Associated parishioners' are those who fulfill all of the above-named conditions for parish membership. With some qualifications, 4.6 percent of the parishioners could be included in this category. They are the most active participants in parish activities and are characterized by total identification with the parish. They interact in it to such an extent that they can view the common goals of the parish as their personal goals.

" 'Parish-sympathizers' are Catholics who fulfill at least five of the conditions of parish membership. They take part in collective activities and express sympathy for the parish and local clergy, but they do not have a 'we' relationship with the other faithful. 37.3 percent of the parish population may be considered to belong to this group. This is the percentage that systematically fulfills the Sunday Mass requirement and declares its solidarity with the parish.

"The next group is that of 'parish users.' They fulfill at least four of the conditions of membership. Parish-users take part more or less regularly in parish activities, but they do not identify with the parish: only 3 percent of this group are regularly practicing Catholics and they express a lack of attachment to the parish. In the case of Nowa Huta–Mogiła, most of those expressing a lack of attachment to the parish are Catholics who do not attend Holy Mass regularly. They represent 34.1 percent of the total group. Altogether, the group of parish-users accounts for 37.1 percent of the whole.

"The fourth group of Catholics, in terms of membership in the parish, are the 'nominal parishioners.' These fulfill one to three of the conditions. The minimum possible comprises baptism, residence in the territory of the parish, and belief in God. The nominal parishioners in the group under study include both 'holiday' parishioners and nonpracticing ones. They represent 21 percent of the total.

"All four types of parishioners coexist alongside one another and give a specific character to the parish population under study. . . .

"The influence of the parish is limited to those who make up the parish community. It has no direct influence on those residents of the parish who are not a part of organized religious life.

"In the conclusion of the study, the bonds of parish membership in a large-city setting were outlined. Among the most significant observations is the conclusion that, in this environment, the 'specific' parish bond is disappearing. This disappearance may be accompanied, on one hand, by the formation of membership in a broader religious community or, on the other, by the severing of the bond of religious membership. In the parish under study, we are confronted more with a situation of developing ties of Church membership where that membership is taking on an 'individualized' character rather than institutional character. This means that for a certain group of believers Church membership does not mean the same thing as acceptance of all of the institutional requirements of religious membership. At the same time, though to a lesser degree, we can observe processes of the abandonment of religious membership in the parish. . . ." (*Report on Materials Censored*, December 1–15, 1974)

The second of the materials challenged was a description of six master's theses [of which three sample descriptions are included in this translation to avoid repetition] containing conclusions about the religious beliefs of secondary school students based on research conducted—with the use of a questionnaire drawn up by the Department of the Sociology of Religion of the Catholic University of Lublin—in various cities: Lublin, Stalowa Wola, Jarosław, Środa Śląska, Będzin, Grudziądz. Selected passages are presented below:

". . . Rev. Ryszard Gołda, *Religious Belief Among Young People in Technical Schools at the Lyceum Level (Based on the Case of the Parish of St. Michael the Archangel in Lublin)*. Lublin: 1970 (master's thesis: typescript in the archive of the Catholic University of Lublin).

". . . The research was carried out in 1969 and covered three secondary technical schools in Lublin: The Energy Technical School, the Chemical Technical School and the Communications Technical School. The sample was chosen by a random drawing. In each school, one-quarter of those students attending instruction and one-quarter of those not attending were separately selected. 314 questionnaires were distributed. . . .

". . . Of the respondents, 3.3% consider themselves to be deeply religious, 74.8%—religious; 13.3%—indifferent to religious matters; 6.3%—unbelieving but attached to religious traditions; and 0.6%—unbelieving.

"In response to the question whether God exists and whether He cares for you, the pattern of answers was as follows:

Does God exist?	Does He care for you?
Yes—76.5%	Yes—57.3%
No—6.6%	No—12.2%
Don't know—13.9%	Don't know—25.2%

"Of those questioned, 32.1% believe that the Church is essential for salvation, 54% that it is only an aid to one's salvation, and 8% that it is not necessary.

"According to the respondents, the most important moral trait is: "to be an honorable person"—69.5%; to observe religious precepts—17.2%; to be progressive—6.0%; and to seek one's own interest—3.7%.

"The following were named as values worth risking one's own life for: defense of the fatherland—76 (25.2%); the saving of human life—70 (23.3%); defense of religion—50 (16.6%); defense of freedom—40 (13.2%). . . .

"60.9% would not be willing to begin married life without a church wedding, 17.2% would, and 16.9% would in certain circumstances. . . .

". . . About 50% of the youth under study were more or less systematic in their religious practice: 49.3% attend Mass each Sunday and holiday, 51.6% go to confession at least a few times a year, 52.2% take Holy Communion a few times a year, and about 50% pray daily.

"The majority of the youth in this study (72%) acknowledge the role of the priest as intermediary in their contact with God. 18.2% do not recognize such a role. For those who do recognize the priest as an intermediary, 67.5% consider him essential as an instructor of faith, 13.9% as a spiritual guide, and 13.9% as the administrator of sacraments.

"Rev. Edward Frankowski, *The Social Conditioning of Religious Attitudes Among Secondary School Youth: A Sociological Study Based on a Survey of Students in Stalowa Wola* [an industrial town], Lublin: 1971 (master's thesis: typescript in archive of Catholic University of Lublin).

". . . The observations were carried out in 1968 in Stalowa Wola. They included students from three secondary schools: the General Lyceum, the Mechanical Technicum and the Medical Lyceum. At that time there were 1,134 students in these schools, 487 (43.0%) of them boys and 647 (57%) girls. The questionnaire was distributed to every third student on the basis of enrollment lists. A total of 380 questionnaires (representing 33.5% of the school population) were distributed. 246 questionnaires were filled out and returned (i.e., 64.7% of the number distributed), 93.3% of them by students attending religious instruction and 6.5% by students not attending. At that time, 87.9% of the secondary school students in Stalowa Wola attended catechism classes.

"Of those surveyed, 25.2% came from very religious families, 71.2% from averagely religious families and 2.4% from indifferently religious families. 11.3% considered themselves to be deeply religious; 83.7%—religious; 2.8%—indifferent; 1.2%—unbelieving, but attached to religion; and 0.3%—unbelieving and concerned that others not believe. The respondents characterized themselves as systematically practicing (57.0%), irregularly practicing (36.3%), observing certain practices (4.8%), or completely nonpracticing (1.2%).

"The pattern of answers to the question of God's existence and whether He cares for one was as follows:

Does God exist?	Does He care for you?
Yes—90.6%	Yes—73.2%
No—0.4%	No—0.4%
Don't know—4.2%	Don't know—23.2%
No answer—0.4%	No answer—3.2%

"Of the young people questioned, 52% believe that the Church is essential for salvation; 45%—that it simply aids one in gaining salvation; and 0.8%—that it is not essential.

"The following were named as values worth risking one's life for: defense of the fatherland—196 (79.6%); defense of religion—185

(75.1%); the saving of human life—167 (68.0%); defense of property—73 (29.7%).

The figure accorded the greatest respect by the youth was the mother (213 respondents—88.6%), then the father (184 respondents—74.7%), then the priest (136 respondents—55.3%). Educators and teachers were mentioned at the very end of the list by about 30 respondents.

"Rev. Czesław Poloczek, *The Religiosity of Secondary School Youth on the Basis of a Survey in Grudziądz*, Lublin: 1971 (master's thesis: typescript in archive of Catholic University of Lublin).

". . . Research was conducted in Grudziądz [an old prewar industrial town] in February 1969. At that time there were 842 young people in the upper classes of secondary school in the community studied. 280 questionnaires were distributed, of which 211 later turned out to be usable in the sample analyzed, 78 of them filled out by boys and 133 by girls. The study covered the two General Lycea, two Pedagogical Lycea, five technical schools and a medical lyceum.

"Of the Grudziądz upperclassmen in this study, 3.3% consider themselves to be deeply religious; 74.4%—religious; 12.3%—indifferent; and 9.5%—unbelievers. Of those surveyed, 65.4% attend catechism classes. 18.9% do not attend at all and 14.9% attend occasionally.

"The pattern of answers to the question of God's existence and care for individuals was as follows:

Does God exist?	Does He care for you?
Yes—66.4%	Yes—39.8%
No—6.2%	No—8.1%
Don't know—27.0%	Don't know—50.7%

"The following were most frequently named as values worth risking one's life for: defense of fatherland—162 (76.9%); the saving of human life—158 (75.0%); defense of freedom—82 (27.0%). In this question, the young people were able to name three values.

"Among the students responding, 63.5% said that they would not become married without a church wedding, 16.6% would, and 19.5% would under certain circumstances.

". . . More than half of those responding (58.3%) said that they believe the teachings of the Church, while 36.0% reject certain teachings. About 48% of those studied experience difficulties in their belief. The reason for these difficulties is ascribed to their environment, especially that of a boarding school. . . .

". . . Based on these observations and the analysis of their results, the author offers the following typology of the youth surveyed: young people with a deep religious belief who accept the teachings of the Church on faith and morals, and observe all obligatory rites and more

—17%; young people with a weakening religious belief—33%; young people who are indifferent or nonbelievers—11%. . . ."* (*Report on Materials Censored,* December 1–15, 1974)

Even in areas in which the party and Church had a common interest, the censors kept announcements of religious activities out of the media and prevented Church officials from publishing statements and guidance on social issues. For example, a major declared concern of both government and religious officials in the mid-seventies was the strengthening of the family and the encouragement of larger families, though the Church and the state justified this policy in different terms. Those who directed the media saw the Church's admonitions about family life as not so veiled criticism of the government's secular morality and an indictment of communism for having failed to promote social order. Statements pointing to the decrease in religious authority as a primary cause of social demoralization were removed even from minor diocesan publications, including a bulletin produced by a local church for its parishioners:

> Issue No. 9–12 of the monthly *Orędownik Diecezji Chełmińskiej* contained an article entitled "Christian Charity Week," which, in its discussion of the "planned activities for the week," made reference to the "wounds of modern man," such as "alienation, loneliness, insensitivity, the rupture of the traditional ties of family and church, a departure from ethical and moral standards, frequent divorces" and so on. A passage was deleted which stated that "the Church sees the cause of all this in the fact that people have turned their back on Christ, who revealed to man that God is the beginning and end of his life here on Earth."
>
> In the same issue of the same monthly, interventions were made in an article entitled "The Bishops' Pastoral Counsel," which discussed the problem of "birth control" and the upbringing of youth. The following passage was deleted:
>
> ". . . Special concern must be aroused by the warping of the outlook of the younger generation that can be seen in various forms of sexual education. Instead of teaching young people from their early years to guide their impulses, by reason and will, with a sense of responsibility for their own acts and co-responsibility for others, they are introduced immediately to the path of least resistance. We ask whether the individuals responsible for this are blind to the consequences that have

---

*As quoted in *Czarna księga cenzury PRL* (The black book of censorship of the Polish People's Republic) (London: ANEKS, 1978), 2:258.

already resulted from this approach to education and social morality, or to the consequences it is likely to have in the future?

"In such a situation, we call on parents to increase their vigilance over the views absorbed by young people and to correct those views of life that are incorrect." (*Report on Materials Censored*, May 16–31, 1974)

One censors' report cites an unpublishable reader's letter containing information about Church-run family counseling centers. Another blocks the publication of an entire book on pastoral family counseling originally published in East Germany. The Polish authorities were obviously more sensitive to the possibilities of Church influence in family life than were their allies. This even though much of the book—according to the censors—was a training manual to prepare priests to help strengthen family life and to encourage them to work with trained lay professionals, which furthered the goals of the state as well as the Church:

Permission was not given for publication of Erwin Heretsch's book *Pastoral Work Among Parents,* submitted by the Center of Social Documentation and Research (1,000 copies). Heretsch's work, published in the German Democratic Republic, is a kind of ideological program for Church influence in family life and the raising of the younger generation. It is an instruction manual for pastoral efforts to shape the family. In his discussion of the religious education of parents, the author tells priests and laymen about the importance of the family and about the problems it faces in light of the social changes that are taking place. "The family is a community of salvation," "a little church," "the place where children receive their first notion and experience of God and learn to honor and love Him." According to the author, "the shaping of the family is a requirement of modern times" and "an important task for the church"; "this issue is as important today as social problems were in the 19th century." The development of families is treated as an "intermediate stage in the religious upbringing of children"; "parents need to be constantly concerned about working with their children." "While helping modern man, the Church can raise the next century's generation of believers." In the "Instruction" section, the author describes various means for encouraging parents' religious development: "small" and "large" family meetings, "family days," seminars, courses and "parents' circles," methods that have been "tested" by pastoral experience in the GDR. The use of modern scientific methods, including audiovisual techniques, is suggested.

In his conclusion to the book, the author discussed the proper preparation of personnel for the religious education of parents, noting, among other things:

". . . Above all, what is important here is the authority that can be conferred by the appropriate knowledge (psychology, pedagogy, sociology). It is also important that this knowledge be based on personal experience. People with insufficient education and priests, despite the best of intentions, cannot provide the level of training necessary. It is therefore essential to find suitable persons among the laity associated with the Church. They must meet high standards. We should mention, first of all, in addition to a general pedagogical background, they need familiarity with the specific problems of working with adults. Until now, most priests and teachers have thought that anyone who teaches children is capable of working with adults as well. They have overlooked the different pedagogy for children and adults. . . . For it is not the leader's task to direct or influence the meetings. Rather, it is his task to continually inspire and 'choreograph' the independent efforts of the adults. . . . We need to apply Makarenko's principle: 'I expect a lot from you because I respect you!' . . . The complexities and variety of contemporary life are so great that it seems necessary to train whole groups of leaders. . . . This is borne out by the results of the training of lecturers.

"Hence the education of parents must begin with the education of the people who will be involved in adult education. This should be carried out on two levels: 1) the training of instructors, 2) the training of class leaders. Each of these courses should include theoretical problems, methodology, practical exercises, and visits by student teachers to one another's classes." (*Report on Materials Censored,* May 1–15, 1974)

The censors were also unwilling to allow any indication that "believers" could be active in regime-supported organizations, even those taking hold in traditionally religious rural areas. So, even though the passage below presented the work of the government-run Rural Youth Union in a positive light, the censors objected:

In Issue No. 22 of *Zorza,* J. Nowojska responded to a reader opinion survey entitled "My Family and Faith" with a statement that was printed under the title "God Brought Us Together." She wrote about her Catholic upbringing, which began at home and was reinforced by religious education classes (which she attended for 13 years) and the Catholic press. A passage reporting on the reader's activities in the Rural Youth Union was blocked. It read in part as follows:

". . . I was elected vice-chairman of the Rural Youth Union. In the summary report evaluating the work of young people in the *powiat,* we were singled out as one of the most active circles. . . . We cleaned up the road running through the village, built a sports arena and helped with the construction of other roads in the village. Through our work, we earned the trust of the older people. . . . I was not able to do all of this by myself. In my prayers, I often called upon the aid of Jesus. I realized that with His help all obstacles can be overcome, as long as we follow His teachings. Jesus can do anything; He can help us to understand the world, and He can help us to love one another and the whole world. He blesses our work, which brings Him joy. He gives us fresh strength and courage. . . . It sometimes happened that parents did not want to let their girls go to dance classes, sports events, outings or parties, but when I went to talk with them everything turned out all right. The parents thought it would be all right if their daughters went along with me. In this way I gained their trust. The girls were very grateful to me. I then approached them to ask if they would go with me to church, help me put together the religious education newsletter. . . ." (*Report on Materials Censored,* May 16–31, 1974)

Church-State Relations

Censorship did far more than try to create the impression—however false—that the Church played no real role in Polish society. It also attempted to create the impression that there were no equal or direct relations between party and state officials on one hand and religious leaders and institutions on the other. Even to have Church leaders publicly acknowledge the permanence of the Communist system was threatening, since it implied the permanence of religion and the necessity of state and party leaders cooperating with it. While government and party officials were negotiating with Cardinal Wyszyński and his representatives on proposed amendments to the Polish constitution, the construction of new churches or the possibility of Church support on social issues, censors' reports show that statement after statement about the need for permanent church-state cooperation or religious support for state organizations was eliminated from published texts.

The minuscule Baptist sect's monthly *(Słowo Prawdy)* included an article on their delegates' visits to Slavic Baptist churches in the United States. The censors allowed some statements by a representative of the Southern Baptist Convention to appear, but as soon as his comments broached the necessity of cooperation between Marxism and Christianity, or touched on discussions of this sort that took place right after the Russian Revolution, they were cut:

> ... A question was raised about a portion of the statement of B. E. Golonka, Vice-Secretary of the Department of Mission Work for National Missions of the Southern Baptist Convention, who spoke of the mutual relationship between Christianity and Marxism, presenting the following view of the future:
>
> "What conclusions do I draw? Communists and socialists have come to the realization that Christianity will remain. Christianity has come to the realization that socialism has a *raison d'être* and will continue to exist, though perhaps in a changed form. It is therefore necessary, in such a situation, to seek a common path of coexistence and mutual understanding. Why destroy one another? Two truths exist and it is necessary to give them support, <u>not to exterminate them. A similar dialogue among students was begun right after the October Revolution by Professor Martinkovskii.</u> ... All those I encounter in my work admit that I have tried to express love for the people who are bringing the new ideology into being. In the American setting, this is pioneer work, since no one has hitherto tried to carry on such a dialogue. And, my last point, I have come to the following conclusion after much thought and work: <u>If Marxism wants to continue to exist, it must join hands with Christianity, and vice versa.</u>" (*Report on Materials Censored*, March 16–31, 1974)

Lay Catholic organizations that attempted to bridge the gap between Catholicism and communism in Poland were in no easier a position. PAX was a pro-Communist organization that had been aided in its formation by, and served as an aid to, the Polish Communist regime. It had been ostracized in the fifties by religious Catholics on orders from the Vatican and the Polish Catholic hierarchy, and supported by the government as a group that would champion the view that Catholicism and communism were not in conflict. Over the years, PAX had been able to build up a rich manufacturing and publishing empire based on religious articles and books, and had engaged in attacks on those who saw communism and Catholicism as ultimately in conflict. The latter view was represented by the Znak organization, centered around its discussion groups and its chief mouthpiece, the weekly *Tygodnik Powszechny*. It was Znak that took the responsibility of maintaining the tradition of Catholic lay humanism in Poland, doing its utmost to prevent Communist ideology from being imposed on the society.

Although both PAX and Znak had been carrying on their discussions for nearly thirty years, neither group had established a *modus vivendi* with the censors in the area of Church-state relations. A summary bulletin issued by the GUKPPiW in the second quarter of 1974 pointed out the failure of PAX journals to present an acceptable picture of Church-state ideological or political relations:

> . . . world-view was clearly separated from ideology, and in more comprehensive deliberations, too, the assumption of a dual world-view —Marxism and Catholic socialism—was adopted *(Kierunki, Słowo Powszechne).* In addition emphasis was placed on the idea that progressive Catholics in Poland were working to "carry out the historical mission of ensuring the future development of Catholicism under the socialist regime," although PAX did make an effort to use the term "unifying force of the Polish working-class party" *(Kierunki).* (*Bulletin of Themes of Materials Censored,* Second Quarter, 1974)

However much PAX may have been pressured to limit its phraseology, the analyses published by Znak were still more objectionable to the censors. An example was a review by A. Micewski in the Znak weekly, *Tygodnik Powszechny,* which made reference to the longtime differences between PAX and Znak. The conflict between the two groups represented far more than an intermural struggle between two lay Catholic organizations. It represented for the censors and for the author of the review the failure of the *modus vivendi* between religion and communism that PAX had advocated and that the state hoped to use to weaken the strong Catholic traditions represented by Znak. This was not the image Polish authorities wanted to appear. Nor did they want it to seem that there was little hope of progress away from strict Catholicism and toward popular support for Communist ideals:

> In *Tygodnik Powszechny*, No. 29, the following text by A. Micewski entitled "Wishful Thinking" was not permitted for publication. It disputes several opinions expressed in the book *Polityka Wyznaniowa* [*Religious Politics*], edited by W. Mysłek and M. T. Staszewski:
>
> "A 500-page book entitled *Religious Politics: Background, Conditions, and Realization,* edited by W. Mysłek and M. T. Staszewski, has been issued by PWN Publishing House. I cannot boast of having read

it in its entirety, something that would demand the patience of a Benedictine, but it is easy to see that the writing of contemporary history, without any time perspective, is as usual a dangerous undertaking. I will deal with just one matter, which came out in a particularly unscholarly way and represents nothing but 'wishful thinking' on the part of Wiesław Mysłek and his colleague. Namely, on pages 344–345 they write: '. . . the whole ideology of pluralism of world-views was formulated in the PAX Society and was, for a long time, ignored by other social Catholic circles. In recent years, however, they have recognized its usefulness and have introduced this slogan to their programmatic statements and proposals. It is difficult to foresee whether all of the above-mentioned processes of eliminating ideological differences will lead as well to an organizational integration, since the animosities between the Catholic organizations have grown stronger during the course of several decades, but in any case one should not eliminate the possibility of the unification of the Catholic social organizations.'

"I rub my eyes in amazement. This represents the height of misinformation about the ideological situation in the Catholic world. And on top of it, all this concern about our unification. Here you have an example of wishful thinking, and probably only the wishes of Wiesław Mysłek, since no one more competent to deal with them has expressed any such wish.

"The difference between the various Catholic groups in Poland is the result not simply of some kind of 'historical animosity,' but, above all else, of a difference in sociocultural and purely political aspirations. It is amusing that the authors appear to praise me precisely for making that distinction. The subsequent differences are the result of a differing understanding of the moral consequences of Catholic belief. Finally, they are linked with ideological principles and political attitudes. The Znak circle does not seek to draw distinctions for their own sake, nor does it deny anyone their achievements, if they are authentic, but it does place freedom and pluralism of Catholic thought and genuine honesty of social views over what are after all unreal political strivings, and tries to express itself in a way that is as close as possible to the truth.

"I do not know how the authors of the book arrived at their thesis about the 'elimination of the differences' between the Catholic groups. I don't want to cite here my own numerous statements bearing witness to something quite different and so I will simply refer interested readers to an article entitled 'Reality or Illusion,' signed by JW in *Tygodnik Powszechny*, No. 10/1154, from March 7, 1971, in which one reads:

" 'The claim about "basic humanistic principles" is—insofar as one can understand it—a pure abstraction. It is contradicted by the real daily life of science and art, by the deeply humanistic works of Poles who are neither Christians nor Marxists. . . . We would not dare to deny the humanism of <u>Maria Dąbrowska, Henryk Elzenberg or Stanisław Ossowski,</u> not to mention an even greater number of individuals [other leaders in Polish culture] who died longer ago or abroad, like <u>Witkacy, Irzykowski, Ajdukiewicz, Tuwim or Gombrowicz.</u> . . .

" 'We are opposed to abstract dichotomies and pairs, to a black and white chessboard as a model of life and value. Life is not black and white. It is often gray. And normally it is, fortunately, multicolored.'

"Not taking into account this kind of very basic enunciation, the authors of *Polityka Wyznaniowa* cite, among other things, the following statements of Jerzy Turowicz [postwar editor of *Tygodnik Powszechny* and leader of Znak] as an example of the 'elimination of differences': 'an enormous portion of our citizenry yearn to live and act within the framework of the organized community which is the Church, and yearn to see the achievement of conditions that will enable the Church to carry out its apostolic mission.'

"Even Wiesław Mysłek should be able to understand that concern about the apostolic mission of the Church, even in its broad sense, is one thing, and political aspirations based on the abstraction of a dualistic society are another. I realize that from the Marxist point of view religion is one's private affair. But one would expect that after 30 years of various discussions Wiesław Mysłek would know that a desire to 'evangelize the world' has nothing in common with the dualistic model of society or with politico-religious aspirations. Catholicism is certainly not just cult, but also a culture, a social morality, and the active presence of Christianity in the world, which by no means should have the character of classical religious parties.

"I will not respond to another of the authors' examples, because it has to do with a speech made in the Sejm by one of the Catholic delegates, who, if he wishes, can answer himself. I will only add that the Catholic organizations do not have the character of religious parties, and the delegates therefore enjoy autonomy in the formulation of their views.

"In short, the authors of *Polityka Wyznaniowa* are not in a position to confirm the thesis that they proclaim, but they draw very far-reaching conclusions from it. Fortunately, they only demonstrate their habit of thinking on the basis of their own desires or, as the English call it, 'wishful thinking.' " (*Report on Materials Censored,* July 16–31, 1975)

The sensitivity of the Polish censors to any suggestions of equality of Church and state, or to any discussion of the connections between them, limited what could be said about the principles or present status of Church-state relations. It also limited what could be said about the past, beginning with restrictions like Regulation No. 78, which prevented all discussion of the initial agreement signed by the Church and the Stalinist authorities in 1950:

> 78. No extensive materials should be permitted concerning the approaching 25th anniversary of the signing of the agreement between the Polish People's Republic and the Episcopate. (April 14, 1975)
>
> Only short notes providing information about the anniversary, without any assessment of the agreement, its content, value, significance and so on may be permitted. (April 2, 1975; canceled June 10, 1975)

The desire to prevent the Church from being portrayed as a pillar of Polish life affected even discussions of early Polish history. The Main Office for Control under Gierek was unwilling not only to permit statements about the enduring strength of religion in Poland despite changes in the economic system under Marxism, but also to permit statements emphasizing the role of the Church in the development of Polish culture long before Marxism:

> Several deletions were made in the text of an interview of Rev. Stanisław Pasierba with Mieczysław Jastrun scheduled for publication in Issue No. 6 of *Więź*. The subject of the interview was "the continuity of Christian inspiration in our literature." Deletions included statements extolling the role of Christianity in the origin and development of Polish culture (e.g., "our cultural life would be inconceivable" without Christianity). A statement was also questioned which expressed the opinion that "it would be shortsighted to believe that the spread of systems based on any kind of doctrine necessarily hinders the influence of religion, which is an intrinsic human characteristic regardless of the economic institutions that prevail at any given moment in history. . . . It is here somewhere that the error of Marxism lies. Changes in the system of production, even the abolition of so-called classes, still do not alter the way men think and feel. Man is older than these issues. Job continues to be Job." (*Report on Materials Censored*, July 16–31, 1975)

Unlike Soviet policy, which has been to represent religion as one of the basic props of the system of repression preceding the Bolshevik revolution, Polish policy has been to remove references to religion and the Church that give them credit for playing a positive and progressive role in society prior to the Communist takeover. In pursuit of this aim, the censors removed certain passages dealing with Church history from the pages of Catholic intellectual journals:

> In a book review entitled "An Auspicious Beginning" (*Tygodnik Powszechny*, No. 29), A. Vetulani discussed Volume I of the work *Historia Kościoła w Polsce* [*History of the Church in Poland*], published in 1974 by Pallotinum under the editorial guidance of Rev. B. Kumor and Rev. Z. Obertyński. The introductory section of the review read in part as follows:
>
> "I am not exaggerating when I say that the appearance of a complete history of our Catholic Church has been awaited long and impatiently by whole generations of Poles, regardless of whether they have a religious or political world-view. For all lovers of the history of our nation are aware of the enormous role that the Catholic Church has played in our history, from the foundation of our state, which almost coincided with the reception of baptism from the hands of Latin priests, through the centuries up to the present day. To be sure, its role has varied during the thousand years of our nation's historical existence, but it has always been present and alive among us. However, despite an awareness of the powerful impact of its principles and hierarchical organization on our society, no one in recent times has undertaken a profound, scholarly presentation of its history. The situation has been all the more paradoxical in that other aspects of our history have been the object of more than one exhaustive, scholarly study. . . ." (*Report on Materials Censored*, July 16–31, 1975)

The censors also removed passages linking the nineteenth-century Church and the left, since the Communist regime identified itself with the latter:

> In Issue No. 49 of *Tygodnik Powszechny*, in the column "Browsing Through the Bookstore," the author "Bibliofil" discussed, among other things, "a valuable book" by R. Bender entitled *Chrześcijanie w Polskich Ruchach Demokratycznych XIX Stulecia* [*Christians in Polish Democratic Movements of the 19th Century*], published by the Center for Social Documentation and Research in Warsaw. The following statement of opinion was deleted:
>
> ". . . Quite apart from its scholarly merits, this book makes the reader, especially the young reader, aware of how very closely every faction, movement and trend in social and political thought during the last century that was labeled as radical or even leftist was related to Christianity, and how many activities and fighters for the cause of

national independence and democracy were Christians or, for that matter, representatives of the official Church establishment. In this respect, Bender's book dots many *i*'s to make up for the vague allusions of much of our postwar historiography." (*Report on Materials Censored*, December 1–15, 1975)

The censors also prevented the publication of sermons that represented the Church as an integral part of the Polish state. A passage in a 1974 sermon by the then Archbishop of Kraków, Karol Cardinal Wojtyła, which discussed the endowment of the University of Kraków by the will of Queen Jadwiga in 1400, was deleted from Church bulletins of official sermons and documents because it stressed the fact that the original core of the university was its theological faculty and because it articulated the message that underlies all these censored historical discussions: the Church predates communism in Poland, and should not be deprived of its rights.

The following passage was questioned in Cardinal Wojtyła's "600th Anniversary of the Birth of Queen Jadwiga" in the weekly *Gość Niedzielny*, No. 12.

"When we mention this, we should not forget that the direct fruit of the Queen's efforts was the establishment of the first Department of Theology in Poland, in Kraków, at the very heart of its oldest university. For this reason, on the anniversary of the birth of Queen Jadwiga, I am organizing special prayers throughout the Archdiocese of Kraków, that theology and theological schools might obtain rights of citizenship in our time. It is a question of our culture's certificate of identity, of the force that defined it for so many centuries, even during the Partitions and the occupation. It is also a matter of respect for the higher education that all priests receive thanks to the initiative of Queen Jadwiga, who petitioned for and received [the right to establish] a Department of Theology from Pope Boniface IX. I have written about this matter many times. In connection with the anniversary of Queen Jadwiga, it again becomes relevant. History, after all, has its rights. We proclaim these rights to everyone: men in power, men of learning and young people in the process of educating themselves. . . ."

The same text was removed from the monthly publication *Apostolstwo Chorych*. (*Report on Materials Censored*, March 16–31, 1974)

Theology as Politics

For Polish censors, religious leaders and journalists, the conflict between Church and state did not begin or end with the Church's role
as a pillar of Polish society. Censorship in the mid-seventies was intent
on weakening the Church by denying its role as a partner. It was also
intent on weakening the Church by complicating its task: news of its
activities were limited, and even parish bulletins and membership
cards were sometimes prevented from being printed. The censors saw
to this, as we have seen, on orders from the party Press Department,
even when the Church and state were committed to the same objec-
tives.

Beyond all this, however, the Church posed an even greater threat.
It was a force in human life whose validity had been denied by Marx.
Religious belief invalidated the Marxist view of history and provided
a haven from the kind of full commitment to "socialist transformation" that Gierek sought. Thus no printed matter was permitted to
suggest that nonbelief was less fulfilling than belief:

> In the text of a sermon entitled "The Mystery of Jesus," forming part
> of an article entitled "Toward an Understanding of the Supernatural:
> Homilies Delivered During the 1975 Lenten Retreat," published in the
> collective work *Z Teorii i Praktyki Głoszenia Słowa Bożego* [*From the
> Theory and Practice of Preaching the Word of God*], Rev. B. Dembow-
> ski wrote the following comments:
> "... For people who do not want to or are unable to recognize the
> truth that God so loved the world that He gave it his only son, the
> person of Jesus Christ will always be a mystery, just as it was for the
> guards who were sent to arrest Jesus and said: 'Never before has any
> man spoken the way that this man speaks.' For if someone feels that
> he wants to and should be an atheist, then what has he to do with the
> person of Jesus Christ? It is possible not to think about Him, and it is
> possible to try not to know anything about Him. This is possible for
> someone born and raised in culture and civilization far removed from
> Europe. In such a place it is indeed possible not to know anything about
> Christ. But what about someone born and raised in European culture
> and civilization? If he wants to think at all, then what is he to do about
> the person of Jesus Christ? About ten years ago, an article appeared
> in *Argumenty* about Jesus of Nazareth, the Prophet. The author of the

article was Leszek Kołakowski. The article ends with a sad conclusion. At the beginning of the article, he stated that 'Jesus was a wonderful man,' almost the same words as of those guards: 'Never before has any man spoken the way that this man speaks.' He was a wonderful man and a man of great faith. However, Kołakowski overlooked the problem that Jesus not only believed in God the Father, but also referred to Himself as being equal to the Father. He ignored this problem altogether. He would only go so far as to say that Jesus was a man of great faith, and added—and this is what is sad—that this great man deceived himself, since there is of course no such thing as God the Father.

"And so it turns out that man is an absurd creature, for here we see that the greatest of all men deceived himself in a tragic manner. The tone of this article is imbued with respect and sadness over the fact that, unfortunately, God does not exist. Well, perhaps it is true. And there we were believing in love, believing that Jesus spoke the truth and was thus not a tragically deranged figure. . . .

"And this is why the Holy Gospel is Good News, and this is why it is sad to contemplate anyone repudiating the fundamental tenet of the Gospel, that God so loved the world that He gave it his only son. During a subsequent discussion of this article, which someone told me about, Kołakowski was reproached for having written an article which concludes that atheism is sad. Kołakowski answered: 'And so, my dear colleague, are you glad that there is no God? This is sad!'

"But we, for our part, are glad that God does exist, and this is joyous news!" (*Report on Materials Censored*, December 1–15, 1975)

The ultimate threat the censors guarded against was the very intimation of the claim made by the following censored poem by a prominent contemporary Polish poet: that unbelief solves no problems which belief does not; that the same human tragedies, which Gierek's propaganda about the new socialist man ignored, have to be faced by all:

The following poem by J. Twardowski, along with the commentary following it, scheduled for publication in Issue No. 12 of the monthly *W Drodze*, was challenged:

> LORD JESUS OF THE UNBELIEVERS
> Lord Jesus of the Unbelievers
> walks among us
> a little bit about Him is known from "Cepelia"*

*A state folkcrafts store.

a little bit from hearsay
He is thoroughly ignored
by the morning paper
unaffiliated with any party
unarmed
a subject of much debate
but avoided
like an old plague victims' cemetery
necessarily drab
hence totally pure
Lord Jesus of the unbelievers
walks among us
sometimes he stops
and stands like a rigid cross
believers and unbelievers alike
we are all united
by undeserved suffering
which brings us closer to the truth.

"Ignored, unaffiliated with any party, unarmed, a subject of much debate, avoided, drab. One might also add 'fashionable' to all these descriptive catchwords. Fashionable and therefore superficial. A stylized religious statue. A film star. A cross pinned to the sweater of a young girl or a bearded young man.

"The Lord Jesus is always willing to be spat upon again and again by our impertinence, indifference, modishness and superficiality.

"Every denial of the truth, every expression of scorn and every refusal to say things that ought to be said is another act of repression directed against Him who is the very embodiment of truth.

"But the dire symbol of the cross, the symbol of suffering and pain, the symbol of ultimate fear, looms over all of us equally. In this sense the terms 'belief' and 'unbelief' are deprived of their power to distinguish between one person and another.

"The truth of suffering and death, the most profound truth of human existence, transcends all beliefs and declarations of faith.

"This is yet another fact that diminishes the value of the petty distinctions that divide us.

"The truth is the same for everyone." (*Report on Materials Censored,* December 1–15, 1975)

8 / CENSORING HISTORY

POLISH HISTORY, marked as it is by conflict with Russia, nationalist struggles and evidence of the shallow roots of communism in Poland, proved no easier for the censors to handle than the present. In Poland, where much of its history was marked by foreign occupation and ignominious defeats, the messages of the past and the moments of glory were something that was transmitted from generation to generation. History was the great measure of right and wrong, heroes and villains, friends and enemies not only in the past but also in the present. Because they could not turn to the past as a source of support for Communist rule, the censors were instructed to erase from historical accounts any embarrassing personalities and trends that might reflect badly on the present and the roots of communism in Poland. This was done in the hope that erasing history from the pages of the mass media and historical literature would erase the national historical memory. Instead, the gaps created by this censorship aroused popular ire. It was the instruction to erase and then repaint the events in the Katyń forest, where at the start of World War II thousands of Polish officers were shot by the Soviets, that triggered Tomasz Strzyżewski's decision to provide the fuel for an attack on censorship and to smuggle out the documents presented in this book. Many Poles, perhaps unaware of the specific censorship regulations yet deeply troubled by the discrepancy between the official version of Polish history and what they had learned in their homes, were driven to seek alternative—undoctored—sources of historical information. During the late seventies this hunger for real history brought large numbers of Polish high school and university students to lectures and classes conducted in private apartments by experts and professors who were prohibited from teaching what they knew in the universities. Their subjects were the history of the Communist takeover, Polish-Soviet relations and the history of the Polish Communist Party. These "Flying University" courses (named after a similar illegal series of courses run during the nineteenth-century Partitions and during World War II, when Polish universities were either closed or barred from teaching politically inconvenient subjects) filled the gaps created by censorship for those who could attend. For the rest of the nation, history was something that was passed from generation to generation and studied from smuggled texts circulated in the West. No amount of erasure and denial by the censors could quell this concern with, and hunger for, genuine Polish history. Holidays that were purposefully ignored by the regime because they did not fit propaganda needs took on even greater national and anti-Soviet symbolism for the population simply because they were being denied.

The censors' office had its own priorities and concerns. Accuracy and truth were not particularly relevant issues. Neither was the originality of historical writing and research. Original research challenged the authorized axioms, and original writing only looked like a clever allegory of the present. In reviewing what was said about history, the censors concerned themselves not only with the past but also with what the past might imply about the present and the future. Their responsibility was as much to cleanse specific facts as to control the overall image of the past. This increased the amount of double-think on the part of the censors. It also made them much more sensitive to what was not said in historical accounts, for history had to be used whenever possible to glorify the present. For example, in any discussion of Russians and Communists not only did censors have to make sure that any mention of events that could be read negatively did not appear, but they also had to see to it that every shred of history that presented the Russians and the Communists in a positive light was included—since Polish history had so little that served this purpose.

The targets of the censors' red pencil went far beyond the newspapers and magazines in which most of the contemporary historical writing appeared. In cleansing history, censors reviewed scholarly journals and books. They watched over guidebooks, encyclopedias and picture albums. And, ultimately, they became the penultimate

arbiters of the public's memories of the dead—the obituaries submitted to newspapers by friends and relatives. Only in their final
marks—their tombstones—were Poles free of the censors' surveillance.

Whether the censors' instructions were to erase or to rewrite the
past, the ultimate problem was that Polish history did not lend itself
to a pro-Soviet or pro-Communist point of view. Few episodes in
Polish history provided suitable raw material for the kind of propaganda sought by the leaders of People's Poland. And yet, precisely
because the present was not glorious, the propagandists *needed* history to help glorify it and to justify the unwelcome rule of the Communists. This was hard to do with a national history that was marked
by struggles between Russians and Poles for land and sovereignty,
struggles in which the Russians were frequently the victors. Even
more difficult was squaring Communist internationalism with the
nationalism that had built up over years of being ruled by occupying
powers while Poland was partitioned time and again among Prussia,
Russia and Austria.

Even the most obscure events took on new color as the past seemed
to parallel the present. When in December 1976 one of Warsaw's
leading theaters was allowed to produce a play by W. Terlecki about
a murder committed by a monk in the nineteenth century, the censors'
directors worried that reviews and discussions of the play could easily
pull its plot out of the past to make veiled references to the present.
So they issued a directive spelling out for censors the potential parallels that they imagined might be drawn from the plot and warning
them to keep these references out of reviews. This was done in part,
according to the directive given the censors, in order to avoid offending religious feelings—the very same feelings the censors were instructed to try to weaken in their censorship of religious subjects. The
production and its plot line, the censors were told, also raised the
more predictable and greater problem of the traditional enmity between Poland and Russia. A not too distant parallel to that play was
The Forefathers, the classic written by Poland's national poet, Adam
Mickiewicz. In 1968 the closing of *The Forefathers* triggered street
demonstrations in Warsaw. At that time the Soviet ambassador felt
that the production used Mickiewicz's hostile view of the tsarist authorities as a device for attacking the Soviet Union, and protested the
production and the wild audience reaction to its specially staged barbs
at the Russians. This time the authorities were willing to permit

Terlecki's play since its staging was not incendiary. But they were clearly frightened enough by all the parallels that might be drawn that they themselves thought of the possible negative interpretations before the play ever opened and issued a regulation to limit the play's publicity and prevent the issues it touched upon from being raised in the media. The regulation was a teaching tool as well. It spelled out explicitly what had to be removed and why, so that the same reasoning could be applied to other cases that the leadership might not manage to anticipate:

> 154. In permitting publication of reviews, discussions and other materials devoted to W. Terlecki's play *Odpocznij po Biegu* [*Rest After the Run*], presented at the Powszechny Theater in Warsaw, the following principles should be adhered to:
>
> In order to avoid potential polemics and accusations in religious publications because of offense to religious feelings and the like, discussions that go overboard in their emphasis on the religious aspects [of this play] (questions of religion in general, assessments of the moral attitudes of the religious, etc.) and all attempts to equate the action of this play with the actual murder committed in Częstochowa before World War I by the Paulist monk should be eliminated. It is undesirable—and this view is in keeping with the conception of the author and director—to attempt to fix the exact place of the event or to mention "its heroes by name."
>
> On the other hand, formulations like the following are permissible: "The author based his account on a real murder committed by a certain monk in a certain monastery somewhere in the Congress Kingdom, etc."
>
> In view of the fact that the action of the play takes place during the period of the partitions (Russian Orthodox tsarist officials act as the judges of a Polish Catholic cleric), all attempts to interpret this play tendentiously on the level of nationalism or to refer it to the contemporary scene (directly or indirectly) should be eliminated.
>
> This instruction is intended solely for the information of the censors. (First version, December 10, 1976; second version, January 5, 1977)

Ironically—given the care with which the propaganda tsars thought out their decision to allow the production in one of Warsaw's best small theaters but to deny the production real literary criticism —the reviews still could not be controlled. Two weeks after the above directive, a second regulation was distributed that stopped any discussion of the play:

156. Until further notice, no reviews, discussions, descriptions or the like should be permitted concerning W. Terlecki's play *Rest After the Run* presented at the Powszechny Theater in Warsaw.

The problems of approving or disapproving the facts of Polish history become even more complicated for twentieth-century events. In the interwar period, Polish communism was hardly a popular force. In fact, it was minuscule and illegal, and Poland was ruled by a rightist, nationalist government whose most heroic moment was repulsing the Red Army, fresh from its own revolution, from Polish lands. The history of the Polish Communist movement was made even more useless for Gierek's propagandists by its identification, before Poland was reestablished as an independent nation in 1918, with the repudiation of Polish nationalism. It was after all Rosa Luxemburg, one of the leaders of the Marxist movement in Poland, who clashed with Lenin over her insistence that nations like Poland should not be reestablished or preserved as independent states.

Poland's wartime and postwar history offered just as little material for the party propagandists. The chief leaders of the Polish resistance during World War II were the non-Communist underground and the Polish army in exile in the West. The role of the Soviets in the war was also more than problematic from the Polish point of view. In 1939 the Soviet Union joined Nazi Germany in a partition of Polish territory and imprisoned countless numbers of Poles in the territories that it had annexed. The historic Polish lands around Lwów and Wilno remained in the Soviet Union after the war; however, much of their Polish population had fled west to Poland at war's end and settled in the formerly German territories given to Poland to compensate for the loss of its eastern lands to the Soviet Union. For these people, the Soviet capture of their lands and their need to flee from Soviet communism were painful memories, still fresh even in the seventies.

Nor did the years of postwar Communist rule provide any moments of glory that the party's propagandists could use. The Communist takeover in Poland was not a smooth liberation. Soviet troops were only momentarily welcomed. The government that they brought with them was not welcomed at all either by the Poles who had survived the war or by the Communist underground that had fought its battles with the Germans from behind the lines in Poland. Toward the end of the war, Poles struggled as much to keep the Soviets from taking control as to destroy the Germans. The ill-fated 1944 Warsaw Uprising was at least in part an attempt by the Polish underground to take control of its capital by itself, before the Soviets could do it and set up their own government there. The Polish underground fighters were slaughtered and Warsaw razed to the ground by the Germans—while Soviet troops sat on the other bank of the Vistula River and watched.

These negative images and the problems of Communist rule in Poland, with its history of a leadership imposed on an unwilling population and faced with the recurrent threat of being unseated, were clearly not what the Gierek regime wanted to claim as its heritage. The problem is exemplified in the Polish leadership's concern, in 1976, over a newly published guidebook to Poland's national cemetery. After the book had been published, the PZPR Ideological Department raised what it regarded as serious questions about what it saw as anti-Communist omissions in the text. It then drafted a critique of the book's organization and of the material that it contained. This critique was then distributed to the censors to provide them with an instructive example of the kinds of errors in content and "tone" that should not have been allowed. The document also provides a clear description of the propaganda chiefs' sense of the uses of history as a propaganda tool:

Main Office for Control of Press,
    Publications and Public Performances
Instruction, Evaluation and Control Group
No. ZI-Pf-132/7/76

                           Warsaw, February 3, 1976
                           C O N F I D E N T I A L
                           Copy No. 24

                Informative Note No. 7

We attach, for the information of censorship groups, an evaluation of Juliusz Jerzy Malczewski's guidebook, *The Communal (Formerly Military) Cemetery at Powązki.* The evaluation was drafted by the PZPR Central Committee's Department for Ideological Education.

The above-mentioned guide by Malczewski was published by the Krajowa Agencja Wydawnicza [National Publishing Agency] in 1975, in an edition of 10,000 copies.

                           Deputy Group Director
                           Janusz Buchalski

Distributed according to the list

Evaluation of Juliusz Jerzy Malczewski's guidebook, entitled *The Communal (Formerly Military) Cemetery at Powązki.*

The guidebook *The Communal (Formerly Military) Cemetery at Powązki* includes an introduction, an outline of the cemetery's history and a discussion of the Avenue of the Worthy (Aleje Zasłużonych), the various sections of the cemetery, the symbolic tombs, headstones, statuary and architecture, as well as an index of names and a plan of the cemetery. The overwhelming majority of the description consists of biographical notes on those buried along the Avenue of the Worthy or in other sections of the cemetery. As the author notes: "This guide is part of a more comprehensive monograph on the cemetery, compiled over the course of several years by a group of historians, archivists and art historians, and is the first publication of its kind written since the war" (page 3). The very publication of this guide should thus be recognized as a positive and socially necessary act.

"The guide was prepared with an actual visitor in mind. It is intended for those who want to tour the cemetery individually, as well as for tour guides. Among those laid to rest here are those who have made important contributions to the life of the capital, soldiers who fell in its defense, and political and social activists and figures in science, the arts and culture whose activity has been of considerable significance to Poland, its history and development. It is the only cemetery of its kind in Poland. Hence its importance not only for Warsaw, but for the nation as a whole" (page 3). It should nonetheless be emphasized that this publication has a number of weaknesses that undermine its effectiveness. It is difficult to agree with the statement of the author that "The notes presented concern the best-known individuals or those most characteristic of a given section of the cemetery" (page 4).

Relatively speaking, the author did his best in his completion of the chapters entitled "Outline of the History of the Cemetery" (pages 5–8) and "Headstones and Graves—Sculpture and Architecture" (pages 52–58). On the other hand, we have reservations about the chapters entitled "Avenue of the Worthy" (pages 9–21), "Cemetery Sections" (pages 21–46) and "Symbolic Tombs" (pages 47–52). What is disturbing, first of all, is the improper proportions of material devoted to those laid to rest in the Avenue of the Worthy and in various other sections of the cemetery, to the detriment of the former. Of the 200 people buried along the Avenue of the Worthy, Malczewski has provided biographical material on only 36 individuals of particular merit. It should be emphasized that many famous party and state figures from the period before December 1974 (the period covered by the guide) are omitted from this list of 36. Many of those omitted were mentioned by E. Gierek at the Seventh Party Congress. These comments apply to an even greater extent to the chapter entitled "Cemetery Sections." The very division of the sections into various groups should give us pause:

Political and Social Activists, Figures from the Fields of Science, Culture and the Arts

Veterans of the January [1863] Uprising [against Russian control]

Soldiers of the Polish Army Who Fell or Died During Wars Between 1918 and 1920 [when the Polish troops fought and pushed back Russian Bolshevik forces]

Soldiers of the Polish Army Who Died in the Interwar Period or Fell in the War to Defend Poland in 1939

Soldiers of the Polish People's Army [postwar title for Polish army]

Soldiers of the People's Guard and People's Army [Communist underground forces during World War II]

Soldiers of the Home Army and the Warsaw Uprising [non-Communist underground force during World War II and the final battle they fought with the Germans to establish themselves in their capital before Soviet troops took over]

The grouping of the sections would not be any great cause for concern if clear criteria had been given for the division and selection of names in the various groups, and if the names suggested by those categories had been retained. For example, the group "Soldiers of the Polish Army Who Fell or Died During Wars Between 1918 and 1920" includes short biographies of seven persons, only one of whom died in 1918 and another in 1919. The rest died chiefly during the interwar period. Among them, for example, is Walery Sławek (page 31), whose biography does not even mention that he was one of the closest collaborators of J. Piłsudski, his personal friend, a joint founder of the Piłsudski camp and a leader of the Nonpartisan Bloc for Cooperation with the Government. As everyone knows, he committed suicide on May 2, 1939.

Far more space in the guide is devoted to soldiers in the defensive war of 1939 than to soldiers of the Polish People's Army. The number of biographies devoted to the latter also suffers in comparison to the former (11 notes on soldiers of the Polish People's Army and 14 on the September [1939] soldiers and others). We find the same to be true when we compare the number of biographies of members of the People's Guard and People's Army with that for members of the Home Army. Biographies of the former take up four and one-half pages, and there are 22 of them in all, while the Home Army, covered in a single page, is represented by 31 biographical notes. Among the soldiers of the Home Army, the author mentions Bronisław Sianoszek, who fought in various bands against the people's government after 1945.

It is a great shame that the author did not devote more space to the 50 Poles who were hanged, most of them activists in the Polish Workers' Party and soldiers in the People's Guard. He presented biographical sketches of only five of them. He failed to mention the names of a number of key activists of the Polish Workers' Party and the People's Guard in Warsaw, hanged on October 16, 1942.

The following names were also omitted: Feliks Papliński, a member of the Initiating Group and a joint organizer of the Polish Workers' Party; Franciszek Wawrzyniak, organizer and secretary of the regional committee of the Polish Workers' Party in Warsaw; Juliusz Kania, a member of the main staff of the People's Guard and a leader of the People's Guard Warsaw city district; Kazimierz Grodecki, one of the organizers and leaders of the Associations of Friends of the USSR and a Polish Workers' Party activist; Izydor Koszykowski, author of the autobiographical novel *Child of the Streets* and an activist of the Polish Workers' Party; Ignacy Romanowicz, a chemical engineer and organizer and director of the People's Guard main staff laboratory. We also have reservations about the tone of the author's statement that "The majority of those killed were Communist activists." He should have written explicitly that 39 of those hanged were Polish Workers' Party activists or soldiers in the People's Guard. This number was established long ago, and is cited in most of the available documentation. On the other hand, the author said far more than was necessary about the Home Army's "Wieniec" sabotage action (October 7–8, 1942) as well as about a second attack on a railroad made by the Home Army on the night of November 16, 1942 (pages 39–40), and moreover it is difficult to determine what action is being described since the author does not place it.

We are also surprised that the symbolic tomb of Canadian pilots has twice as much space devoted to it as to a similar tomb of soldiers of the First "Kościuszko" Infantry Division, who died in the battles for the liberation of Praga. The author has devoted several lines to the Canadian pilots themselves, but most of his account pertains to the air support for the people involved in the Warsaw uprisings, and this action is not directly related to the subject matter of the guide. On the other hand, the discussion of the symbolic tombs and the grave architecture and sculpture of the cemetery deserves a favorable assessment. It also seems that the selection of the ten pictures of cemetery monuments and graves was a good one, except for the fact that the quality of some of the pictures is not very good.

In all, the cemetery guide gives the impression of being a rather haphazard compilation of data of various kinds. The general and historical sections have, to their credit, the virtue of offering visitors to the cemetery the opportunity of becoming well acquainted with it. On the other hand, the biographies have been carelessly selected and are presented haphazardly. The guide's instructive, informative, and ideological and political virtues are somewhat dubious, given its present form. After all, the significance of a publication of this kind stems from the fact that an important part of patriotic education is becoming acquainted with the national past through the deeds and fate of those who have gone before. The author and the publisher (Krajowa Agencja Wydawnicza) have the responsibility of seeing to it that this publication corresponds to historical truth and the socialist character of the goals of patriotic education.

The subtleness of history and the importance of monitoring not only what was included but also what was omitted required that the censors be reminded by reports like the one on the cemetery guidebook or the one below, on the children's encyclopedia of what they should have considered. In both these cases, the books had passed review by their own editors and censors yet were found lacking by high party officials who learned of their existence only after receiving their copies. In both cases, therefore, the censors were warned and instructed to minimize the damage by controlling the books' reviews. In the case of the children's encyclopedia, the censors were informed that only glorified history was to be presented to the new generation of Poles, and that no child was to be exempt from information about the achievements of Polish communism:

Main Office for Control of Press,
    Publications and Public Performances
Instruction and Documentation Group
Nr ZI-Pf-131/2/77

Warsaw, February 11, 1977
C O N F I D E N T I A L
Copy No. 29

Informative Note No. 2

In connection with Regulation No. 167, we are informing you that a number of criticisms have been made of the content of *Encyklopedia dla Dzieci* [*Encyclopedia for Children*]. They concern, among other things: the selection of historical figures to be discussed (omission of a number of names, while including, for example, Ignacy Mościcki [president of Poland in the interwar period, 1926–39] as a pioneer of

Polish chemistry); the absence, under the heading "Capital," of any discussion of the role of the Polish Army and the Soviet Army in the liberation of Warsaw; improper treatment of the topic "PZPR" (omission of the role of the Polish Workers' Party and the names of key party activists); and the omission of various entries relating to the working class.

For these reasons, it has been determined fitting to direct reviews of the book in such a way that they will be balanced and not completely favorable.

Vice-Chairman
Edward Adamiak

Distributed according to the list
63 copies made

Before the Communist Takeover: An Embarrassed Silence

The task of the censors was a complicated one when it came to dealing with articles on the interwar period, when Poland enjoyed its first moment of statehood after 123 years of total partition. The leaders and heroes of the interwar period, like Marshal Józef Piłsudski, who ruled Poland and led the Polish army in its "miraculous" victory against the Russian forces in 1920, and Wincenty Witos, the leader of the Polish Peasant Party, were hardly pro-Soviet or pro-Communist. Indeed, the history of the period begins with a war between Poland and the newly formed Communist state in Russia—a war that ended in 1920 with Piłsudski driving Bolshevik soldiers back from the gates of Warsaw and out of the country. Like that war, the profiles of the leaders of Poland before World War II did not lend themselves to the needs of postwar propaganda. Poland was led by men who were basically nationalists and anti-Communists, and who feared Russia above all else. The Communist Party in Poland had almost no popular following. The membership it did have was drawn largely from Jews and other ethnic minorities who were unwelcome in the Polish government. Even worse, from the point of view of the Gierek propaganda machine, the party and its leaders were annihilated on the eve of World War II on Stalin's orders, because he found them unmanageable. And yet another thorny issue from this period was the lack of close relations between bordering East European nations.

Journalists and writers who could remember the interwar period, and the people who led Poland's cultural and political establishment in those years of independence, were angered by the distorted pictures of this period, so important in Polish history and national consciousness. One, Antoni Słonimski, the senior poet and leader of the literary establishment in the postwar period, decried, in a censored article that he tried to publish in one of Poland's regional intellectual monthlies, the falseness with which this period and its intellectual leaders were presented. His protest dealt specifically with the picture painted of interwar Warsaw society, but it was a reflection of a far broader objection that he often voiced—an objection to distortions that were forced by censorship on what could be written. This protest he voiced not only in journals where the circulation was small enough that there was some chance it could slip into print, but also at writers' meetings and intellectual gatherings.

In the Wrocław monthly *Odra,* No. 4, we challenged A. Słonimski's "Prototypes," in which he called for a "clearing up" of views about the interwar period and a "defalsification" of assessments made about these years and of evaluations of certain figures in the political and literary world. Below are some excerpts:

"Today, after 30 years of People's Poland, it is worth considering the kinds of traditions we have adopted and should adopt concerning the recent past, the two decades between the wars.

"It seems to me that the primary task is to arrive at a true picture of these not too distant years of independence. Unfortunately, until now we have not written a comprehensive political, social, artistic and moral history of this period. We reach out sporadically and chaotically to various books and notes. . . .

"I think that it would be worthwhile to look at those victims of distortion closest at hand, and I consider it my duty to defend one of the friends of my youth.

"It would be worthwhile to unmask the false legend about Wieniawa [an adjutant to Piłsudski and leading interwar Polish diplomat] as a ladies' man and swaggerer in the Gascon style, a legend that continues to maintain itself, presenting us with a false image of this colorful and tragic figure of the twenty-year interwar period. . . .

"After the war, Wienawa's archetype became his caricature. The myth has been maintained as a picture of the prewar years. It has become one of the requisites of that unbearable [bourgeois] 'Old Warsaw' like Adria [a nightclub], Ordonka, a two-horse carriage with rubber tires, or pigeons in Mariensztat. His patriotic character has been forgotten. . . .

"We can probably afford to let Wieniawa be himself in Poland, and there is no reason to obliterate the differences in the political points of view of Maria Dąbrowska [a highly respected interwar writer] and Wanda Wasilewska [Communist writer in the interwar period]. One may criticize or oppose our recent past, but what is the sense of criticizing the past if one is dealing with false, unreal or imaginary archetypes?

"Long years of friendship link me with Maria Dąbrowska, but I must confess that it is difficult for me to recognize her in the currently published fragments of her memoirs.

"For today's reader, Dąbrowska has become someone entirely different for the reason that her views are presented in a one-sided way, destroying the dichotomous frame of mind typical of the progressive intelligentsia of that period. A lecture she never gave is ascribed to her, and despite the fact that there is incontrovertible evidence that such a lecture was never given, this false information has never been corrected. In this way, we draw close to the goal which, Gombrowicz noted: 'Is based on the idea that in order not to change too much one rather shades, alters bit by bit, adding a little here, taking away a little there until, for no clear reason, the honorable thoughts of a man who has spent his whole life struggling to think in a serious manner are turned into dirt.' (*Diary, 1961–66,* p. 145)

"I warn you against these notes, for they not only provide an incomplete image, but lose the atmosphere, distort proportions. . . .

"Let's forget about silly 'Old Warsaw.' We should rather remember those who rebuilt prewar Poland after one hundred years of bondage, who succeeded in joining together the three partitions and laid the basis of our present-day culture and learning. Maria Dąbrowska can defend herself. No film version can destroy *The Wedding* or Żeromski's *Ashes.* Writing about Wieniawa, I tried to recall a difficult thing, the Polish prewar intelligentsia, full of its own specific character, formed by generations of contact with European and national culture. These are delicate things, material that is easily lost. But it is important that we remember that our forebears were not like the stone statues on Easter Island, incomprehensible, all facing in the same direction and indistinguishable from one another." (*Report on Materials Censored,* March 16–31, 1974)

Since many writers and political figures of the interwar period had represented points of view that were not only anti-Communist but often right-wing, the censors of the Gierek era were charged with preventing their being treated as outstanding figures of Polish history.

The censors' error in allowing the publication of a book honoring some interwar political figures connected with the right served as a tool for teaching the censors how to do their work properly:

2. The publishing house Wydawnictwo Literackie has issued a work by Adam Grzymała-Siedlecki entitled *Those Who Were Not Bid Farewell* [*Nie Pożegnani*] (Kraków, 1972). This is a collection of reminiscences about writers who perished in the years 1939–45 in battle, in concentration camps, etc., or who died a natural death and—in the opinion of the author—were not, because of the conditions of the occupations, given a fitting farewell as outstanding contributors to Polish culture. "Feeling the painful wrong done to these most worthy among us, I resolved to honor them someday, at the very least with my own humble pen," says the author in his introduction.

Among these "most worthy from among us," outstanding figures of Polish culture, patriots and good citizens, the author included more than fifty portraits, many of them activists of a nationalist-clericalist political persuasion: Antoni Potocki—a National Democratic ideologist, collaborator of Roman Dmowski; Stanisław Pieńkowski—a contributor to the National Democratic papers *Gazeta Warszawska* and *Myśl Narodowa*; Stefan Kołaczkowski—editor of the quarterly *Marchołt* and a close friend of the nationalistic periodical *Myśl Narodowa*, which supposedly "cultivated Polish reality with an ideological plow, pulled out the weeds from it, and plowed the richer soil of the spirit"; Józef Birkenmajer, characterized by the author as a "zealous Catholic, who found in religious teachings a harmony with his own natural feelings"; Count Edward Krasiński; and Countess Marta Krasińska. Stanisław Piasecki, a prewar figure in the National Radical Camp and the founder, publisher and ideologist of *Prosto z Mostu*, was characterized as follows:

"Establishing as a cover a café in the ruins of the Warsaw Philharmonic, a café which, moreover, served as a place for meetings between members of the Underground, he began, already in November of 1939, to publish a secret periodical ([GUKPPiW note:] Reference to the conspiratorial organ *Walka*, which appeared between 1940 and 1944 in Warsaw as the central organ of the National Party, Stronnictwo Narodowe), one of those papers which, for more than five years, kept the country in a state of revolt and gave it the strength to continue. . . ."

Some of the writers described by the author as "most worthy" were connected with right-wing groups. To group them together under the single heading "those who were not bid farewell" gives the book, as a whole, an undesirable tone, suggesting that people like Antoni Potocki, Stefan Kołaczkowski, Count Edward Krasiński, Stanisław Piasecki and others should occupy a permanent, worthy place in the history of Polish culture and that they somehow wait until the present day for that act of recognition, a fitting farewell (or perhaps even political rehabilitation).

The Peasant Party had been the leading party during the Interwar period and in the wartime government-in-exile in London. Its leader during the immediate postwar years was Stanisław Mikołajczyk, who entered into a coalition government with the Communists and was later forced by them to flee Poland. For Polish censors, all of this meant that any mention of a Peasant Party leader could be interpreted as a demonstration of support for prewar, non-Communist leaders who opposed a Communist takeover in Poland. Hence:

20. In the event that obituaries of former activists of the peasant movement are presented for publication, the National Committee of the Peasant Party [i.e., the present-day state-controlled Peasant Party] or, in local areas, the voivodship committee should be consulted before granting permission. (This applies particularly in the case of activists from the interwar period or during the first few years immediately after liberation.)

This regulation allowed censors selectively to limit statements in obituaries that referred to unmentionable interwar events or that gave an unduly prominent place to the activities of the Peasant Party. It also left open the option of not printing an obituary or detailed statement honoring a prewar non-Communist politician.

The history of the left in prewar Poland was an almost equally difficult topic to handle as the right, for it was never more than a nationalist force using "socialist" as a title. As pointed out by one censored article presented for publication in *Więź*, the liberal Catholic intelligentsia monthly of the Catholic Intelligentsia Clubs:

"The collapse of the revolution of 1905 brought about an ideological crisis for all varieties of social radicalism in Poland, a crisis that has not been given sufficient attention or emphasis in our modern historiography. Beginning in 1907, the possibilities of socialism ceased to be fascinating <u>even</u> for many of its former advocates. After his experience with the Battle Organization, Piłsudski devoted himself to building up a military liberation. The PPS [Polish Socialist Party, 1892–1948] Faction and the Left Wing [Lewica] became bogged down in disputes <u>that</u>

were often positively Talmudic. And soon, social problems were over-shadowed by the struggle for independence.

"Basically, concern with resolving Poland's social problems was very slow in coming. The year 1920 [when the Bolshevik army was driven back by Piłsudski's Polish army] proved that as far as the national question went, resolving social problems was then very much in the background.

"The socialist-revolutionary mentality, born at the end of the 19th century and linked to an earlier set of radical-democratic convictions and values professed by the Great Emigration (and through it to the slogans of the French Revolution), but brought to life chiefly by the idea of socialist revolution predicted by Marx, addressed itself to the exploited classes of society. Initially, in the Social Democratic Party of the Kingdom of Poland and Lithuania [the left wing of the Polish Socialist Party and the Polish Communist Party], all hope was placed on the international proletariat with the call "Workers of all countries, unite!" But beginning in the 1890s those among the socialists who clearly emphasized national identity proved to be more popular. In this Polish Socialist mind-set, Polish workers were the key. The uppermost values of this group became social equality and social justice applied not only to the distribution of material and cultural goods, but to political power as well. At the foundation of the group's ideology was its conviction that class struggle was the only true mechanism of historical changes. This inclined them to reject categorically the idea of a proletarian solidarity transcending national boundaries. Since the situation of the nation required such solidarity, the Polish socialist was faced with a drastic dilemma, resulting from his dual spiritual affiliation." (*Report on Materials Censored,* March 16–31, 1974)

The battles during the two decades of independence between the more popular and highly anti-Communist socialist parties and the tiny Communist Party, which enjoyed no popular support, were likewise difficult to square with the party's propaganda needs. Hence virtually all socialist activity during the prewar period became nonhistory. As is clear from the portions of the passage below that were accepted, censorship not only managed to silence history but often transformed it by deleting important details:

Passages portraying anti-Soviet sentiment among Polish socialists during the interwar period were deleted from J. Czajkowski and J. Majchrowski's essay, "Stanisław Dubois" (*Tygodnik Powszechny,* No. 12), which dealt with the career of this activist.

"... Despite the fact that he did not want to fight in Byelorussia or the Ukraine, he entered the war in 1920 as a volunteer in the Polish Army, helped to defend Warsaw and won the Cross of Valor. . . .

"... The Sixth Congress of the Communist International advanced the notion of 'social fascists,' a term that encompassed the entire socialist movement, 'the chief obstacle to the Communist parties' struggle against capitalism'; the different stand the socialists took concerning [Wera] Kostrzewa and [Adolf] Warski [prewar Communist Party leaders] became the reason for their removal from the party leadership. 'The Flames,' the radical leftist PPS groups allied with it and, later still, the Youth Organization of the Workers' University Society were considered by the Communist parties to be 'a device intended to draw the revolutionary masses away from the Communist movement.' Finally, it became difficult for most Polish socialists to adopt the Communist slogan of alliance with the Soviet Union and the necessity of supporting and defending the USSR against potential aggression on the part of the capitalist countries, since their own awareness had developed in the course of a struggle against the Russian tsar, who had been a symbol of oppression and servitude for generations. . . ." (*Report on Materials Censored*, March 16–31, 1974)

The complicated nature of the Polish Communist Party's own early history made coverage of it a difficult task. Ideally, the censors preferred that it not be discussed at all, for to talk of the prewar Communist party was to talk of a party that fit the desires neither of the Polish population nor of the Soviet Union. Most of the Polish Communist Party leadership had been internationalist, insisting, in a land of nationalists, that national boundaries were not relevant for the new socialist state. In the fights for control that went on after Lenin's death in the Soviet Union (January 1924), the Polish Communists were supporters of Leon Trotsky. After Trotsky lost to Stalin in his bid for power (in 1927 he was expelled from the Soviet Union), the Polish Communists continued to be outsiders in Stalin's Comintern, the international organization of Communist parties. To the majority of the Polish population, though, they seemed to be the Russians' servants. This image was reinforced when the Polish Communist Party went along with Comintern instructions and advocated that Germany get back some of the land it had lost in World War I (a demand that served the interests of the German Communist Party but hardly helped the image of the Polish one). At the same time, the Polish Communist leaders never advocated, to the degree that other East

European Communists did, Stalin's policy of doing everything to serve the interests of the Soviet Union. As a result, Stalin perceived them as Trotskyite opponents, the Polish population saw them as enemies of the nation's very existence, and the rulers of Poland dealt with them as enemies to be jailed even as they offered their support.

All of this left little positive to be said about the PZPR's forebears. Consequently, the censors found themselves frequently making decisions to allow or even to forbid material that was later questioned, since history was far clearer and more negative in its messages than the images the masters of Gierek's propaganda needed. In an effort to guide the censors in their task, the Main Office Department of Instruction put out an instruction sheet with an example of an article about Stalin's 1938 dissolution of the Polish Communist Party that a censor had allowed to appear in *Polityka*. On review, the censor's decision had been criticized within the censors' office but, finally, upheld. As the instructive note pointed out, the article and information were certainly too sensitive for a mass-circulation paper that pandered to the broadest group in the population. But it was tolerable —if only that—in a journal like *Polityka* (with its liberal line that served to placate the intelligentsia) as long as the censors did not look to this as a precedent for automatically approving other articles on the subject. In addition, though the moment in the Polish Communist Party's history described in the article was its nadir, the article skirted the issue of the villain in the dissolution of the Polish Party, some of the reasons for its destruction (the party's identification with internationalism and its independence from the Stalin line) and the impact of its dissolution in 1938, one year before Poland was attacked by the Germans, which caused the party to be weak during and after World War II. Even without these elements, however, the fate of loyal Communists—their being jailed or killed for their commitment—was embarrassing. The text, included below, is also an example of the review that went on of individual censors' decisions.

TRAGIC FATE OF CLOSE FRIENDS

In time, our group of regular contributors (to a children's periodical, published by Przeworski) was joined, thanks to his knowledge of the English language, by a translator and copier of texts (which came out of the mouths of cowboy heroes shooting from two Colts like a cloud of steam on a cold day). That translator signed himself Jan Hłasko, and he had gotten his knowledge of the language not from the Methodists [who ran the most respected English school in Warsaw], but from nine years of study in prison cells, where there had been lessons in many fields, based not only on textbooks, but on the live words of fellow prisoners. He ended his studies in September in Tarnów [prison], the place where he was released. Before his release, in July 1939, it was his lot to live through the greatest tragedy of Poland's Communists: the dissolution of the Polish Communist Party by a resolution of the Comintern [under Stalin].

"We lived through it on the outside. And while it is true that none of the four of us, not Władek or Wanda or Marian, was singled out, it was impossible for us not to be affected by the tragedy of some of our closest friends and comrades of so many years, who experienced that decision in various ways.

"How was it experienced by comrades in prison cells, or those struggling in Spain?

"Some accepted the Comintern decision with gritted teeth, as one eudures physical pain or surgery without anesthetic. They were clearly not in agreement with it, but they remained silent, perhaps because of an internal habituation to party discipline, or perhaps because they saw for whose mill grist would be provided by their protest or any attempt to establish a new organization or continue the old one in isolation from the international Communist movement. There were others who accepted the resolution not only out of an inner sense of party discipline based on deep trust in the representatives of the Communist parties in the Comintern, but because they did not feel themselves called or competent to question the facts that had influenced this undoubtedly very difficult decision. And there were others who broke down completely.

"Years later the memoirs were written. Some, full of dignity, and often real civic courage, would not lie about past behavior. And the memoirs of those 'who knew better,' memoir writers who, beating others' breasts only, affirmed that they 'always knew, that they had known already at that time.' And since history, after many twists and turns, makes certain things straight, what does one more scapegoat matter? Where do these double-jointed people come from? Only from among those who broke down right away, or from those who immediately and stubbornly refused, internally, to give in? I don't know. These are not after all simple matters. One cannot cram everyone into the same labeled drawer. People passed through various phases before and after the Comintern decision. It sometimes happened that some of the most fanatic sectarians after years [of party service] learned, in a sudden revelation, as if illuminated suddenly by the secular equivalent of the Holy Spirit between Thursday and Friday or Saturday and Sunday, what horrible sins they had committed. And they fell immediately into a kind of revisionist neophytism, negating everything from before. And it was just as intolerant a neophytism as when they had passed sentence for the slightest sign of dissidence or doubt before—an intolerance that enabled them to believe that such-and-such a comrade from the same punishment cells could turn out to be a provocateur.

" 'Jan Hłasko' was released 'with his things' after the dissolution of the party and after his own additional tragedy. In the common cell they had spoken about the trials that had taken place in Moscow in 1937. Naturally, the Polish prisoners were not provided with copies of the Soviet press with a full stenogram of the legal proceedings. And at that time Romek, or the later Jan Hłasko, had said, out of sincere human suffering over incomprehensible events, 'Oh, if only we could see the stenogram!'

" 'Aha! You have doubts . . .' It was already not a question, but rather a condemnation. Exclusion from the 'community' in the political prisoners' cell. A sentence that could not be appealed. There no longer was any higher party court of appeal. Not inside the cell or outside it. There no longer was any party at all.

"He had a choice of two other cells. One of genuine renegades, of those who had signed declarations renouncing their Communist activity—a special document for the prosecutor And the criminal cell. He chose the latter. That was also an answer.

"When he picked up his things from deposit, the head of the prison proposed, just one more time, like the Tempter: 'And perhaps you would like to sign that declaration? After everything your own comrades did to you?'

"The answer was that it was 'none of his —— business.'

And then he was released. His friends outside, those who knew him, had no doubts about his position or about the psychosis that clearly explained the judgment of his comrades, despairing, yet somehow acting in good faith, trying to save themselves from breaking down, or perhaps from doubt? Some of them years later experienced that sudden appearance of the secular Holy Spirit. Others maintained their self-respect by telling the truth. In their daily illegal activities they had come up against just such contrived and perfidious deeds, including those of genuine provocateurs. They simply believed that the party would be born again after this careful verification, that the cause and the struggle continued everywhere that fascism and imperialism were being attacked, whether abroad or at home And that they had to, and wanted to, be in the very thick of the fight.

"That was probably in the middle of September 1938. In the garden, just cleared of a heavy growth of thistles and burdock, the petals of some kind of flower arrangement purchased in Ulrich's shop were turning yellow. It was too late to weed and cultivate the garden, and perhaps I would not have been equal to the task presented by such a neglected garden. So I just put one flower bed in order, so as to have a starting point for a vegetable and flower garden in the future."

The evaluation of materials dealing with the fate of Polish Communists after the dissolution of the Polish Communist Party is unquestionably a complicated and difficult task. In our opinion, the doubts raised by the censorship review in the case of these passages are not sufficiently convincing to have rejected them. At the same time, we feel that permission for the publication of the above text in *Polityka* should not be taken as a precedent in the censorship of materials of a similar nature. Each text taking up the complex and painful problems associated with the history of the Polish Communist Party should be examined individually, and a decision must take into account the character of the publication, the type of material, the author, the level of the potential audience, the time of publication, etc. (*Instructional Materials*, No. 1, February 1974)

World War II: Glory and Silence

Of all the events in twentieth-century Polish history, World War II was the most significant both for the future of Poland and for the lives of its people. The country suffered enormous losses: approximately six million of its citizens were killed. At the outset of the war, Hitler and Stalin divided up Poland between them. During the war, Polish armies fought against the Axis along with Soviet and Western allied forces. Inside the country, the non-Communist underground forces of the Home Army led a valiant and costly resistance struggle against the occupying forces. Among the other, smaller underground groupings was a Communist force, the People's Army, which along with the Soviet forces that "liberated" Poland did not support the Home Army. In fact, during the Warsaw Uprising, led by the Home Army, at least in part to ensure that Poles and not Soviet troops liberated the capital city and therefore laid claim to controlling Poland, Polish efforts were undermined because of the refusal of Soviet forces to support the fighters. At the end of the war, despite their efforts, Poland was shifted some 150 miles to the west, a Communist government was installed in power and the Soviet Army was stationed throughout the country. Some units of the Home Army continued to fight after the war's end to prevent a Communist takeover. Thus the war served as one further impetus for hostility between Poland and Russia. The underground struggles of the war had created a whole series of non-Communist heroes who fought in the anti-German, anti-Communist underground. (And one's wartime affiliations and activities with the tiny Communist underground or the much larger non-Communist underground continue to be important criteria for Poles in determining who one is and whether one is to be trusted.) The experience of German aggression during the war continues to serve as a justification of the Polish-Soviet alliance for the "protection" of Poland today and in this respect, German atrocities have been brought up again and again in postwar Polish propaganda. Yet the Gierek regime made official peace with West Germany, and so had to avoid offending the Germans with shrill attacks on German atrocities. As a result, even the glories and tragedies of the war, which remained fresh in the population's memory, had to be touched up.

The official version of the war and the resistance has, not surprisingly, been a flawed one. Only in the second half of the sixties was recognition given to the valor of the Home Army, in an attempt to get support from the many men and women who had been associated with it. Even that concession, however, was far from a blanket permission for references to the Home Army. In 1974, thirty years after the ill-fated Warsaw Uprising, notices of privately organized commemorations or obituaries of fighters who had taken part in the uprising were explicitly banned from the media:

> 34. Obituaries, advertisements and other types of announcements in the press, radio, television, or printed notices of funerals describing planned assemblies in cemeteries or around monuments, sites of battles, etc., on the occasion of the outbreak of the Warsaw Uprising or various episodes of it by veterans' groups, detachments, etc., of the Home Army and other right-wing organizations that took part in the Warsaw Uprising *may not be permitted for publication.*
>
> On the other hand, obituaries and other information about religious services taking place inside of churches may be permitted. (August 26, 1974)

To protest these prohibitions was forbidden. It was also forbidden to protest the refusal of the Polish authorities to allow underground fighters who were not part of the Communist force to be given full military honors (the Polish authorities continued to refuse to allow battles of the Polish Home Army or the Polish Scouts to be treated as a part of Polish military history and ceremony, although for many of the men who fought them they were their highest and most glorious achievement):

> At the conclusion of a commemorative article entitled "Henryk Józef Bagiński, 1888–1973," published in Issue No. 11 of *Więź* (in the section entitled "Problems of Modern Polish History"), authors E. Muszalski and B. Studziński, after describing the sociopolitical, professional and military career of a man who, in their opinion, "served the motherland well," made the following remarks:
>
> "Burial ceremonies were held on December 13, 1973, in accordance with the soldierly wishes of the deceased, at the Powązki Military and Communal Cemetery in Warsaw, where he was laid to rest in the midst of so many other soldiers. The many hundreds of mourners who attended the ceremony included professional colleagues and wartime comrades of the deceased, representing several different generations now residing in Warsaw, along with others who came from as far away as the Baltic coast. Despite the three timely obituaries published in *Życie Warszawy* and *Słowo Powszechne*, and even despite telephoned announcements, the military and scouting banners that would have inclined over the fresh grave were missed. A sad thing." (*Report on Materials Censored*, December 1–15, 1975)

The massacre of 8,000 Polish officers (the total as established by Western historians) in the Katyń forest by the Soviets during the war was not simply an event passed over in silence by the media during the seventies. The Germans had, after all, found the mass graves and brought the massacre to international attention. The silence of the fifties and sixties in Poland's media had not erased the issue from Poles' memories. Thus Polish censors were instructed in detail to follow the line laid down in the *Great Soviet Encyclopedia*, a line that shifted the blame from the Soviets to the Germans by stating that the massacre took place not in 1940, when it did, but in 1941, when Germans occupied the area held until then by Russians. In addition, they were to determine whether any discussion of the event in a particular context was even necessary:

Main Office for Control of Press,
  Publications and Public Performances
Instruction, Evaluation and Control Group
No. ZI-131/2/75

Warsaw, January 14, 1975
C O N F I D E N T I A L
Copy No. 25

Informative Note No. 2

In connection with Regulation No. 21/IX concerning materials about the death of Polish officers in Katyń, we offer the basic outlines of the assessment of this matter found in the *Great Soviet Encyclopedia* and the communiqué of the special commission created by the Soviet authorities in 1943.

The Polish officers interned by the Red Army in September 1939 in camps in the Smolensk area fell into the hands of the Germans, who took over this area in August 1941. These officers were shot by the Nazis in the autumn of 1941 and were buried in mass graves in the Katyń forest.

Immediately after the liberation of the Smolensk area by the Soviet army in September of 1943, work was begun by a special commission composed, among others, of N. Burdenko (chairman), member of the Academy of Sciences; Aleksy Tolstoi, member of the Academy of Sciences; Metropolitan Nikolai; W. Potiomkin, member of the Academy of Sciences. The commission established that, as part of their general program for the physical extermination of the Slavic nations, the Nazis murdered about 11,000 Polish officers at Katyń. The execution was performed by a special army unit known as the Staff of the 537th Labor Battalion.

At the beginning of 1943, in connection with the deterioration of Germany's military situation and the rising military power of the Soviet Union and the progressive consolidation of the anti-German coalition, the Nazis decided to try to stir things up, and ascribed their own crimes to agencies of the Soviet leadership. The Germans were interested in covering up their own crime and setting members of the anti-German coalition at loggerheads with one another, particularly the Russians and the Poles. It should be recognized that the Nazis partly achieved their goal. Referring the Katyń matter to the International Red Cross, the émigré Polish government worsened already difficult relations to a point where the Soviet government broke diplomatic relations with the Sikorski government [the Polish government-in-exile in London] on April 25, 1943.

The perpetrators of the Katyń massacre were finally revealed in a communiqué published on January 24, 1944, by a special commission created by a decision of the Soviet Extraordinary State Commission to establish and investigate the crimes of the German Fascist invaders.

It has been previous censorship practice to remove all information about Katyń as the place of death of Polish officers during World War II. The present regulation establishes the scope of information and type of materials in which such information may appear.

At the same time, we note that it would not be useful to take up the matter of Katyń on a broad scale in historical writing or, especially, in the press in general. In addition, any material that goes beyond the scope of the matters regulated by the prohibition should be referred to the GUKPPiW administration prior to the making of a censorship decision.

Vice-Chairman
Tadeusz Ratajski

Distributed according to the list

Like the achievements of the non-Communist Home Army, victories won by the London-based Polish army-in-exile also were not allowed to be given full play. In the case of a passage reprinted from a wartime underground journal, the censors were interested in the exclusion of statements alluding to these soldiers' belief that their victories would help to ensure Poland's independence:

> On the occasion of the 30th anniversary of the battle of Monte Cassino [a major battle won with heavy casualties by the Polish army fighting in the west in which the Polish troops captured the Italian mountain monastery], Issue No. 20 of *Tygodnik Powszechny* ran an article entitled "The Battle of Monte Cassino in Underground Publications," which contained passages from articles published in underground periodicals during 1944. The following passage from the introductory article in *Biuletyn Informacyjny,* No. 21 (May 25, 1944), was deleted:
>
> "As far as the political aspect of this victory is concerned, it is no less clear than the military aspect. Rarely during the past five years has Polish blood been shed for such a worthy purpose as it was at Monte Cassino. This victory will do more to secure the independence and integrity of the Republic than any maneuvers undertaken by diplomats and politicians. . . ." (*Report on Materials Censored,* May 16–31, 1974)

On the other hand, the censors clearly considered it good taste and good propaganda to portray life during the war in simple and heroic terms. The fact that a few Poles survived by collaborating with the Germans while others suffered for opposing the occupation was not a permissible topic in the Polish media. The only acceptable image of occupied Poland was one of universal resistance (even though the censors were unwilling to give the Home Army its due):

> The following passages in the memoirs of T. Byrski, entitled *Theater-Radio* (PWN, edition of 3,000 copies), concerning cultural life in Warsaw during World War II, were suppressed:
>
> ". . . On the political front, the year 1942 was truly the blackest year for the whole world. It marked the beginning of public executions in Warsaw, and yet at the same time small public theatrical companies were springing up everywhere. And it is interesting to note that there were actors who took this kind of work, and even tried to defend it.
>
> ". . . There were prominent actors who openly urged their colleagues to keep on pursuing their careers, arguing that any resistance was a sign of hypersensitivity and stupidity, since an actor has to act, and if he ceases to do so, he ceases to be an actor. Of course, they were not disturbed in the least that other aspects of our cultural life had withered away, and that most of their fellow countrymen had to accept a very different and often thankless kind of work. The statement of one of these actors is well known: 'I had acting jobs during the occupation and am still acting today. Those who did not work in those days are not working now—so what can you say?' Unfortunately, it has to be said, most regretfully, that the clearance process [after the war] was conducted in a most unfair manner: it was a cruel ordeal for fourth-rate thespians, but an easy one for the great and famous who had actually proven themselves to be of puny stature during the time of national testing. Maria Zarębska told me how once during the occupation she had gone into a café with a pack of cigarettes that she intended to sell to the patrons in order to make some money to live on (she was quite literally dying of hunger at the time). A prominent actress firmly asked her to leave, noting that such things were not allowed there, in such a refined café. Unfortunately, one could go on and cite many other examples of this kind. I cite them here to show that there were other ways to misbehave than simply acting in the public theaters. But then it is never too late to mend one's ways, and some people took advantage of this. For example, the writer, whose name was still not very well known at that time, who recruited people to work for the German radio but subsequently wound up in Auschwitz. Gold traders, black marketeers and freeloaders of various kinds later came back from the German camps to shining reputations in People's Poland as suffering patriots. (*Report on Materials Censored,* December 1–15, 1975)

At times, as the review office indicated, the zeal of individual censors to properly orchestrate events could go too far. For example, censors were chided for having criticized the publication of a photograph of General Berling, commander of Polish forces organized in the Soviet Union, swearing his oath before a Catholic priest. They had based their criticism on the assumption that the picture made Berling seem religious and dependent on Church support. Their superiors pointed out, however, that the picture was a common one that hardly needed to be removed from a journal intended for a Catholic audience:

> The censors' review for the journal *WTK* characterized as a political mistake the permission given for publication of an archival photograph with the caption: "Oath of Chief of the First Division, Gen. Zygmunt Berling. The oath administered by Rev. Major Wilhelm Kubusz." The photograph was used as an illustration accompanying the text of a conversation with the former chaplain of the First Division of the Polish Army.
>
> It should be noted that this photograph has been published several times in material concerning the establishment of the Polish People's Army. It would be difficult now to refuse to allow a *Catholic* periodical to recall the religious aspects of that military act.

The decision of the Great Powers about the relocation of postwar Poland—the granting of former Polish territories to the Soviet Union and the taking of land from Germany—was always to be treated as a just and long-awaited act. Detailed descriptions of Poland's losses to the Soviet Union in the transfer could not be allowed. Equally heretical was the suggestion that Poland should have gained more territory in the west (at the expense of present-day East Germany) and that the Stalinist Polish leader Bierut was party to the conference where Western leaders like Churchill perceived that the Poles were gaining less than the Russians and losing more than the Germans. This, even though Bierut was made to look like the leading Polish negotiator at Potsdam, which he was not:

> In an article entitled "The Poles at Potsdam" (*Polityka,* No. 30), M. Turski wrote about the participation of the Polish delegation in the Big Three talks of July 1945. The author quoted, among other things, notes kept by Churchill on his meeting with the Polish representatives.
>
> " 'Bierut testified that it would be a terrible mistake if Great Britain, having entered the war for the sake of Poland, were now to show

a lack of understanding for her claims. They are humble and, in light of the need for peace in Europe, Poland does not demand more than it has lost. It would require the resettlement of only one and a half million Germans (in both Germany and East Prussia). Only that many have remained. New lands are needed to resettle four million Poles from the lands east of the Curzon line as well as about three million who will return from abroad, but even then Poland will be smaller territorially than before the war. It has lost rich agricultural fields around Wilno, valuable forests (it was always rich in timber), and oil fields in Galicia. . . .

" 'I reminded Bierut that there was no argument about giving Poland those parts of East Prussia that lay to the south and west of Königsberg, but he stated that the Germans, who lost the war, would lose only 18 percent of their territory, while Poland would lose 20 percent. . . .' " (*Report on Materials Censored,* May 16–31, 1975)

Reconstructing Communist Rule

Presenting the years of Communist rule in Poland in a positive light proved to be the most irresolvable problem for censors in the midseventies. Not only had the Communists failed to fulfill their promises, but they had failed to establish themselves as Poland's rightful rulers. The immediate postwar years saw a brutal civil war against the Communist takeover; Stalinist leaders were overthrown after workers' riots in 1956; in 1968 the Gomułka leadership was seriously attacked by adversary factions from within the Polish United Workers' Party (as the Polish Communists had renamed themselves in 1948) and then overthrown after workers' riots in 1970, which brought Gierek to power.

Postwar Polish politics also provided fuel for the fires of Polish anti-Russian feeling: in the years after the war, Poland's leaders supported and aided the Soviet Union despite the devastation of their own lands, and tailored their own policies to fit the needs and instructions of the Soviets.

In the mid-seventies, the history of Communist rule in Poland became an especially problematical issue: 1974 marked the thirtieth anniversary of the establishment of Communist Poland, and writers, journalists and editors, naturally drawn to its commemoration, found little to say that made both the present and the past look good. Furthermore, by the mid-seventies Gierek's industrialization drive and his campaign to promote political loyalty on the part of the population began to seem less a step toward a better future and more a return to the dark past of Stalinism. Even the years of Gomułka's leadership appeared in a more positive light as Gierek's promises to improve the economy and the government rang more and more hollow. Since journalists and writers could not resort to silence, however, the censors' tasks were extremely sensitive and complicated. They had to rely on their own sense of what was or was not politically acceptable, and found many of their decisions on historical articles questioned upon higher review.

The *Bulletin of Themes of Materials Censored* and the other censors' reports document how the thirtieth anniversary of the Communist takeover forced censors to block much information about the troublesome events in the history of Communist Poland. Ironically, these were the events about which Poles knew the most and had the deepest feelings. The censors' work, then, did not—could not—create new images. It merely created media which over half of the Polish population, the generations that had lived through World War II and the years of Communist rule that followed, clearly recognized as propagating falsehoods:

5. Interventions in the Field of Modern History

Most of the interventions in this area involved the elimination of texts, views and opinions that did not assess the sociopolitical changes of the last thirty years in a proper fashion. In the items challenged, all of the negative aspects of that period were generally presented, and extremely strict political criteria were used to evaluate those events. Another common theme was the "periodization" of the history of the last thirty years—"from error to error"—which was treated by many authors as a basic fact and an inherent feature of the socialist path of national development. Accents of this sort appeared both in serious scholarly writing and in the journalism of the central and regional press.

In the bimonthly *Oświata Dorosłych,* for example, we challenged the view that "twice, in Poznań in 1956 and Gdańsk, Gdynia and Szczecin in 1970, tragic demonstrations by the working class produced a healthy effect. They helped to bring about a change in the political and governmental leadership. . . ."

The greatest intervention was made in items dealing with problems of the early period in the development of People's Poland.

In one item, an author wrote about the degradation of the Sejm in the 1950s when, deprived of any real power, it "merely served as an ornament adorning the established program of the political system." It was further stated that "the then accepted model of party influence on the Sejm greatly narrowed the Sejm's freedom of action and absolutely bound the hands of party members, even on specific issues" (W. Skrzydło, "Some Problems of the Leading Role of the Party vis-à-vis a Socialist Parliament," *Annales* of Marie Curie-Skłodowska University, Vol. 21, 1974). In another item, it was noted that the distortions of the 1950s manifested themselves, *inter alia,* in a limitation of the role of the Sejm, "the superordinate position of the government and an excessive growth of the activities of the government," "bureaucratic ailments in the operation of the state machinery" which led to the "hypertrophying of the function" of the security apparatus and its "dominance over other bodies of the state machinery" (A. Burda, "Characteristic Features of the Evolution of the Political System of the Polish People's Republic," Proceedings of a scholarly session organized by Marie Curie-Skłodowska University, June 15, 1974).

In yet another item it was written, *inter alia,* that "centralized, inflexible and bureaucratized public ownership of the means of production in conjunction with incorrect information produced an economy of artificial shortages, bottlenecks and waste of the basic factors of production" (*Contract as an Instrument in the Planning of Market Production,* published by Adam Mickiewicz University in Poznań). Similar criticism was found in K. Bajan's *Agricultural Policy of the Polish People's Republic.* He stated that "agricultural policy ([GUKP PiW note:] even after 1970) had a number of adverse consequences, not only in the field of agriculture, but in the national economy as a whole," which resulted in "general dissatisfaction on the part of the working class and resistance on the part of the village."

Another object of intervention was extremely blatant criticism of our educational system in Poland from 1945 to 1957, when "the role of the school was reduced to the upbringing of consumers of propaganda," and educational policy was characterized by "the primacy of propaganda over education." Some of those publications cited official documents from those years. In one, an excerpt from an address by W. Bieńkowski was cited: "anarchy and irresponsibility have appeared in our school system . . . the teacher, subject to political censorship, has ceased to be a teacher and has become a bureaucrat for the transmission of programmatic formulae and political encyclicals . . ." (B. Ratus, *The Didactic and Upbringing Activities of Pedagogical Lycea in People's Poland*).

Similar things were said about the development of culture, the period 1950–1955 being characterized as the "most barren period during the last three decades" *(Zeszyty Muzyczne).*

Other books and press items included statements like the following: "Before 1956, Poland was not a mother to all, but rather, for many, was a stepmother, inspiring fear, plagued with suspicion and severely punishing"; in 1956, "for the second time since the war, people felt really free"; "in the new ideological situation predominating in the party (at the end of 1948), scholarly research on the history of the Polish Workers' Party became impossible. . . . Even in the Department of Party History, research was kept to a minimum. . . . The dominant view treated all organizations not related to the Polish Workers' Party as the 'camp of Polish reaction' "; "for many years, the Home Army was a taboo subject"; and so on.

We also challenged the expression of the opinion that the policy of the Polish Workers' Party and the Polish Committee of National Liberation in the Rzeszów area "caused bitterness among many activists and undermined the authority of the organs of revolutionary power" and "could not win the rural population over to the idea of democratic rule," while "a condition for getting a job in a factory was joining the party" (E. Olszewski, "The Beginnings of People's Power in the Rzeszów Region," in *Polska Partia Robotnicza* [*The Polish Workers' Party*], published by PWN).

Similar statements about "blatant errors," "the lack of trust for the new leadership in rural areas," about the "danger" and the "plague of looting" in the reclaimed territories appeared in several other items, chiefly in the press.

We questioned a call that appeared in *Kultura* for the pardon of some right-wing groups from 1945. Looking back on the last three decades, the author wrote, "It would be good if some historical themes returned in a somewhat bolder form, if only because many issues that were once sensitive and emotional have cooled down today and become purely historical issues." *Szpilki* proposed another such initiative, launching its crusade with an article entitled "The Afflictions of the 30th Anniversary."

Most of the interventions in press coverage related to the 30th anniversary [of Communist rule] nonetheless involved the deletion of opinions, notes and information tending to maintain in the mind of society a view of the history of People's Poland as one characterized by periodic cycles of struggle against a continuing series of distortions.

For example, drastic assessments "comparing life styles in two different periods of our 30-year history" were challenged. They compared the sociopolitical climate of the 1960s—"bombastic phraseology, no implementation of constantly repeated demands, empty rhetoric, drowsiness, boredom . . . a fierce power struggle"—with the attitude of the average Pole in 1973—"in social life, a lack of great ideas forces us to tread constantly the wrong tactical paths . . . it is in just this way that such an idea takes shape" *(Tygodnik Kulturalny).*

The form and substance of worker self-management were also subjected to very critical judgment. In a challenged article in *Polityka*, for example, it was argued that the working class is prevented from performing the role in government that it does in theory—the function of co-manager and co-owner of enterprise. Among other things, the author pointed to the supposed existence of a "kindling point" resulting from the "unrealized democratic ambitions of the workers, who are anxious to have their voice be heard in fact, not just in theory."

Other publications had eliminated from them, among other things: assessments that denied the economic achievements of the first few years following liberation ("the mechanization of the mines was given little consideration at the top and was sabotaged at the bottom . . . exports were limited, as were deliveries to the population and, finally, to industry. . . . Thus it was necessary to give up planned construction, so that one link after another disappeared, and by 1956 the whole economic plan was blown away" *(Życie i Nowoczesność)*; balance sheets of economic losses resulting from Poland's new eastern border *(Kierunki)*; and deliberations concerning the causes of the events of December [1970] *(Żołnierz Wolności).*

On the other hand, objections to newspaper and magazine articles as well as monographs about the interwar period and the war itself were only sporadic. For example, questions were raised about the very flattering view of the interwar agrarian reform, which was described as "beautiful" ("after the land redistribution life in the countryside was organized anew, integration was carried out, improvements were made, new fences were built and the peasant received the keys to a farm ready for use"), as well as about a critical assessment of the activity of the Polish Communist Party, whose policy "accelerated the outlawing of 'Self-Help' societies and led to a narrowing of the circle of party allies in rural areas" *(Kalendarz Lubelski).*

Clearly nationalistic accents led to the challenging of extensive sections of P. Bobko's *Memoirs and Notes* published by LSW. Excerpts concerning old antagonisms between the Polish and Czech populations of Cieszyn in Silesia were deleted from it. In his conclusion, the author wrote, "We may still live to see the desired restoration of the situation of October 31, 1918 [when Poland was reestablished with the division of Cieszyn between the Poles and Czechs]."

Other, infrequent cases of intervention included the deletion of information concerning repression against Polish citizens by the Soviet authorities *(Tygodnik Powszechny, Kalendarz Lubelski)* and a passage from an account of senseless persecution of German civilians by Poles

(Literatura). (*Bulletin of Themes of Materials Censored,* Second Quarter, 1974)

The censors' interventions shown above reflect only a small portion of the material that was submitted about the history of Communist Poland, only to be rejected or questioned. The literary journal *Życie Literackie,* associated with the Moczar faction in the mid-sixties, was unable to publish statements indicating the level of Soviet control and involvement in Polish affairs in the years immediately after World War II. The statements in question were from the memoirs of a well-known Polish general who had been military attaché in the Polish embassy in London after the war. Despite his prestige in the Communist military, the statements were not allowed to appear:

> The following passages were deleted from an installment of the memoirs of General J. Kuropieski, entitled "The Return of Polish Soldiers from the West" (*Życie Literackie,* No. 12), from an account of the victory parade in London in which "all of the states at war with the Germans at the end of the war were invited" to join:
>
> "During the last days of May, I expected the arrival of the Polish delegation from one day to the next. In the end, I received a telegram announcing a definite time for the arrival of their plane. On the appointed day, Ambassador Strassburger [a prominent Polish leader in the London government during the war] sat with me for several hours at the airport in Croydon. For nothing. No one arrived, even though we had not been informed in advance.
>
> "It was not until our return to the embassy, when it was already evening, that we learned that we were not going to take part in the parade, just as the Soviet Union was not going to (something I had learned several days earlier from the Soviet military attaché, Col. Gorchkov). . . . I was very annoyed by this decision not to take part in the parade. At the time, I could not determine any reason for the cancellation of the flight. Our absence made it even more difficult for me to rid myself of premonitions and even ill will. Unreconciled émigrés used the failure [of the delegation] to arrive as an argument for proving a lack of independence in even the most superficial of matters, and complained that the great contribution of Polish soldiers in the West was being intentionally played down." (*Report on Materials Censored,* March 16–31, 1974)

Nor was it possible to refer to the Soviets' insistence that Poland turn down Marshall Plan aid or to popular dissatisfaction with the policies of the new Communist government, even if such statements were balanced with positive assessments of that regime:

> In R. Jarocki's article "Heavy Industry Instead of Chocolate" (*Kultura i Ty,* No. 4), the author presented "the feelings of Polish society on the question of whether or not to accept the Marshall Plan 26 to 28 years ago." In that article, we read the following:
>
> "Why am I talking about this? Well, it seems to me that even today the question of the benefits of the Marshall Plan—and this is in reference only to those years—which we passed by creates various misunderstandings. It is said that the Soviet government influenced Poland to reject offers of American assistance. In certain circles during the years when this matter was a current and timely one, people spoke about this with bitterness, a bitterness that was sometimes clearly anti-Soviet. . . .
>
> "Let us look at the situation of that period through the eyes of Western correspondents such as the representative of that great newspaper the New York *Times.* . . . That reporter moved freely about Warsaw and through the countryside. He talked with whomever he wished, including people who did not hide their disapproval of the new Polish regime. But the American wrote that while it was difficult for him to find people willing to bestow their affection on the new government, or even any real sentiment, most of his private informants spoke with respect about the group in power. . . .
>
> "During the lifetime of one generation, Poland has become an industrial as well as agricultural country. The source of financing for investments for years on end was so-called 'internal accumulation,' i.e., a restriction of consumption. . . . Group B industry, comprising light industry (agricultural and food-processing industry), housing construction, services, trade and tourism, all of which were related to consumption and individual comfort, were restricted to the very limits of the endurance of society. The socioeconomic crisis of 1956, the difficulties of 1960–70, and finally the crisis at the end of 1970 were, among other things, obvious signals that society, especially the younger generation, which had grown up after the war, did not agree with economic growth based solely on the giving up of various things. . . ." (*Report on Materials Censored,* March 16–31, 1974)

Many of the policy decisions of the Stalinist period were repudiated during the "Polish October" of 1956. Peasants left their collective farms and reestablished their own private farms. Forced heavy industrialization with virtually no investment in consumer goods was tempered. For years following 1956, Stalinism was automatically blamed for Poland's problems. Yet twenty years later it seems that Stalinist policies, judging from the censors' reports smuggled out by Strzy-żewski, were nevertheless still protected from criticism. When a discussion of them appeared, it was simply censored out. *Report on Materials Censored* for the first two weeks of December 1974 included two articles on the economic policies of the Stalinist period. One, by Władysław Machejek, the editor-in-chief of *Życie Literackie,* sought to probe the causes of Poland's economic difficulties. It also suggested —indirectly—that there had never been a real examination of the roots of Poland's economic failure:

> "November 29. Hilary Minc, whose name is associated with many of the projects of the first postwar Three-Year Reconstruction Plan and the Six-Year National Development Plan, was buried today in Powąz-ki Cemetery. . . . For a long time to come, historians and economists will be trying to find out what stopped the momentum of this recon-struction and development drive in satisfying the needs of the popula-tion at large. Was it just the 'Cold War,' or was it also, among other things, the dogmatic line that prevailed after the autumn of 1948? . . . As a politician, Hilary Minc was swept away by the wave of retribution in 1956 that sought to settle scores with 'errors and distor-tions.' " (*Report on Materials Censored,* December 1–15, 1974)

Another series of passages removed by the censors were part of a study on agricultural policy in Lower Silesia (a region next to Gierek's Silesian power center) during the years of Stalinist collectivization. The ideas in the article were so offensive to the censors that, even given the fact that the study and its results had the support of the *województwo* leadership, they were blocked for the second year in a row from what, at best, was a little-known publication. The article was to have come out in the *Report of the Activities of the Wrocław Aca-demic Society* and, according to the publishers, to be reprinted later as a book subsidized by the Wrocław government. What made any publication of this study and its conclusions so unacceptable was that it was an attack on the postwar creation of state farms in the empty, formerly German lands, the area where collectivization had seemingly had the most success and had continued into the sixties and seventies. Such an attack not only made light of past Communist agricultural policies and achievements in one of the only areas in Poland that was not privately farmed, but also had troubling present-day implications given the fact that the Gierek leadership's long-term goal was the gradual collectivization of private plots throughout Poland as they were left empty and unfarmed when aging peasants left or died. The concern about criticism of what little collectivization existed in Poland and, by implication, of Gierek's policies for the future was strong enough to override considerations of the regional leaders' support for this presentation, its repeated submission and the minuscule audience that this publication would reach:

> The summary of a work by W. Kluska entitled "The Basic Rationale of the Agricultural Policy of the PZPR in Lower Silesia During the Period 1949–1956" was disapproved for publication in Issue No. 28 of *Sprawozdania Wrocławskiego Towarzystwa Naukowego.* According to an announcement made by the editors of *Sprawozdania,* "this work will be issued in book form as a publication of the Wrocław Academic Society, the costs of publication being covered by the Wrocław Voivodship Administration." In this summary version, the author presented views that she had expressed earlier in a paper entitled "Plans for Rural and Agricultural Development in the Policies of the PZPR, 1949–1956," which was challenged last year when it was scheduled for publication in Issue No. 106 of *Zeszyty Naukowe Akademii Rolniczej.* The author criticized the agricultural policies of the PZPR in Lower Silesia, emphasizing that "PZPR policy lacked relevance to the realities of the situation at that time," and that "the model of rural and agricultural organization established by the Unification Congress" [when the Polish Workers' Party incorporated the Polish Socialist Party in 1948, establishing its full control of politics in Poland] lacked all relevance to the "actual conditions in the Lower Silesian countryside." The full text of the "précis" is as follows:
>
> "By analyzing party documents (resolutions, speeches of representatives, instructions), one can reconstruct the working out of models for rural life and agriculture during different periods. This report uses the terms 'model' and 'pattern' in such a way as to explain the lack of correspondence between the policy of the PZPR and the social reality of those years. While there is a relationship between the elements identified as 'models' and 'patterns,' this relationship may vary from that of synonyms to that of complete antonyms.
>
> "The model of rural life and agriculture worked out by the July-August Plenum of the Central Committee of the Polish Workers' Party and subsequently confirmed by the Unification Congress affirmed that 'under conditions of a people's democracy, the struggle between the

rural capitalists and the small and middle peasantry will not only continue, but grow sharper as well.' The model of rural social structure contained in the Declaration was far from the real rural situation in Lower Silesia. This model did not take into account the special characteristics of these lands, the problems connected with stabilization and so forth. It is also important to note that it ignored the differences in culture, customs and even language between the various groups of immigrant population.

"To what extent were these special characteristics taken into account by the program of the Lower Silesian party organization? The beginning of 1950 brought with it a full and precise application of the program of 'struggle against kulak [rich peasant] resistance, and constant and systematic struggles to 'politically isolate' the kulaks. In the name of these goals, all forms of cooperative ventures were abolished in the countryside and independent owners of larger farms were excluded from the self-government organizations.

"The social and agrarian structure of the Lower Silesian countryside, which had been formed as a result of the [postwar] settlement, was characterized by a predominance of medium-sized and large farms. The average 'figure' here was the owner of a medium-sized or large farm. The percentage of farms of fewer than 5 hectares (39.1%) was fewer than the national average (57.2%).

"Given the social structure of the Lower Silesian countryside, it proved difficult to activate the rural poor, much less to make a political force out of them. The prevailing tendencies among the peasantry tended rather to emphasize a commonality of interests. Slogans of class struggle thus did not find fertile soil among the peasantry here. The party was transformed gradually from a political force outlining the major directions of development and mobilizing and winning over the broad ranks of society to the realization of its program into an administrative force taking the place of the state apparatus. The work of the voivodship during this period was characterized by growing mistrust and lack of respect for skill. This led to a halting of economic development and a deepening of the sense of temporariness, and hindered the processes of integration and adaptation. Moreover, it did not encourage the transformation of the peasants into farmers.

"In the second half of 1952, when there began to be talk in Poland of the need to provide aid for agriculture, in Lower Silesia there continued to be talk about an 'orgy of speculation' on the part of the kulaks, about an 'opportunistic distortion' of the true sense of party guidelines and so on. Lower Silesian activists did not perceive their failures (a decline in productivity in livestock breeding as well as in the cultivation of crops). They did not see that the model outlined by their program was not bringing them closer to the peasantry. The Second Congress of the PZPR (in Lower Silesia) continued to speak chiefly about 'class struggle' and the 'isolation' of the kulaks.

"Nineteen forty-nine was the first year of experience in the establishment of production cooperatives. In Lower Silesia, much attention was given at the time to cooperatives of newly settled parcels of land and to the strengthening of the 35 production cooperatives established on this basis. Much was said about the refinement of the various forms of cooperation between neighbors and the growth of agricultural production.

"The end of 1949 and the beginning of 1950 brought with them a new set of principles. The slogan 'a production cooperative in every community' began to be advanced. The party's goal became the establishment of production cooperatives. An exaggerated importance was given to class struggle and to the threat to people's power represented by the kulak. The year 1950 in Lower Silesia saw the proclamation of a kind of race to establish production cooperatives. Praise was bestowed on those Communist party secretaries who could report the greatest number of newly established cooperatives.

"The model of production cooperative advanced in the 1950s was in clear contradiction to the development of peasant agriculture. A realization of the existing patterns of rural life is of particular importance for successful party activity." (*Report on Materials Censored*, December 1–15, 1974)

Not only could the policies of Poland's early leaders not be criticized, but even reports on the difficulties of daily life during the early years of Communist rule—something about which every adult Pole had clear memories—were also frequently excised or altered. No mention could be made of the very obvious problems involved in reorganizing a party whose internal lines of communication had been shattered when some activists fought in the underground in Poland and others spent the war in the Soviet Union. Nor could any reference to the maneuvers of the Polish Communist Party (then called the Polish Workers' Party) to assure itself a strong position in the postwar elections be permitted, even in a scholarly work:

The following passages, *inter alia*, were challenged in a book by J. Naumiuk entitled *The Polish Workers' Party in the Kielce Region*, published by Książka i Wiedza [the PZPR book-publishing house] in an edition of 3,000 copies [an extremely limited edition]:

"The organizational work of the Voivodship Committee during the first days after liberation was carried out in an atmosphere of tension. This was due to the fact that three people showed up, each contending for the post of first secretary. The fact that they had supposedly been sent by the Central Committee certainly must have had a depressing effect on First Secretary J. Kula, making him aware of the provisional nature of his position. Accordingly, on January 26 he sent an alarming letter to the Central Committee, asking for a clarification of the situation.

"Letter of J. Kula to the Central Committee of the Polish Workers' Party in Lublin, January 26, 1945. In this letter, Kula asked: 'Write and tell me who is supposed to be the secretary of the Voivodship Committee of the Polish Workers' Party in Kielce, since three people have come here and are wrangling with each other for the job, even though they do not yet have party membership cards. What am I supposed to do about this? Am I supposed to clear out, or am I supposed to stay in Kielce and wait on tables in the local cafeteria? As a party member and a soldier of Lenin, I do not intend to relinquish my post until I am ordered to do so by the Central Committee. I am not going to give in just because someone has a whimsical urge to play king of the mountain.'

"As a result of the Polish Workers' Party's (PPR) anti-Mikołajczyk propaganda campaign, the creation of the 'New Liberation' [Nowe Wyzwolenie] wing of the Polish Peasant Party, and the general political situation in the country, the Kielce organization of the Polish Peasant Party was overcome by a mood of disorientation and passivity. Many Polish Peasant Party members quit the party and declared their willingness to join the Polish Workers' Party. But in keeping with the recommendation of the executive committee of the Polish Workers' Party Voivodship Committee, they were urged either to join the New Liberation Polish Peasant Party or to stay in the regular Polish Peasant Party and engage in anti-Mikołajczyk activities, with the promise that they would be accepted into the Polish Workers' Party after the elections. Nevertheless, the Polish Peasant Party still had considerable influence among the peasantry, and it had established bridgeheads in various government organs, especially in the people's councils and rural social organizations. The Polish Workers' Party devoted a great deal of attention to demolishing these in the course of the Sejm election campaign, while at the same time warning the democratic [Communist front] faction not to underestimate the Polish Peasant Party.

"In conjunction with the intensification of its propaganda campaign to further curtail the Polish Peasant Party influence in local government organs, the PPR launched an initiative calling for personnel changes in the traditional local government positions of *starosta*, deputy *starosta* and *wójt*. Numerous staff changes were also made in the *gmina* offices in order to get rid of Polish Peasant Party members. . . .

"Numerous Polish Peasant Party members, known to have an unswervingly negative attitude toward the party and the other parties of the democratic bloc, were removed. In Kielce Voivodship, a total of 30,437 persons, or 3.3 percent of the adult population, were stricken from the voter registration lists.

"In the final days before the elections, certain district election commissions were reshuffled in order to get rid of Polish Socialist Party members suspected of maintaining contacts with the Polish Peasant Party. These suspicions were not always justified, and this led to friction between the PPR and the Polish Socialist Party in Kielce Voivodship. The Voivodship Committee of the Polish Socialist Party lodged a protest against these actions. It would seem that the above-mentioned tactical maneuvers of the PPR directed against members of allied parties were, at least in certain cases, totally unnecessary. They caused dissension and discord in the cooperative efforts of both workers' parties in the course of the Sejm election campaign. . . ." (*Report on Materials Censored,* December 1–15, 1975)

The lives and the actions of prewar Communists and their fate after the Communist takeover were also not the stuff of good propaganda in postwar Poland. One censored article, the story of the daughter of a prominent prewar Communist Party figure who was a history doctoral candidate, violated a number of taboos. The girl's father was, apparently, a member of the prewar Communist Party disbanded by Stalin. He was also one of the Communists who fought in the Communist underground during the war. When the Communists who came back to Poland at the end of the war from the Soviet Union took over, he and many of his fellow underground fighters—including Gomułka himself—were jailed, and only freed after Stalinism was discredited and after Gomułka was brought back into the party leadership in response to unrest among workers and disaffected intellectuals.

The story of the girl's mother was no more acceptable. Her infidelity, even for political reasons, was unacceptable, as was her marriage of political convenience. And, after the war, her inability to work because of her husband's position was not an aspect of Stalinism that the Gierek leadership was willing to condemn or even admit to. Finally, the article went on to suggest that the usual dismissal of Piłsudski's military government as a fascist regime did not take into account the complexity of reality.

Interventions were made in 20 texts dealing with historical problems. Several interventions concerned assessments of the earliest years of People's Poland and of certain events that took place during World War II.

In Issue No. 21 of *ITD*, G. Nawrocki, in an article entitled "Mésalliance," told the story of a young girl, an intellectual enthralled by the "genius of the Great Witold" (Gombrowicz [an eminent Polish writer]) and a university graduate, who is afraid to marry an ordinary construction engineer because he "won't even consider getting a higher education." Interventions were made, *inter alia*, in the following passages:

"Our heroine is not in the least a grotesque intellectual, but an authentic intellectual, getting a doctorate in history. A lovely girl working for a doctorate. Could there be anything nicer?

"Why in the field of history? Perhaps because her father is a piece of living history. Before the war he was in the Polish Communist Party and spent his time in prison, not long, to be sure, but after all. And still today, people even more famous than he, who were once in power but have since left it, when they see him on the street, run across the street in his direction, glad to see him, and call out 'Hey, Stefan!' He was active during the war, and after it as well, in the Rzeszów region. He fought against the UPA, the WIN [anti-Communist guerrilla bands fighting for Polish independence], and something else. That was in 1949. In 1957 he went to work in a publishing house. From 1949 to 1957 there was an interruption, but fortunately the interruption did not last long. As a result, she came to know him only after she had started school and was in the second grade. Before that she had only heard about him. He came back just in time to provide a proper life for her younger brother, born in 1958. . . .

"Our heroine knows that she will not have the kind of biography that her father does, but why should anyone need a biography? Her father's biography? Perhaps her father's biography helped her when she decided to study history, but who will her biography be of any use to? Her mother's biography is also complicated; her father's of course is complicated, but unambiguous. Her mother worked for the security administration. For professional reasons she infiltrated a [presumably anti-regime] gang, and for professional reasons she became the fiancée of its leader. There is still a photograph at home of three young people wearing bandoliers and carrying guns. In the middle is the girl's professionally affianced mother. She is no longer alive, nor are the two people standing on either side of her. The mother betrayed her fiancé for professional reasons. Then she married the girl's father, also for professional reasons, but in a different sense. It was simply the marriage of two colleagues. Then the father went off with his toothbrush and towel.

He was in a sanatorium, the mother said. So the mother stopped working, and if it had not been for friends and relatives, it's hard to imagine how she would have survived those eight years. Only in 1957 did she begin to receive an income, when the girl's father began to work in the publishing house.

"And so her father's past and his historical leanings were the reason for her decision to study history. And her studies went like a fairy tale —a high average, and even a publication in a scholarly periodical. She wrote her doctorate on the period of the Second Republic, but, despite her father, she chose to write on the 'sanacja' regime [name of the authoritarian regime set up after Piłsudski, Poland's military leader and hero, staged a popular coup d'état in 1926, taking power from Poland's democratically elected leaders]. Who today would try to defend the *sanacja* regime? She certainly did not intend to. She only noted, where appropriate, that the *sanacja* was not fascism, and that such a view would be an oversimplification. And even if it was, then what kind of fascism was it, since Italian fascism was not the same as German? There is no reason to try to justify the *sanacja:* the facts speak for themselves. But why should one reach right away for the label of 'fascism'? Of course, one should look at the past in a critical way, but why slander it?" (*Report on Materials Censored*, May 16–31, 1974)

The publication of a series of reminiscences about the resettlement of the Polish population at the end of World War II as a result of the change in Poland's boundaries, and the search by much of the population for housing and new opportunities, alarmed the censors. To talk of chaos and of hoodlums who frightened women and children was to say that the Communists had trouble asserting their control. And it reminded Poles that lands once at the center of Polish life were now in the Soviet Union, while Poland received in exchange territory that had been under German control for centuries. This was an especially significant and sensitive issue for the men of Gierek's leadership, since Silesia, Gierek's power base, had been one of the territories that Poland got from the Germans and where many ethnic Germans remained. The issue of postwar boundary changes and resettlement was also of concern to the Gierek leadership in the mid-seventies because it was in the process of acting on its agreement with West Germany to allow ethnic Germans to leave Poland in exchange for payments by the German government. Discussions of who inhabited these former German territories (their numbers, ethnic backgrounds and migration patterns), as well as the conditions under which Germans had

moved to Germany or had been forced to remain in Poland right after
the war, could, in the eyes of the Gierek leadership, complicate the
negotiations. This was, after all, a matter of earning hard currency.
And to talk of the problems that faced Poles who tried to leave the
parts of Poland that had been taken over by the Soviets was to paint
a black picture of the Soviet Union. Hence, while a Wrocław publishing house was permitted to print a limited edition of a
work dealing with the "repatriation" of the Polish population after
the war, the censors were instructed to consult with the directors of
the Main Office for Control before permitting the study to have a
broader audience:

> 56. The Institute of History of the Polish Academy of Sciences, acting
> through the agency of the Ossolineum, has published a book by Krys-
> tyna Kersten entitled *Repatriation of the Polish Population After the
> Second World War.*
>   The publication contains many statements that are in contradiction
> with the current aims of propaganda work. Therefore, the GUKPPiW
> administration should be advised of any reviews, studies, etc., related
> to this book. Minor mentions and bibliographical notes may be permit-
> ted without restriction.
>   This prohibition is intended solely for the information of the censors.
> (November 23, 1974; canceled February 4, 1976)

The censors forbade the publication of a series of memoirs about
the chaos that resulted from the movement of Poles into the former
German territories. Some people came to the new land simply to make
their fortune, settling the empty territories and taking over what the
Germans had left behind. Other settlers had been displaced from their
homes in what for generations had been Poland's eastern territories
(until the Hitler-Stalin pact and the postwar allied agreements ceded
this land to the Soviets), and were escaping the repression in their
former homelands. (Many Poles from the eastern territories had been
arrested and shipped to Siberian exile at the start of the war, and many
others lost their land when the Soviets took over at the war's end.)
They, too, went to the western territories in the hopes of taking over
the land and property vacated by departing Germans. For ethnic
Poles who had been living for generations in the lands that before the
war belonged to Germany, these were especially trying times. They
were often attacked by the newcomers, who regarded them as Ger-

mans, not Poles, as they saw themselves. As a result, the western territories, hailed by the new regime as a land of opportunity that would witness the glorious development of communism, were convulsed by ethnic and political strife. So, though the chaos was something that had touched almost every Pole and though the memoirs cited below contained no reference to even the existence of Communist rulers or Communist policy, the troubled times in the western territories were not to be recorded:

In his diary *My Path Through Life,* published by "Pojezierze" in an edition of 7,000 copies, W. Steffen, a teacher at Adam Mickiewicz University in Poznań, described, among other things, living conditions in Warmia [a former German territory] immediately after the cessation of hostilities in 1945. The following passages were deleted:

"I set out for Tomaryny in Ostroda Powiat. I wanted to find out what was happening with my family. My sister Barbara owned a grain mill in Tomaryny, situated in the middle of the woods in the picturesque Pasłęka Valley. . . . They were, as it were, all sitting on top of a volcano, for soon 'pioneers' [from the east] turned up in the area. Most of them were just hoodlums who had set out in search of loot and plunder. They harassed the local residents in the most outrageous manner. One time they showed up at my sister's place brandishing weapons and proceeded to rob them of all their best clothes. A couple of days later they came again to take what was left. When they couldn't find anything, they locked up the adult women in another room and held pistols up to the chests of the children, threatening to kill them if they didn't tell where their mothers had hidden the clothes. They carried off literally everything they could find, including the livestock. The one cow the family managed to save from these thieves had to be hidden in the cellar. When my sister Joanna showed them her carefully preserved membership card from the Union of Poles in Germany and little volumes of Warmian Polish folk songs given to her by my brother Augustyn, she received the reply that one heard every day: 'You're all a bunch of Hitlerites, to hell with you!'

"Living conditions in Warmia at that time were deplorable. In entire villages there was not a single man to be seen. They had either died in the war or been carried off to the far corners of the globe, whence they never returned. The abandoned women lived with their children in terrible poverty. . . . But the greatest plague were the malicious denunciations. Wanting to get control of farms by calling them German properties, the 'pioneers' denounced the owners of these farms, accusing them of having been members of some Hitlerite organization, which resulted in the arrest of many innocent people. Let me cite one drastic example of this. After I had arrived at my sister's place, an elderly Mazurian showed up one day and asked us to sign a petition to the security authorities appealing for the release of his wife, who was under arrest. He told me the whole story of the horror that he and his wife had lived through. Despite his protests, a newcomer from Mazovia had moved into his house, brazenly declaring his intention to take over the old man's farm, even though he had no right to do so. He raped the old man's wife in front of him, and after a while he accused the pair of having been Nazis. Both were arrested. The husband was released after a few weeks, when it turned out that the accusation was totally groundless, but his wife was still under arrest. In the Recovered Territories during that period there was no jurisdiction that could protect the indigenous inhabitants against accusations of this kind. Things got somewhat better after legitimate settlers from the Lwów and Wilno regions [territories taken over by the Soviet Union] began moving into Warmia. Their attitude toward the Warmian Poles was much more sympathetic than that of the 'Mazovian pioneers.' But sadly, many Poles who had risked their lives fighting to preserve the Polish ethnic character in Warmia during Prussian times had not been able to withstand this period of great trial. They moved to the west in search of a more tranquil life. What an ironic fate! Poles driven out by other Poles!"

The "Pojezierze" Publishing House also submitted the memoirs of a rural schoolteacher entitled *When There Was No Love* (proposed edition: 4,000 copies). Interventions were made in the following passage, which describes the author's return from a concentration camp to her native village in the vicinity of Olsztyn:

" 'Times are so bad. There is not a drop of milk or a single egg to be found in the house. There isn't a single cow in the whole village, to say nothing of chickens. . . . They plundered everything. They stole everything. They still keep coming and stealing whatever they can lay their hands on. They even stole all of your things, which I was keeping for you. And who are these people? Poles!' she said indignantly. 'They say we're Hitlerites, Huns! It's a good thing your father didn't live to see this.'

" 'Don't talk like that, Mother. Certainly not everyone is aware that Poles live here, too.'

" 'They don't know?' she exploded. 'But there's a Polish flag hanging on the building!'

"We approached the house. The red-and-white national flag greeted me from afar, flapping gaily in the breeze, heralding the beginning of a new chapter in my life. . . ." (*Report on Materials Censored,* December 1–15, 1975)

The rule of Gierek's predecessor, Władysław Gomułka, who ruled Poland from 1956 until the December riots of 1970, also presented the censors with a challenge. The censors' reports available to us contain no references to the events of 1956, when workers and intellectual unrest brought a wave of liberalization to Poland and forced the Communist leadership to bring Gomułka back from house arrest as the only leader who could get the support of the population. Nor do they contain articles about Gomułka's moves to reassert party control in 1957 and end the euphoria of wide-ranging and sharply critical discussions in the media, proposals for workers' councils in factories, and hopes that Poland would break with the Soviet Union. Journalists who had experienced both the euphoria and the gradual reinstitution-alization of Communist control did not see this "stabilization" positively, but clearly the taboos on explicit discussion of these topics were so ingrained that no one even attempted to treat those years of Polish history. Reports on the later years of the Gomułka era were also circumscribed: by the mid-seventies, the honeymoon with Gierek had ended, his promises of better leadership, a better life and more democracy had worn thin, and attacks on the failures of the Gomułka regime could easily raise the implicit question "How different are things today?" Furthermore, since Gierek and his men had been prominent in the Gomułka leadership, attacks on the Gomułka regime were attacks on them as well.

Similarly, the period of factional strife within the party between the nationalist Moczarite forces and the Gomułka leadership, that brought with it purges in the bureaucracy and the party as well as the 1968 student strikes that came to symbolize the struggle, became nonevents. This was not a struggle in which Gierek had been a leader, nor had it led directly to his takeover. But it involved the kind of inner party turmoil that Gierek was not willing to tolerate. To discuss it (and implicate some of the men who held high positions under Gierek) was simply not acceptable. Nor was it acceptable to deal with the shifts in personnel that had resulted from the largely anti-Semitic attacks on many of Poland's leading bureaucrats and public figures. After all, many of those who had benefited from the purges were officials of Gierek's Poland, whose tenure began in 1968. To talk about them as beneficiaries not of their own achievements but of the purges of bureaucrats and officials, as the censored sections of the following article did, would have called their ability into question. Furthermore, to talk of the Propaganda Department (under Stefan Olszowski, a temporary ally of Gierek and Poland's foreign minister in the mid-seventies) as somehow involved with the 1968 purges hardly portrayed either the propaganda bosses or Poland's foreign minister in a good light. The following article was an anomaly. It made reference to a time that established journalists knew instinctively could not be discussed in the media.

"Notes from My Journal, 1968–1970" is the title of a collection of excerpts from the diary of H. Worcell [a postwar author], published in the monthly *Sigma* (No. 11). Interventions were made in the following passages:

"November 4, 1968—There was a general meeting of our department yesterday. A new administration was elected, and . . . to my complete surprise, I was elected the new chairman! I don't know whether this should worry me or make me happy. After all, I have no experience in this area, and I have never been a member of the administration before. I am not acquainted with any of the people in authority. It is interesting that I was selected in response to pressure from the Department of Propaganda (especially on the part of Kuszewski), even though I am not a party member. What kind of tactic is this? . . .

"May 21—It is nonetheless grueling to have to go continually on these overnight trips. It's the traveling late at night, at one or three o'clock in the morning. . . . And the nights themselves are troublesome enough, as was the case, for example, yesterday in Polkowice, in a workers' hotel, where they started raising a fuss about wages, and about the lack of real socialist democracy. And what could I say to counter their arguments, when I can see it myself? . . ." (*Report on Materials Censored*, December 1–15, 1974)

The censors were sensitive to any reappearance of anti-Semitism (a recurring phenomenon despite the fact that the country had been largely emptied of Jews as a result of World War II and the anti-Semitic campaigns of the postwar years). Hence, when the pro-Communist but also nationalistic PAX group tried to publish a book containing a passage presenting Jews in an unfavorable light, the initial response was to reject it. This decision was later reviewed and criticized for being oversensitive to the book's portrayals of anti-Semitism during World War I, since these incidents occurred before the Communists took over:

In a book by Czarnowski entitled *Fragments of Memoirs*, submitted by the PAX Publishing Institute, along with a number of appropriate interventions, the following underlined items were needlessly deleted:

"I waited for the train for a rather long time. My unusual greatcoat and, even more, my sword with its protruding hilt excited interest among the travelers waiting on the platform. They were primarily <u>Jewish</u> rabble, curious and obtrusive. I kept myself off to one side and answered with reluctance when anyone accosted me. On the bench next to me sat a woman in an advanced stage of pregnancy, along with an old woman and a little girl. They spoke to each other in Polish, using a dialect that was strange to me. As it turned out, they were *góralki* [inhabitants of the mountainous regions of southern Poland] from the Zakopane area and were waiting for the same train as I was. Finally, the train arrived. I wanted to help the woman to board the train, but before it had stopped a crowd of <u>Jews</u> pushed onto the cars with such force that both women were shoved aside, the pregnant one nearly falling beneath the wheels of the still-moving car. I was so enraged that I could hardly see. Knocking down a few <u>Jews</u>, I pulled my revolver out of my pocket and snarled:

" 'I'll shoot unless you let this woman board the car!' In the twinkling of an eye, the crowd dispersed, and the police appeared. The result of the whole affair was that the women and the <u>Jews</u> set off in the train, while I was invited to the police station.

"After the details of the matter had been made clear, the chief politely informed me that he was forced to confiscate my revolver and punish me for an infringement of public order.

"I responded that, in the first place, not I but the <u>Jews</u> had violated the peace, by trying—in violation of the rules—to board a still-moving train. . . .' "

The passage of the memoirs cited here relates to the period before World War I, and hence it is unreasonable to assume that Czarnowski's account could be related to any conceivable accusations of anti-Semitism in Poland.

Likewise, intervention in the following passage concerning the Black Hundreds in Russia was also unnecessary:

"The forces of reaction sensed the danger, and sought, at all costs, to crush the sprouting revolutionary tendencies. Grasping at all possible means, they began to organize the dregs of society into units of the so-called 'Black Hundreds,' about whom I have already written in my discussion of Nowogród. Here, as in other cities, pogroms were organized. <u>And the famous slogan of that period, 'Beat the Jews, the intelligentsia, and the students!' was widely proclaimed.</u>" (Unnecessary interventions) (*Instructional Materials*, No. 1, February 1974)

The history of the Soviet Union was no less problematical for the censors than Polish history. A short history of the Soviet Union was initially approved and published. Apparently, the work had not explicitly crossed any of the limits censors had been trained to maintain, but when top officials in the censorship office reviewed the book they found that its condensation of Soviet history oversimplified and distorted important questions from the point of view of the Polish party. In order to prevent further mistakes of this kind, the work's "misrepresentations" and the "proper" interpretation of the issues in question were set out in detail in a set of instructional materials prepared for the censors:

In the set of Nonperiodical Publications, approval was given for the publication of a book by A. Czubiński entitled *Land of the Soviets: Years of Struggle and Victory*. This small, 180-page book contains a rich store of information on the more than 50-year path of socialist construction in the Soviet Union. The book was written on the occasion of the fiftieth anniversary of the formation of the Union of Soviet Socialist Republics, celebrated in 1972. It sought to assimilate, recall and analyze anew the Soviet experience, since, as the author noted in the introduction, "the experience of socialist construction in the USSR has enormous practical significance for the Polish people today."

The book was published by the "Iskry" Publishing House in an edition of 30,000. It was intended largely for younger readers, often, undoubtedly, still in the process of establishing their views concerning the major problems of the contemporary world. Hence the type, range and form of the information about the first socialist country in the world that this book provides for such a reader is a matter of unusual importance.

We have noted these problems at the outset, for some of these circumstances—along with others—will play an important part in our critical assessment of Czubiński's work. The publication of this book in a large edition intended for younger readers was an important political mistake. It is to be feared that the reaction of some readers to this work will be an ambiguous one, not necessarily useful from the point of view of the goals of the political education of society.

The author's efforts to incorporate a large amount of information in a small book has necessarily led to the presentation of this information in an extremely condensed, if not telegraphic, form. There was no place for an elucidation of the sociohistorical background, a description of the development of historical processes or commentary on particular events.

Passing on to more detailed matters, we wish to draw attention to certain basic errors, which should have been questioned as part of the process of preventive censorship of *Land of the Soviets*.

1. In Czubiński's treatment, the greatness of V. I. Lenin as leader of the October Revolution and head of the Bolshevik Party and Soviet state has been implicitly diminished. Naturally, the author does not deny Lenin's leading role, but he also gives attention to other figures to an extent hitherto unknown in popular historical literature in the Soviet Union and our country. The majority of these were people who appear on later pages of this study as the organizers of anti-party factions. An example of information of this kind is provided by the following passage:

"During the Civil War, alongside the five-member Politburo (Lenin, Stalin, Trotsky, Kamenev, Bukharin), an increasingly important role came to be played by the Organizational Bureau of the Central Committee. In accordance with the accepted division of labor, Lenin and Kamenev were in charge of the government and the Politburo; Trotsky —military affairs; Bukharin—press and propaganda; and Stalin—organizational matters. The Eleventh Congress of the Russian Communist Party (b) in the spring of 1922 made changes in the statute, broadened the membership of the Central Committee, and established a party general secretariat. The membership of the Politburo was increased to include Tomsky (trade unions) and G. Zinoviev.

"During the revolution and civil war, Trotsky was the first Commissar for Foreign Affairs, and then the Chairman of the Council of Defense and Commissar of the Army and Navy . . ." (p. 55).

2. Czubiński devotes a large part of his book to discussions of divisions within the Communist Party, to the formation and liquidation of factions, the growth of the cult of personality and the subsequent return to Leninist norms in the life of the party and state. These dramatic events, presented in condensed form, have a particularly strong effect on the reader. For example, the author saturates his two-page account of the trials of 1935–38 with a mass of detail, listing a whole series of names as well as the numbers of condemned party and state leaders and military commanders.

Providing simple information and offering greatly condensed material without any accompanying commentary, the author increases the number of question marks. For example, describing the return to Leninist norms in party and state life after the 20th Congress of the CPSU, he writes:

"Wrongly condemned party figures were rehabilitated, and in 1954 the officers condemned in 1937 (among whom Tukhachevsky was most prominent) were likewise rehabilitated. On the other hand, the leaders of the Trotskyite-Zinovievite opposition and other party factions were not rehabilitated. . . .''

If it was necessary to include the information about the un-rehabilitated leaders of the Trotskyite-Zinovievite opposition here, then an explanation should have been offered as to why. In many other places as well, the reader finds himself asking for an explanation. One can, moreover, assume that a significant part of this book's audience is being confronted with information about struggles within the party, the cult of personality and its consequences for the first time.

3. The condensed treatment of these matters has as its result a situation in which the reader of *Land of the Soviets* does not know, in fact, the basis for the mistaken anti-party conceptions of particular factions. Indeed, in some cases, he may even come away with a sense that the position of a particular faction was a correct one, as, for example, in the case of the oppositionist platform of the Bukharin group in the face of the call for the mass, speeded-up collectivization of agriculture.

Describing the agrarian revolution of 1929–33, Czubiński criticizes the wisdom of the forms of socialization of the village adopted in the Soviet Union, supporting his assessment with data on the decline in agricultural production.

By drawing attention to just a few aspects of Czubiński's *Land of the Soviets,* we wish to emphasize that its publication in its present form was a serious mistake, particularly on the fiftieth anniversary of the USSR. The book draws out all of the difficult moments in the history of the USSR and exposes internal divisions in the direction of the CPSU, ones about which its readers had, in many cases, probably never even heard. A compilation of information of this kind, without an exhaustive commentary, must of necessity create a false, gloomy picture of the history of the Soviet Union. The subtitle of the book is *Years of Struggle and Victory,* but in Czubiński's treatment the victories have been drowned out by the errors, internal struggles, abuses of power and the like. This is an extremely harmful approach. In popular literature, which is by its nature abbreviated in character and intended for a mass audience, one should not permit a piling up of abbreviated information concerning difficult and often tragic events. This applies to more than simply the Soviet Union. Such problems may, on the other hand, be taken up in comprehensive works of a scholarly nature, which permit a description of these in a broader sociohistorical context, with appropriate commentary. (*Instructional Materials*, No. 1, February 1974)

The writing of history in any system is never just a report of past events as they happened. As these documents illustrate, however, history for the Polish regime and others in the Communist world has a far greater symbolic value for their leaders than it has elsewhere. Polish history did not provide a basis for Soviet-Polish friendship or for the support of the Communist Party. With the exception of the brutality of the Germans during World War II, Polish history, reported as we know it in the West, countered the images that the Communists tried to put forward. It thus served to weaken rather than encourage support for the party and for any alliances with Poland's Communist "brother states." So the censors attempted to cut out all this history, or to re-form it.

History also played a major role as a veil for criticisms of present-day events. By the mid-seventies most comparisons with the past hardly shed a favorable light on the present. There were too many similarities between problems of the past and those of the present. Furthermore, by the mid-seventies, as the Gierek regime tightened the reins, the parallels that could be drawn with the Stalinist era began to appear. All of this led censors to check carefully each historical report for allusions and notions that, though a part of Polish history, were unacceptable in the context of Gierek's policies.

Ironically, even though the media audience during the seventies was drawn increasingly from the postwar baby boom generation, with little or no firsthand experience of Poland's prewar or even Stalinist past, censoring history did not erase it for them. Images and events were transferred verbally from person to person, generation to generation. Instead of becoming less significant, historical events grew more symbolic, more and more emotionally charged, until in the spiral of events in 1980, when the victory of shipyard workers in Gdańsk opened the possibilities for free discussion of Poland's past, the writing and rethinking of the country's history became as imperative a goal as programming its future for workers and intellectuals alike.

9 / CULTURE

The Final Conundrum

THE FIELD of cultural affairs posed the greatest puzzle for the Polish censors. Propagandists demanded of Polish culture that it perform two contradictory roles: as a safety valve for intellectual discontent, and as a flattering mirror of Polish society. When he took power in December 1970, Gierek reached out for support from the artistic community by putting an end to the blacklisting of intellectuals who had criticized the Gomułka regime in the late sixties and by establishing a new journal, *Literatura,* to give them a forum. He also began to invest in the development of new theaters, television and film facilities and in better funding for writers and artists. These gestures made him seem a savior to Poland's cultural community, but his liberal image ended as quickly as it had begun when writers and other cultural figures showed they had no intention of giving the regime and its policies their unconditional support.

The cultural policy that reigned was as contradictory as the roles that were assigned to it. On the one hand, those who controlled Polish culture recognized, however grudgingly, that some cultural freedom had to be granted to Poland's intellectuals simply to placate them. Thus a number of books, films, plays and cabaret sketches presenting an unadorned image of present-day realities, and alluding to the shortcomings of socialism, were allowed to appear. On the other hand, books and productions permitted by this conciliatory policy were allowed only a small, select audience and often were not allowed to be mentioned in the mass media. Writers and artists were thus cut off from the public. Fewer and fewer Western books were translated. And while the Gierek regime spoke of the importance of culture, it was clear that technology and science were far more important (though having a book or novel published was a status symbol for members of the political establishment—even if the party had to protect the work from critical reviews). These policies, according to many in the Polish artistic community, meant isolation from new ideas from outside Poland. And, while toying with the intellectuals, for the population as a whole the Gierek leadership sought to provide a "culture" that would inspire without challenging anyone or anything. Intellectuals found this policy of carefully controlled criticism for the few and positive cultural propaganda for the masses an insidious threat to the quality of Polish culture.

The treatment of cultural issues in the Polish media was characterized by a number of ironies. The Polish leadership sought to court the Polish communities abroad and reassure the West that Communist rule had not brought with it a decline in Polish culture. On the other hand, Polish cultural figures were seen as dangerous symbols of alternatives to the regime's leadership and prestige, and the media were not permitted to report, for example, on the activities or work of prominent Poles living and working abroad—if they did not support the Gierek regime. Plays were funded and produced, books printed and posters (even those for party congresses) selected, printed and reproduced as postage stamps only to be recalled, criticized or treated with an obligatory silence in the mass media.

Contradictions of this kind were in part the result of differing perceptions and views at different levels of the party and state hierarchies. In part, too, they reflected the philosophy that some things were all right for the few but not for the masses. As a result, silence often shielded critical artistic creations so their appearance would go unnoticed outside the artistic community. The other option, to criticize something publicly, could draw attention to and pique public interest in the target of the criticism, a development that would hardly serve the propaganda directors' interests.

The kinds of topics censored in books, poems, films, plays and cabaret sketches did not differ greatly from those censored in media discussions of political, social, economic, religious and historical questions. The censors simply read especially carefully between the lines of literary works to make sure that nothing that could not be said explicitly was being implied. The rules that the censors were given in regard to culture were concerned not with the revelation of information about cultural affairs—except to mask its general decline—but with who and what could be mentioned, how, and in what context.

Our information about the censors' actual work on books and dramatic productions is more limited in these documents than is our information about their work in the mass media. Most reported instances of censorship in the cultural field involved media commentary on culture or references to censored productions. There were some cases reported of censors cutting passages from literary works or ordering cuts to be made in scripts after reviewing dramatic and cabaret productions. The censors' interferences in public performances were especially difficult to document since they often involved changes in nonverbal elements, such as suggestive staging, or in the general ambience. The documents also contain a number of indirect references to censors' involvement in decisions about whether books should be published, plays produced or films shown, as well as discussions of books and productions that were completed but kept out of the media to reduce their audience.

The Freezing of Polish Culture

Mass media commentary on cultural affairs in Poland was far more closely watched than was cultural life itself. Long before it was clear to most of the population that Gierek's promises of social and economic reform would not be fulfilled, the artistic community was feeling the cutbacks in funding for culture and the increasing restraints on their freedom of expression. Gierek was far less interested in courting the cultural community than in courting the technocrats. As soon as it became evident that artists and intellectuals would not sing the praises of Gierek's policies, investment in and tolerance of Polish culture dwindled. Since most contemporary writing was or at least could be taken as a reflection of contemporary reality, that writing became less publishable as reality appeared less glowing. In addition, as new policies were made and pressure was exerted for strong party control, artists and writers felt compelled to oppose the new policies. And the Gierek élite came to see deviance on one issue as opposition on all. Critical writing was tolerated only from a select few whose acquiesence could be won by the regime only by a modicum of respect for their tastes. In no time at all, cultural products came to be a burden, not a benefit, to the regime. Rather than bear the burden, Gierek's leadership tried to create an alternative "good" culture by engineering it. The rest, however much it was an integral part of Polish society, they decided to consign to oblivion.

Much of the artistic community railed at the subsequent restrictions and at the failure of the Gierek regime to provide for Polish culture. The artists' disaffection was expressed from early on, but most of the criticism appeared only in *Report on Materials Censored*. According to the bulletin summarizing the general trends in materials censored during the second quarter of 1974, the artistic community raised cries of alarm about Gierek's cultural policies already in the early seventies. It continued to face the same problems, raise the same issues and see its complaints kept out of the media for the remainder of the decade:

> [Current] cultural policy was accused of interfering with artistic creativity (especially in literature and poetry), and of making light of or ignoring altogether the opinions of artistic groups. It was stated that the basic conditions necessary for cultural development are not subject to change, but that our model of cultural development is based, in effect, more on the administration of culture [by bureaucracies] than on the steering of its development.
>
> In another journalist's opinion, "even a beginning writer knows that the reward of reprinting a book is given not to those books that have the most success with readers, but to those that are correct" *(Argumenty)*. In another place, it was written: "In our country there are special conditions and relationships" within the framework of which "there exists a penalty unknown elsewhere of prohibiting the publication of works by authors who have committed some sin or other." Therefore, it is stated, "there are a lot of writers who (unfortunately) follow the path of least resistance and know how to 'tell which way the wind is blowing' " *(Kierunki)*.
>
> Similar opinions about the "ailments" of literary life were also eliminated from various statements, articles and works by the younger generation of poets, the so-called "generation of 1968–70." The challenged statements by these young writers expressed the conviction that there exists in our country a "system of imposed" consciousness, of cultural leveling, and a limitation of creative possibilities. For example, it was stated that "the pressure of nonartistic types of speech—mass, noisy, orchestrated forms, obediently pursuing designated goals without any question as to their moral value—pushes poetry into the realm of silence, or at least into a culturally fruitless limitation of its goals" *(Tygodnik Powszechny)*. Similar views in another Catholic publication

were also challenged. In the opinion of a leading representative of the young literary movement, S. Barańczak, the existing criteria of value "have been falsified and distorted. . . . The force brought to bear against consciousness must, sooner or later, develop into physical force. To take note of this and to give warning is the role of poetry" *(Więź)*. Concerning the tasks and role of the young poets, it was also written that [their works] must break through "the shell of falsification," take "a polemical position vis-à-vis the mass means of command," and strive to create a body of values that "can act as an alternative to the defeated system of thought" *(Tygodnik Powszechny)*. These same accents appeared in another item recounting a meeting between officials and representatives of the "younger generation of writers." [The article] referred to "young literature's distrust of official ideologies" and to its "right to publish opposing statements in the press" *(Tygodnik Powszechny)*. *(Bulletin on Themes of Materials Censored,* Second Quarter, 1974)

Although the regime's intention to have cultural products centrally planned and engineered, just like everything else in the society, was an open secret, the censors were unwilling to let references to this state of affairs appear in print. Nor was information about the misuse of funds by cultural officials any more fit for print than such misuse by other officials:

In an article entitled "Culture and Its Consumers" *(Kierunki,* No. 19), departing from his observations on the May Book Fair, W. Głogowski analyzed various aspects of culture from the point of view of both artists and consumers. Passages containing criticism of certain aspects of current cultural policy, including the question of "the administration" of culture, were deleted:

"One can see to what an extent methods drawn from other areas are being introduced into cultural policy and the administration of culture. . . . Increasingly, the model of the hard sciences is being applied to the humanities, something that is naturally not always good for them. The same is true in the cultural field.

"In foreign and domestic policy, or in economics, exact planning is necessary, with a set hierarchy of values, the elimination of all imbalances, and great consistency of approach. In cultural policy, such methods do not always lead to the best results. The establishment of a unified hierarchy of values may lead to the destruction of culture; a rigid personnel policy, to a lifeless Parnassus. If this were to come to pass, Parnassus would have a large number of artists sitting on it who should have ceased to be there long ago. On the other hand, those who should be there could not be. The artistic career ladder has already been artificially truncated. This is the result of defeatism, various psychological complexes, and an increased reliance on connections that abounds in the cultural world even under the most normal of conditions. The misunderstanding involved in treating cultural goals in too literal a manner is much the same as viewing a lyric poem and the lead article in a political newspaper as belonging to the same category, as having interchangeable values.

"Culture can develop only through the conflict of values and tendencies. We shouldn't think that the laws of the dialectic, of progress through contradiction, do not apply to us. In directing cultural policy, we should not try to weaken such confrontations or round out the sharp corners of contradiction. We should only see to it that in those conflicts clean tactics are used, that art is not used for aims that have little do do with it. . . .

"The greater the attention we attach to culture, the more resources we allocate to it and the more people we employ in its dissemination, the more carefully must we review, every day, the influence of the organizational apparatus charged with bringing culture closer to society.

"At this point, we are getting into the problems of the administration of culture. And, as in the case of cultural policy, we are confronted here with the danger of an excessively mechanical and literal use of methods taken from the field of economics, whereby quantitative data are viewed as an indicator of development and their sums as an indication of real gain. . . .

"It is relatively easy to assemble impressive statistics in the cultural field, but it is much more difficult to achieve really satisfactory results. It is well known that people working in cultural institutions of various kinds fabricate statistics [about what is produced]. . . . Directly linked with administration is finance, and when administration has too much faith in statistics, financing can be absolutely absurd. It is in fact impossible to calculate how much money is spent on culture, or whether too much or too little is being expended, since much of the money allocated for culture is used for completely different purposes [a reference to the personal use of state funds by many top-level bureaucrats or administrators]. How is it that the coordination of these matters exists more on paper than in real life, or that some institutions still manage to set up copiously "watered" [alcoholic] excursions that involve miles of travel for no reason at all? Events of this sort are usually paid for out of cultural funds." (*Report on Materials Censored,* May 1–15, 1974)

Other reflections on the state of Gierek's cultural policy were equally revealing and, for the censors, equally unacceptable. It was simply not permissible for writers to tarnish the officially promoted image of the regime as one devoted to fostering culture. When a group of top-level directors of publishing houses whose appointments required Politburo approval *(nomenklatura)* pointed out that the economic crisis had brought with it a paper shortage which, in turn, meant a limitation on the number of books that could be published, the censors balked. Such comments, especially when they came from the regime's own cultural experts and bosses, were too revealing of the economic predicament in which the country found itself as well as of the government's failure to keep its promises in the area of cultural policy:

> Among the participants in a debate on the needs and capabilities of our publishing industry in view of the worldwide "paper shortage," published in *Polityka*, No. 49, were representatives of the Executive Administration of Publishing Houses, the Institute of Books and Reading in the National Library, and the directors of two publishing houses. After being informed of our objections, which were shared by the Department of Propaganda, Press and Publications of the PZPR Central Committee, the editors of *Polityka* deleted certain phrases from statements by:
>
> A. Wasilewski, director of the State Publishing Institute (PIW): "We realize that, notwithstanding our good intentions, the present crisis has managed to frustrate the ambitious plans of party and government organs for, say, the last two years. In any event, however, this crisis is also affecting the most affluent countries, where, as I could see at the Frankfurt Book Fair, publishing houses are reducing their staffs and cutting back on publication plans. But cutting back production in countries where the annual publishing industry output amounts to eight to ten copies per capita is one thing, and cutting back production in a country where the average is four copies per capita, <u>as is the case in Poland,</u> is something else again. <u>The devil will have carried off the thin man before the fat man has even had a chance to slim down.</u> Naturally, we are in favor of conservation measures. . . ."
>
> A. Kurz, director of the Literary Publishing House (Wydawnictwo Literackie): "I, too, have mixed feelings about this problem. Things were moving along more smoothly than ever before in terms of the industry's ideological and program planning (I am referring here to the Politburo's resolution of June of this year concerning the growth of the publishing industry), when <u>all of a sudden,</u> a <u>threatening</u> situation

developed in the country's paper supply. And what we should really be thinking about now is not simply how long <u>this paper shortage crisis will last,</u> but also what <u>it</u> implies, since it may be that it is not merely a transitory problem, but a structural one that is a function of our whole way of life. <u>In this case, ad hoc conservation measures will not be of very much help, since they produce few results and a great deal of confusion in the bureaucratic machinery.</u> <u>Conservation measures are, of course, necessary, but they will only enable us to save the situation for half a year. And then what?</u> . . . We have had a program based on a differential in book prices. On the one hand, you have library books, which are rather expensive and hardbound; on the other, you have inexpensive paperbacks for the mass reading public. It was the State Publishing Institute who launched this program. <u>But in a situation where there is no paper, the inexpensive paperbacks are the books that are placed in the greatest jeopardy, since there is a shortage of the paper stock needed for large printings.</u>" . . . (*Report on Materials Censored,* December 1–15, 1974)

Indications of the inconsistencies of Polish cultural policy, however apparent they were to those who supervised culture, were not to be revealed. When someone pointed out that a book supporting leftist educational methods did not appear, even after it had been widely discussed and heralded in the press, the remark was deleted. The press discussion and the threat posed by a book advocating very nontraditional and nonbureaucratic teaching methods led officials involved in education to raise objections to its publication, and convinced party cultural managers to have the book withdrawn. The translation from English simply never moved from the final stages of production to the distribution of even the 300 copies customarily produced for research libraries and for distribution to top party and government leaders and party scholars. Its fate was not atypical. Such "censoring of the audience" by allowing but not actually completing the production of a book for unexplained or technical reasons became a common way to handle internal conflicts over whether something should appear or not and the pressures for publication of sensitive topics or powerful authors. In many ways, this tactic proved more effective than even explicit censorship: once a book appeared on a list of publications, even if there was a "delay in production" and the book wasn't really made available, nothing could be done. Other publishers could not be sought, and changes could not be made because the work was formally already published. Nor could clear protests be raised about censorship: no one forbade a book; it was just that no action was taken. The Helsinki Conference Final Act was originally published in just this manner, in only a few copies and with even fewer distributed. The result, of course, was that it was not available to the Polish public and remained a much spoken of but unrecorded document:

> The following letter from a reader, entitled "Where Are These Books to Be Found?" was deleted from Issue No. 50 of *Kultura:*
>
> "I was highly pleased to learn of the State Publishing Institute's decision to publish I. Illich's *The Community Had No School.* The series of newspaper articles devoted to this great thinker did a good job of preparing readers to receive this work. The fact that the introduction to the work was written by Professor Suchodolski makes this book even more interesting, and is indicative of the care with which the publishers approached its publication.
>
> "However, several months have gone by, and the work is still not to be found anywhere. I am writing to you gentlemen to ask for an explanation. Is this book going to be published, and if so, when? If not, why? Why is the cultural affairs press, which had devoted so much space to articles describing the contents of the book, which is as interesting as it is controversial, suddenly silent on this subject, as if it were indifferent to the book's fate?
>
> "P.S. Here is an entirely different problem that demands an explanation. Copies of the *Final Act* of the Helsinki Conference on Security and Cooperation in Europe, the impending publication of which was announced long ago, are not available in the bookstores. This is the document described by E. Gierek in *Życie Warszawy* as a 'great charter of peace.'" (*Report on Materials Censored,* December 1–15, 1975)

When discussions on the state of culture in Poland were allowed to take place, the censors were frequently given directions on when, how and where such a discussion should take place. When these press discussions came from writers and journalists themselves, the Press and Culture departments of the party frequently stepped in to specify what should be the "last words" in the discussion. This meant that prominent cultural figures were often able to speak their minds, but their words had only a muted effect since what they had said could not be repeated or taken up in further, open discussions. To prevent protest by prominent figures against the muting of their statements, the censors were instructed not to inform anyone of the regulations governing this policy in justifying their decision to those who protested. All of this ensured that cultural discussions would come to the "proper" conclusions and have few reverberations in society.

The two-article debate below took place between two regime figures, but even their presentations were judged too problematic by the propaganda supervisors. The editors of the Warsaw daily that allowed the initial article to appear were directed by the Central Committee Press Department officials to order a suitable concluding article to the debate. This ensured that the article presenting the correct line would appear in a mass journal. Journalists and editors often referred to such an article with the initials of the Bureau of Sanitation services—an article to cleanse the error that had been made in publication:

> On January 15, 1976, there appeared in *Życie Warszawy* an article by W. Sikorski entitled "Discussion, or the Passing of Sentence," which sharply argued with the assessments of a number of critics of Polish literature expressed in an editorial discussion published in *Literatura*, No. 2, 1976. A response to [Sikorski's article] appeared in an article by J. Putrament, "Kuciapów," published in the fourth issue of the weekly *Literatura*.
>
> *No reprints or discussion of "Kuciapów" should be allowed.*
>
> The final article, which will bring an end to this series of polemics, will be a response to J. Putrament's article and will appear in the near future on *the pages of Życie Warszawy.*
>
> The content of this instruction is intended solely for the information of the censors. (January 29, 1976; canceled April 12, 1976)

Vanishing Acts

The principles governing all the censors' decisions in the area of culture were the same as those for censorship in other fields: "With silence, all will be forgotten" and "He who is not with us is against us." But those who directed the censors' work knew that there were degrees of opposition and treachery. They also worked in an atmosphere, however much they wished to deny it, in which Poles were well aware of who had been prominent and left Poland and who spoke against the Polish regime both in the West and at home. As a result, censorship regulations on cultural issues varied depending on who was involved, the topics that were presented and the publications (and their audiences) in which something was to appear.

The names that the censors wished would disappear from Polish consciousness were those of prominent Poles (many of them at one time members of the political and intellectual establishment) who left Poland either immediately after the Communist takeover or in the mid-fifties and in 1968, when Poles of Jewish origin and other dissidents were pushed to emigrate. Similarly, Poles who lived abroad and criticized Polish Communists either in émigré radio broadcasts or publications, or in Western political discussions, were blacklisted. Finally, the regime wanted to deny the existence of those living in Poland who dared criticize the regime from their position as highly respected members of the Polish intellectual and cultural establishment. For these individuals, censorship meant far more than having a critical statement or article removed. It meant becoming a blacklisted nonperson for one's public.

The "disappearances" of prominent Poles were not required to be uniformly complete, however. There were gradations and degrees of "disappearance" determined by whether any mention could be made of an individual, provisions as to how much neutral or positive information could be given, in what types of publications, at what level the appearance of various names had to be approved, and in what context such references were to be placed. Although the censors' regulations were more haphazard than rational, it appears that the more political and immediate one's activities, the more one was denied media coverage. Those who directly attacked the Polish regime to Polish as well as to Western audiences, whether they remained in Poland as members of the cultural establishment or did so from abroad, were not allowed even passing references in any publications. Others, less critical and public in their attacks on the regime or more undeniably established in Western nations' politics, were permitted limited mention in low-circulation journals and books. For those who had left Poland as members of the postwar establishment élite, treatment was carefully weighed. In all cases, individuals found that it was not their works that were censored but their very existence.

To the Gierek leadership, the broadcasters, publishers and émigré leaders who attacked Poland from abroad were the most serious threats. The regime had a highly classified transcription of all the Polish-language radio broadcasts and all the émigré articles on Poland in émigré journals as well as a classified translation series called *Poland in Western Eyes.* Material from these sources was distributed to top party leaders, leaders of the propaganda apparatus and top editors so that they could in turn counter the information that these sources made available to Western and Polish audiences, and the critical views of Polish affairs they disseminated. But in the Polish media, before its own people, the Gierek leaders elected to simply pretend that the émigré radio stations and journals on which so many even in the "establishment" relied for information did not exist. So, even as journalists listened to Radio Free Europe and the British Broadcasting Corporation's Polish-language service, and read Polish émigré publications like the highly respected Paris *Kultura* (a Polish-language journal that publishes literature and critical political reports from and on Poland) and talked openly of what they had heard or read, they were blocked from mentioning in the media either the broadcasters and writers on whom they themselves relied or the radio stations or émigré publications they used. The regulation below was followed by a list of fifty-eight individuals that included the Polish commentators for Radio Free Europe and the BBC, as well as writers and editors of émigré journals such as the Paris *Kultura,* the London-based *Orzeł Biały* and other smaller journals, all of whom were non-persons. The list also included Stefan Korboński, head of the Assembly of Captive Nations, an American anti-Communist lobbying group, and a prominent member of the World War II underground; Zbigniew Jordan, a member of the Freiburg Soviet Institute in West Germany who worked on Polish affairs; and Feliks Gross, an American sociologist and head of the American Polish Institute of Arts and Sciences. The regulation read as follows:

2.c. All references, other than critical ones, to the names and works of the following writers, scholars and journalists residing abroad (most of them collaborators with enemy publications and centers of anti-Polish propaganda) should be unconditionally eliminated from the press, radio and television, as well as from nonserial publications of a non-scholarly nature.

On the other hand, in scholarly works (books, periodicals and special works) published in small editions for a limited circle of readers, and in memoirs and special works (e.g., historical monographs), the names of the persons listed below, the titles of their works and short statements concerning them, as justified by the nature of the publication, may be permitted.

This also applies to bibliographies, lists of names, indexes and so on. In publications in which the persons listed below are mentioned, the criteria provided in part 2a. should be followed.

2a. In purely scholarly publications, where justified by the nature of the material, permission may be given to include the titles of publications not permitted to circulate in the Polish People's Republic, and the names of Polish institutes operating abroad under émigré sponsorship in notations, indexes and bibliographies.

According to many journalists, the impact of this regulation was far broader in practice than its specific limits. Rather than have any mention that appeared negative be construed by their bosses as positive, the censors simply did not allow these individuals or their journals and stations to be mentioned at all. Only in direct attacks on these émigré sources could they surface, for then the censors could be sure that there was a higher directive that sparked the journalists' attacks.

Those who had once been members of the establishment and then left Poland were also targeted to be treated as nonpersons by the mass media. Many of these émigrés had been forced to leave when they were attacked in the anti-Semitic campaign that swept Poland in the mid-sixties, even though they had spent their working lives either in the Communist Party or in Poland's artistic community. Out of Poland, most continued to be representatives of their homeland's intellectual life, using their experiences and expertise on various areas of Polish life to write in the West. For some, like those listed in the regulation below, total disappearance was not feasible: they had made irreplaceable contributions to scholarship and culture under the Communists. The censors were therefore instructed to allow brief mention of their work and criticism of it in the mass media, as well as broader discussion of them and their work by scholars and intellectuals in books and scholarly journals. A complete ban on references to these figures by their intellectual colleagues (many of whom had been their contemporaries or their students) would have only made them more conspicuous by their absence.

Section IX. Culture.

1. No positive exposure may be given to the names and scholarly contributions of the following persons in the press, radio or television:
   Bronisław Baczko
   Włodzimierz Brus
   Leszek Kołakowski
   Krzysztof Pomian

On the other hand, brief information on the subject of works published by them and all material criticizing their work may be permitted.

In nonserial publications and scholarly, sociopolitical and specialized periodicals, their scholarly work may be permitted, and their contributions may be referred to (or cited), provided that normal censorship guidelines are observed. The above-mentioned names and the titles of their works may also be permitted in bibliographical works, lists of names, annotations, commentaries and so on. . . .

ɔ. References to the names and works of the persons listed below should be eliminated from the press, radio and television, and from nonserial publications of a nonscholarly nature. This restriction does not apply to purely scholarly publications, critical discussions, bibliographies, indexes or lists of names, in which the names of and titles of works by the persons listed below may appear when appropriate:

Zygmunt Bauman
Zbigniew Brzezinski (canceled December 18, 1976)
Edward Etler
George Flemming (Jerzy Działak)
Aleksander Ford
Henryk Grynberg
Piotr Guze
Marian Hemar
Łukasz Hirszowicz
Nina Karsow
Roman Karst
Julian Katz-Suchy
Jan Kott
Karol Lapter
Michał Mirski
Aleksander Peczennik
Roman Palester (canceled February 11, 1977)
Stefan Ritterman
Kalman Segal
Dawid Sfard
Szymon Szechter
Leopold Tyrmand
Andrzej Wirth
Stanisław Wygodzki
Eugeniusz Żytomirski
Krystyna Żywulska
Andrzej Brycht
Witold Wirpsza

Although he was not an émigré member of Poland's intellectual community, Zbigniew Brzezinski, who was born in Poland, was included on this list. This regulation allowed his foreign policy analysis and his role as adviser to the Democratic Party on foreign affairs to be discussed in academic circles. When times changed and he became a clear choice for a high-level foreign policy post, the ban was lifted altogether: the Polish regime hoped that by currying favor with a Polish-American in the U.S. administration, Polish national interests would be given special consideration. Furthermore, to continue to blacklist Brzezinski would give the Carter foreign policy apparatus far less positive press than the Poles normally tried to give new and potentially useful U.S. administrations.

Other Polish émigrés, such as Oskar Halecki and Władysław Pobóg-Malinowski, authors of works on Polish history published in the West but banned in Poland, or the Polish-born writers Stanisław Kot, Czesław Miłosz and Marek Hłasko could be discussed in more widely circulated Polish media. Yet the censors were reminded:

> 2a. On the other hand, the work of the above-mentioned persons should not be allowed to be overrated, nor should they be presented in too favorable a light.
>
> In publications directly concerned with the life and work of any of the above-mentioned individuals, a short sketch of that individual, including the position he has taken or now holds toward our regime, should be provided in the preface, epilogue, or in an annotation, if this is not done in the text itself.
>
> In the specialized, cultural, literary or sociopolitical press, articles, essays and works concerning the above-mentioned persons may be permitted, provided that the principles provided above are followed.
>
> On the other hand, their names and the titles of their works should be eliminated from the daily press, radio and television, except when such information is critical in nature.

Remaining in Poland was no guarantee that one would remain a person in the media. Authors and intellectuals who opposed Gierek's policies disappeared from the media without ever having emigrated. Two of Poland's most controversial writers from this period were singled out for special control. These men, Kazimierz Orłoś, a leading young writer, and Stefan Kisielewski, the Catholic intellectual community's leading critic and satirist, had close ties to those who formed Poland's then tiny dissident community. They also published in Western émigré publications the articles and works that they could not get past the censors in Poland, a clear violation of the rules of the game for Polish writers. Publishing in what were considered "enemy publications" made them special targets. Orłoś was young enough that the censors could relegate him to oblivion, but Stefan Kisielewski was such an established figure in Polish intellectual life that his disappearance would have been too obvious to too many people. All the censors could do was carefully monitor everything he wrote. His articles, however, were so complex, and he was such an experienced adversary of the censors, that his works were not entrusted to regular censors (even to those specially trained to work on Catholic periodicals) but had to be handled by the heads of the censors' office.

The regulation specified that:

> No work by Kazimierz Orłoś may be permitted for publication.
>
> All conceivable publications concerning this author should be approved by the GUKPPiW administration on an ad hoc basis.
>
> Any publications by Stefan Kisielewski may receive permission for publication only after prior consultation (each time) with the GUKP PiW.

For *Tygodnik Powszechny,* where Kisielewski usually published, this meant that even the usual one-week wait for the censors to pass their decision on the paper was extended when his articles were submitted.

A censorship regulation written after top intellectuals protested the constitutional amendments of 1976 summarily removed some of the most prominent among them from public view. The censors were instructed to refer mention of any of these individuals to the heads of the censors' office for approval. At the same time, the censors were told to keep the regulation itself a secret. These individuals were thereby to be denied the recognition that would be accorded them by being "openly" blacklisted. (Nonetheless, news of the de facto blacklisting spread through the country's intellectual circles almost immediately.) In this case, as in others, absence from the media did not entirely remove these figures from cultural life; however, they could no longer perform publicly, even as members of orchestras, and writers suddenly had their works known only by word of mouth. Many did continue to write and publish under pseudonyms. Some became active contributors to dissident publications. And when Gierek's regime collapsed in 1980, many reappeared as leaders of various intellectual groups or as advisers to the Solidarity unions.*

Prohibitions and limits regulated not only people whose names were prevented from appearing in the media, or whose existence could be revealed only to the few, but also the appearance of various works that were published or produced in Poland or other Soviet bloc countries. In addition, Poland had books on its publication lists that were not available to its population. Some, like the supplement to *The Dictionary of Polish Authors* and *The Political Archive of*

*Those listed in this regulation were as follows:
1. Jerzy Andrzejewski [writer]
2. Stanisław Barańczak [writer]
3. Jacek Bocheński [writer]
4. Kazimierz Brandys [writer]
5. Marian Brandys [writer]
6. Witold Dąbrowski [poet]
7. Andrzej Drawicz [Russian literature translator]
8. Jerzy Ficowski [poet]
9. Józef Hen [writer]
10. Zbigniew Herbert [poet]
11. Andrzej Kijowski [literary critic]
11. Stefan Kisielewski [columnist]
13. Jacek Kleyff [cabaret actor and author]
14. Jonasz Kofta [cabaret actor and author]
15. Julian Kornhauser [writer]
16. Wanda Leopold [writer]
17. Edward Lipiński [prewar economist]
18. Jan Józef Lipski [writer]
19. Andrzej Mandalian [writer]
20. Jerzy Markuszewski [theater personality]
21. Ryszard Matuszewski (canceled August 16, 1976) [theater critic]
22. Artur Międzyrzecki [poet]
23. Halina Mikołajska [actress]
24. Wojciech Młynarski (canceled October 16, 1976) [poet]
25. Zygmunt Mycielski (canceled October 16, 1976) [music critic]
26. Marek Nowakowski [writer]
27. Jan Pieszczachowicz (canceled February 27, 1976) [literary critic]
28. Jan Pietrzak (canceled April 21, 1976) [cabaret producer and writer]
29. Antoni Słonimski (canceled October 16, 1976) [writer]
30. Michał Sprusiński (canceled October 16, 1976) [literary critic]
31. Jan Józef Szczepański [writer]
32. Irena Szymańska [publisher, Czytelnik publishing house]
33. Stanisław Tym (canceled October 16, 1976) [playwright and actor]
34. Jerzy Waldorff [music critic]
35. Wanda Wilkomirska (canceled October 16, 1976) [violinist]
36. Wiktor Woroszylski [poet]
37. Adam Zagajewski [writer]

Ignacy Paderewski (the Polish pianist who led the campaign for Polish independence before World War I and who was Poland's first prime minister after Poland was reestablished as a self-governing nation in 1918), were never sent to bookstores but were sold to those who had been notified that they would be available and allowed to sign up and pay in advance to purchase them in so-called "closed sales." All of this was intended to placate some and affect very few. (In fact, it only irritated those who were able to get the books. They were the only ones who knew a given book existed and so saw the permission to publish it as a cynical sham: the book would never reach its true audience and would receive no press coverage.) The censors were told:

> 20. A supplement to *The Dictionary of Polish Authors* published in 1963 will be issued soon by the State Scientific Publishing House (PWN). This supplement will be distributed exclusively according to the system of closed sales.
>
> No permission should be given for criticism of the manner of distribution or to demands for an increase in the size of the edition or a reprinting. (See Informative Note No. 42/74) (December 13, 1974; canceled May 6, 1976)

> 22. In 1973–74, the "Ossolineum" Publishing House issued *The Political Archive of Ignacy Paderewski* in a small edition. The book was distributed by means of closed sales.
>
> No criticism should be permitted concerning the size of this edition or the means of its distribution. All critical assessments of the contents of this book should be referred to the GUKPPiW administration. (July 8, 1975)

Certain objectionable books, films and theatrical productions either slipped through censorship or were permitted because they were the work of prominent figures or of individuals protected by prominent political figures. In these cases, the Press Department sought to mute their impact and distribution by limiting mention of their existence in the media. One such case involved a number of films made by prominent Polish writers and producers. References to them were forbidden—despite the fact that state monies and resources had been invested in their production and that official approval of the scripts had been given before production of the films was begun:

16. *No material* (information, descriptions, reviews, reports, demands for showings, etc.) concerning the films listed in the attached annex, which will be continually updated, should be permitted. (See Informative Note No. 9/75)

ADDENDUM TO REGULATION 16 OF SECTION IX

1. Polish feature films:
    1. Diabeł [*Devil*], directed by Żuławski
    2. Ręce do Góry [*Hands Up*], by Skolimowski
    3. Długa Noc [*The Long Night*], by Nasfeter
    4. Czarna Parzenica [*Black Embroidery*], by Komorowski
    5. Zasieki [*Barbed Wire*], by Piotrowski
    6. Ile Jest Życia? (Losy) [*How Much Life Is There? (Fates)*], by Bratny (canceled March 25, 1976)
    7. Przeprowadzka [*The Move*], by Gruza
    8. Pełnia nad Głowami [*Full Moon Overhead*], by Czekalski
    9. Indolencja [*Indolence*], (amateur film)
2. Polish documentary films:
    1. Meta [*The Goal*]
    2. System [*The System*]
    3. Człowiek Który Wykonał 550% Normy [*The Man Who Fulfilled His Quota 550%*]
    4. Trudności Bardzo Obiektywne [*Very Objective Difficulties*]

NOTE: The titles and very general descriptions of the content of the documentary films may be permitted for publication.

The reasons for the dual censorship standard—allowing something to be published or produced, yet forbidding any discussion of it in the media—varied. In the special case of a novel written by the editor-in-chief of the Kraków literary journal *Życie Literackie*, Władysław Machejek, long a member of the political establishment, the very publication of the book was clearly only a result of his personal political position. Yet Machejek, editor of one of Communist Poland's oldest cultural weeklies, had tarnished the party's image. So the censors were not even allowed to handle the book's treatment in the press nor could the publishers do anything to encourage readers. They were instructed that:

> 90. All discussion, reviews and the like concerning Władysław Machejek's four-volume *I Wait for the Last Word,* soon to appear, must be approved by the PZPR Central Committee's Department for Press, Radio and Television before permission to publish is granted.

Publisher's announcements, notes and the like should have all favorable emphasis or promotion of the book eliminated from them.

The publication of sections or excerpts should not be permitted in any periodicals (other than *Życie Literackie*).

This instruction is intended solely for the information of censorship groups. (First version, May 22, 1975; this version, June 14, 1975) (See Section IX, Regulation 26) (Canceled February 4, 1976)

As a result, the censors eliminated references to the book and its contents:

In Issue No. 50 of *Argumenty,* an interview of T. Hołuj by E. Żurek entitled "Tadeusz Hołuj: Not Just About Himself" was published. The following passage from the writer's replies was eliminated, in accordance with the appropriate directive:

"[Question] Could you mention a few of the literary works, prose works, that have made a strong impression on you?

"[Answer] I can say something about ones that I find interesting. I would certainly have to mention Władysław Machejek's *I Wait for the Last Word.* I have some reservations about the book's artistic form and even about its ideological value, but it is the only book ever written about the lives of people directly involved in the life of the party. . . ." *Report on Materials Censored,* December 1–15, 1975)

K. T. Toeplitz, a regular contributor to leading official papers, was able to have a compilation of his writings published but, similarly, not discussed in the media. In his case, however, the top censors were allowed to pass judgment:

99. No reviews or discussion of K. T. Toeplitz's book *Substitute Packaging,* published by PIW, should be permitted without prior consultation with the GUKPPiW administration.

Only short bibliographical notes may be permitted without consultation.

This instruction is intended solely for the information of the censors. (June 14, 1975; canceled January 22, 1976)

Leaders in the literary or scholarly establishment who took nonconformist positions were treated very carefully by the censors when it came to press coverage. For example, the position of a leading inter-war writer who had left Poland for the West after the war and then returned in the fifties was considered so problematic that no regular censor was empowered to make decisions on materials dealing with him:

> 45. All publications concerning the person or work of Melchior Wańkowicz dealing with more than purely literary problems (e.g., descriptions of him as a person of great courage, a politician, an activist, a national hero, the conscience of the nation and the like) should be held up and referred to the GUKPPiW administration. (This version, September 13, 1974; canceled March 19, 1975)
>
> All publications evaluating the creative work or the sociopolitical views of M. Wańkowicz should be referred to the GUKPPiW administration.
>
> On the other hand, the creative writing and other works of M. Wańkowicz published in People's Poland may be permitted to appear without prior consultation, so long as the normal censorship rules are observed. (This version, March 19, 1975; canceled January 22, 1976)

The death in 1976 of the often outspoken chairman of the Polish Writers' Association, Antoni Słonimski, posed similar problems. Słonimski held a prominent place as a leader in postwar Polish literature, both as a writer and as head of the Writers' Union. But at the time of his death he was also involved in protests against restrictions on Polish literature and intellectuals. As a result, the media were to treat him with what can best be described as muted respect. Rather than leave his death open for coverage by all, making it a national political event, only those who traditionally handled literature and literati were allowed to do their own reporting. To this end, the following instructions carefully outlining what could appear and where were drawn up and distributed to individual censors:

> 141. In connection with the death of Antoni Słonimski, the following censorship principles should be adhered to:
>
> 1. The whole press may publish the PAP communiqué;
>
> 2. Życie Warszawy will publish obituaries by the Ministry of Culture and Art, publishers and organizations, and reminiscences by St. R. Dobrowolski (without reprint rights);
>
> 3. The central literary press, certain regional publications, and the cultural editors of Polish Radio and Television will issue appropriate material and obituaries (after having them approved by the Department for Press, Radio and Television of the PZPR Central Committee);

4. All individual editors' recollections, commentaries, notes and the like must be approved by the Department for Press, Radio and Television of the PZPR Central Committee. (July 5, 1976; canceled October 16, 1976)

In another case, the censors were confronted with a book on the social history of World War II that was certain to excite a great deal of interest among Poles. It had already been awarded the highest honors by the Polish chapter of the international writers' association the PEN Club, a legal organization in Poland. But neither the book nor its author had completely followed the official line. The censorship authorities therefore decided that while the book was newly on the market they would carefully orchestrate its media treatment. Normally a book on the war, and especially one giving a factual discussion of the Polish underground and the Warsaw Uprising, would command a broad, popular audience. By permitting only one or two intellectual journals to give the book any publicity, the authorities radically limited its readership to those who were part of the chain of literary or scholarly gossip on books and at the same time satisfied the intellectual community that already knew about the book and the award:

62. The current number of *Tygodnik Powszechny* contains, as an exception to normal procedure, information about a symposium devoted to Władysław Bartoszewski's book *The 1,859 Days of Warsaw*. Any reprintings of this information, discussions or interviews with participants in the symposium, or reviews or further discussion of Bartoszewski's book should be referred to the GUKPPiW administration before permission is granted.

On the other hand, bibliographical notes and short informative notes about the book may be permitted. (January 21, 1975) (See Regulation No. 26 of Section IX) (Canceled February 4, 1975)

84. The PAP communiqué concerning the award of the annual Mieczysław Lepecki P.E.N. Club Prize to W. Bartoszewski for his book *The 1,859 Days of Warsaw* that appeared in the April 29 issue of *Życie Warszawy* may be permitted for publication *only* in the cultural periodicals and *Tygodnik Powszechny*. (April 29, 1975; canceled July 13, 1975)

Censoring Fraternal Culture

Promoting culture from Poland's Soviet bloc neighbors was not a simple matter. However much talk there was of developing cultural ties within the Soviet bloc and of fraternal relations, those who manipulated the Polish media in the Press Department and the leadership of the GUKPPiW carefully reviewed each import to make sure it did not contain material that was "unsuitable" for the Polish audience. For, as the censors were told,

> The fact that [a book] was published in the Soviet Union cannot be used as a justification since the inhabitants of the Soviet Union think differently from the Polish reader. Every state, in conducting its domestic policy, handles its problems in different ways. The officials of a given country, in permitting reference to be made to various sensitive subjects, have their own citizens in mind above all. Furthermore, in relations among countries of the socialist bloc, the principle has been adopted, on the basis of reciprocity, that information about the domestic difficulties in one country will not be provided [in the media of another]. (Informative Note No. 5)

The occasion for the above explanation was the book *Meetings with Icons,* which referred to the sorry state of Orthodox churches in the USSR. From the perspective of their superiors, the censors responsible for its translation and publication had failed to consider its potential interpretation in the Polish context. They had failed to recognize that while the destruction of Russian Orthodox churches in the Soviet Union was relatively accepted there, in Poland any discussion of this would open the door to all sorts of parallels to the problems of Church-state relations in Poland. The censors were therefore informed of the serious error in judgment that had been made in the decision to publish the book, and the case was used as an instructional example. The rules of the game, they were to remember, and the expectations of society differed widely between the Soviet Union and Poland. To prove how the Russian book shed, by reflection, a negative light on Polish officials' respect for the Church, the Instruction, Evaluation and Control Group in GUKPPiW also appended a review that used the Soviet book to attack Polish officials' mistreatment of religious symbols:

Main Office for Control of Press,
    Publications and Public Performances
Instruction, Evaluation and Control Group
No. ZI-Pf-132/5/76

> Warsaw, January 23, 1976
> C O N F I D E N T I A L
> Copy No. 29

Informative Note No. 5

Attached is the censors' review of V. Soloukhin's book *Meetings with Icons* (Appendix No. 1), issued by Wydawnictwo Literackie in Kraków in 1975 and awarded the PAX Włodzimierz Pietrzak Foreign Prize.

There have been several cases of intervention in press reviews of this book. These consisted largely of eliminating citations from the work. (We are also attaching, in Appendices 2 and 3, typical examples of interventions, from *Więź* and *Tygodnik Powszechny.*)

As a result of a second review by the Instruction, Evaluation and Control Group, it was determined that the permission granted by the delegated censorship group in Kraków for publication of this book was an error.

> Deputy Group Director
> Janusz Buchalski

Distributed according to the list

Appendix No. 2:
In his article "On Icons and a Few Other Matters," T. Chrzanowski presented his reflections after reading V. Soloukhin's *Meetings with Icons.* The underlined passages below were deleted.

". . . All I know about the author is what the book jacket tells me and what he writes about himself in the book. The information is not too encouraging: a graduate of the Gorky Literary Institute (strangely enough, I do not have much faith in literary training schools of that kind). . . . The author of *Meetings with Icons* describes things that make your hair stand on end. The terrible extent of the damage done in the Russian provinces after the revolution, a situation that continued unchecked until only recently. But even in our country the destruction was severe, and not just because of the fires of war, but also because of the deep changes in the structure of the state and society. All such changes are bound to produce devastation, but when they are accompanied by revolutionary ideological change, the devastation is still greater since every revolution carries with it a strain of iconoclasm in the broadest sense of the word. [The book describes] 100 Russian churches that are falling into ruin along with the objects they contain. In our country, too, a number of churches are being destroyed, and the furnishings of rural manor houses have ceased to exist. Several large residences (Pszczyna, Łańcut, Nieborów) have been salvaged to some extent, but Polish manor houses like the 'Rychter-Janowska' have in essence ceased to exist. A few dozen architectural shells have been preserved, but how much of the old interiors and furnishings have survived? I know of three, maybe four houses in this condition. . . .

"Soloukhin captures Leningrad, with its marvelous, pristine, original form, the expression of a particular epoch, which still preserves its old planned stone outlines along the banks of the Neva. And he is so bold as to say that Leningrad is more beautiful than Moscow. This statement, completely obvious to me, barely makes it out of his mouth (or typewriter), and he considers it proper to document his opinion. Hence he cites various favorable opinions of Moscow and admits that it is a beautiful city, but . . . that it is no longer that most beautiful city of hundreds of golden domes. On page 16 there begins an enumeration of the destruction, performed largely in the 1930s. I am omitting the beginning and cite only the later parts of the text: 'I will list only the examples more schematically: A church from the 16th century at the corner of Kirov Street and Dzierzynski Square—destroyed. An empty square remains. The church of Florus and Laurus (1651–1657) on Kirov Street, diagonally across from the main post office—demolished. Now an empty, neglected square. A church from the 17th–18th century at the corner of Kirov and Markhlovski Street—demolished. [In its place,] plywood stalls. A church from 1699 near the Gate—demolished. Now a square. A church from the 16th century at the corner of Dzierzynski Street and the Kuznetskii Bridge—demolished. Now an empty square covered with grass. A belfry surmounted by a pavilion dome dating from 1685 on Hertsen Street—demolished. Now small squares. A church dating from 1696 on Pokrovka—demolished. Now a square.'

"And so on. As can be seen from the above remarks, we have come full circle. We have to fight and to be apostles, to threaten and persuade, and above all, despite deeply rooted clichés, despite those frightened by any new resistance, despite [the lure of a] cheaper popularity, we must present some facts that are often unknown or not familiar.

"In our country there is a 'fad for icons,' and it is considered good taste, in homes at a certain level of society, to hang pictures of this type which have been looted from the Bieszczady Mountains [in Poland] or appropriated from the Balkans. . . . Icons in the homes <u>of the members of certain strata of society</u> are like a gas lamp or a flatiron with a heater: a snobbism that <u>even under socialism</u> is not something we should be ashamed of. . . .

"Collecting calls for a certain fervor. . . . But fervor cannot and must not go hand in hand with arbitrariness or a lack of scruples. <u>In our country, where unfortunately the sense of ownership of any kind is as light and fleeting as cigarette smoke,</u> even pseudo-collecting 'gives rise to sin,' and makes thieves out of ordinary people. . . .

"Social awareness of the past and its documents is what I would consider a basic aspect of the proper development of conservationist thinking. Although a lot is supposedly going on in our country in this field, our <u>whole</u> society is still at only a low level of awareness. If the ruins of the palace in Świecie (and dozens of other palace ruins) have provided free entry to our fellow countrymen for years on end, if our city fathers feel true joy at being able to [illegible] the more beautiful and [illegible] dumps . . . then this probably means just one thing: that there is no public concern about the protection of historic monuments in our country, even though we are supposedly proud of the Old Towns of Warsaw and Gdańsk, and even though there supposedly is a 'Polish School of Conservation.' . . ."

Not only did the Polish censors have to watch fraternal culture for potential reinterpretations based on the Polish mind and situation, as well as for potential negative images of other states in the bloc, but they also tried to wash fraternal culture clean of anything that would offend Polish sensibilities. So, for instance,

Parts of a film produced in the GDR entitled *The Reed,* which blamed Poland for the hardships suffered by displaced persons, were deleted from the film. (*Report on Materials Censored,* July 16–31, 1975)

Every effort was made to eliminate open criticism of books and films imported from elsewhere in the bloc—criticisms that could imply a negative view of the societies which had produced them. Hence the censors removed from the following passage the barbs aimed at Soviet cultural controls and the Soviet film industry:

A passage containing a negative assessment of the Soviet film *Monologue* was eliminated from M. Hołyński's "Love of Male Beauty" (*Politechnik,* No. 12), which described [the films shown at] "Confrontation 74" [a yearly film festival in Warsaw]. The passage read as follows:

". . . the only film produced by the democratic countries that received the praise of the critics. It is noteworthy that the film did not reflect the country in which it was made. The film was strong in its defense of tradition. Its hero, a likable professor from Leningrad, says: 'I am a representative of the old Russian intelligentsia. And this is my home, which I have inherited from my forefathers.'

"Not everybody liked it. In the words of a clean-shaven, short-haired man in a suit: 'This film was annoyingly poor. The Americans were already making films of this sort back in the days of silent movies. In my life I have seen about 20 Soviet films, and I do not care what relationship *Monologue* has to other Soviet films. I want to be able to compare it to normal [Western] films. And from that point of view it fails completely, as a collection of naïve, obvious facts.' " (*Report on Materials Censored*, March 16–31, 1974)

Likewise, the censors sought to protect a Czech film sent to Poland from critical treatment of its artistic quality in the media:

Assessments critical of the Czech film *Days of Betrayal*, describing it as "irritating" from an aesthetic point of view, and "consistently flat in its treatment" of everybody "from Hitler to Gottwald," were deleted from another article devoted to "Confrontation 74," entitled "Imagined Miracle," which was written by J. Pałasiński. (*Report on Materials Censored*, March 16–31, 1974)

Discussion of cultural developments elsewhere in the Soviet bloc which presented negative views of those societies was prohibited, just as was other criticism. According to the censors' reports, for example,

In T. Żolsiński's review of A. Drawicz's book *Invitation to a Journey* in *Literatura na Świecie*, No. 11, a book offering "several biographical and monographical studies of Soviet writers," including Mayakovsky, Zoshchenko, Olesha, Bulghakov and many more young writers" (Yevtushenko, Tarkovskii, Samoilov), deletions were made in a passage discussing the "ruination of writers" as a result of conscious efforts to "ignore their works." (*Report on Materials Censored*, December 1–15, 1974)

The authorities were also often unwilling to offend their allies by publishing or mentioning in Poland things that had been forbidden elsewhere in the bloc. So, for instance,

Mention of A. Solzhenitsyn's book *Cancer Ward,* published by the Instytut Literacki in Paris [the leading émigré publishing house] in a translation by J. Łobodowski, was deleted from the "Bibliography" section of *Rocznik Literacki* (published by PIW, edition of 1,000 copies), in accordance with regulations. (*Report on Materials Censored,* May 1–15, 1974)

And in keeping with the practice of Soviet cultural authorities:

5. The publication of the works of Vladimir Voinovich, Vladimir Maksimov and Nadezhda Mandelshtam should not be permitted, nor should any mention, discussion or information about these writers or their works be permitted. (*Report on Materials Censored,* May 1–15, 1974)

. . . Short items relating to Osip Mandelshtam may be permitted in the media, but the GUKPPiW should be advised if any of his works are submitted for publication.

The content of this prohibition is intended solely for the information of censors. (New version, February 11, 1976)

Bringing the Curtain Down

Censorship of the media also extended to the presentation of dramatic works. Whatever the supposed degree of spontaneity or rehearsal, each and every aspect of all public performances in Poland was closely monitored. Before a show could open, the censors in charge observed the dress rehearsal and passed judgment on everything from the words to the gestures, staging and costuming. After all, in 1968, the staging of a Polish classic had triggered a wave of student demonstrations. This particular production of Adam Mickiewicz's classic *Forefathers* had emphasized the work's anti-Russian accents, and Warsaw audiences had cheered loudly. When objections were raised by the Soviet ambassador, the play (whose production, under a leading Polish director, had been approved by the censors) was closed, and Warsaw's students took to the streets in protest against this kind of cultural censorship. Gierek's censors were unwilling to risk another incident of this kind.

For dramatic productions, however, censorship and the threat of closing were measures of last resort. The government provided all the funds for culture in Poland, and therefore, when a theater company decided to stage a particular play or to put on a new cabaret show (or even a new routine), permission had to be obtained from the Ministry of Culture (and by implication the Cultural Department of the Central Committee). The ministry examined each request in terms of who was involved, what the costs were and how this production fit in with its own plans for the direction of cultural programming. Directors and theater heads all knew that the ministry's decisions on a given production were a reflection of its past experiences with a company and with the production itself. They were therefore anxious not to allow themselves to become "notorious causes," as did a small experimental theater in Puławy. The result of that theater's independence was its dissolution, as described in the following censorship regulation:

> 12. Arguments and discussions about the decision to close the Experimental Theater in Puławy as a result of grave improprieties in its operations (e.g., cooperation with the clergy, failure of the theater managers to adhere to the directions of the censors) should not be permitted for publication.
>
> The content of this regulation should not be revealed to editorial boards.

Only after all the preliminary controls had been exercised did the censors have their say. Censors assigned to handle theatrical performances and party and government officials were the audience for the first dress rehearsal. And as they watched, they censored.

As in every other aspect of Polish cultural life, the decisions of the censors on dramatic productions were far from consistent: what was good for one audience was not necessarily considered suitable for another. Larger theaters had far less leeway than their smaller, experimental offshoots. Internationally prominent directors and actors could go much further than unknown fledgling artists. This was all part of the well-known "facts of life" for the artistic community. It was also a hurdle that artists tried to circumvent—much to the distress of the censors, who reported this trend in the bulletin for the second quarter of 1974:

> As a footnote to the problems of the operation of student cabarets, we should note the attempts made here and there to get around the regulations concerning control. There have been instances where various

student cabarets have tried to put unaccepted texts into the program and present them, and there have also been attempts to avoid the obligation of respecting the approval of a program given in its home territory when it is being presented outside of the cabaret's home territory. For example, the Jelita cabaret program of Gdańsk Polytechnic was not submitted for approval before being presented at the Białystok "Start-74" student cabaret festival. Similarly, the Pod Budą Cabaret of the Agricultural Academy in Kraków made guest appearances in the hall of the Voivodship House of Culture in Kielce without the approval of the Kielce representatives of GUKPPiW. The Polish Socialist Students' Union school council of the Higher School of Economics in Wrocław also failed to go through the formalities when it invited the Poznań Tey Cabaret and the Warsaw Pod Egidą Cabaret to appear at the Wrocław "Ekonomalia" festival. (*Bulletin of Themes of Materials Censored,* Second Quarter, 1974)

Polish theaters were able to put on lavish productions and keep companies of actors because of the subsidies provided for the arts. Under Gomułka, what was provided was left for the artists to administer. So, when the Gierek leadership took steps during the mid-seventies to make theaters function more like economic enterprises, the move was criticized. In one censored interview, the director of the Stary (Old) Theater in Kraków, J. P. Gawlik, criticized this new policy, just as his colleagues in other branches of the arts had attacked similar policy changes. Not surprisingly, the censors deleted his statement,

> . . . published in Issue No. 49 of *Kultura* under the heading "Doomsday for the Polish Theater," which expressed the opinion that the new law regulating the management of Polish theaters forces directors to run their theaters on a commercial basis "to a greater extent than before," and that "the spectre of commercialization is beginning to pose a threat to the social and ideological missions of Polish drama . . . inasmuch as ideology still seems to be more flexible than the science of accounting." (*Report on Materials Censored,* December 1–15, 1974)

In the documents available from the mid-seventies there are reports of censors refusing permission for specific plays to be staged because they honored the "beat" culture of the 1950s or raised the sensitive issue of the need for Christian values in society. In the latter case, the censors ordered the removal of all Biblical passages from one production. Normally, even in theater productions geared to tiny intellectual audiences, the same rules that applied to the mass media about honoring deviance or religion were enforced:

> Permission was denied for a presentation of Allen Ginsberg's *Howl*, the text of which was submitted by the Polish Socialist Students' Union campus council at the University of Warsaw (the work was to have been presented by a student theatrical group from the Department of Polish and Slavic Philology). In the work, the author, one of the leading representatives of the beatnik movement in literature, presented the fundamentals of hippie ideology. Its criticisms of American society basically express such ideas as "the generation's best minds consumed by insanity," "purging their dreams with drugs, nightmares, alcoholism," etc. (*Report on Materials Censored,* May 1–15, 1974)

> The Estrada Theater of Warsaw Voivodship submitted the script of a program of music and poetry entitled "After All, One Should Fall in Love Again." The substance of this performance, a commentary on the dehumanization of modern man, lost in a world "consumed by individual and collective egotisms that are the source of antagonism, wars, conflicts of interest, or, in a word, hate," included a demand for the creation of a world of "harmony, justice and peace," based on the Christian ethic. Among the passages challenged were "A Psalm of David," "The Epistle of St. Paul to the Corinthians," an article by Archibishop A. Kozłowiecki entitled "Hate Is Senseless" and an address by Pope Paul VI. (*Report on Materials Censored,* May 16–31, 1974)

On the other hand, the censors' documents are also testimony to the fact that productions which veiled some of their political relevance did get presented in small theaters. Often these theaters, whose tickets were available to only a select few, were extensions of larger theatrical institutions that produced conventional dramas for their mass public. Whether the censors who gave their imprimatur to such sideline productions were aware of their covert political implications or not, the censors who watched the media sought to keep reviewers from making those implications clear. For example:

> In an article entitled "Political Impacts" (*Kierunki,* No. 50), K. Głogowski reviewed K. Estreicher's play *Three Conversations with Colonel Ulysses,* produced by the Theater for the Advancement of Contemporary Drama under the auspices of the Nowy (New) Theater, and R. Bratny's show *Three in a Straight Line,* produced by the Little Stage

of the Popular Theater [Teatr Powszechny]. Interventions were made in the following passages concerning:

—*Three in a Straight Line:* ". . . Bratny and Huebner do not gloss over the cruelties of the period of history that ended not so long ago, the period of the civil war [when Poles fought against a Communist takeover]. They reveal the diversity of personal attitudes characteristic of that period, the abuse of power, and instances where laws were broken for opportunistic reasons, purely for the sake of cultivating good personal relations. They also show the continuity of personality defects: the lawbreaking opportunist Col. Sandomierski (played very convincingly by Henryk Bąk) is still an opportunist years later as the head of a film production unit—ruthlessness stemming from a fear of one's superiors, from a lack of 'backbone,' is ruthlessness all the same. This is why the people who come to power at turning points in history are not always the most qualified, but are simply more cunning than everybody else. And they end up pushing out those who refuse to abandon their personal integrity or agree to absurdities and lawlessness against the power they represent." . . .

—*Three Conversations with Colonel Ulysses:* ". . . This is a very strange one-act play. Estreicher uses period costumes, which nonetheless are merely a cloak for the very contemporary reflections of a humanist who manages to show us the timeless mechanisms of history in their true light. . . . Consequently, the sufferings of Aeneas, Troy's minister of foreign affairs, after the fall of that city, reminds us of our own suffering after the collapse of the Warsaw Uprising." . . . (*Report on Materials Censored,* December 1–15, 1975)

Curtains to Cabarets

Whatever the criticisms and negative images of Polish realities that managed to appear on the Polish stage, the true center of social commentary lay elsewhere. In cafés and nightclubs all over Poland, amateur and professional groups created drama and comedy out of Poland's political and social failings. Cabarets had been the source of the freest and sharpest political criticism in Poland since the days of the partitions. On tiny stages, cabaret troupes acted out an ongoing series of skits and jokes that took reality to task. Their humor and bite were based on suggestive costumes, plays on words, quickly spoken dialogue and rapid movements. Often the cabarets thrived on spontaneity, something the censors saw only as deliberate defiance of their authority. For the censors and the Gierek leadership, satire was a threat. No matter how few people could be crowded into the cabarets or how out of the way the productions were, the censors were vigilant to prevent their barbs from going too deeply into the problems that existed in Poland. They had their work cut out for them, for, as a student newspaper for technical universities tried to point out, contemporary politics and problems were the stuff that cabarets were made of:

> "as is well known from accounts and observations of the revivals [of theater] that took place after October [1956] and December [1970] . . . the farther we are removed in time from these dramatic events, the less interesting the work done in the theater becomes. . . . due to the absence of political upheaval and to the stabilization of the consumer goods market, productions have become mediocre and dull. . . ." (*Report on Materials Censored,* May 16–31, 1974)

Whatever criticism and satire the censors failed to purge from the cabarets, they were careful to prevent from being repeated or reported in the media. As a result, though word of new satirical routines and jokes spread rapidly through the intellectual community that frequented the cabarets, it never really reached a larger audience. Because of the censors' actions, cabarets lost much of their political punch and audience draw (in the mid-seventies, though tickets were hard to get to cabarets, they were more available than they had been in earlier years and than they would be in the Solidarity era) and their punch lines were not recorded for those who could not attend. Nor did they get the publicity necessary to generate new audiences. Still, the cabaret troupes survived. And as the social and economic situation grew worse by the mid-seventies, they found, despite the increasing strictness of the censors, more and more subjects crying out for criticism. Cabarets were reported to have been censored for satirizing all manner of phenomena, including

1)*The mass media*

The following poem was removed from a production by R. M. Groński entitled "Early Friday Morning," which was submitted for approval by the A. Fredro State Theater in Gniezno:
—The News Song
Tweedledum and Tweedledee,
Like two peas in a pod,
Entrenched behind their office doors.

So squished and scrunched up,
That you can't tell who is who.
Who gave you life,
You paper men
With hearts cut out of newsprint?
Who gave you life,
You paper men—
Guidelines and arguments?

Who gave you ears,
You paper men,
And eyes flushed with lies?
All those days spent in government offices
And you are awash in a sea
Of everyday events written up in fine print.

Who gave you life,
You paper men,
With ears cut out of newsprint?
Who gave you life,
You paper men—
Guidelines and arguments?
Who gave you life,
You paper men
Made of desks and fear?
Who gave you the right
To exchange the flag
For a weathervane?

(*Report on Materials Censored,* December 1–15, 1975)

The Powiat House of Culture in Słupsk [a small coastal town] submitted a concert hall program prepared for the anniversary of the liberation of Słupsk and the 30th anniversary of the Polish People's Republic. We challenged Cz. Szewczyk's skit, "New Method," which was supposed to represent a dialogue between an editor and a leading cattle breeder who had achieved splendid results by using a new kind of feed. Here are some excerpts from that skit:

EDITOR: What are the ingredients of this new high-grade fodder?
BUMPKIN: The ingredients? . . . It is composed of daily papers, weeklies, monthly periodicals, and quarterlies. . . .
EDITOR: If I understand you correctly, you are feeding your animals wood pulp, paper.
BUMPKIN: Oh, no! My animals won't eat just any paper. I give them newspapers.
EDITOR: Just ordinary newspapers?

BUMPKIN: No, not ordinary ones. They're made into chopped feed, silage, fodder, and also dried feed, in place of hay. But they have to be fresh. Once I gave them a piece of wastepaper that was two years old, and they got sick.

EDITOR: And how do you get the papers? Do you subscribe?

BUMPKIN: I feed the ones to be fattened for slaughter with a special mix: one part *Perspektywy* to three parts *Żyjmy Dłużej* [*Let's Live Longer*]. This makes them feel better and causes a noticeable increase in weight.

EDITOR: Have you noticed any adverse side effects from the use of your new fodder?

BUMPKIN: No adverse side effects, but there are additional benefits, like I told you. They don't kick. They don't move around while being milked. And if somebody yells, 'Move!' they don't pay any attention. You have to say, 'Pardon me,' and then they move. . . .

(*Report on Materials Censored,* May 1–15, 1974)

2) *The housing shortage*

The Construction Workers' Administration attached to the Municipal Administration of the Union of Socialist Youth in Wrocław submitted the script of a production to be presented on "Construction Workers' Day," written by J. Jankowski. The following passages, *inter alia,* were deleted from it:

—From a poetic composition entitled "How to Lose Weight":

"The question of how to lose weight is a key problem facing our national economy, since finding a solution to this problem would enable us to resolve all of our difficult housing problems. For example, a family of four persons slims down and converts their four-room apartment into two two-room apartments, thereby creating another two-room apartment to help meet the needs of the state housing allocation office. Six hundred thousand Wrocław residents reduce to the point where their dimensions are equivalent to a population of 300,000, thereby doubling the size of our housing stock.

—To lose weight,
This is our national cause.
Łódź, Poznań and Warsaw
Are losing weight.
To lose weight:
This means to take the lead.
The fatter part of the nation
Is losing weight.
To lose weight
And be like a board or a stick.
Lose weight!

Until there is nothing more to lose.
And then there will be lots of room
For those who forgot to lose weight.
(*Report on Materials Censored,* December 1–15, 1974)

3. *Gierek's "economic maneuver"*

The "Świdnica Basement" Young Workers' Club, under the Voivodship Administration of the Union of Socialist Youth, submitted a program entitled "A Walk and a Song." We challenged three numbers: J. Pietrzak's "Communiqué," D. Pietryk's "Reception in Color" and "Szpilki's *Little Economics Dictionary*" by Z. Lewandowicz and A. Potemkowski.

Here are some of the "terms" from the last number:

BANKRUPTCY—Insolvency. Inability to pay debts.

"In a socialist system, there is fortunately no such thing as bankruptcy, and so this is a completely theoretical notion. In the event of financial difficulty, an enterprise simply shifts to categories of planned deficit. There is some conjecture that this clever method of avoiding bankruptcy was actually developed in this country. . . ."

ECONOMIC INCENTIVES—Means of material encouragement used to improve the effectiveness of the work of a unit or entire group. They are usually in the form of money.

"There are instances in history where economic incentives have produced the anticipated, but not the intended, effect."

EXPORT—Sale of goods abroad or the rendering of services for a foreign party in return for a fee.

DOMESTIC EXPORT—Sale of goods or rendering of services to domestic parties for foreign exchange, as, for example, in the case of the Polish Savings Bank.

"Export is a very important matter, since export rejects are widely sought on the market and highly appreciated by customers. Unfortunately, despite great efforts, we have not yet managed to provide everyone with an adequate supply of export rejects. . . ."

INVESTMENTS—Outlays intended for the creation and expansion of fixed assets.

"An example of a profitable investment might be the hanging of a piece of metal with the inscription 'Express' on a bus, thus making it possible to raise bus fares. The investment is amortized very quickly, to everyone's satisfaction. . . ." (*Report on Materials Censored,* May 1–15, 1974)

4. *Official ceremonies*

And here is Jan Pietrzak's [the head of Poland's most famous and consistently critical cabaret, Pod Egidą, in Warsaw] "Communiqué":

"According to the Polish Press Agency, a government delegation of

the Paltic Federation arrived today in the capital of Central Amitosis.
Heading the delegation is the First Chairman of the Great Supreme
Council of the Paltic United Revolutionary Worker-Peasant Organiza-
tion in Alliance with the Working Intelligentsia. At the station, the
Secretary-General of the Permanent Presidium of the All-National
Assembly of the Working Populace of Cities, Villages and Settlements
and Part of the Citizenry Residing Outside of Towns, Villages and
Settlements of the Central Republic of Amitosis greeted the delegation.
Welcoming addresses were given by: the First . . . and the Secretary.
. . . In the afternoon, the First Chairman . . . treated the Secretary-
General . . . to luncheon. On the other hand, in the evening hours, the
Secretary-General . . . gave a dinner in honor of the First Chairman.
. . . During the dinner, toasts were proposed by: the First Chairman
and the Secretary-General. . . .

"Tomorrow, in the morning hours, official talks will begin between
the delegations, which are headed by: the First . . . and the Secretary. . . .

"Tomorrow, during the afternoon hours, we will issue the next
communiqué and give comprehensive information about this interesting political event." (*Report on Materials Censored,* May 1–15, 1974)

Cabaret programs that hit too hard, too clearly and too often were
simply forbidden completely, especially when they were produced by
amateur student or worker groups who couldn't fight the decision.
Their supervisors were themselves far from deeply committed to the
cabarets. This made such censorship even easier. The censors watched
these informal groups closely because, even though the audience for
such groups was small, they were drawn from the very workers and
students the Gierek regime wanted to convince that everything was
all right. In one case:

A script from the cabaret "Dynamo," entitled "Three Times Like
This," was challenged in its entirety. The script had been submitted
through the departmental council of the Polish Socialist Students'
Union attached to the Department of Economics and Social Science of
the Main School of Planning and Statistics. The script portrayed our
social and political institutions in a malicious and critical manner, with
references to personnel policy, the quality of propaganda and "uncompromising" journalism, and the new system of stipends. It pointed out
the superficiality of the slogans about a "new Poland," characteriz-
ing it as an illusory antidote to compensate for the shortcomings
of our society, and it derided the constitutional rights and duties of

the citizens of the Polish People's Republic, pointing to limitations of civil liberties through programming "from above" and the total surveillance of society. (*Report on Materials Censored,* May 16–31, 1974)

Major cabaret groups posed a far greater problem for the censors. These were well-established institutions that had long exercised the right to satirize society and were a basic part of the intellectual milieu. Hence they could not simply be shut down the way the more ephemeral factory and student cabarets could. Established cabarets did not appear and disappear as the members of their companies came and went. Particular acts, songs and routines could always be deleted, but the news of such censorship often spread and became a "cause" in and of itself. And so the authorities generally let such cabarets produce satires to placate the intellectuals, while trying to keep their programs and very existence a secret, in part by limiting audiences through making tickets hard to get and the number of performances as small as possible.

When Warsaw's most established cabaret, Pod Egidą, broke with unwritten protocol regarding the heroes of the past and satirized the perquisites and pretensions of some underground resistance fighters of World War II, it got great play in the media. It was, after all, an act of nonconformism that attacked the last revered institution in Poland. Or rather, it would have, had the censors not intervened.

Main Office for Control of Press,
  Publications and Public Performances
Instruction, Evaluation and Control Group
No. ZI-Pf-132/6/76

> Warsaw, January 30, 1976
> C O N F I D E N T I A L
> Copy No. 25

Informative Note No. 6

During the past few days, several publications *(Kultura, Szpilki, Polityka, Zarzewie)* have presented for publication materials devoted to Jan Pietrzak and the Pod Egidą Cabaret. On the basis of the KTT feature in *Kultura,* No. 4, and the response of Jerzy Urban, which was to appear in *Polityka,* No. 5, it may be concluded that this concurrence is not a mere coincidence. In view of the fact that there are an increasing number of attempts to publish items on this subject, and in light of the nature of the programs of the Pod Egidą Cabaret, we have eliminated a review of the cabaret's program from Issue No. 5 of *Szpilki,* along with related drawings and four sets of song lyrics. After learning of our opinion, the editors of *Polityka* removed J. Urban's article, entitled "The Pietrzak Affair," from Issue No. 5, and the editors of *Zarzewie* removed M. L. Szwajkowska's article "Call for an Open Life" from Issue No. 6.

Deputy Group Director
Janusz Buchalski

enclosures: 4
Distributed according to the list

Guarding and Remaking Film Images

With film, as with books and dramatic productions, the censors could control production and distribution, as well as critical reception. Censors and cultural authorities often limited the number of films that could be produced, and were quite critical of films once they had been made. At the same time, however, film was an exportable product, so the censors were told not to allow Polish movies that might be exported to be attacked in the mass media. One of the major concerns was filtering out any criticism of the Polish film industry:

A number of critical comments were also made concerning Polish cinematography. For example, the following was written about the current situation in the film industry, and particularly the production of films for television: "Generally, screenplays were delayed, especially when they concerned contemporary problems. Nor is the making and approval of a film any kind of guarantee of quick distribution" *(Słowo Powszechne).* In another item, the statement was made that "the level of professionalism of our film industry has been behind the times for so long that no one can even imagine it being otherwise" *(ITD).* The way in which screenplays are approved was criticized even more strongly. In one case, it was stated that "there has been an increase in the number of reviewers," a situation the author termed "disturbing." It was noted that "a similar setup existed in the past and was sufficiently discredited at that time." It was also stated that "the pre-release screening for representatives of the film industry was losing its importance," since assessments of films "are formed and developed by people not involved in the creation of the image . . ." *(Życie Literackie)*.

It was also written that "If we could measure the vitality of the Polish film industry and cinematic culture by the number of personnel changes in this field, we would undoubtedly be the greatest cinematic power in the world." Film periodicals were characterized as "petty periodicals," whose quality, in the wake of the most recent personnel changes, "has reached its nadir" (DKF publishing house of Wrocław Polytechnic). *(Bulletin of Themes of Materials Censored,* Second Quarter, 1974)

The censors refused to permit even veiled references to the fact that films were submitted to any kind of censorship:

These critiques, a review of reviews, and the passage printed below were deleted from B. Seidler's article "Filmmakers' Conference" *(Życie Literackie,* No. 19), which contained an account of the Third Congress of the Filmmakers' Association:

". . . 'The greatest stain on our honor are the films that are lying on the shelves,' Kawalerowicz [film director] told the congress, adding quickly that this opinion has not been expressed by everyone in the film industry because many of these films are unknown [even] in the cinematic milieu, or are shrouded in myth or ambiguous evaluation. The decision to hold back a film always creates a stir in our milieu, and for a director it is a moment of personal tragedy. The highly emotional way in which such a decision is received by the film team and by the cinematic milieu in general is due largely to the absence of clear and authentic information about the criteria used in deciding whether a film is to be released. And yet the profession would probably benefit the most from a discussion of those films that exhibit the most extreme errors. A clarity in both critical and positive assessments of film is one of the basic elements necessary for activating and mobilizing the profession." . . . *(Report on Materials Censored,* May 1–15, 1974)

Some films, even after having been reviewed by the heads of Polish Television, who included some of Gierek's closest associates, were not approved by the censors. Or they were considered sensitive enough to warrant special instructions for their coverage in the mass media. For example, a short satirical series on the foibles of Polish factory managers caused a sensation, so the party daily had to step in to provide a "proper" ideological interpretation:

Main Office for Control of Press,
Publications and Public Performances
Instruction, Evaluation and Control Group
No. ZI-Pf-132/39/75

Warsaw, December 23, 1975,
C O N F I D E N T I A L
Copy No. 24

Informative Note No. 38

A review of the television series *The Directors* appeared in *Trybuna Ludu* on December 22, 1975. The opinions and commentary on recent Polish history (particularly the December events [the workers' strikes of 1970 over price increases, which resulted in Gierek's takeover]) that it contained are a model for dealing with these matters in other reviews of the series. The presentation of *The Directors* on television does not imply an opening of press discussion of the political problems of recent years or a change in our criteria for evaluating material on this subject.

Group Director
Julian Pelczarski

Distributed according to the list

Other films, including those by world-famous Polish directors such as Andrzej Wajda, were allowed to be produced and shown to limited audiences. But, like many books and theater productions, they were not acknowledged in the media. When reviews were permitted of Wajda's film *Man of Marble,* about the fate of idealistic and not so idealistic workers during the Stalinist era, they had to have the approval of the Press Department of the Central Committee:

168. Until the setting of a date for the premiere of the new film directed by Andrzej Wajda, *Man of Marble,* all material (statements, reviews, reporting, interviews, showing schedules and so on) concerning this film may be published only after editors have received the approval of the Department of Press, Radio and Television of the PZPR Central Committee.
This instruction is intended solely for the information of the censors.

This film clearly did not correspond to the needs of the Gierek propaganda system. But cinema, in general, in contrast to theater or even cabaret, was also viewed by the Polish authorities as an ideological tool, and they were concerned not only with controlling or screening out negative images, but with finding ways to enhance the propaganda value of films through well-orchestrated media film criticism. In connection with this goal, a number of theaters began to preface the Western films they showed with a short ideological reinterpretation of their content.

Something very similar was attempted with Wajda's earlier (1975) film, *The Promised Land,* a cinematic version of Władysław Reymont's classic novel about industrialization and urbanization in nineteenth-century Poland. Even the experts of the Central Committee's Committee for Ideological Education became involved, seeking to provide a reinterpretation that would make the film useful as propaganda in Poland and abroad. The document below represents their attempt to deal with the film version of this classic tale about three young men (a dispossessed member of the Polish gentry, a Jew and a German) who try to capitalize on the opportunities offered by the new weaving industry in the booming textile city of Łódź in the latter half of the nineteenth century. Their friendship and their falling out, as well as their reactions to the problems of ownership and competition, provide the film with its major theme. The censors, however, were instructed to manage reviews so that they followed the lines sketched out in the document below:

Main Office for Control of Press,
   Publications and Public Performances
Instruction, Evaluation and Control Group
No. ZI-Pf-132/18/75

Warsaw, July 16, 1975
C O N F I D E N T I A L
Copy No. 24

Informative Note No. 18

I am attaching, for the information of censorship groups, "Comments on the Discussion Concerning A. Wajda's Film *The Promised Land,*" drawn up by the Department of Ideological Education of the Central Committee of the PZPR.

Group Director
Julian Pelczarski

Distributed according to the list

Comments on the Discussion Concerning A. Wajda's Film *The Promised Land*

A. Wajda is one of the four Polish film directors who have reached a position of high status in the world at large. He is one of the two (Zanussi being the other) who work in Poland. His cinematic and theatrical work as well as the interviews he has given permit us to conclude that he has no ideological or political commitment to our side. Rather, he has assumed the position often taken by artists, that of the "unbiased judge" of history and the present, believing that he has both the right and the ability to add a measure of humanism and morality to all of the world's problems, and that to do this he does not need either Marxism or any other sociophilosophical system [to support him].

In *The Promised Land*, Wajda's personal point of view happened to coincide with a class interpretation of history. This was a new and unexpected development in his career.

As a result, these two developments—i.e., the view of Wajda justified by his earlier work and the surprising change in *The Promised Land* —have been a cause for confusion in our film criticism, which even at best has never been very strong in terms of either its content or its political point of view. Three extreme approaches to viewing this film have appeared as a result:

1. Emphasis of the nationalist element. Both extreme and naïve points of view have been represented here: Sweden did not want to allow the film to be shown, feeling that it contained various anti-Semitic elements, a view shared by some in this country. B. Nosal and B. Krzywobłocka, on the other hand, feel that Wajda elevates the virtues of the Jewish characters at the expense of the Poles, a viewpoint that is also shared by many viewers. Lost in an analysis of Wajda's intent, B. Nosal went so far as to conjecture that the film was referring to March 1968.

2. Emphasis of the class element. In this case, it is stressed that Wajda has been successful in portraying a period of history and understood the growing class exploitation and class awareness in a very dramatic way, with much sympathy for the working class.

3. Emphasis of the aesthetic element and on artistic matters.

If we look at *The Promised Land*, without involving ourselves in earlier assessments of the director or with the repercussions evoked by the film, we find that the film expresses a proper ideological point of view, convincingly presented, and that the work's nationalistic elements do not drown out its class analysis. If the film is viewed from this perspective, Borowiecki is the least distasteful figure of the three, with more positive characteristics than the other two, the German and the Jew. Somewhat confused by this fact, B. Nosal, contradicting his earlier assumptions, has tried to determine whether Wajda is attempting to portray a model of a man in an epoch of accelerated economic development.

But not only the film, but the opinions circulating about it in society must be considered as a social fact. It must be remembered that this film evoked an especially great emotional response because, rightfully or not, it was interpreted in a nationalistic fashion. And it must be taken into consideration that this film was condemned for being pro-Semitic and anti-Polish. Drawing the attention of society to these questions has had its undoubted advantages, if only the greater sensitivity with which the scholarly community subsequently viewed certain historical works of a dubious character. In the case of *The Promised Land,* however, this sensitivity may lead to certain losses in the area of propaganda.

In discussions of this film—both published and unpublished—a kind of special "struggle over Wajda" has been apparent. Those who remember Wajda's earlier work are mistrustful of this film and its class point of view, seeing behind its seemingly correct class position another element: anti-Polishness. Others are alarmed by Wajda's adoption of the ideals of apoliticism and neutrality vis-à-vis the present system. Pro-Zionist circles are also alarmed, seeing in the film an attack on the values they espouse.

The international popularity of Wajda increases the propaganda value of his works. It would seem, therefore, that *The Promised Land* should be used for propaganda purposes, in two different ways.

First, it is not often that one is confronted with a Polish film that combines an effort to portray aspects of historical materialism on one hand with a high degree of aesthetic achievement on the other. And here, after all, Wajda has portrayed the exploitation of the working class, the solidarity of capital, and the ideals and dedication of the representatives of the growing working-class movement. (It is noteworthy that he does not deal with the nationality of the worker activists, precursors of the class struggle.) Both for a younger viewer in this country and for one abroad, for whom Wajda's name is an important recommendation, the film is a good lesson in our way of thinking.

Secondly, it should be cautiously emphasized that Wajda has made clear his class point of view.

Such a point of view, by reinforcing what has happened, may help to distance Wajda from those circles that are unwilling to see art as politically committed, and may bring him closer to our propaganda art circles.

It would seem useful to slowly quiet the discussion concerning this film, and not permit people to bring up nationalist elements—which are essentially secondary—but to emphasize the class elements and perhaps the aesthetic elements. Exaggerated praise for Wajda should be avoided absolutely. It is the work that should be praised, not the author. Wajda must not be turned into the bard of Marxism, but the objective, ideological educational value of *The Promised Land* should be emphasized.

Warsaw, February 4, 1975

Why a Cultural Crisis?

In all these areas—books, theater, film—the censors tried to maintain images that accorded with the leadership's demands. To this end, they had to excise inappropriate images from the past as well as the present. At the same time, they felt it necessary to allow some cultural productions to serve as a vent for social discontent. This meant, in theory, compliance with the adage of Antoni Słonimski, "Either books or sausage," allowing discontent to express itself largely in the field of culture. But the Gierek leadership was not too willing to make the simple trade-off: of a measure of cultural self-expression for social peace. By the mid-seventies the economy was so overextended that the funding of cultural activities would have forced the regime to divert funds and resources they wanted to use for industrial investment. It should also be remembered that the members of this leadership were "engineers," for whom culture was ultimately expendable if it could not be used to create a new society. What this meant for the censors was that they had to not only ban "questionable" material, but also limit the audience for certain artistic events to those who seemed to need a richer cultural fix in order to be satisfied. Ultimately, the censors attempted to black out enough criticism and discussion to create an illusion of cultural development and freedom when neither existed in Poland in the mid-seventies or would exist until the fall of the Gierek regime in September 1980.

10 / **CONCLUSIONS**

C ENSORSHIP, intended by Gierek and his predecessors to strengthen and ensure their rule, ultimately helped make it impossible for a Communist Party leadership to rule Poland. Instead of creating popular support for communism and Communist leaders, the censored media convinced the population that "the press lies" and that so do the Communist leaders who control it. Instead of giving the rulers greater control over the minds of the ruled, the gaps between reality and media images left Poles with no alternative but to create their own independent media. Instead of making Poles feel that they were one with their leaders, censorship made them feel that their world and that of their rulers did not intersect. Instead of streamlining policy making by keeping it from being mired in endless debates, censorship mired policy makers in ignorance. Instead of giving the leaders control over their own government, censorship protected the failing economy and the growing bureaucracy from public scrutiny. In the end, then, the leadership's investment in developing a massive bureaucracy of censors carefully directed by trusted party men to deny all failures in the system was one of the things that cost Gierek and his men their power and left his successors with so little authority that they could not stop Solidarity or be equal partners in negotiations with them.

The workers who struck the Gdańsk shipyards in 1980, like the rest of the population in Poland, were avid consumers of the media the censors reviewed so carefully. But the more they read and saw, the less they believed either the media or their bosses and the less attention they paid to their specific messages. In research done in the mid-seventies, those who claimed to have read the press often did not remember what they had read or even how the papers they claimed to have read looked. As pointed out by a group of establishment intellectuals who organized themselves in 1978 to search for explanations of Poland's problems and a way out of Poland's growing crisis, in their report on "Experience and the Future of Poland":

> A Polish citizen experiences the meanderings of politics and planning more or less as he experiences changes in the weather: as important changes he must adapt to but whose causes—wholly external—are not worth exploring more deeply, since he has no way of influencing them. . . .
>
> What is more, this system has created something that is more dangerous than indifference and cynicism, something that surely was not intended: it has created a state of collective *informational* psychosis. One week a couple of fires break out in a capital city of one and a half million people [Warsaw]: well, then, some mysterious arsonist must be on the prowl! Perhaps it is a sign of a power struggle [in the leadership]! Or posters are put up—as they are every year—announcing a call-up for military service: well, then, it must be a general mobilization; they are sending our boys to Vietnam! Or what about the explosion in the General Savings Bank at the Rotunda [an explosion at the center of Warsaw's main business district in 1979 that the Warsaw government blamed on a gas leakage]? Obviously a time bomb, dynamite, sabotage, a provocation!*

To fill the voids that caused this "information psychosis," Poles turned to sources that the censors did not control. They made careful and regular use of the various Polish-language broadcasts from the West, such as Radio Free Europe, heard by 17 million Poles weekly; the Voice of America, heard by nearly 9 million Poles weekly; and the BBC Polish broadcasts, heard by almost 7 million weekly.† Beyond these Western broadcasts, Poles depended on their own observations and gossip with friends and co-workers. This made family dinner conversations, social gatherings, plant and professional club meeting rooms, and even buses and crowds standing in long lines important media for Poles searching for information they could not find in the mass media controlled by the censors.

*Experience and the Future Discussion Group, *Poland Today* (Armonk, N.Y.: M. E. Sharpe, 1981), p. 25.
†The Board for International Broadcasting, *1983 Annual Report*, p. 17.

After the workers' strikes of June 1976, a group of dissident intellectuals formed KOR, the Workers' Defense Committee, one of whose purposes was to aid workers fired or jailed for participating in these strikes and to see to it that information about the government's actions, censored from the regular press, did circulate. They took it upon themselves to develop an elaborate and reliable series of journals independent of the censors. With these, and a lengthy list of books and university-level courses conducted in private apartments beyond the censors' reach (the "Flying University"), they tried to combat what they felt was the government's use of censorship to create an ignorant population that could be manipulated and made to follow orders. By the end of the seventies, these independent publishers were producing some thirty regular journals filled with information, critical analysis and literature that would not have been tolerated by the censors. Rather than succumb to the veil of silence that the authorities attempted to pull around them and their publications, most of the authors and publishers of Poland's uncensored or independent press listed their names and addresses in what they published. For, they contended, while censorship was beyond the law, their work was perfectly within the letter of the law.

The audience for Poland's parallel, independent media was far larger than the number of copies of any given journal that could be printed on an eclectic assortment of homemade, stolen and smuggled printing equipment—with ink and paper taken from state supplies by printers, bought from sympathetic salespeople in stores or concocted from whatever could be found. With volunteers and paid employees working in basements and various apartments odd and long hours to avoid drawing the attention of the police, who could arrest them and confiscate their equipment, these publishers were able to put out 200 copies of individual books and over 7,000 copies of major monthlies, such as the *KOR Information Bulletin,* at a time. Clearly, no underground publisher could match the resources and reach of journals supported by the government and doing its service. But the publications earned enough respect to be sought after, passed from hand to hand, and discussed by individuals from far outside the opposition movement itself. By the dissident publishers' own estimates, for every copy of a periodical they could print there would be at least thirty readers and countless numbers of other Poles who heard reports and readings from its pages over Western radio broadcasts. Despite all of this, however, dissident publications did not penetrate far beyond

Poland's intellectual centers. But for those who could either get copies or hear, through friends or from Western radio broadcasts, about the issues they raised, these journals satisfied some of their hunger for information and for discussions of the failings and viable alternatives to current government policies.

Where the opposition press was concerned, the Gierek regime found itself with few alternatives in the late seventies. It could do little beyond harassing those who were involved, for any sterner measures would spark popular indignation and protests, or alarm their much-needed Western creditors about human rights violations in Poland. Also, the myopia of those who ran the regime's media establishment prevented them from competing with the new, uncensored and more credible presses of the dissidents. Instead, the government's continued unwillingness to admit its errors and move out from behind the shield of the censors created the ground for the work of the opposition and only helped it grow stronger.

In the end, the information blocks censorship put up succeeded not only in weakening the Communist leaders' authority but also in weakening the traditional role and authority of establishment intellectuals: journalists and writers were *not* the leaders of revolution and change in Poland in 1980, as they had been in earlier years. The reasons for this were complex. Because for the most part only those who wrote what the regime wanted or would tolerate could get their work published, the writers who were published came to be regarded by their readers as mere handmaidens of the regime. They had no way to communicate to their readers that much of what they had tried to say had been penciled out by the censors. Readers made it clear to journalists that they no longer saw them as their best advocates in the system as they had when they regularly contacted journalists by letter or in person with requests that they intervene to solve their problems. By the late seventies, readers no longer trusted the official media enough to turn to the press openly for help with problems. The number of letters and requests for help that came to the media declined at the very time when the problems of daily life were increasing. Readers had come to have so little trust in the media that they even refused to sign their names to the letters that they did send, and turned to journalists less and less frequently for protection.

Censorship further weakened the intellectuals' potential for leadership by denying them the very stuff of their work: facts and the interchange of ideas. Most intellectuals and policy makers could not even get essential data to make and defend their decisions. In every area, information was unavailable or was forbidden. According to the 1978 report of establishment intellectuals, "Experience and the Future of Poland," "even those who arranged purchases of licenses and machinery, those who spent this borrowed money, did not know the figures of the national debt."* Party Central Committee members not in Gierek's inner circle found their statements censored in the press and found themselves being ordered about by party propagandists or discussing policies without knowing what was really being considered. For instance, the potential problems of and the best propaganda approach on the 1976 price increases were discussed with leading party journalists and editors three days prior to their announcement with none of those gathered in the party conference hall being told what the price increases would be.†

Censorship and the world it created cut intellectuals off from far more than just their traditional public forums and the information they required. It also cut them off from each other and from the top leaders they were supposed to advise. If they elected not to publish in the dissident publications so as not to be blacklisted from publishing in establishment journals, they had little chance to have others outside their own circles know what they were really thinking and doing. Nor were they able to serve as funnels of information for the Gierek leadership. As censorship colored the images that were printed in the media, it colored the information that the leadership received. As less and less could be published, journalists made less and less of an attempt to find out and reveal what was happening in the society. Managers and bureaucrats didn't need to worry about whether their mistakes would be revealed. And, ultimately, neither Gierek nor the men around him wanted to hear what was going wrong. In the end, Poland's intellectuals were walled off by the political bureaucracy, at once corrupt, ineffective and immutable. For them, as long as this bureaucracy existed, there could be no real change. By the end of the seventies, writers and journalists considered both as preparing for a transformation of socialism, as the regime demanded, and engaging in direct criticism of it, as they often said they would like to, as purposeless. Gierek and those around him had come to believe in

Poland Today, p. 24.

†Mieczysław Rakowski, *Rzeczpospolita na progu lat osiemdziesiątych* (The Polish People's Republic on the threshold of the eighties) (Warsaw: Państwowy Instytut Wydawniczy, 1981), p. 250.

the fantasy land they insisted be communicated to those they ruled.

The victories of the shipyard workers in Gdańsk in August 1980, and the others all over Poland who followed their lead, spelled the end to Gierek's fantasy. With the signing of the accord between the government and the workers' strike committee in Gdańsk on August 31, Polish government officials conceded to Polish workers the right not only to strike and have an independent union to protect the economic gains they had been promised, but also to have a media system open for a variety of viewpoints. To ensure that this actually happened, government negotiators and Solidarity leaders concluded that there would have to be a special censorship law written and passed by Parliament.

When Edward Gierek was ousted and the accords allowing independent trade unions, the right to strike and more open media as well as economic concessions were put into effect, Polish journalists and media officials found themselves working in an entirely new situation. No longer did the Polish public simply hunger for information; now they demanded it. If the old established media did not provide it, citizens wrote and printed their own papers. From the broadcast of the signing of the Gdańsk accords by Mieczysław Jagielski, the head of the government negotiating team, and Lech Wałęsa, Solidarity's leader, brandishing an oversized souvenir pen from the Pope's trip to Poland, to the open discussions of Poland's economic mismanagement, the return of discussions on Poland's historical heritage and the long feature interviews with Solidarity's various regional leaders, there was no question but that the face of the old Polish media was transformed after August 1980. Even mention of censorship ceased to be censored. Articles and broadcasts that journalists never thought would appear suddenly appeared. And, as time went on, new journals representing a whole spectrum of views joined the lists of publications from established government publishing houses.

On closer scrutiny, however, the transformation of the media was not simple or unambiguous. Neither the censorship bureaucracy nor the party officials who had directed the media were willing simply to cede power and allow the media to run free. Even as the party's leaders fell into disgrace and Poles at every level took action to get the kind of information they had sought for so long, the censorship bureaucracy that filtered and planned the media's messages remained in place. Only its orders and a few of its top bosses were shifted. Just as orders were changed in the seventies when new orders were more convenient, the censors' directives were changed whenever the battle plans to rein in Solidarity changed. For example, though Polish television had broadcast the signing of the Gdańsk accords, photographs of the ceremony were not initially approved by the censors. And as the battle between Solidarity and the government continued, what was publishable one day or in one journal often was not allowed the next day or in another journal. Therefore, though the battles within the party and government were so heated that journalists could appeal the strictures placed on them at the behest of one group or leader to others within the leadership, journalists were still not the masters of their own media. Censorship did not end or limit itself; it continued to protect its bureaucratic masters even as it was a target of attack.

The first few months after the accords between the government and Solidarity's new leaders had been signed were filled with euphoria over the appearance of information and criticism that could never have appeared in the Gierek era. But the euphoria was short-lived. It soon became clear that the appearance of negative reports in the press could not be equated with real press freedom. Nor, perhaps, was the commitment of some journalists and their editors to a freer press sufficient to combat the party leaders' determination to hold the line, a determination strengthened by the conviction that "he who does not control the media, does not control power."* Journalists found themselves able to report as they wished, but only in organs that the party leadership did not consider important. What they could do in media like television and *Trybuna Ludu,* the central party paper, which the party leaders saw as their own, remained ultimately the decision of the party leadership.

For all the activity of Solidarity units within Polish radio and television, and for all the freedom of discussion and criticism that reigned within their offices, when air time came, radio and television still remained the organs of the party leadership. Initially, Polish radio was allowed to report the dramatic victories of Solidarity and the bitingly critical discussions that went on all over Poland with little interference from their censors. Parts of television programming also turned to the kinds of subjects that had long been prohibited. Cultural programming enjoyed a renaissance: not only were new programs aired that could not have been even proposed before, but canister after

---

*The statement has often been used by top leaders in the Jaruzelski government in arguing with journalists for greater restraint.

canister of films that had been shelved by the censors were brought out and aired. Television news, however, was carefully managed. Not even the regular censors were trusted to review all of its programming. The top party official in charge of the media and propaganda came every second or third night to review the prime time news just as his predecessor had reviewed the nightly news in the seventies. The distortions that the increasingly conservative and intransigent men who directed the party's propaganda insisted on in television reports about Solidarity and its disputes with the government became a leading irritant to the Solidarity leaders. To much of the population, for whom television was the prime news source, the gulf between reality and reporting was overriding proof that the media still lied, even as they relished the critical information that appeared elsewhere, or the flowering of cultural programming on television. For even when creative and critical programming was allowed on television and radio, be it broadcasts of parliamentary debates or cultural affairs programs about Poland's minorities or long-banished moments of Polish history, it was usually done with the lowest budgets and in the least popular time slots.

For the print media, the controls also became more and more obvious as the conflicts between Solidarity and the government became more insoluble. When the police beat up demonstrators in the Bydgoszcz incident of March 1981, television news roundly condemned the demonstrators, and Polish newspapers and periodicals were instructed to follow this example. In fact, many elected either not to report anything or to try and include their own version of the events—versions that differed dramatically from the official police whitewash. By this time, even the print media were less and less able to go their own way on issues that the censors and their bosses designated as important. Journalists found themselves hamstrung on critical issues by galley sheets returned from the censors' office with phrases and entire articles marked out in a censor's red pencil. Individuals fought with the censors to have their articles published. They also barraged the party leadership with public protests from groups in the journalists' association over the continuation of irrational and excessive censorship. All these protests succeeded, at best, in allowing a few articles to appear. They did not stop the censors. In fact, journalists found that they had very few means by which to ensure that they could do their jobs as they felt they should be done. All they could do was make public protests about the increasing pressure on them to distort their reporting; enforce among themselves a code of ethics that prohibited journalists from attacking each other or lying; and, when no other alternative was available, simply refuse to publish rather than present distorted information. Beyond this, many journalists, including the heads of the Association of Polish Journalists, were serving as negotiators between Solidarity, leading political organizations of intellectuals, and the regime.

By January 1981, printers had grown so incensed about the steady increases in the censors' red marks in the copy they had to set in type that they took matters into their own hands. Initially, they threatened to leave blank spaces in the copy whenever the censors had cut something. As a compromise, after frantic negotiations with the government and journalists, they agreed merely to mark the missing censored passages with three dots. When that did not discourage the censors, the printers went on strike. They delivered to Poland an almost "newspaperless Friday." A few issues of the party and military papers appeared on the stands owing only to the help of the military's own printers. In this action, the printers did not have the support of most of Poland's journalists, who saw it as an unprofessional incursion in their work. So, after leaving Poland without a press for a day, the printers in Warsaw went back to work, having demonstrated to the public and the government their fury over the continued censorship of the press. What remained was a very real sense of the threat of further printers' strikes in response to censorship decisions that they would not accept.

The strength of the censorship bureaucracy and the weakness of established journalists' and editors' efforts to combat it made it necessary in the minds of Solidarity activists to create and control their own media. From the very start, just as the strikes began, the authorities attempted to quell them by cutting off all telephone contact between striking workers and the outside. So, striking workers communicated with strikers in other cities and with the rest of Poland through messages scrawled on the walls of trains running from region to region. In large striking factories news sheets were printed with whatever equipment was available. These early union bulletins soon spawned a vast Solidarity media system, often ephemeral and never censored. Individuals and groups simply got paper from any source they could and found an available mimeograph machine to reproduce their "paper." The telex network that the Gierek regime had created to tie factory managers with their bosses in the central ministries was turned by the workers into a vast national news network. Solidarity's national bodies had their own news services and had even begun, in 1981, to produce cassettes with news and information that they played in factories during breaks.

But this groundswell of spontaneous communications did not fill the needs of the Solidarity organization any more than the increased information allowed in the mass media satisfied Poles' information hunger. The union leadership battled continuously with the government for the right to produce its own official weekly and for access to its own television program. The demand for access to television never got anywhere. Solidarity was allowed to set up offices in radio and television stations; the government promised to give Solidarity air time as a part of the regular programs and to include its representatives in discussions, but the government was never really willing to turn over time on its most powerful media to Solidarity. Giving Solidarity access to its own weekly was a more acceptable concession for the government. So, in April 1981, after much jockeying on both sides over the size of the paper, its circulation and the composition of the editorial staff, Solidarity's own official weekly, *Tygodnik Solidarność,* was born. Like other new journals springing up all over Poland to represent Solidarity groups and various professional groupings, *Tygodnik Solidarność* struck down all the old barriers and habits of self-censorship. Like these other journals, too, *Tygodnik Solidarność* was staffed primarily by Solidarity activists and new writers who had little or no experience as censored and self-censoring journalists. Those who were used to writing for the establishment press were in the minority, following the lead of the new recruits rather than controlling them. From the beginning, *Tygodnik Solidarność* served as far more than a union journal recording union business and official debates. In addition to publishing a complete record of the Solidarity Congress meetings and other official union activities and speeches, *Tygodnik Solidarność* provided a forum for discussing events in Polish history that had never before been raised publicly. Its pages were covered with revelations of the corruption and bad management that had mangled the Polish economy, as well as criticisms of the party and government authorities that were unthinkable elsewhere. After weeks of arguing with the censors, for instance, an interview with a former censor on life in the Main Office was published. Workers, professionals and economists from the universities also used the pages of *Tygod-*

nik Solidarność to argue alternative methods of saving Poland's economy as well as to review political life and move ahead into a new form of socialism.

Initially, all of this happened because *Tygodnik Solidarność* had a staff of both experienced and novice journalists who were unwilling to tolerate interference from the censors. They and the censors knew that behind the weekly stood a phalanx of Solidarity members who were willing to fight and strike for the independence of their own organ. The censors themselves were far less aggressive in censoring *Tygodnik Solidarność* than they were with respect to other journals except the large-circulation regional Solidarity publications (which began as spontaneous worker publications and became official regional organization organs if not government-licensed journals). Furthermore, having 10 million Solidarity members as backers gave those who worked on the journal a sense of another kind of power: they did not feel compelled to engage in the self-censorship that many established journalists and writers felt was necessary. In their debates with the censors and press officials who controlled not only what they could publish but also how they published and distributed their journals the editors held the trump card—they could threaten strikes of their printers and their union.

Solidarity did far more than create its own media. It broke with the established media. Even during the strikes of the summer of 1980, many Polish journalists who had appeared as supporters of the Gierek regime and its policies were simply not allowed to enter the striking shipyards and factories. Even their promises of support were viewed with suspicion. When the Solidarity Congress was held in August 1981, the meeting halls of Gdańsk were crowded with foreign television crews; Polish television was not allowed in. Its manipulated and distorted presentation of the news had so incensed Solidarity officials that they refused to allow Polish television to cover their convention unless they could review and approve any coverage of their own activities. This was something that the government refused to grant Solidarity. As a result, Polish television was forced to buy the British Broadcasting Corporation's reports on the congress in order to report the events of the day at the congress on their own seacoast. And, as a matter of principle, both before and after the convention, Solidarity officials in different plants and offices often directed journalists as to what they could cover and to whom they could talk—just as their predecessors from the party had. All of this further complicated the

information problems that were faced by government officials, journalists and Solidarity leaders alike. The relentless pressures exerted by
the Main Office for Control and the indefatigable, unceasing attempts
of the party's propagandists to transform events by manipulating their
descriptions had, through a curious, circuitous process, turned others
in the society into censors as well.

As the media changed and the censors and their bosses tried to stem
the tide of change, journalists and writers engaged in an examination
of their past failings and their hopes for the future. From the first
round of strikes in July 1980, journalists had to face the huge gulf
between what they could say and the compelling events they watched
all around them. They reported to their fellows what they knew that
censorship would not allow them to report to their readers. In response to their own sense of failure and the demands of the society,
the Association of Polish Journalists called an Extraordinary Congress in November 1980 to assess and realign their professional world.
Former opinion leaders in the profession, unable to publish for years
during the Gierek regime because they were too critical, were elected
to replace the loyal bureaucrats who had headed the association under
Gierek. In the course of their congress, the 337 delegates attacked
themselves as well as the ponderous and intrusive bureaucracy of the
censors for having created a media establishment that was neither
believed nor effective. They pressed for new institutional structures to
protect them and their work from outside interference so that they
could be real partners in politics, guiding and reflecting both the
population and the party leadership's views. In the end, they committed themselves to seeing to it that Poland had multiple sources of
information and that they would not have their thinking and writing
limited by either the official censors or the internal censors they had
each developed after many years of writing for the Polish press.

The Extraordinary Congress was only the beginning of the battle
for the Association of Polish Journalists. When the censors and party
propagandists allowed them to publish less and less, the association's
leaders spoke up publicly much more than they had before about the
censors' controls. By August 1981 censorship and direction had returned in such force that the association's top leaders drew up a
protest letter attacking the failure of the government to meet either
its promises or the demands of the population regarding media policy.
Ironically, only the Solidarity weekly could and would publish this
letter, whose appearance marked the beginning of the final battle

between the leaders of the journalism profession and those who controlled party propaganda. The letter's authors who were still party members, including the president of the Association, were all ousted from the party. Attacks on the letter and its authors were published in government-controlled papers all over Poland. Petitions were gathered both for and against the letter, with those who supported its views far outnumbering its opponents. And the censors increased their control over the media while government and party officials abandoned all attempts to work with the Association.

Paralleling the spontaneous moves for change in the media (and the attempts by party propagandists and censors to stop them) were discussions between representatives of intellectual organizations (such as the Writers' Union and the Association of Journalists), Solidarity leaders and government officials on the establishment of the censorship law. The goal of their negotiations conducted from September 1980 to August 1981, was to fulfill the agreements made in response to the striking Gdańsk workers' third demand, that the government

> respect freedom of expression and publication, as upheld by the Constitution of People's Poland, and . . . take no measures against independent publications as well as . . . grant access to the mass media to representatives of all religions.*

To this end, the government had promised not only that the Polish media would be made accessible to different points of view and to the Church, but also that a law would be put before Parliament to regulate censorship so that it protected only the legitimate "interests of the state." This was promised for October 1980, but there was so much disagreement over what the limits and controls on censorship should be that no drafts could be put up before the Polish Parliament until the end of July 1981. Even then, the divergences between the government proposal and the proposal drawn up by representatives of intellectual groups and Solidarity were so great that two drafts had to be presented for the Parliament to consolidate—the first time such a level of dissension had to be resolved in the Parliament.

For all of this disagreement, there was agreement among intellectuals that some degree of censorship was a necessity because of Poland's

---

*As translated in Abraham Brumberg, ed., *Poland: Genesis of a Revolution* (New York: Random House, 1983), p. 287.

position in the middle of the Soviet bloc, where too much deviance would bring a Soviet invasion. As one of Poland's most respected journalists said in the Parliament days after the initial accords were signed (in a speech that was censored because it was not deemed fit to be made public in its entirety):

> No reasonable person in Poland with a sense of responsibility demands today the complete abolition of censorship. What is needed is to limit its areas of responsibility, its powers and its criteria of evaluation, as well as to establish a procedure for appealing its decisions.*

Achieving these goals was not easy. Not only did more immediate demands of Solidarity's battle to establish itself push the regulation of censorship into the background in the winter and spring of 1981, but there were real differences between what the government felt was necessary and appropriate and what the group of intellectuals proposed "for the society" in their draft, which represented the views of Solidarity, the Church and intellectual organizations. These intellectual groups tried to use their expertise with censorship to devise a system where (1) interventions would be limited to only what was necessary (in light of Polish political realities) and (2) the censorship bureaucracy itself would be controlled by institutions other than the party and state bureaucracies. To achieve the latter goal, they insisted that the Main Office for Control be subordinate to the Parliament rather than to the Council of Ministers, as proposed by the government draft. The council, they pointed out, merely represented the ministries' vested interests in uncritical discussion. In the end, they compromised. The law, passed in August 1981, made the censors subordinate to the collective head of state, the Council of State, elected, at least formally, from the Parliament. To further ensure that the censors were independent of the administration and political élite, the law also provided for an independent review commission only one-third of which was to be selected by the prime minister and the rest of whom were to be representatives of the various political and social organizations.

To achieve the other objective—that interventions be limited to only what was necessary—the intellectuals and Solidarity leaders

---

*From a speech by Karol Małcużyński, a prominent journalist and delegate to the Polish Parliament, on September 5, 1980. The partial text was printed in *Słowo Powszechne*, September 10, 1980.

required of the government that there be clear specifications of what, who and by what process material could be censored. In order to prevent the kind of reinterpretation of "national security information" that had been used by the censors to justify their removal of everything from unflattering pictures of Gierek to reports of religious events, the censorship law listed ten specific catagories of information that could be removed. These were attempts to prohibit the Polish media from overstepping the bounds of Soviet tolerance. The censors were empowered basically to prevent anything that

—appealed for the overthrow, slander, ridicule or degradation of the Polish constitutional system;

—struck at the constitutional principles of the foreign policy of the Polish People's Republic and its alliances;

—disclosed information that constitutes state secrets, including economic secrets or official secrets concerning defense and the armed forces;

—publicized morally harmful topics, especially alcoholism, drug addiction, cruelty and pornography.

Because both the Polish constitutional arrangements and foreign policy principles were based in part on ensuring Soviet tolerance of Polish decisions by recognizing the leadership of the Communist Party and enshrining the Soviet's lead in foreign policy, these provisions attempted to ensure that the media would refrain from questioning the outer limits of the status quo in Poland.

With the new censorship law the censors also lost their right to review many of the publications and kinds of information that appeared in Poland. They were prohibited from tampering with the records of parliamentary discussions and speeches; court decisions; official forms and laws; maps, statistics and texts issued by official government agencies; music and art; and publications for members of the Church, unions and various professional and special-interest groups. Since union publications included all of Solidarity's journals, most of which were taken at least as seriously as the regular Polish media by the Polish population and by the Soviets, the law also allowed for individual journals to be put under the censors' control if they continually violated the "national interests" spelled out in the law.

The mass media were to remain censored, but they, too, gained a measure of protection. Censors' interventions could now be indicated by dots or blank spaces in the final copy, so that readers did not think that journalists or writers were the ones responsible for gaps in information or criticism. There were also specific limits imposed on how long a piece could be held by the censors before it had to be either approved or disapproved. This prevented the censors from using their old tactics of simply censoring by not ever either approving or disapproving, until the article or film in question lost its currency. As a further protection, journalists and writers were officially given the right they had long insisted on with their editors, to approve the publication of censored pieces, so that they did not find their names attached to something that had been censored into having a new meaning. There was also a provision for an administrative review court to which editors and writers could go to protest the censorship of their works and get an impartial hearing. This freed them from the vicious circle of having to appeal to the party officials who were the ones directing the censors and giving them instructions in the first place.*

The new censorship law was never really fully tested. In the two months between the time the law went into effect (October 1981) and the declaration of martial law, however, a number of cases concerning censorship were appealed to the courts. All were decided in favor of the right of journals to publish as they had planned. The necessity for these court cases was in itself an indication of the censors' refusal to be cowed by any legal regulations. And there were other indications that even as the Polish Parliament legalized a highly circumscribed form of censorship, the Jaruzelski regime went about limiting the media in other ways. Prices for newspapers and magazines were raised while paper allocations were cut. Supplies for television's more controversial broadcasts also dried up in the fall of 1981. And every journalist who spoke out or broached new, sensitive subjects was a target of attack: expulsion from the party or sharp, personal criticism in one of the conservative papers that had come to life in response to Solidarity's growth.

The declaration of the state of war by the Jaruzelski government on December 13, 1981, was the final demonstration of the threat a freer press held for the rulers of Poland. The media and journalists along with Poland's licensed hunters (who had the right to keep weapons)

---

*"The Law on the Control of Publications and Public Performances," issued June 16, 1981, as printed in *Zycie Warszawy*, August 21, 1981, Section IV (*Zycie i Nowoczesność*). For a discussion of the different proposals, see *Censorship: Issues and Documents*, Radio Free Europe, Polish Situation Report/23 (December 20, 1980), pp. 35–48.

were the only two groups other than Solidarity attacked directly in the initial declaration. All mass media but the military daily, *Żołnierz Wolności,* the central party daily, *Trybuna Ludu,* and radio and television were suspended from publication. Journalists who had been leaders in their own association and in Solidarity were interned or sought for internment. In fact, of all the professional groups in Polish society, it was the journalism profession that had the largest percentage of its membership detained. Ironically, their numbers included even some who had escaped the worst of the censors' cuts in the seventies, while others who had battled with censorship in the seventies, like Mieczysław Rakowski, Teodor Toeplitz, Wiesław Górnicki and Jerzy Urban, held prominent places in the martial law regime.

Martial law meant far more than a return to media control and an end to the hopes for change that Solidarity had given rise to. It involved a direct attack on the Polish media itself as well as an assault on Solidarity. Not only were many journalists interned, but most of the Polish media were simply suspended. Before a paper could resume publication or a television journalist return to work, each individual had to go before a verification committee and attest to his or her loyalty to the system and support for the suspension of Solidarity. Many refused to do this, while others were considered too tainted by their activity in the opposition even to be allowed this option. With the exception of journals like the Catholic *Tygodnik Powszechny* that had always battled the censors, few journals or journalists that had dared criticize the government in the heyday of Solidarity reemerged. Some traditional weeklies and monthlies that had published in Poland for years, such as *Literatura* and *Kultura,* had too few "trustworthy" staff members willing to continue to work in the Polish media system to reappear. Professional journals associated with professional groups like sociologists and historians who had taken a lead in the renewal disappeared for more than a year. Other journals—for example, *Polityka*—returned to the newsstands but with only part of their traditional staff members. According to estimates of former leaders of the Association of Journalists, over one-fourth of the nearly 10,000 journalists in Poland left the profession or moved to more marginal positions. Some went on early retirement. Many others decided to take on "honest work" making jewelry, selling books or working in other nonprofessional jobs. And some stayed in their profession but, either because they were blacklisted or because they would not condone the regime by staying in their old high-profile jobs, went to work on obscure journals like hunters' magazines, the journal of the Blind Artisans' Cooperative or the small Catholic journals that appeared. These marginal publications became havens for some of Poland's former leading journalists. But for all their new-found fame in the population, they had tiny circulations and virtually no guarantee of support, so they were not effective platforms for discussion.

The traditional media were now peopled with newcomers and less-established journalists who were afraid to take the risk of challenging the authorities, or established journalists who felt they should go along with martial law and the subsequent post-martial law regime. Neither the one nor the other gave the censors as much to censor. Instead, in the early months of martial law, as the workers rioted and demonstrated against the martial law regime and the suspension and eventual dissolution of their union, the mass media—dailies and television news—returned to most of the old formulas of Gierek's "propaganda of success." One difference was that this time the media stressed the hardships of life and blamed them on Solidarity.

The concession that the Jaruzelski regime did make to the lessons of the Gierek period and the explosion of Solidarity was to allow diversity of opinion to appear in weeklies and other limited-circulation journals. This they did in part as a requirement for getting experts to participate in their regime. For instance, when Czesław Bobrowski, one of Poland's leading economists, was asked by Wojciech Jaruzelski to set up an advisory commission on economic reform, he agreed to do so only under the condition that he have access to the media and that he be able to have the results of the commission's findings, however critical, published. In part, too, at least some of the leaders recognized that, for all their fury over what they regarded as the excesses of the media under Solidarity, the economic and political problems were virtually unresolvable without more open discussion than had been allowed in the seventies. And so discussion went on in some of the media, and new journals, many supported by both the conservative and liberal wings of the party as well as the Church, began to appear. Ironically, the relative freedom of many of these journals has not grown with the ending of martial law. New editors took over and the limits of censorship became clearer.

None of this initial apparent tolerance either abated intellectual fury and rejection of the regime or signaled a real rapprochement of the government with the nation's intellectuals. The first assault was the total disbanding of Poland's postwar Association of Journalists in

March 1982, scarcely three months after the declaration of martial law. The substitute organization that appeared, and the continued discussion over the fate of other intellectual organizations, did nothing to reduce the fury and alienation of journalists both in and out of the profession. And then, in preparation for the ending of martial law and the return to "normal" legal procedures which was to follow, the leaders once again moved to explicitly ensure their ability to control the media. The unions of actors, artists and finally writers, all of whom had been involved in preparing the new censorship law and fighting for freedom of expression in Poland, all were disbanded in the spring and summer of 1983 after over a year of suspension. A move was made to introduce a press law in Parliament that would have left journalists with little ability to protect their sources and to establish a supervisory press board to exert political control. Both the pro-regime Association of Journalists and the Church objected strongly to this and it was tabled. In addition to enchancing the powers of the police and security apparatus, Parliament was forced to pass revisions of the censorship law that added general clauses to each of the specific points under which censorship was allowed, making it possible to justify most kinds of intervention by reference to the loose language of the law and reducing the number of things that were free of censorship. Thus union papers, artistic exhibits and scholarly books were once again under the control of the censors. This was done, according to Jerzy Urban, the government press spokesman, to close off all possibilities of a reappearance of the press explosion of the Solidarity period.

Despite the tightening up of censorship, and although the repression of martial law dealt a severe blow to the system of dissident publications, it did not succeed in controlling the minds of the population or in creating media that fully served their interests. After sixteen months of relative freedom, Poland's former opinion leaders had either disappeared from the view of the wide public audience or were permanently disgraced in the eyes of most Poles by their cooperation with the regime and its media. This highlighted the isolation of the Jaruzelski leadership. It made cooperation and compromise impossible. And Poles were much more open about their disgust with the manipulation of the media than they had been before the days of Solidarity. Papers that previously had always been bought and read (even though usually not believed) now sat in newsstands. In some small towns, television sets were turned facing out the window and people took walks in the street during the evening news program to demonstrate their displeasure. But none of this affected the censorship process and the media it produced. Rather than back down, the Jaruzelski regime continued to rule with sporadic threats and public attacks on Solidarity. As their predecessors had, many in the Jaruzelski regime preferred to rely not on equal discussion with those they ruled, but on the kind of control and distortion the documents in this volume were intended to provide in the seventies, though with a greater emphasis on admitting that there were problems and opponents. And all this meant that, just as it had been in the mid-seventies, political change was both "an absolute necessity and an absolute impossibility"* for Poland in the early 1980s.

*Poland Today, p. 138.

APPENDIX

Polish Publications

"Annales" UMCS
  Annals of the University of Maria Curie-Skłodowska in Lublin
Apostolstwo Chorych (Mission to the Sick)
  Church publication for the sick
Archiwa, Biblioteki i Muzea Kościelne (Archives, Libraries and Church Museums)
  Publication concerning church archives, libraries and museums
Argumenty (Arguments)
  Social and cultural weekly of the Atheists' Association
Barwy (Colors)
  Social and cultural monthly for the Mazowsze region
Biblioteka Kaznodziejska (Library of Ethical Teachings)
  Religious publication for priests published in Poznań
Biuletyn Informacyjny (Information Bulletin)
  One of the most influential and long-standing news leaflets circulated by the underground Polish Home Army during the German occupation
Biuletyn Specjalny (Special Bulletin)
  Limited-circulation news bulletin published by the Polish Press Agency
Biuletyn Towarzystwa Kultury Moralnej (Bulletin of the Society of Moral Culture)
Budownictwo—Zeszyt Naukowy (Construction—Research Report)
Chrześcijanin w Świecie (The Christian in the World)
  Monthly published by a small Catholic group
Collectanea Theologica
  Quarterly published by the Polish Theological Society
Currenda
  Official bulletin, Roman Catholic Curia in Tarnów

Człowiek i Światopogląd (Man and World-View)
  Monthly published in Warsaw
Dookoła Świata (Around the World)
  Popular weekly magazine with emphasis on geography and travel
Dziennik Ustaw (Legal Reports)
  Official list of laws (including texts) passed by the Sejm (Polish Parliament)
Echo Celulozy (Cellulose Echo)
  Factory paper for independent newsprint workers
Ekonomista (The Economist)
  Quarterly published by the Economists' Association, Warsaw
Express Wieczorny (Evening Express)
  Popular tabloid evening newspaper
Forum (Forum)
  Weekly of selected translations from the foreign press
Gaz, Woda, Technika Sanitarna (Gas, Water, Sanitary Techniques)
  Monthly
Gazeta Białostocka (Białystok Gazette)
  Local newspaper circulated in the district of Białystok
Gazeta Handlowa (Trade Gazette)
  Weekly
Gazeta Olsztyńska (Olsztyn Gazette)
  Daily
Gazeta Robotnicza (Workers' Gazette)
Gazeta Warszawska (Warsaw Gazette)
  Daily
Gazeta Zielonogórska (Zielona Góra Gazette)
  Local newspaper circulated in the district of Zielona Góra
Głos Glinika (Voice of Glinik)
  Paper published by a machine works factory in Glinik Mariampolski, a
  district of Gorlice
Głos Pracy (Voice of Work)
  Daily of the Central Board of Trade Unions
Głos Wybrzeża (Voice of the Seacoast)
  Daily of Gdańsk
Gość Niedzielny (Sunday Visitor)
  Popular weekly on Catholic problems, published by the Roman Catholic
  Curia in Katowice
IKP (Ilustrowany Kurier Polski) (Illustrated Polish Courier)
  Bydgoszcz daily
Innowacje: Przegląd Techniczny (Innovation: Technical Review)
  Weekly published by the Polish Technical Organization (engineers' associ-
  ation)
ITD (Etc.)
  Students' weekly

Kalendarz Lubelski (Lublin Almanac)
  Published annually
Katecheta (Catechist)
  Bimonthly for teachers of Roman Catholic classes in schools
Kierunki (Directions)
  Weekly of the progressive Catholic movement
Koksochemik Wałbrzyski (Coke Chemist of Wałbrzych)
  Factory paper printed in Wałbrzych
Kraśnik Fabryczny
  Factory paper printed in Kraśnik Fabryczny
Kronika Diecezji Przemyskiej (Chronicle of the Przemyśl Diocese)
Kronika Diecezji Sandomierskiej (Chroncile of the Sandomierz Diocese)
Kultura (Culture)
  Cultural and social weekly
Kultura i Ty (Culture and You)
  Popular cultural monthly for youth, for distribution in community centers
  and libraries
Kurier Polski (Polish Courier)
  Daily sponsored by the Polish Democratic Party
Kwartalnik Historyczny (Historical Quarterly)
  Scholarly quarterly published in Warsaw by the Historical Association
Literatura (Literature)
  Cultural and social weekly
Magazyn Rodzinny (Family Magazine)
  Family monthly published by the Polish Society for the Family
Monitor Polski (Polish Monitor)
  Official register of government resolutions and decrees
Myśl Narodowa (National Thought)
Nasze Sprawy (Our Affairs)
  Factory paper from a chemical works in Inowrocław
Nowe Drogi (New Roads)
  Ideological journal of the Polish United Workers' Party
Nowa Kultura (New Culture)
  Cultural weekly published prior to 1956
Nowy Medyk (The New Medical Student)
  Journal published in Warsaw by medical students
Odgłosy (Comments)
  Social and cultural weekly from Łódz
Odra (The Oder)
  Cultural and social monthly published in Wrocław and circulated through-
  out the country
Orędownik Diecezji Chełmińskiej (The Chełmno Diocese Advocate)
Oświata Dorosłych (Adult Education)
  Monthly

Perspektywy (Perspectives)
 Political and social weekly
Plon (Harvest)
Pobrzeże (Seacoast)
 Sociocultural monthly from Koszalin
Podkarpacie (From the Carpathians)
Politechnik (Polytechnician)
 Weekly for students of technical academies
Polityka (Politics)
 Influential political and social weekly
Po Prostu (Plainly Speaking)
 Radical student weekly published in Warsaw through 1957
Postęp w Rolnictwie (Progress in Agriculture)
Prakseologia (Praxis)
 Quarterly
Prawo i Życie (Law and Life)
 Lawyers' Association weekly
Problemy Alkoholizmu (Problems of Alcoholism)
 Published by the Polish Society Against Alcoholism in Warsaw
Problemy Rad Narodowych (Problems of National Councils)
 Publication of the Institute of State and Law
Prosto z Mostu (Straight Talk)
Przegląd Historyczny (Historical Review)
 Popular historical quarterly published in Warsaw
Przegląd Kulturalny (Cultural Review)
Przegląd Sportowy (Sports Review)
 Sports daily
Przemysł Chemiczny (Chemical Industry)
 Monthly
Przyjaciółka (Girl Friend)
 Women's weekly intended especially for less-educated readers
Przyjaźń (Friendship)
 Journal of the Polish-Russian Friendship Society
Radar (Radar)
 Youth magazine
Rocznik Biblioteczny (Librarians' Annual)
Rocznik Chrześcijańskiej Akademii Teologicznej (Christian Theological Academy Annual)
Rocznik Katolickiego Uniwersytetu Lubelskiego (Annual of the Catholic University of Lublin)
Ruch Muzyczny (Musical Movement)
 Specialized musical magazine
Sad Nowoczesny (Modern Orchard)
 Monthly on orchard cultivation

Sigma (Sigma)
Monthly student paper of the Wrocław Polytechnic
Słowo Ludu (Word of the People)
Kielce daily
Słowo Polskie (Polish Word)
Wrocław daily
Słowo Powszechne (Popular Word)
Daily of the Christian society PAX
Słowo Prawdy (Word of Truth)
Baptist Church publication, bimonthly.
Sprawozdania Wrocławskiego Towarzystwa Naukowego (Reports of the Wrocław Scientific Association)
Stilor Gorzowski (Gorzów Polyester)
Factory paper printed in Gorzów
Stolica (The Capitol)
Cultural weekly devoted to historical and present-day Warsaw
Student (The Student)
Students' weekly published in Warsaw
Studia Philosophia Christianae
Studia Socjologiczne (Sociological Studies)
Journal of the Polish Sociological Association
Studia Theologica Varsaviensia
Sygnały (Signals)
Railway workers' weekly (a factory paper by the same name was also published monthly in Bydgoszcz)
Szpilki (Needles)
Satirical weekly
Sztandar Młodych (The Youth Banner)
Party youth daily
Technika + Ekonomika + Organizacja = Postęp (Technics + Economics + Organization = Progress)
Publication of the industrial automation equipment plant in Ostrów Wielkopolski
Tempo (Tempo)
Daily sports journal, Kraków
Trybuna Ludu (People's Tribune)
Official Communist Party daily
Tygodnik Demokratyczny (Democratic Weekly)
Weekly of the Democratic Party
Tygodnik Katolicki (Catholic Weekly)
Religious weekly published in Lublin for the western territories from 1948 to 1953
Tygodnik Kulturalny (Cultural Weekly)
Weekly on social and cultural problems, published in Warsaw

Tygodnik Morski (Marine Weekly)
Tygodnik Powszechny (Popular Weekly)
  Weekly of the Christian society Znak
Walka Młodych (Battle of Youth)
  Socialist youth weekly published in Warsaw
W Drodze (On the Way)
  Religious monthly
Wektory (Vectors)
  Warsaw journal
Wiadomości (News)
  Social and political weekly, Wrocław
Wiadomości Diecezjalne Łódzkie (Łódź Diocesan News)
Wiadomości Zachodnie (Western News)
  Monthly published in Szczecin
Wieczór Wrocławia (Wrocław Evening)
  Popular evening daily circulated in Wrocław
Wieś i Rolnictwo (Village and Agriculture)
Więź (The Link)
  Highly intellectual Catholic monthly
WTK (Wrocławski Tygodnik Katolicki) (Wrocław Catholic Weekly)
  Cultural Catholic weekly printed in Wrocław
Za i Przeciw (For and Against)
  Christian Social Association weekly
Zeszyty Muzyczne (Musical Reports)
Zeszyty Naukowe Akademii Rolniczej (Research Reports of the Agricultural
  Academy)
Zeszyty Naukowe Katolickiego Uniwersytetu Lubelskiego (Research Reports of
  the Catholic University of Lublin)
Zielony Sztandar (The Green Banner)
  Daily of the United Peasant Party
Znak (The Sign)
  Catholic monthly published in Kraków by the Catholic Deputies' Club
  (Znak)
Zorza (Dawn)
  Progressive Catholic weekly on family problems, published by PAX
Żołnierz Wolności (Soldier of Freedom)
  Polish People's Army daily
Życie Gospodarcze (Economic Life)
  Economic weekly
Życie i Nowoczesność (Life and Modernity)
  Economic weekly supplement to *Życie Warszawy*
Życie Literackie (Literary Life)
  Literary weekly published in Kraków
Życie Warszawy (Warsaw Life)
  Nonparty Warsaw daily

Selected Rand Books

Bagdikian, Ben H., *The Information Machines: Their Impact on Men and the Media,* New York: Harper & Row, 1971.

Bretz, Rudy, *A Taxonomy of Communication Media,* Englewood Cliffs, N.J.: Educational Technology Publications, 1971.

Dinerstein, H. S., and Leon Goure, *Two Studies in Soviet Controls: Communism and the Russian Peasant; Moscow in Crisis,* Glencoe, Ill.: The Free Press, 1955.

Downs, Anthony, *Inside Bureaucracy,* Boston, Mass.: Little, Brown and Company, 1967.

Fainsod, Merle, *Smolensk under Soviet Rule,* Cambridge, Mass.: Harvard University Press, 1958.

George, Alexander L., *Propaganda Analysis: A Study of Inferences Made from Nazi Propaganda in World War II,* Evanston, Ill.: Row, Peterson and Company, 1959, Westport, Conn.: Greenwood Press, 1976.

Goldhamer, Herbert, *The Soviet Soldier: Soviet Military Management at the Troop Level,* New York: Crane, Russak & Company, 1975.

Hosmer, Stephen T., and Thomas W. Wolfe, *Soviet Policy and Practice Toward Third World Conflicts,* Lexington, Mass.: D. C. Heath, 1983.

Johnson, A. Ross, Robert W. Dean and Alexander Alexiev, *East European Military Establishments: The Warsaw Pact Northern Tier,* New York: Crane, Russak & C82.

Kecskemeti, Paul, *The Unexpected Revolution: Social Forces in the Hungarian Uprising,* Stanford, Cal.: Stanford University Press, 1961.

Kolkowicz, Roman, *The Soviet Military and the Communist Party,* Princeton, N.J.: Princeton University Press, 1967.

Leites, Nathan, *Soviet Style in War,* New York: Crane, Russak & Company, 1982.

——, *The Operational Code of the Politburo,* New York: McGraw-Hill Book Company, 1951; Westport, Conn.: Greenwood Press, 1972 (reprint of 1951 ed.).

Pye, Lucian W., *Chinese Commercial Negotiating Style,* Cambridge, Mass.: Oelgeschlager Gunn & Hain, 1982.

Rush, Myron, *The Rise of Khrushchev,* Washington, D.C.: Public Affairs Press, 1958.

Smith, Bruce Lannes, and Chitra M. Smith, *International Communication and Political Opinion: A Guide to the Literature,* Princeton, N.J.: Princeton University Press, 1956.

Wolfe, Thomas W., *The SALT Experience,* Cambridge, Mass.: Ballinger Publishing Company, 1979.

——, *Soviet Power and Europe, 1945–1970,* Baltimore, Md.: The Johns Hopkins Press, 1970.

INDEX

About the Author

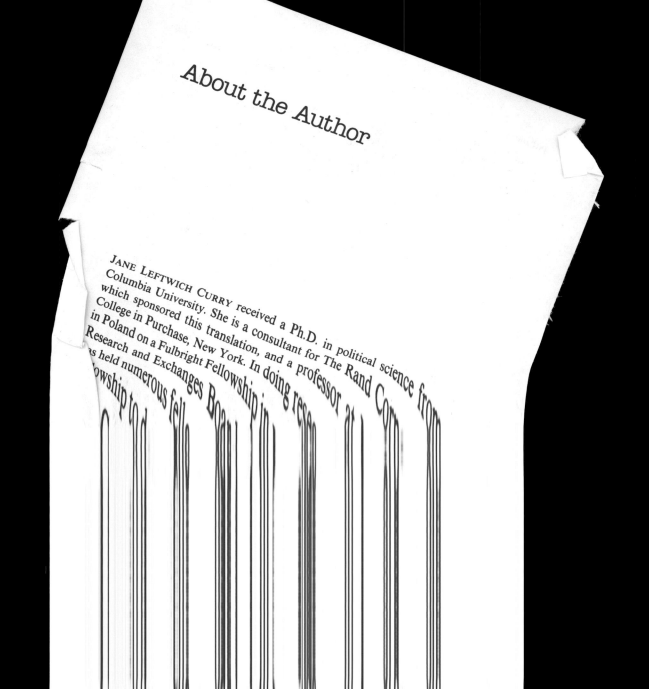

JANE LEFTWICH CURRY received a Ph.D. in political science from Columbia University. She is a consultant for The Rand Corporation, which sponsored this translation, and a professor at Corning College in Purchase, New York. In doing research for this book in Poland on a Fulbright Fellowship in 1976 and from the International Research and Exchanges Board in 1974 and 1975, Dr. Curry held numerous fellowships to do research in Poland, including a fellowship to do work on the Polish press.

About the Author

JANE LEFTWICH CURRY received a Ph.D. in political science from
Columbia University. She is a consultant for The Rand Corporation,
which sponsored this translation, and a professor at Manhattanville
College in Purchase, New York. In doing research on Poland, she was
in Poland on a Fulbright Fellowship in 1969–70 and on an International
Research and Exchanges Board Fellowship in 1974–75 and 1983. She
has held numerous fellowships, including a Rockefeller Human Rights
Fellowship to do research on "Socialist Perceptions of Human Rights."

Dr. Curry has also edited *Press Control Around the World* (with Joan
Dassin; Praeger, 1982), *Dissent in Eastern Europe* (Praeger, 1983) and
Polish Dissident Writing: An Annotated Bibliography (Praeger, 1983).
Currently, she is completing a volume on the Polish journalism profes-
sion and the roots of the Polish crisis.